Vauxhall Victor FD 1600, 2000 1967-72 Autobook

By Kenneth Ball
Graduate, Institution of Mechanical Engineers
Associate Member, Guild of Motoring Writers
and the Autopress Team of Technical Writers.

Vauxhall Victor 1600 FD 1967-69
Vauxhall Victor 1600 Super 1969-72
Vauxhall Victor 2000 FD 1967-69
Vauxhall Victor 2000 SL 1969-72
Vauxhall VX 4/90 1969-72

Autobooks

Autopress Ltd. Golden Lane Brighton BN1 2QJ England

The AUTOBOOK series of Workshop Manuals is the largest in the world and covers the majority of British and Continental motor cars, as well as all major Japanese and Australian models. For a full list see the back of this manual.

CONTENTS

ISBN 0 85147 279 6

First Edition   1970
Second Edition, fully revised   1971
Third Edition, fully revised   1972
Reprinted   1972
Reprinted   1973

780

Printed and bound in Brighton England for Autopress Ltd by G Beard & Son Ltd   A

ACKNOWLEDGEMENT

My thanks are due to Vauxhall Motors Ltd. for their unstinted co-operation and also for supplying data and illustrations.

I am also grateful to a considerable number of owners who have discussed their cars at length and many of whose suggestions have been included in this manual.

Kenneth Ball
Graduate, Institution of Mechanical Engineers
Associate Member, Guild of Motoring Writers
Ditchling Sussex England.

INTRODUCTION

This do-it-yourself Workshop Manual has been specially written for the owner who wishes to maintain his car in first class condition and to carry out his own servicing and repairs. Considerable savings on garage charges can be made, and one can drive in safety and confidence knowing the work has been done properly.

Comprehensive step-by-step instructions and illustrations are given on all dismantling, overhauling and assembling operations. Certain assemblies require the use of expensive special tools, the purchase of which would be unjustified. In these cases information is included but the reader is recommended to hand the unit to the agent for attention.

Throughout the Manual hints and tips are included which will be found invaluable, and there is an easy to follow fault diagnosis at the end of each chapter.

Whilst every care has been taken to ensure correctness of information it is obviously not possible to guarantee complete freedom from errors or to accept liability arising from such errors or omissions.

Instructions may refer to the righthand or lefthand sides of the vehicle or the components. These are the same as the righthand or lefthand of an observer standing behind the car and looking forward.

CHAPTER 1

THE ENGINE

1:1 Type, features, models, capacities

The engines fitted to the FD series Victor, VX4/90 and Victor 2000 are four-cylinder in-line overhead camshaft units with the cylinders inclined towards the nearside at an angle of 45 deg. The layout can be seen in **FIGS 1:1** and **1:2**.

The cast-iron crankshaft is carried in five bearings, end float being controlled by a flange on the rear bearing. The bearings are split in line with the horizontal sump face, that is at an angle of 45 deg. to the cylinder bores. A spring-loaded oil seal is provided at the front end of the crankshaft and a two-piece lip type oil seal at the rear. The solid skirt pistons have offset gudgeon pins which are an interference fit in the connecting rods.

A housing bolted to the cylinder head carries the five-bearing overhead camshaft and inverted bucket type tappets, as shown in **FIG 1:3**. The tappets incorporate wedge-type adjusters for valve clearance. The camshaft housing has a double-skinned pressed-steel cover. Steel wool packing between the skins acts as sound insulation

and also as a filter for the crankcase ventilation system. This comprises a large diameter hose from the camshaft housing to the air cleaner with a smaller branch pipe to the inlet manifold to provide ventilation at low engine speeds. The camshaft is driven from the crankshaft by a toothed rubber belt as shown in **FIGS 1:1** and **1:2**. The belt also drives an auxiliary shaft carried in a housing forming part of the cylinder block casting. The auxiliary shaft drives the fuel pump, distributor and oil pump. Belt tension is maintained by means of an adjustable jockey pulley. On later engines a protective cover is provided for the camshaft drive belt. The water pump, which is mounted on the cylinder block, is driven from the crankshaft by a conventional V-belt which also drives the generator or alternator.

The cylinder head is shown in **FIG 1:4**. Inlet and exhaust valves are positioned alternately along the length of the head. Each valve has an individual port, with the inlet ports on the offside or upper side and the exhaust ports on the nearside of the head. To compensate for the

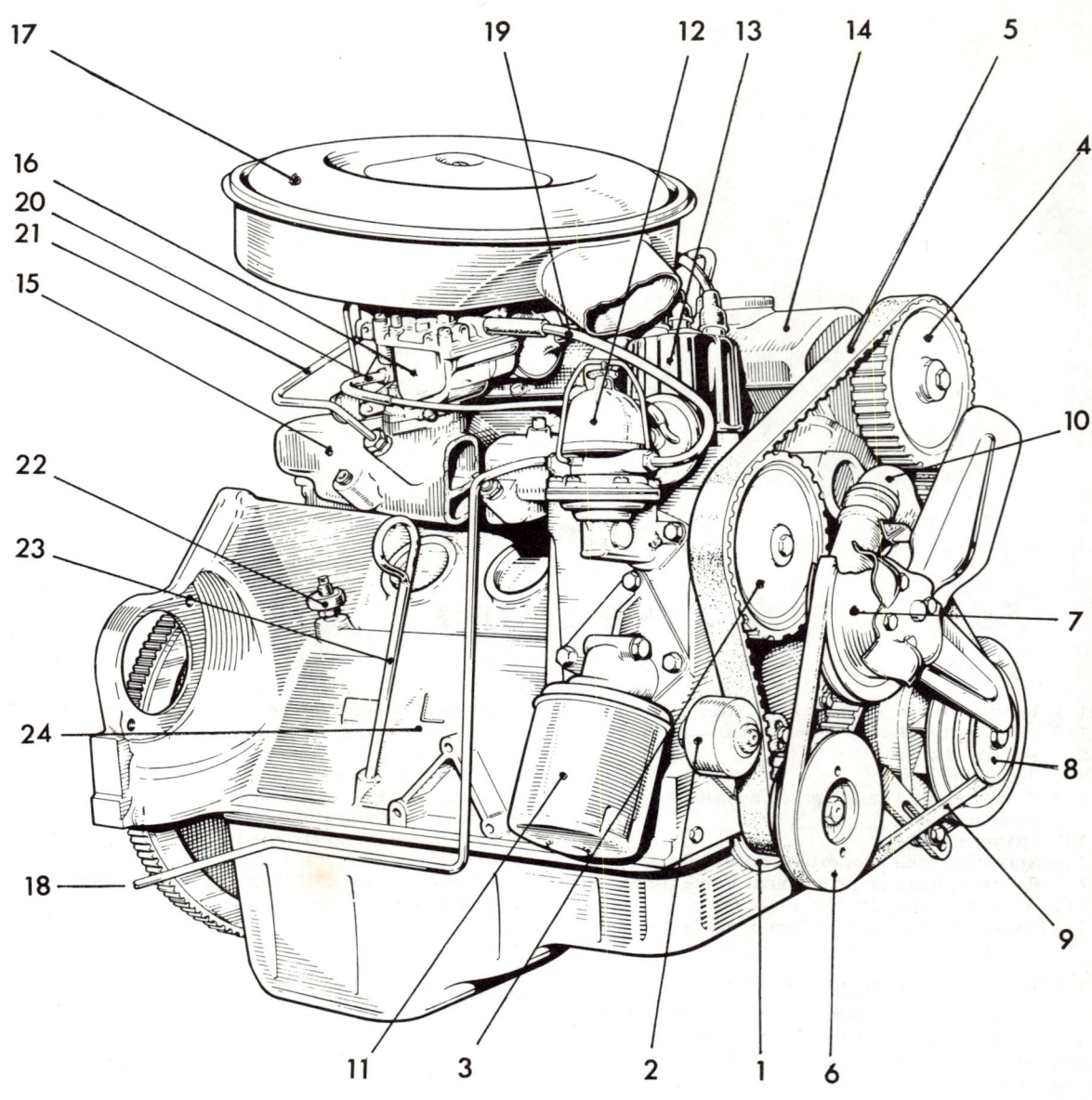

FIG 1:1 Vauxhall OHC engine. Part-sectioned offside front view

Key to Fig 1:1   1 Crankshaft timing pulley   2 Jockey pulley   3 Auxiliary shaft pulley   4 Camshaft pulley
5 Camshaft drive belt   6 Crankshaft fanbelt pulley   7 Fan pulley and water pump (on cylinder block)
8 Alternator (or generator) pulley   9 Fanbelt   10 Water pump inlet elbow (bolted to head)   11 External oil filter
12 Petrol pump   13 Distributor   14 Camshaft housing cover   15 Inlet manifold and water jacket   16 Carburetter
17 Air cleaner   18 Petrol pipe, tank to pump   19 Petrol pipe, pump to carburetter   20 Vacuum advance pipe
21 Low speed breather pipe   22 Oil pressure warning lamp switch   23 Dipstick   24 Letter L denoting 2000 cc (Letter
S denotes 1600 cc)

FIG 1:2 Vauxhall OHC engine. Part-sectioned nearside front view

absence of a hot-spot, a full-length hot water jacket is incorporated in the inlet manifold, shown in **FIG 1:5**. **FIG 1:6** shows the arrangement of the sparking plugs which are of a special pattern with tapered seatings to provide a gas-tight joint without the use of washers. The plugs are screened by a heat-shield of insulating material fitted between the exhaust manifold and the cylinder head. A special socket tool, No. VR.2040 is needed for plug removal and a torque wrench must be used when tightening the plugs.

The oil pump supplies oil through a full-flow filter to the main oil gallery and through drillings in the cylinder block to the crankshaft and auxiliary shaft and through the cylinder head to an oil gallery in the camshaft housing to lubricate the camshaft bearings, cams and tappets.

The engine is produced in two capacities, differing only in the bore size. The engine fitted as standard to the Victor FD is of 85.73 mm bore and 69.24 mm stroke, giving a capacity of 1599 cc. The larger engine is of 95.25 bore and

69.24 mm stroke, giving a capacity of 1975 cc. This engine is the standard fitment for the Victor 2000 which at the same time has a more elaborate specification.

Throughout this manual the engines will be referred to for convenience as '1600 engine' and '2000 engine' respectively, the car models being briefly designated as 'Victor 1600' and 'Victor 2000'. It should be noted that the larger engine is available as an option on the standard Victor, but in this case certain items in the Victor 2000 specification, including servo-assisted disc front brakes, pre-engaged starter and alternator are automatically included. This model will be referred to as 'Victor fitted with 2000 engine'.

Both the 1600 and 2000 engines are available in high-compression (8.5 1) and low-compression (7.3:1) forms, identified by the code letter H or L respectively, stamped on the cylinder block near the distributor. On early engines a second letter identifies the bore size, S for the 1600 and B for the 2000 engine. On later engines the letter S for the

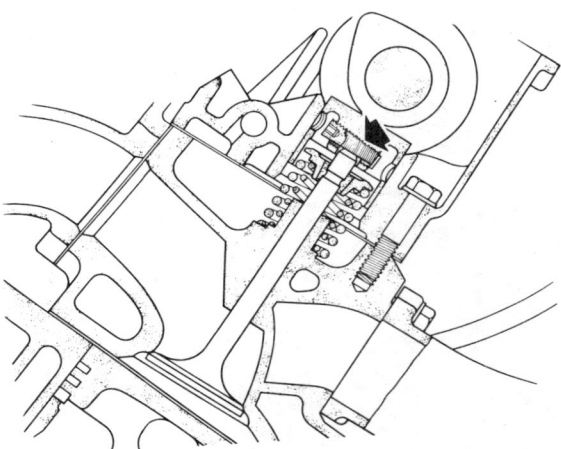

FIG 1:3 Section of tappet showing tapered adjusting screw (arrowed)

1600 or L for the 2000 is cast on the cylinder block near the dipstick as shown in **FIG 1:1**.

In the following instructions the cylinders are numbered from the front end of the engine, No. 1 cylinder being next to the radiator.

1:2 Working on engine in car. Jobs requiring engine removal

The following parts can be removed and refitted with the engine ih the car:

Cylinder head and valves, camshaft, camshaft housing and seal, carburetter and inlet and exhaust manifolds, auxiliary shaft and seal, fuel pump, distributor, oil pump, water pump and thermostat. Detailed instructions will be found in the appropriate Sections.

Attention to the clutch and flywheel, or to the flexplate on automatic models, is possible after removal of the gearbox or transmission, leaving the engine in position. The gearbox or transmission must in any case be removed prior to engine removal.

For removal of the sump, connecting rods and pistons, or for attention to the crankshaft and main bearings, the engine first is removed from the car as described in the next Section.

1:3 Removing engine

On all models the gearbox or transmission unit must be removed before removing engine. On cars fitted with over-drive, before starting any dismantling operations, drive the car in third or top gear, engage overdrive, then disengage the overdrive with the clutch pedal depressed. Further details will be found in **Chapter 6**.

To remove the engine on all models proceed as follows:
1 Disconnect both leads from the battery. Remove the
    bonnet. Disconnect the breather pipe and remove the

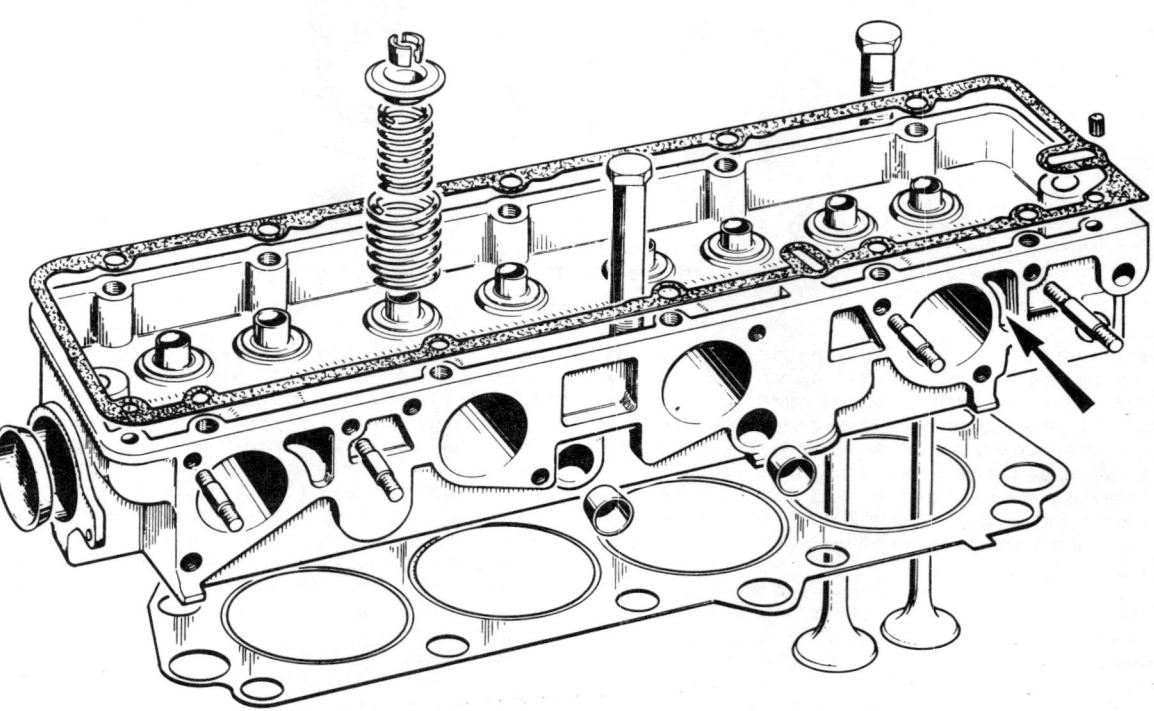

FIG 1:4   An exploded view of the cylinder head showing the four inlet ports. The arrow shows one of the two passages connecting with the water jacket in the inlet manifold (see FIG 1:5)

air cleaner. Remove the heater air duct.

2 Drain the cooling system, saving the liquid if antifreeze is used. There are two drain taps, one in the radiator bottom tank and one at the rear lefthand side of the cylinder block. Both taps should be opened and the filler cap removed.

3 Disconnect the radiator hoses and heater hoses. Remove the radiator and also the horizontal shield covering the space between the top of the radiator and the front panel.

4 Disconnect the petrol pipe from the inlet side of the fuel pump, plugging the pipe to prevent fuel loss.

5 Disconnect the heavy cable from the starter and remove the engine earthing strip. Disconnect the wires from the engine temperature gauge unit and oil pressure switch. Disconnect the white/blue and white wires from the ignition coil. On cars with pre-engaged starter, also disconnect the three brown wires, white red and white/blue wires from the starter solenoid.

6 Disconnect the exhaust pipe from the manifold.

7 Remove the gearbox or transmission. For detailed instructions, reference should be made to **Chapter 6** for cars fitted with manual gearbox or to **Chapter 6a** for cars fitted with automatic transmission. Note that for engine removal purposes the manual gearbox is disconnected from the clutch housing (bellhousing) so that the clutch and housing can be removed with the engine. Where an overdrive is fitted this is removed with the gearbox as a unit. On cars fitted with automatic transmission, the converter housing takes the place of the clutch housing but forms a unit with the transmission, so that only the flexplate remains on the engine after transmission removal.

8 Support the engine in a sling arranged as shown in **FIG 1 : 7**.

9 Remove the bolts and nuts from each of the two front engine mountings.

10 Make a final check to ensure that no wires or other connections between the engine and the frame have been overlooked.

11 Lift out the engine.

12 On cars fitted with automatic transmission, the engine after removal must not be allowed to rest on the flexplate as this may distort the plate and render it unserviceable.

1 : 4 Removing and servicing camshaft and auxiliary shaft

FIGS 1 : 1 and **1 : 2** show the layout of the toothed belt drive from the crankshaft to the single overhead camshaft and the auxiliary shaft. The latter drives the distributor, oil pump and fuel pump. The glass-fibre reinforced toothed rubber belt does not stretch appreciably in service and periodic adjustment should not be necessary. A jockey pulley, incorporating a sealed ballbearing, is provided to facilitate installation and removal of the belt. If, however, incorrect adjustment is suspected, check the belt tension midway between the camshaft and auxiliary shaft pulleys. A load of 10 lbs at this point should give a deflection of .30 inch. Adjust if necessary by slackening the jockey pulley bracket bolts shown in **FIG 1 : 8**. Tighten the bolts securely and recheck the tension. An overtightened belt will whine, while a slack belt will wear rapidly.

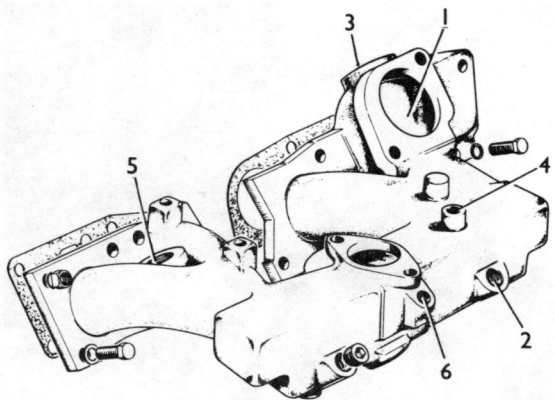

FIG 1 : 5   Inlet manifold and hot water jacket showing connections

Key to Fig 1 : 5
1 Thermostat housing
2 Tapping for water temperature unit   3 Car heater hose connection   4 Brake servo vacuum connection (disc brake models)   5 Water pipe to water pump connection
6 Low speed breather pipe connection

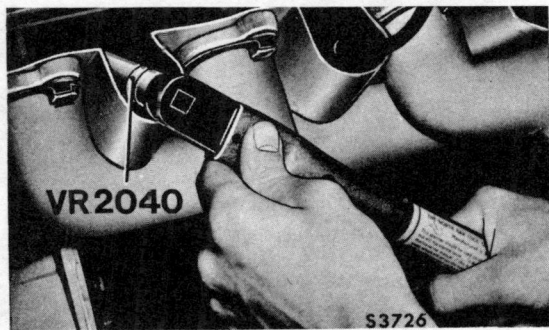

FIG 1 : 6   The special type sparking plugs require the use of tool No. VR.2040 in conjunction with a torque wrench. The sparking plug heat shield is also shown

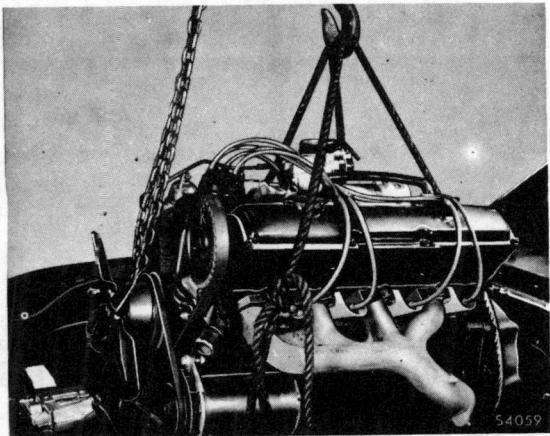

FIG 1 : 7   Removal of engine with clutch and clutch housing attached (cars with manual gearboxes)

FIG 1:8 Jockey pulley for camshaft drive belt

FIG 1:9 Timing marks. For special precautions when removing drive belt on 1600 high-compression engines see text

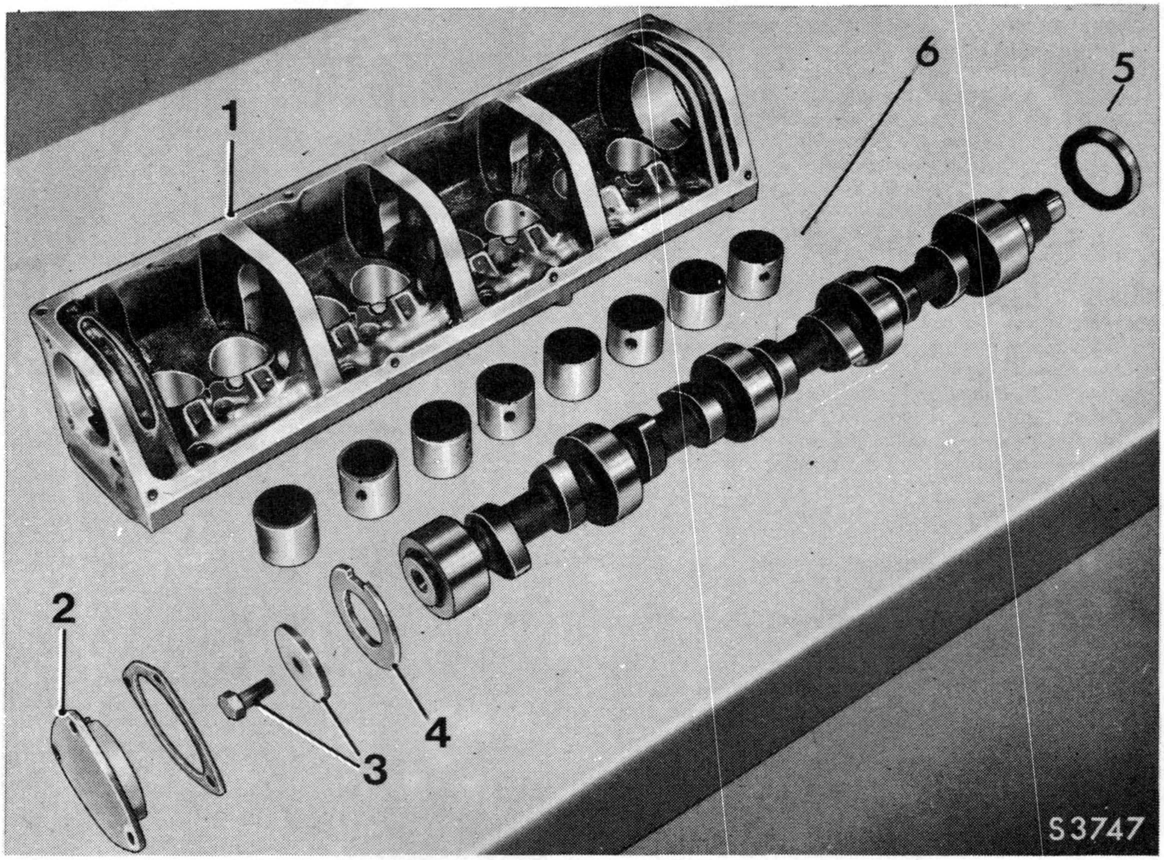

FIG 1:10 Exploded view of camshaft assembly

Key to Fig 1:10   1 Camshaft housing   2 Housing end cover   3 Retaining bolt and plain washer
4 Thrust washer   5 Camshaft seal   6 Tappets

To remove the drive belt proceed as follows:

1 Disconnect both leads from the battery.

2 On later cars remove the drive belt cover. This is secured by two nuts and can be withdrawn after removal of the fan pulley and crankshaft fan pulley. See **Chapter 4** for details.

3 If the belt is to be used again, it should be marked with a chalked arrow showing the direction of drive so that it can be installed as originally fitted.

4 If it is intended to remove either the camshaft pulley or auxiliary shaft pulley, the retaining bolt in the pulley centre should be slackened before releasing the drive belt. Each pulley is keyed and is a push fit on its shaft.

5 On 1600 high-compression engines, before removing the drive belt, ensure that the timing mark 1 in **FIG 1 : 9** on the crankshaft pulley is approximately 90 deg. before the TDC pointer 2 on the jockey pulley bracket. Afterwards the engine must not be rotated whilst the drive belt is off, or the valve heads may foul the pistons at TDC.

6 Slacken the jockey pulley bracket bolts. The drive belt can now be slipped off the pulleys. For removal of camshaft or attention to auxiliary shaft this will be sufficient. If however the drive belt is to be completely removed, the fan belt must first be removed in order to allow the drive belt to be withdrawn between the crankshaft and generator pulleys. Full instructions for this will be found in **Chapter 4**.

FIG 1 : 10 shows the components of the camshaft assembly. The camshaft and tappets operate directly in the housing 1 secured to the cylinder head by ten bolts located inside the housing. An oil gallery extends from front to rear of the housing. The camshaft is retained by an end cover 2, a retaining bolt and washer 3 and a thrust washer 4 which controls the end float. The camshaft is sealed at the front end by a spring-loaded lip-type seal 5. The housing has a double-skinned pressed-steel cover (see **FIG 1 : 1** item 14) which is secured by eight screws.

The camshaft oil seal can be renewed without removal of the camshaft as follows:

1 Remove the drive belt and camshaft pulley as previously described, ensuring that the pulley centre bolt is slackened before releasing the belt, and observing the

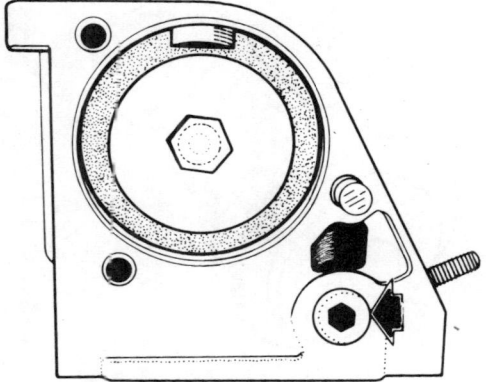

FIG 1 : 12 Camshaft oil gallery end plugs

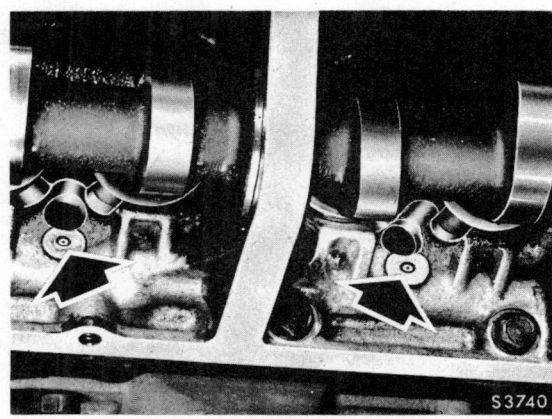

FIG 1 : 13 Camshaft oil jet holes

special precautions described for 1600 high-compression engines.

2 Prise out the old seal, taking care not to damage the seal land on the shaft.

3 Smear the lip of the new seal with anti-scuffing paste and install the seal open side first. Drive in the seal until it contacts the abutment face in the housing. Refit the pulley and drive belt and set the valve timing as described in **Section 1 : 7**.

To remove the camshaft assembly:

1 Remove the drive belt as previously described, observing the special precautions given for the 1600 high-compression engine. The pulley may remain on the camshaft unless dismantling of the camshaft assembly is intended, in which case the pulley nut should be slackened before releasing the drive belt.

2 Disconnect the breather hose from the camshaft housing cover. Remove the eight screws to release the cover. Removal of the cover gives access to the ten bolts securing the camshaft housing to the cylinder head. Slacken these bolts evenly and in turn to release the housing.

3 The tappets and screw assemblies are graded in relation

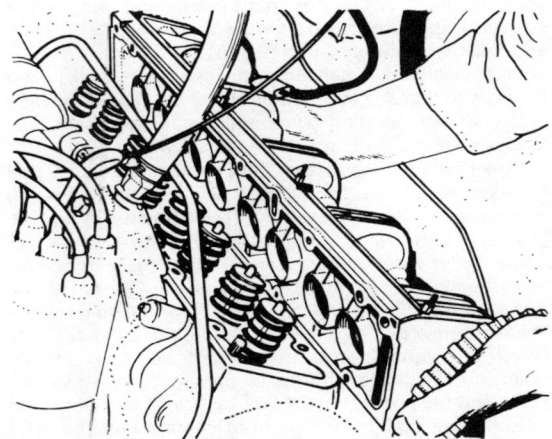

FIG 1 : 11 Removal of camshaft housing. The housing must be tilted as shown to prevent tappets falling out

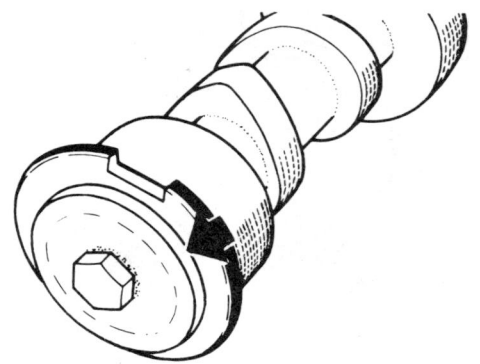

FIG 1:14 Camshaft end float

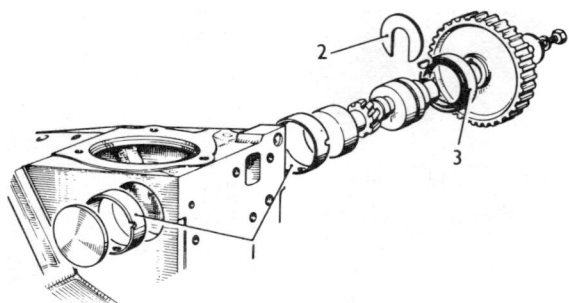

FIG 1:15 An exploded view of the auxiliary shaft components

Key to Fig 1:15

2 Thrust washer   3 Oil seal   1 Auxiliary shaft bearings

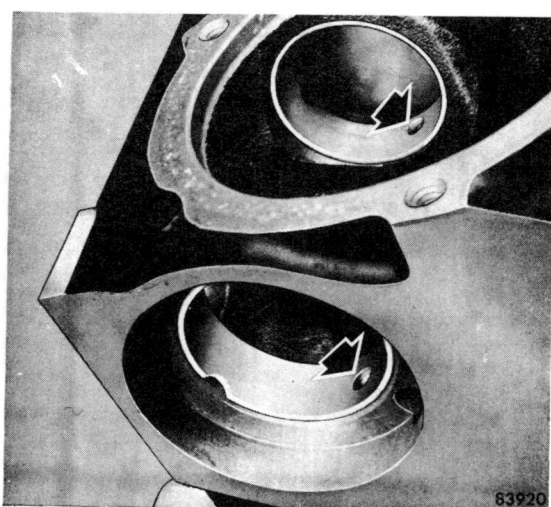

FIG 1:16 Auxiliary shaft bearings. Oilways are indicated by arrows

to their corresponding valves and should not be mixed. Therefore when removing the camshaft housing, turn it on its side as soon as the tappets are clear of the valve springs, as shown in **FIG 1:11**, to prevent the tappets dropping out. The tappets should then be stored in their correct order to ensure installation in their original bores.

To dismantle and service the camshaft assembly:

1 Referring to **FIG 1:10**, remove the housing end cover 2. This is retained by three screws. Remove the retaining bolt and washer 3, holding the front end of the camshaft in a soft-jawed vice. On no account must the camshaft pulley be held in a vice for this purpose.

2 Remove the camshaft oil seal 5 and withdraw the camshaft through the front of the housing.

3 Unscrew the end plugs from the oil gallery (see **FIG 1:12**). Referring to **FIG 1:13**, the gallery oil feed passage from the cylinder head and the oil jet holes must be cleared by blowing out with compressed air. When refitting the oil gallery end plugs smear the threads with jointing compound.

4 Referring to **FIG 1:14**, temporarily assemble the thrust washer and plain washer on the camshaft using the original bolt. The shaft end float should be .001 to .007 inch and will be equal to the clearance between the plain washer and the thrust washer, as indicated by the arrow.

5 Smear the camshaft journals, housing bores and cams with graphited oil and install the camshaft in the housing. Fit the thrust washer and plain washer and secure with a new retaining bolt. The bolt has a nylon insert and must always be renewed. Before fitting the rear cover, position the thrust washer with its slot uppermost as shown in **FIG 1:12**.

FIG 1:15 is an exploded view of the auxiliary shaft components. The shaft is supported in an annexe to the cylinder block by two bearings 1 and driven by the camshaft drive belt. The shaft provides a drive to the distributor and the oil pump and also incorporates an eccentric which operates the fuel pump. A thrust washer 2 and a lip-type oil seal 3 retain the shaft in the cylinder block.

The oil seal can be renewed without removal of the shaft, but it will be necessary to remove the auxiliary shaft pulley. Slacken the pulley retaining nut before releasing the drive belt. On high-compression 1600 engines the same precautions must be observed as previously described for belt removal. Prise out the seal, taking care not to damage the land on the shaft. Smear the new seal with anti-scuffing paste and install open side first. Drive in the seal to contact the thrust washer.

To withdraw the auxiliary shaft, remove the pulley and drive belt as previously described. Remove the fuel pump (see **Chapter 2**), the distributor (see **Chapter 3**) and the auxiliary shaft seal. If the auxiliary shaft gear is worn or damaged, the distributor gear should also be renewed. When removing bearings, the expansion plug sealing the rear bearing will be driven out with the bearing. When installing new bearings, ensure that the bearing with the offset oil hole is fitted to the housing rear bore. The oil holes must coincide with the oil passages in the cylinder block and the notches in the bearings must face outwards as shown in **FIG 1:16**. The front bearing must be flush with the face of the housing counterbore. Replacement bearings are ready finished to size and do not need reaming.

Install a new expansion plug behind the rear bearing using jointing compound to ensure an oil tight joint. When installing shaft, lubricate the shaft journals and bearings with a graphited oil. Locate the thrust washer A shown in **FIG 1 : 17** in the shaft groove. Ease the shaft into position so that the slot in the thrust washer engages the dowel in the cylinder block. The thrust washer controls the end float of the shaft which should be .002 to .008 inch. Install the shaft oil seal as previously described.

1 : 5 Lifting the head

To remove the cylinder head with the engine in the car proceed as follows:
1 Disconnect both battery cables.
2 Disconnect the breather pipe from the camshaft housing cover and the inlet manifold. Remove the air cleaner.
3 Drain the cooling system as described in **Chapter 4**. Referring to **FIG 1 : 5**, disconnect the following from the inlet manifold: the thermostat elbow 1, temperature gauge switch wire 2, heater hose 3, vacuum servo hose 4 (disc brake models only) and the water pump pipe connection 5.
4 Disconnect from the carburetter the feed pipe, vacuum advance pipe and throttle and choke controls.
5 On cars with automatic transmission disconnect the downshift linkage rod from the throttle lever, and remove the bracket from the manifold, taking care not to alter the adjustments. (If rod or cable adjustments are disturbed, reference should be made to **Chapter 6a** for instructions).
6 Disconnect the HT cables and remove the sparking plugs, using the special tool VR.2040 shown in **FIG 1 : 6**.
7 Remove the bolt securing the water pump elbow to the cylinder head (see **FIG 1 : 18**).
8 Remove the exhaust manifold from the cylinder head. The manifold is secured by eight bolts which are locked by tabs on four locking plates. Access to the four lower bolts is from underneath the car and is made easier if the front nearside wheel is removed. **The car must be firmly supported during this operation.**
9 Remove the camshaft assembly as described in **Section 1 : 4**. Note than on 1600 high-compression engines, after the removal of the drive belt the crankshaft must not be rotated until the camshaft assembly has been removed.
10 The inlet manifold can be removed with the cylinder head, using a long socket wrench to reach the cylinder head bolts. If the inlet manifold is to be removed separately before lifting the head, withdraw the thermostat to give access to one of the securing nuts located inside the manifold as shown in **FIG 1 : 19**.
11 Slacken the cylinder head bolts a little at a time in the reverse order to that shown for tightening in **FIG 1 : 28**. Lift off the head and remove the gasket.

1 : 6 Servicing the head, attention to valves

FIG 1 : 4 shows the cylinder head and valve components, viewed from the offside of the engine. Exhaust and inlet valves are positioned alternately throughout the length of the head. Each valve has an individual port, the inlet ports

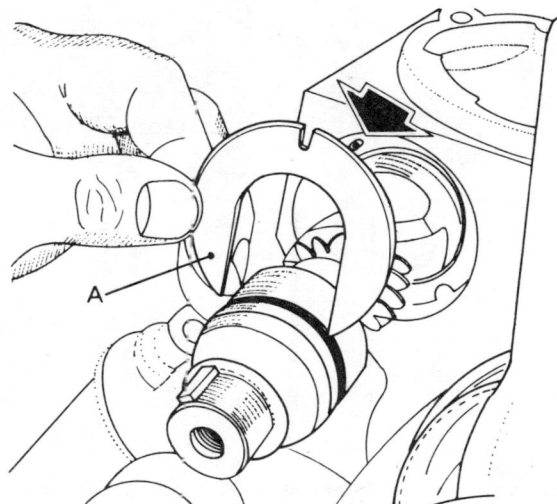

FIG 1 : 17 Auxiliary shaft showing thrust washer (A) and the locating dowel (arrowed)

FIG 1 : 18 Water pump inlet elbow. The water pump is attached to the cylinder block but the elbow is secured to the cylinder head by the bolt (arrowed) which must be removed before removing head

FIG 1 : 19 Access to one of the nuts securing the inlet manifold is obtained by removing thermostat elbow and withdrawing thermostat from housing. The stud threads and copper washer (arrowed) should be smeared with sealer on reassembly

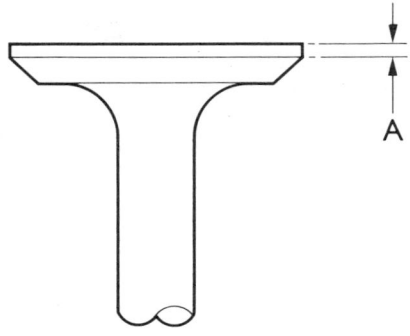

FIG 1:20 Valve head thickness indicated by dimension **A**

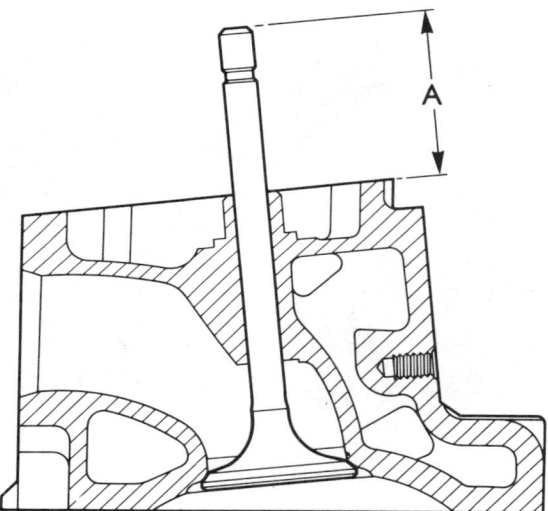

FIG 1:21 Valve stem assembled height A must not exceed 1.13 inch

being on the offside and the exhausts on the nearside.

If the inlet manifold has not already been removed from the head, note that the thermostat must be withdrawn to provide access to one of the securing nuts as shown in **FIG 1:19**.

When decarbonizing, scrape most of the carbon from the head before removing the valves, to prevent damage to the valve seats. Clean the piston crowns, leaving about a quarter of an inch at the outer edges and taking precautions to prevent loose carbon from blocking the oil transfer passage A in **FIG 1:26**. To remove the valves, compress each of the double springs with a suitable valve tool so that the split cotters can be removed and the springs released. Valves and their parts should be stored

so that they can be refitted in the same positions if serviceable.

Inspect the valves for burnt or cracked heads and the valve faces for pitting. Check the valve stems to see whether the clearance is within the limits shown in Technical Data. No valve guides are fitted, the stems operating directly in the head. Valves are supplied with standard stems or with .003, .006 or .012 inch oversize stems. The stems are stamped with numbers showing the oversize in thousandths of an inch. The bores in the head must be reamered to suit, reamers Z.8500, Z.8501 and Z.8502 accommodating .003, .006 and .012 inch over-sizes respectively. To ensure an accurate bore at the valve port, ream from the top of the cylinder head.

New inlet valves have an aluminium coating fused to the seat face. No attempt should be made to remove this coating by polishing or grinding. Refaced valves may be used again providing the dimension A shown in **FIG 1:20** is not less than .025 inch for inlet valves or .035 inch for exhaust valves. When refacing valves the minimum amount of metal should be removed, otherwise the tappet adjusting screws may not have sufficient range of movement. The refacing of valves and seats can be more efficiently carried out by a service agent. The valve assembled height A in **FIG 1:21** must not exceed 1.13 inch. If it exceeds this maximum with a refaced valve, check with a new valve. If the maximum height is still exceeded the valve seating is too deep and the head is unfit for further service. The valve stem tip must not be refaced as this could prevent the correct valve clearance from being obtained.

Before refitting the valves, make sure that all traces of loose carbon have been removed from the head and ports and that the valve stems and valve stem bores are perfectly clean. Lubricate the stems with a mineral oil containing colloidal graphite. It is advisable to fit a set of new valve springs, as weak springs can cause premature burning of valves and seats and other more serious trouble.

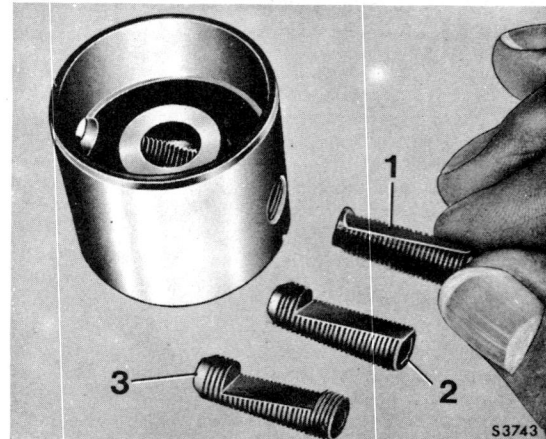

FIG 1:22 A tappet and the three types of tapered adjusting screw available

Key to Fig 1:22　　　1 Standard　　2 First undersize
3 Second undersize

If new valves are fitted a set of new split cotters should also be fitted. In other cases examine the existing cotters. They have an internal projection to engage in a narrow groove in the valve stem shown in **FIG 1 : 21**. Any cotters showing signs of wear at this point should be renewed. When fitting the valve springs, ensure that the tapered hole in the valve spring collar is clean. Compress the spring and after inserting the split cotters release the spring slowly, making quite sure that the cotters are fully home.

Before refitting the cylinder head as described in the next Section, temporarily fit the camshaft assembly to the head and adjust the valve clearances. **The final adjustment of clearances is carried out on a hot engine, but a preliminary check is necessary, especially if the valves and seats have received attention, as there may be insufficient range of adjustment on the existing tappet screws. These cannot be removed without removal of the camshaft housing from the head.**

FIG 1 : 3 is a sectional view of the valve gear showing how the clearance is adjusted by turning the wedge-shaped tappet screw, indicated by the arrow. **FIG 1 : 22** shows one of the bucket type tappets and the three sizes of tappet screw available. To adjust, first rotate the camshaft so that the appropriate cam peak is at 180 deg. to the tappet. Rotate the tappet until the access hole for the tappet screw is in line with the cutaway in the housing as shown in **FIG 1 : 23**. The access hole can be distinguished from the hole in the opposite side of the tappet by a groove, arrowed in the illustration. **FIG 1 : 24** shows the clearance adjustment being carried out using tool No. VR.2041.

The correct clearance (hot) is .007 to .010 inch for inlet valves, .010 to .013 for exhaust valves on early type camshafts (identified by a groove as shown in **FIG 1 : 25**) and .015 to .018 for exhaust valves with late type camshafts. The tappet screw must be turned through one complete turn, clockwise to decrease clearance or anticlockwise to increase clearance. One turn is equivalent to a difference of .003 inch. If the correct valve clearance cannot be obtained with the existing tappet screw, note that screws are available in standard, first undersize and second undersize as shown in **FIG 1 : 22**. When checking the clearance (cold) prior to fitting the cylinder head, the aim must be to select a screw which will allow a sufficient range for

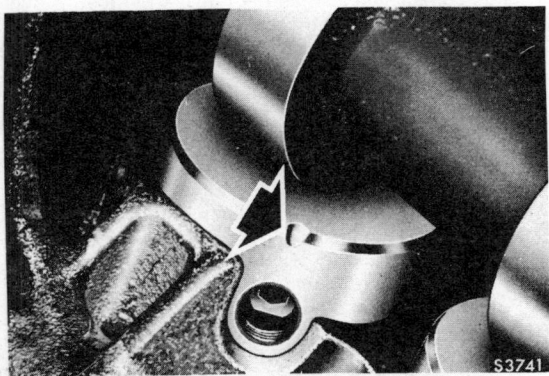

FIG 1 : 23 Tappet adjusting screw access hole can be distinguished from opposite hole by notch (arrowed) in tappet

FIG 1 : 24 Adjusting valve clearance using tool No. VR.2041. One turn of the screw alters clearance by .003 inch

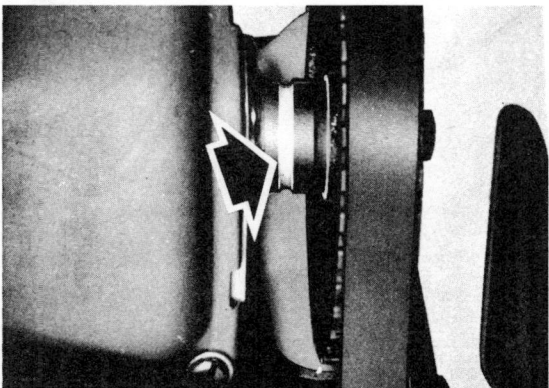

FIG 1 : 25 Groove in camshaft (arrowed) identifies earlier engines which have a different exhaust valve clearance

subsequent adjustment in either direction. Before installing a screw, smear the threads with graphited oil.

Note that when final adjustment is carried out on an assembled engine, the engine must be at working temperature but **the operation must not be carried out with the engine running.**

1 : 7 Refitting head and camshaft. Valve timing

Before refitting the cylinder head the reader is advised that certain gasket sets do not require any additional sealing compound. These gaskets will have a warning included in their wrappings.

1 The inlet manifold can be fitted to the cylinder head before or after refitting the head. In either case note the following points:
(a) Ensure that the manifold studs are tight in the cylinder head.
(b) Before installing the manifold gaskets, smear sealing compound on both sides of the gaskets around the two holes corresponding with the water passages between head and manifold, shown in **FIG 1 : 4**.

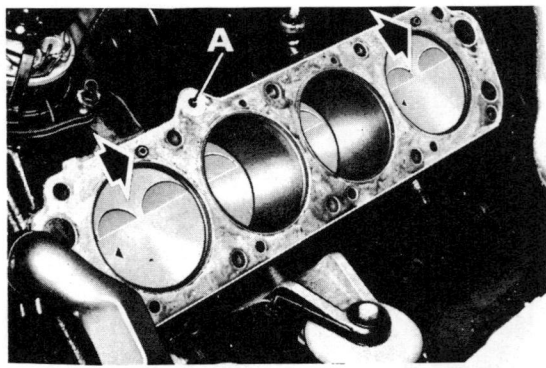

FIG 1:26 Top of cylinder block showing head gasket dowels (arrowed) and camshaft oil passage at A

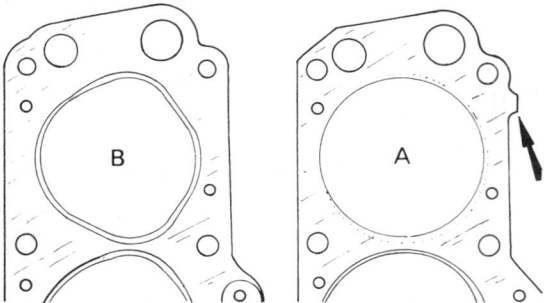

FIG 1:27 Cylinder head gaskets. Gasket **A** for 2000 engines has circular apertures and an identification tab (arrowed). Gasket **B** is for 1600 engines

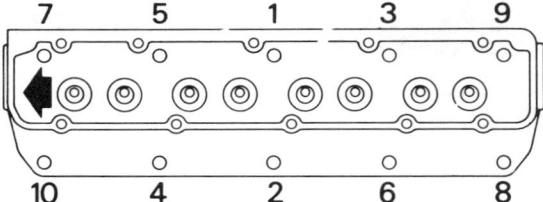

FIG 1:28 Cylinder head bolt tightening sequence. Arrow indicates front of engine

FIG 1:29 Camshaft drive timing marks

(c) Use a new copper washer on the stud inside the manifold (see **FIG 1:19**) and smear stud, washer and nut with sealing compound.

(d) Tighten manifold bolts and nuts evenly.

2 Remove the camshaft assembly if this has been temporarily fitted to the head for valve clearance adjustment as described in **Section 1:6**, taking care not to damage the gasket.

3 Ensure that the faces of both cylinder head and cylinder block are clean and dry and that the oil transfer passage A in **FIG 1:26** is clear.

On early engines the joint between the two oil transfer passages is sealed by an O-ring located on a hollow spring pin. This pin should protrude .12 inch from the head face. On later engines a combined dowel and restrictor with a larger O-ring is used. Two spring pins, at either end of the block are made longer to ensure that they enter the head before the dowel.

4 Ensure that the correct type of cylinder head gasket is used. **FIG 1:27** shows gasket A for the 2000 engine and gasket B for the 1600. Smear the gasket with Wellseal jointing compound and locate the gasket on the dowels, arrowed in **FIG 1:26**, on the cylinder block.

5 Recheck that the oil transfer passage A is clear as there is a risk of its becoming choked with jointing compound. Cylinder head bolts should have clean dry threads. Install the cylinder head and tighten the cylinder head bolts gradually and evenly in the sequence shown in **FIG 1:28** to a torque of 83 lb ft.

To install the camshaft assembly:

1 On 1600 high-compression engines, it is essential for the crankshaft to be in the position shown in **FIG 1:9**, before installing the camshaft. The crankshaft pulley timing mark 1 should be approximately 90 deg. before the TDC pointer 2 on the jockey pulley bracket. This will ensure clearance between the valve heads and the pistons prior to setting the valve timing.

2 Ensure that the gasket between the camshaft housing and cylinder head is in good condition. Locate the gasket on the dowels at each end of the cylinder head and ensure that the oil transfer passage from the cylinder head to the camshaft is clear and that the aperture in the gasket is aligned with it.

3 Lubricate the tappets with graphited oil and install each in its correct bore. Install the housing on the cylinder head, taking care that the tappets do not drop out during the process.

4 The ten securing bolts for the housing should have clean dry threads and should be tightened gradually and evenly to a torque of 15 lb ft.

To refit the camshaft drive:

1 If the camshaft pulley or auxiliary shaft pulley have been removed they should next be refitted. Ensure that the shafts and pulley bores are clean and that the keys and keyways are undamaged. The pulleys are a push fit on the shafts. At this stage it is sufficient to hold the pulleys by hand while tightening the centre securing bolts.

2 Rotate the camshaft and auxiliary shaft pulleys so that the timing marks, indicated by arrows in **FIG 1:29,** are positioned as shown and in line with the pulley centres. The auxiliary shaft pulley has a V-shaped mark on its rim and the camshaft pulley a circular mark on its rim. Other marks on the pulleys should be disregarded.

3 Rotate the crankshaft clockwise, using a wrench on the crankshaft pulley bolt, so that the timing mark 1 on the pulley is aligned with the upper (TDC) pointer 2 on the jockey pulley bracket as shown in **FIG 1 : 30**.

4 Maintaining the position of the crankshaft, auxiliary shaft and camshaft timing marks, fit the drive belt to the pulleys in the original direction of drive shown by the chalk marks and temporarily adjust the jockey pulley.

5 Rotate the crankshaft at least one revolution clockwise until the crankshaft timing mark again aligns with the TDC pointer. If the engine is turned too far, do not turn it back, but again turn clockwise until TDC is reached. This will ensure that the run of the belt between the camshaft and the crankshaft is correctly tensioned against the resistance of the camshaft.

6 If camshaft pulley or auxiliary shaft pulley have been removed, the centre retaining bolts can now be finally tightened.

7 Check the belt tension. A load of 10 lbs applied midway between the camshaft and auxiliary shaft pulleys should give a deflection of .3 inch. Adjust as necessary by means of the jockey pulley. Correct tension is essential.

The fitting of the remaining components to the engine is a reversal of the removal procedure, but the following points should be noted:

1 When refitting the exhaust manifold note that the sparking plug heat shield also acts as the manifold gasket and should be in good condition. Renew the lockplates, each of which secures two bolts. Tighten the eight bolts evenly and securely and bend up the tabs of the lockplates.

2 On cars with automatic transmission reference should be made to **Chapter 6a** for method of checking throttle downshift linkage adjustment.

3 When installing the special type sparking plugs, it is essential to use tool No. VR.2040 in conjunction with a torque wrench as shown in **FIG 1 : 6**. The plugs have tapered seatings and are used without washers. The specified torque of 15 lb ft must not be exceeded.

4 Temporarily install the camshaft housing cover. Refill the cooling system and run the engine at fast idling speed until it reaches normal working temperature. Remove the camshaft housing cover and finally adjust valve clearances as described in **Section 1 : 6**. Carry out the adjustment as quickly as possible while the engine is still hot. **On no account must the engine be running while adjusting clearances.**

5 Fit the camshaft housing cover. Tighten the screws evenly and afterwards check for oil leakage.

1 : 8 Removing and refitting oil pump

FIG 1 : 31 is a sectional front view of the engine showing the main features of the lubrication system. The oil pump is mounted in the cylinder block and is driven from the distributor, which in turn is driven from the auxiliary shaft shown in **FIG 1 : 2**. Referring again to **FIG 1 : 31**, the attaching bolts 1 pass through the distributor flange and the oil pump flange securing both to the cylinder block. Two projections on the pump bottom cover contain the outlet port 2 and the inlet port 4, and engage in recessed ports in the cylinder block. The pump draws oil from the sump through a suction pipe and strainer 5 and feeds it through an external fullflow filter to the main oil gallery 3 and also through drillings in the cylinder block to the crankshaft, auxiliary shaft and to an oil gallery 6 in the

FIG 1 : 30 Crankshaft timing mark and pointer

camshaft housing. From the latter, oil passes to the cams, camshaft bearings and tappets. Two types of pump are used, a vane type and a rotor type. These are interchangeable as complete units. An oil pressure relief valve is fitted in the pump body. The valve is retained by a cover which is secured by peening of the pump housing and is not to be removed.

Owing to its position the oil pump can be removed and refitted without sump removal. Removal of the sump and the suction pipe and strainer however involves engine removal and is described in **Section 1 : 9**.

To remove the oil pump:

1 Disconnect both battery cables.

2 Disconnect the breather pipe from the air cleaner and remove the air cleaner.

3 Remove the distributor as described in **Chapter 3**.

4 Remove the fuel pump as described in **Chapter 2**.

5 Using a lever as shown in **FIG 1 : 32**, raise the oil pump sufficiently to release the bottom of the pump from the ports in the cylinder block.

6 After releasing the bottom of the pump, turn the pump body through 90 deg. to clear the auxiliary shaft as shown in **FIG 1 : 33** and lift out the pump. **FIG 1 : 34** shows the pump after removal.

Refitting of the oil pump is a reversal of the removal procedure but the following points should be noted:

1 Fit new O-rings, indicated by arrows in **FIG 1 : 34**, to the pump bottom cover before installing the pump. Smear oil in the ports in the cylinder block to assist entry of the O-rings. Fit the pump flange gasket with its adhesive side to the cylinder block.

2 After installing the oil pump, fit the upper gasket with its adhesive side to the pump. This gasket is omitted on later engines, but the joint should be sealed with Hylomar SQ32/m

3 To ensure correct ignition timing, fit the distributor as described in **Chapter 3**.

4 When refitting the fuel pump ensure that a gasket is placed each side of the heat insulator (see **Chapter 2**).

1 : 9 Removing sump and oil strainer

Although it is possible to remove the sump (oil pan) with the engine in the car, this involves removal of the complete front axle assembly and calls for equipment which is unlikely to be available to the owner. Refitting of the sump from below also presents difficulties.

Removal of the engine is therefore recommended in all cases where the sump is to be removed. Proceed as follows:

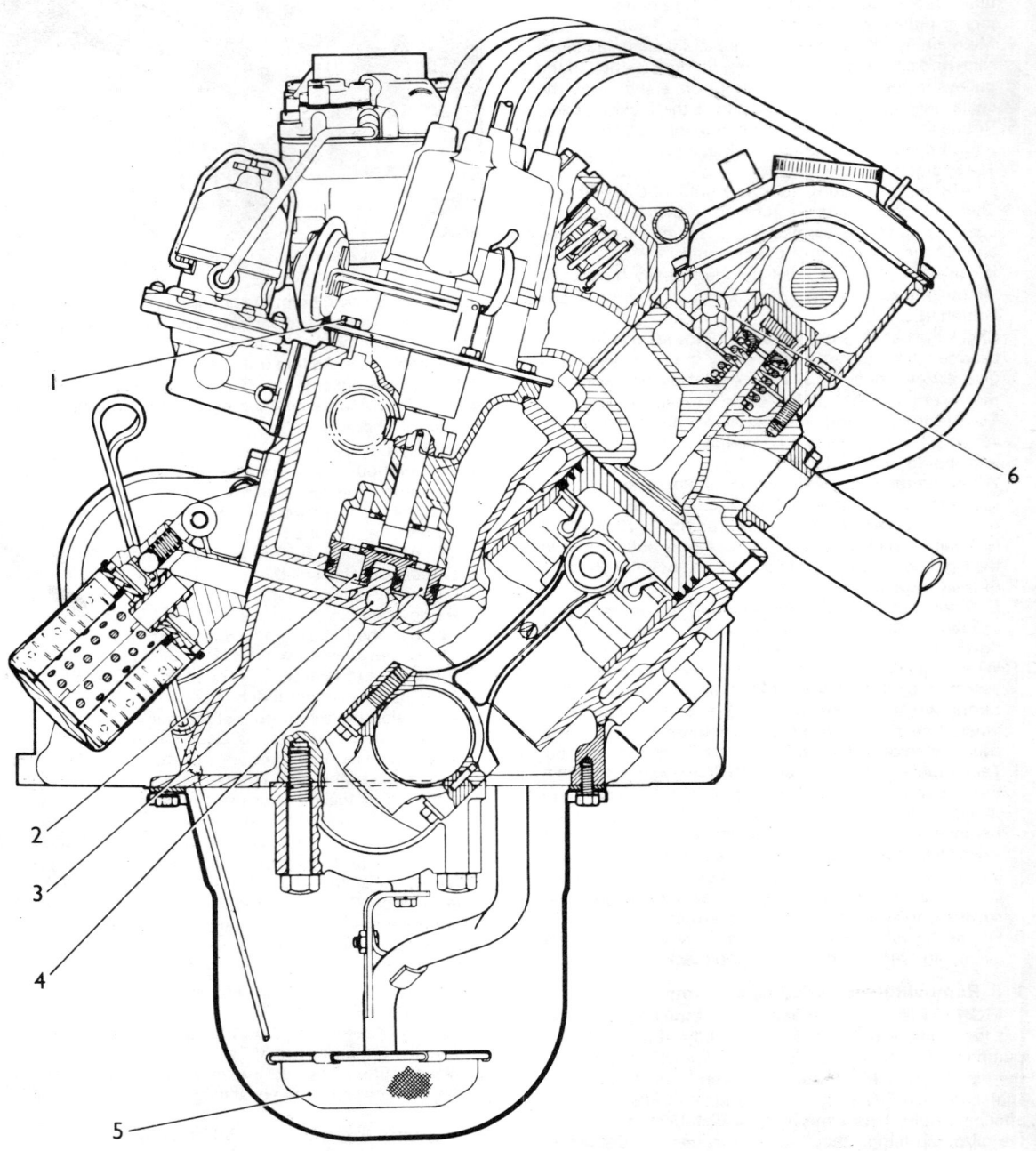

FIG 1:31   Cross-section of engine (front view) showing lubrication system

Key to Fig 1:31   1 Distributor attaching bolts   2 Oil pump outlet port   3 Main oil gallery   4 Oil pump inlet port
5 Oil strainer   6 Camshaft housing oil gallery

1 Remove the engine as described in **Section 1:3**. Drain the oil from the sump.
2 Invert the engine. This will be facilitated if the cylinder head if first removed, as described in **Section 1:5**. In any case, any major operations such as removal of pistons and connecting rods require both the head and sump to be removed.
3 Undo the bolts securing the sump to the block and remove the sump and gasket.
4 The oil strainer gauze can be removed by bending back the securing tabs. It should be washed in paraffin using a brush or compressed air. Rag must not be used.

1:10 Removing clutch and flywheel, or flexplate

On cars with manual gearbox, the gearbox is removed as described in **Chapter 6**, leaving the clutch, clutch housing and withdrawal mechanism attached to the engine. The clutch, clutch housing and withdrawal

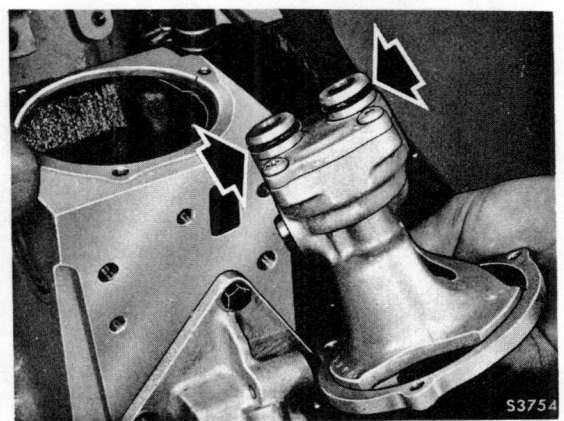

FIG 1:34 Oil pump showing O-rings (arrowed)

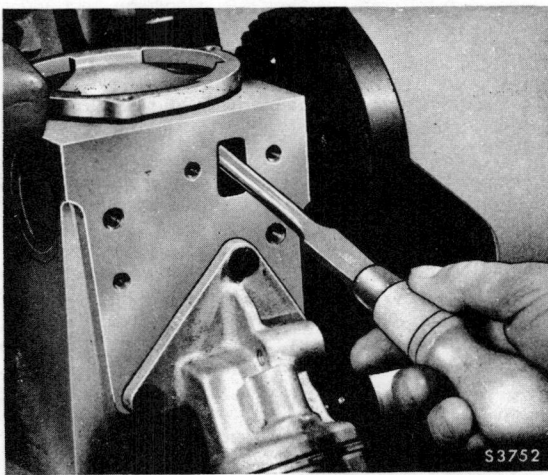

FIG 1:32 Oil pump removal, first stage

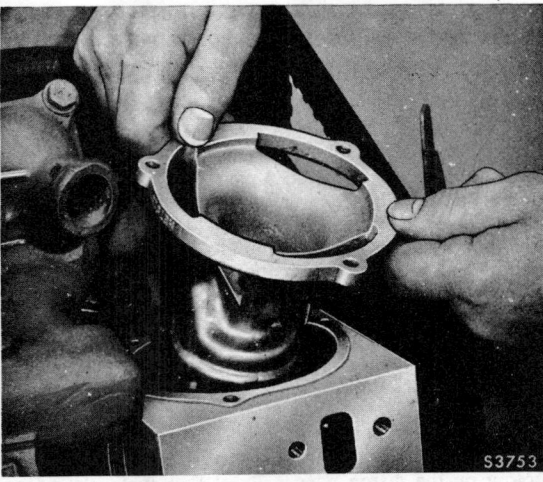

FIG 1:33 Oil pump removal, second stage

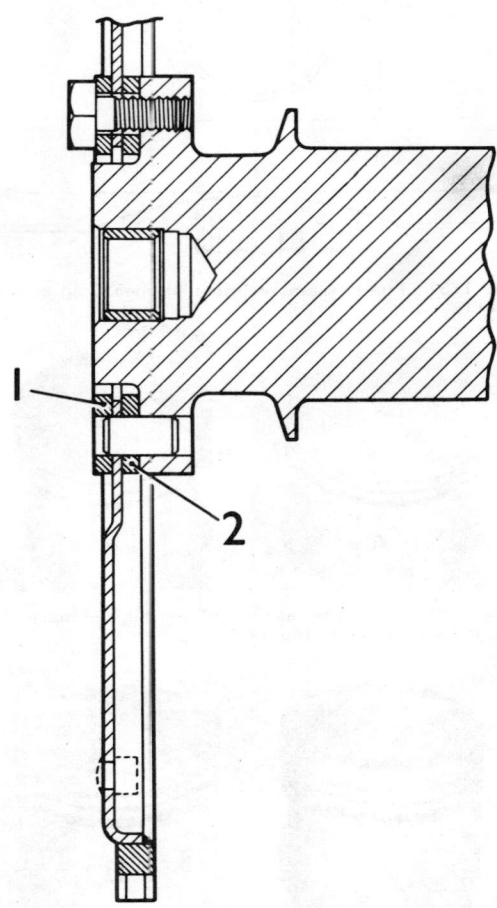

FIG 1:35 Flexplate (automatic transmission) showing installation on crankshaft with distance pieces 1 and 2

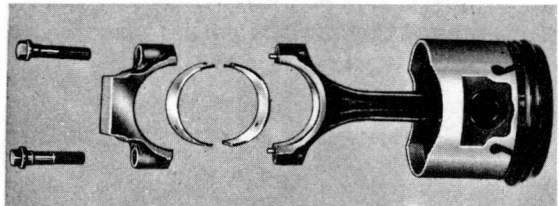

FIG 1:36   Piston and connecting rod assembly

FIG 1:37   Piston diameter must be measured as indicated

FIG 1:38   Low-compression (A) and high-compression (B) pistons for 1600 engine

FIG 1:39   Low-compression (A) and high-compression (B) pistons for 2000 engine

mechanism can next be removed as described in **Chapter 5**. This operation can be carried out with the engine in or out of the car. Engine removal was described in **Section 1:3**.

The flywheel can then be removed after removal of the bolts securing it to the crankshaft flange. Support the weight of the flywheel and keep it square during removal. The flywheel has a shrunk-on starter ring gear located in a shallow groove in the periphery. Renewal of the ring gear should be entrusted to a service agent. When refitting the flywheel, take the weight and keep it square in the same way as when removing. Tighten the securing bolts evenly to a torque of 48 lb ft.

On cars with automatic transmission, access to the flexplate, shown in **FIG 1:35**, is obtained after removal of the transmission as described in **Chapter 6a**. The starter ring gear is welded to the flexplate and if the teeth are worn or damaged the flexplate should be renewed. When refitting the flexplate the flange carrying the starter ring gear must be towards the crankshaft and the distance pieces 1 and 2 located as shown. Tighten the bolts evenly to a torque of 48 lb ft.

1:11   Splitting big-ends, removing rods and pistons

For removal of connecting rods and pistons, the engine must be removed from the car and the cylinder head and sump removed as described in previous Sections.

FIG 1:36 shows a piston and connecting rod assembly. Before splitting the big-ends, mark each piston and connecting rod assembly and its cap with the cylinder number. Do not use a file or punch as such marks can lead to a fatigue failure. Numbers or symbols found on rods and caps indicate matching pairs but not the cylinder number. Piston crowns are marked 'Front' or with an arrow indicating the front, also a small figure indicating piston graded size.

Unscrew the big-end bolts and remove the caps and bearing shells. Keep these to their respective rods and caps. Place the engine on its side. Remove the carbon from the top of each bore and withdraw the pistons upwards with their connecting rods. Carefully remove the piston rings. The gudgeon pins on early engines are an interference fit in the connecting rods and no attempt must be made to remove them. For replacement, the complete assembly of piston, gudgeon pin, connecting rod and cap is supplied. Bearing shells can be renewed if the dimensions of the crankpin and the connecting rod housing bore are within the limits given in Technical Data. Note that rods or caps which have been 'taken up' by filing cannot be renewed on an exchange basis.

On later engines provision is made for removing the gudgeon pin if necessary, using tool No. VR.2506, which comprises a support base, removal pilot, installation pilot with a spring and a drift.

To remove the gudgeon pin, fit the removal pilot to the support (without spring) and locate the pin on the pilot so that the flat on the support aligns with the recess in the piston. Press the pin out using the drift until it bottoms on the pilot, then remove the pilot and remove the pin.

Before fitting a piston to a connecting rod, ensure that the grading colour on the gudgeon pin is the same as the colour on the piston boss. Lubricate all mating surfaces with a graphite oil.

Fit the spring and installation pilot on the support and then position the piston so that the recess in the piston lines up with the flat machined in the support. Polish the machined faces at the end of the connecting rod eye and heat it evenly to a temperature of 230° to 260°C (at this temperature the metal should be a dark straw colour and heat should be applied to the eye only).

With the connecting rod eye at the correct heat, locate it on the pilot inside the piston, making sure that the oil hole in the rod is on the same side as the arrow cast inside the piston.

Press the gudgeon pin through the eye in the connecting rod using the drift until the pilot bottoms on the support and hold this position for about 30 seconds to allow for cooling.

Examine the cylinder bores for scoring or wear. The diameter should be measured at the point of maximum wear, just below the highest point of piston travel. This can only be accurately measured by means of a cylinder gauge. If the bores are scored or the wear exceeds .010 inch the cylinder block must be rebored.

1:12 Pistons, rings and gudgeon pins

For production purposes, pistons are graded into eight sizes numbered 1 to 8 (stamped on the piston crown) representing variations of .00025 inch in an overall range of .002 inch. For replacement purposes, standard pistons are supplied in grades 5 to 8. Oversize pistons of .005, .020 and .040 are available. As the piston skirt is ground both oval and tapered, it is essential that the piston size is measured at right angles to the gudgeon pin and .30 inch from the bottom of the skirt as shown in **FIG 1:37**.

Four types of piston are used, identifiable by the shape of the crown. **FIG 1:38** shows pistons for the 1600 engine, A being low-compression and B high-compression type. **FIG 1:39** shows low-compression (A) and high-compression (B) pistons for the 2000 engine.

The vertical clearance of piston rings in their grooves should be checked. If the grooves are badly worn, new piston and connecting rod assemblies will be required.

If pistons and connecting rods are still serviceable and cylinder bore wear is within the specified limits, new piston rings should be fitted. The slight ridge round the top of the cylinder bore must be removed before fitting new rings. Check the gaps in the new rings, placing them about $1\frac{1}{2}$ inch down the bore and squaring up with a piston. The gap must on no account be less than that specified.

Fit the piston rings in the following order:
1 A scraper ring in the bottom groove. The scraper ring spacer must be fitted in the groove so that the coloured ends A and B in **FIG 1:40** do not overlap but have their ends engaged as shown. Position the ends of rails C and spacer equally around the piston.
2 Fit the stepped ring in the centre groove, with the stepped face, marked 'Top' to the top of the piston.
3 Fit the plain compression ring in the top groove. This ring is molybdenum faced and it can be installed either way up.

1:13 Removing crankshaft and main bearings

The crankshaft is carried in five main bearings, end float being controlled by a flanged rear bearing as shown in **FIG 1:42**. Shell-type bearings are used. On production

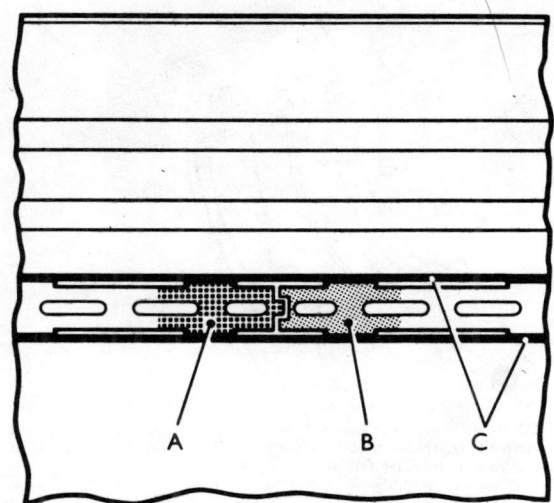

FIG 1:40 Showing correct method of fitting scraper ring

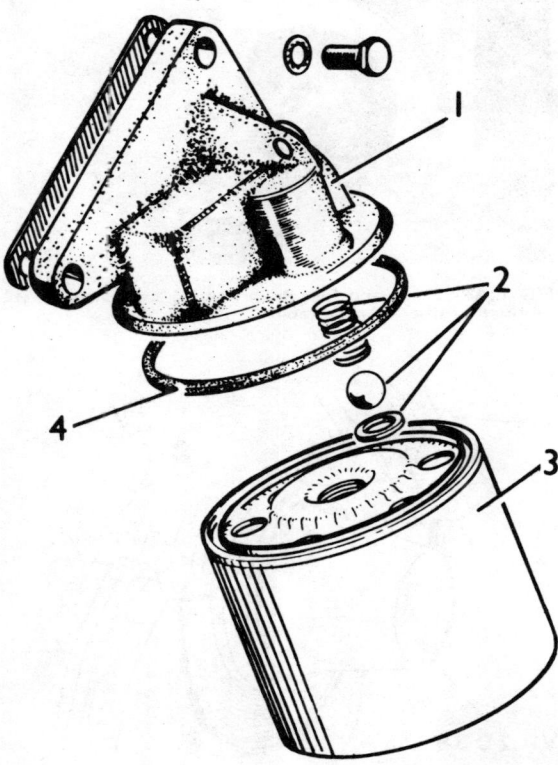

FIG 1:41 An exploded view of the external oil filter

Key to Fig 1:41   1 Adaptor   2 Bypass valve
3 Throw-away filter   4 Sealing ring

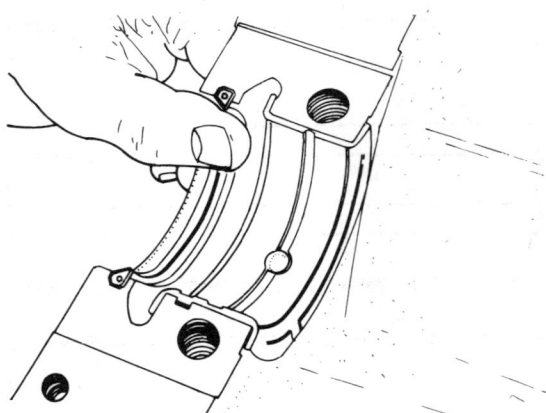

FIG 1:42 Crankcase half of rear main bearing showing flanged bearing shell which controls end float. Also shows method of fitting rear seal

S3929

FIG 1:43 Front and rear main bearing cap faces must be flush with crankcase face

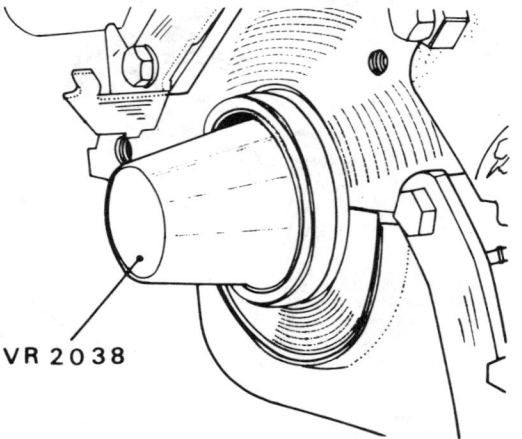

VR 2038

FIG 1:44 Fitting front main bearing oil seal using seal protector tool No. VR.2038

engines these are whitemetal lined for the 1600 engine and copper/lead lined for the 2000. Copper/lead bearings may be used as replacements on both types of engine, but bearings of different materials should not be mixed.

It is possible to remove the crankshaft leaving the pistons and connecting rods in the bores. The engine and sump are removed and the big-ends split as described in previous Sections. Normally, however, the engine will be completely stripped, the cylinder head and pistons being removed as described. The flywheel or flexplate must also be removed.

Before removing the crankshaft, check the end float to determine if the rear bearing flanges are worn. End float is best checked by means of a dial gauge and should be .002 to .010 inch.

Mark the main bearing caps to ensure that if serviceable they are refitted in the same positions. Remove the main bearing bolts and caps, also keeping each shell with its own cap. Lift out the crankshaft and discard the oil seals. Remove the bearing shells from the crankcase, again noting their respective positions.

The crankshaft main journals and crankpins should be checked for wear and ovality. If worn below the specified limits or badly scored, the crankshaft must be reground and undersize shells fitted. In production engines, crankshafts with .010 inch undersize main journal and/or crankpins may be fitted as an alternative to a standard size shaft. Crankshafts may be reground to .010, .020 or .040 undersize. Note that undersize rear main bearing shells are oversize on width to allow regrinding on rear journal flanges. An equal amount must be removed from each flange face to ensure correct location of crankshaft in relation to the crankcase. Fillet radii and crank throw must be within the specified limits. Dimensions will be found in Technical Data but regrinding will of course be entrusted to a service agent, who will also be able to check the shaft for truth by mounting between centres. Crankshaft oilways should be cleared by forcing petrol or paraffin through them under pressure.

1:14 External oil filter

A fullflow oil filter is mounted on the offside of the cylinder block as shown in **FIGS 1:1** and **1:31**. **FIG 1:41** shows the adaptor 1 which is bolted to the cylinder block. The filter is of the throw-away type, the paper element being integral with the casing 3. A rubber sealing ring 4 is fitted in a recess in the casing attachment face. A spring-loaded bypass valve 2 is located in the adaptor and ensures that oil will still flow to the main oil gallery in the event of the filter element becoming blocked.

The filter should be renewed every 6000 miles. Unscrew the filter casing from the adaptor and discard. Ensure that the new rubber sealing ring supplied with the replacement filter is correctly located in the casing recess. Smear the sealing ring with oil and tighten the filter by hand only. Check for oil leaks when the engine is running. Check the sump oil level and top up as necessary to replace the small quantity of oil in the filter. Two alternative types of filter are fitted but they are interchangeable.

1:15 Reassembling stripped engine

Before starting the work of reassembling the engine ensure that all components are scrupulously clean. If the block has been rebored pay particular attention to any corners where swarf could have collected. On a major overhaul the plugs should be removed from the main oil galleries and the galleries blown out with compressed air. Waterways in the cylinder block and head should be flushed out with water and any rusted core plugs renewed. New gaskets and oil seals should be fitted throughout the engine.

Refit the crankshaft as follows:

1 Check the crankshaft end float as described in **Section 1:13**.
2 Fit the crankcase halves of the main bearing shells in the crankcase and lubricate them with engine oil. The flanged shell is for the rear bearing.
3 Referring to **FIG 1:42**, remove any oil from the rear main bearing oil seal groove. Smear the periphery of the crankcase half of the seal with jointing compound and press the seal firmly into the groove as shown, with the lip towards the front of the engine. Smear the seal lip with anti-scuffing paste. Fit the other half of the seal to the rear main bearing cap in a similar manner. A rear seal of braided fabric is used on later engines, which should be pressed into its groove by rubbing with an implement such as the handle of a hammer and the ends cut off flush or to a maximum excess of .02 inches. Smear the seal liberally with the recommended lubricant.
4 Install the cap halves of the main bearing shells in the caps and lubricate with engine oil. The flanged bearing shell goes in the rear bearing. Fit the caps and bolts, having oiled the bolt threads. Take care when fitting the rear bearing cap not to damage the seal.
5 Before fully tightening the cap bolts, ensure that the faces of the front and rear caps are flush with the machined faces of the crankcase as shown in **FIG 1:43**.
6 Tighten the main bearing cap bolts to a torque of 83 lb ft.
7 Install the front main bearing oil seal as shown in **FIG 1:44**. The lip of the seal and the crankshaft land should be smeared with anti-scuffing paste and the periphery of the seal coated with jointing compound. Use the protector VR.2038 to guide the lip of the seal, open side first, over the crankshaft land as shown. The seal must be driven in flush with the crankcase face and the main bearing cap.

FIG 1:46 Fitting sump oil seals. Bostik 771 should be applied to the crankcase surfaces indicated by arrows

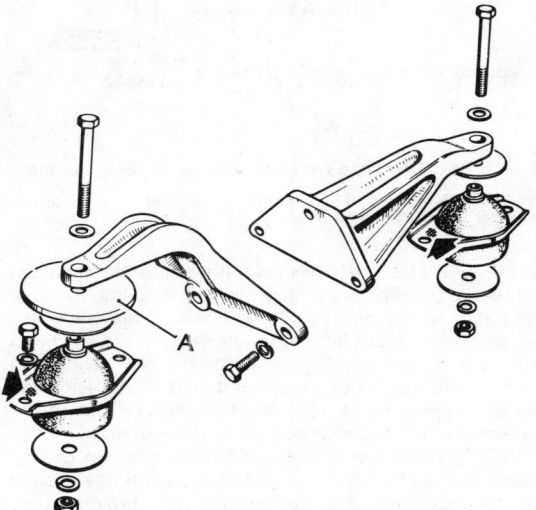

FIG 1:47 Front engine mountings showing (A) heat shield fitted to nearside mounting. Arrows indicate spots of paint identifying nearside mounting (yellow) and offside mounting (blue)

Fit the piston rings in the order described in **Section 1:12**. Lubricate the gudgeon pins, cylinder bores, pistons and rings with clean engine oil. Using a piston ring compressor, install each piston through the top of the cylinder bore, ensuring that the arrow or the word 'Front' on the piston crown faces the front of the engine. Piston ring gaps should be evenly spaced round the bore. When refitting original pistons, fit each in its original bore.

Lubricate and fit the big-end bearing shells to the connecting rods and caps. Assemble the caps and shells so that the pairing marks coincide. Note that there is an oil hole through the shell and the connecting rod for cylinder wall lubrication on the thrust side. Install the big-end bolts with oiled threads and tighten to a torque of 47 lb ft.

Before fitting the sump, if the oil strainer and pipe have been removed ensure that a new sealing ring, indicated by

FIG 1:45 A new sealing ring (arrowed) must be fitted to the oil suction pipe on reassembly

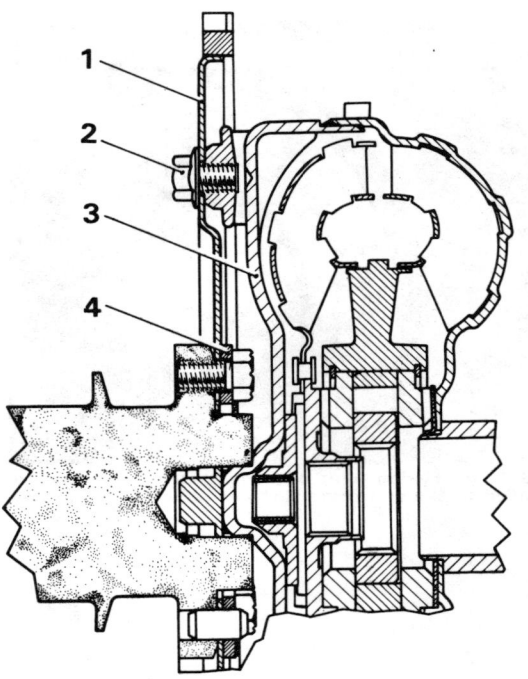

FIG 1:48 Flexplate fitted to GM automatic models

Key to Fig 1:48   1 Flexplate   2 Bolt   3 Torque
converter   4 Distance plate

the arrow in **FIG 1:45**, has been fitted and that the front
and rear of the pipe are secured by the supports. Remove
any traces of old jointing compound from the crankcase
and sump joint faces. Fit new sump seals to the front and
rear main bearing caps. Ensure that the seal grooves in
the caps and the stepped faces of the crankcase are clean
and dry. Apply Bostik 771 sealer to the surfaces of the
crankcase where the shaped ends of the seal fit, as shown
in **FIG 1:46**. When pressing the seal into the groove
ensure that each end of the seal is pressed firmly against
the stepped face of the crankcase as shown. Apply
jointing compound to the sump gasket areas of the crankcase and over the ends of the seals. Fit new sump gaskets
overlapping the seals and install the sump. Jointing compound is not used on the sump side of the gasket. Tighten
the bolts evenly.

Refit the oil pump, flywheel, cylinder head, camshaft
and drive belt as described in the appropriate Sections of
this Chapter. Refitting of distributor and timing the
ignition are described in **Chapter 3**. For installation of
clutch and clutch housing reference should be made to
Chapter 5.

On cars with automatic transmission, the weight of the
engine must on no account be allowed to rest on the
flexplate after this has been refitted to the crankshaft.

1:16 Refitting engine in car

Refit any components removed from the engine after it
was taken out of the car. Examine the engine mountings
to ensure they are in good condition. Note that a stiffer
front mounting is used on the nearside to support the
offset weight of the engine. The nearside mounting is
identified by a spot of yellow paint on the top flange as
indicated by the arrow in **FIG 1:47**. If the bolts securing
the mounting brackets to the crankcase have been removed,
clean the bolt threads and internal threads and smear with
sealer before refitting. When installing the nearside
mounting ensure that the heat shield A is located flange
downwards between the engine support bracket and the
mounting upper washer as shown.

The engine should be slung in the same way as for
removal, as shown in **FIG 1:7**. Refitting is then a reversal
of the removal procedure. The gearbox or automatic
transmission should be fitted as described in **Chapters 6**
and **6a** respectively.

On both types, refill the engine and gearbox or transmission with the recommended oil and refill the cooling
system. Ensure that all wires and controls are properly
connected before starting the engine. On cars with automatic transmission the throttle downshift linkage should
not be overlooked. Details will be found in **Chapter 6a**.

The valve clearances will have been roughly set (cold)
during engine assembly. The engine should be started up
and run at a fast idling speed to reach working temperature
and the clearances finally adjusted as described in
Section 1:6. The camshaft housing cover is then refitted.
Recheck oil and water levels and check for leaks, also
setting the idling adjustment as described in **Chapter 2**.

1:17 The flexplate, GM automatic transmission

Refer to **FIG 1:48**. On models fitted with GM Automatic transmission a flexplate 1 is bolted to the crankshaft flange to provide a drive via the torque converter 3
to the transmission. The converter is attached to the
flexplate by the three bolts 2.

It is necessary to remove the transmission/converter
assembly to gain access to the flexplate.

The starter ring gear is welded to the flexplate and if a
new ring gear is required the complete assembly must be
renewed. When fitting the flexplate to the crankshaft it
should be noted that the flange carrying the starter ring
gear is away from the crankshaft. Do not omit the
distance plate 4, and tighten the bolts evenly to the
specified torque.

1:18 Fault diagnosis

(a) Engine will not start

1 Defective coil
2 Faulty distributor capacitor (condenser)
3 Dirty, pitted or incorrectly set contact breaker points
4 Ignition wires loose or insulation faulty
5 Water on sparking plug leads
6 Corrosion of battery terminals or battery discharged
7 Faulty or jammed starter
8 Sparking plug leads wrongly connected
9 Vapour lock in fuel pipes
10 Defective fuel pump
11 Overchoking
12 Underchoking
13 Blocked petrol filter or carburetter jets
14 Leaking valves
15 Sticking valves
16 Valve timing incorrect
17 Ignition timing incorrect

(b) Engine stops

Check 1, 2, 3, 4, 10, 11, 12, 13 and 15 in (a)
1 Sparking plugs defective or gaps incorrect
2 Mixture too weak
3 Water in fuel system
4 Petrol tank vent blocked
5 Incorrect valve clearance

(c) Engine idles badly

Check 1 and 5 in (b)
1 Air leak at manifold joints or vacuum connections
2 Slow-running jet blocked or out of adjustment
3 Air leak in carburetter
4 Over-rich mixture
5 Worn piston rings
6 Worn valve stems or stem bores
7 Weak exhaust valve springs
8 Ignition timing too far advanced

(d) Engine misfires

Check 1, 2, 3, 4, 5, 8, 10, 13, 14, 15, 16, 17 in (a); 1, 2
   and 5 in (b)
1 Weak or broken valve springs

(e) Engine overheats (see **Chapter 4**)

(f) Compression low

Check 14 and 15 in (a); 5 and 6 in (c) and 1 in (d)

(g) Engine lacks power

Check 3, 10, 11, 13, 14, 15, 16 and 17 in (a); 1, 2 and 5
   in (b); 5 and 6 in (c) and 1 in (d). Also check (e) and (f)
1 Leaking joint washers
2 Fouled sparking plugs
3 Automatic advance not working

(h) Burnt valves or seats

Check 14 and 15 in (a); 5 in (b) and 1 in (d). Check (e)
1 Excessive carbon around valve seat and head

(j) Sticking valves

Check 1 in (d)
1 Bent valve stem
2 Scored valve stem or stem bore
3 Incorrect valve clearance

(k) Excessive cylinder wear

Check 11 in (a) and see **Chapter 4**
1 Lack of oil
2 Dirty oil
3 Piston rings gummed or broken
4 Badly fitting piston rings
5 Connecting rods bent
6 Oil squirt holes in connecting rods blocked

(l) Excessive oil consumption

Check 5 and 6 in (c) and check (k)
1 Ring gaps too wide
2 Oil return holes in pistons choked with carbon
3 Scored cylinders
4 Oil level too high
5 External oil leaks. Check (s)
6 Ineffective valve stem oil seals

(m) Crankshaft and connecting rod bearing failure

Check 1 in (k)
1 Restricted oilways
2 Worn journals or crankpins
3 Loose bearing caps
4 Extremely low oil pressure
5 Bent connecting rod

(n) Internal water leakage (see **Chapter 4**)

(o) Poor circulation (see **Chapter 4**)

(p) Corrosion (see **Chapter 4**)

(q) High fuel consumption (see **Chapter 2**)

(r) Engine vibration

1 Loose generator or alternator
2 Fan blades out of balance
3 Defective front mounting rubbers
4 Front mounting rubbers fitted to wrong sides

(s) External oil leaks

1 Defective oil seals on crankshaft, camshaft or auxiliary
   shaft
2 Defective sump oil seals and/or gaskets
3 Loose oil filter or incorrectly fitted sealing ring
4 Badly-fitting camshaft housing cover

(t) Water leakage

See **Chapter 4**
1 Leaks at inlet manifold water jacket gaskets and internal
   nut

NOTES

30

CHAPTER 2

THE FUEL SYSTEM

FUEL PUMP

2:1 Fuel pump operating principles

Both the 1600 and 2000 engines are fitted with the AC type FG mechanical fuel pump, shown in exploded form in **FIG 2:1**. The pump is bolted to the crankcase annexe and the pump rocker arm 13 is operated by an eccentric on the auxiliary shaft, as shown in **FIG 1:15** in the previous Chapter. Referring again to **FIG 2:1**, the other end of the rocker arm operates a link 12 pivoting on the same spindle 6 but not attached to the rocker arm. The link pulls the diaphragm 1 downwards against its spring 2, drawing petrol in through the inlet valve 14. The spring then pushes the diaphragm upwards, closing the inlet valve and forcing petrol through the outlet valve 15 into the pipe and carburetter.

As soon as the carburetter float chamber is full, its needle valve closes and the back pressure on the pump holds the diaphragm down. A small spring 10 keeps the rocker arm in contact with the eccentric and it continues to reciprocate but without operating the link. A gauze filter screen 19 in the filter bowl 21 traps any dirt before it reaches the inlet valve. There is an oil seal 4 below the diaphragm to prevent entry of engine oil. A heat insulator 9 is fitted between the pump body 5 and the crankcase. A gasket 8 is placed on each side of the heat insulator to prevent oil leakage.

2:2 Routine maintenance

The fuel pump filter should be removed periodically for cleaning. Referring to **FIG 2:1**, unscrew the thumb nut to release the wire bail 22 and remove the glass filter bowl 21. Wash the bowl and the filter screen 19 in paraffin and dry with compressed air. Refit the bowl, but before tightening the thumb nut ensure that the bowl is centred so as to enter the recess in the upper cover 17 thus making contact all round with the gasket 20. Renew the gasket if suspect, as leaks at this point will prevent the pump from operating.

2:3 Dismantling pump

To remove the pump, disconnect the two fuel pipes from the pump, plugging the inlet to prevent leakage. Remove the two bolts attaching the pump to the crankcase and lift away the pump complete with two gaskets and the heat insulator. Dismantle the pump as follows:
1 Remove the filter bowl and screen.

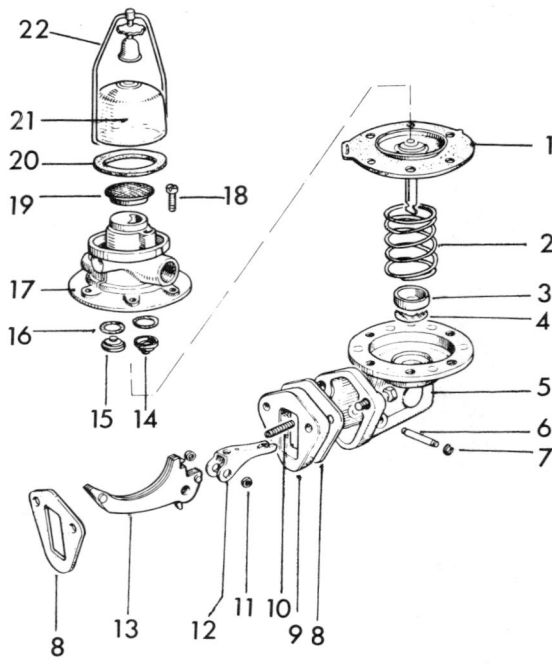

FIG 2:1   An exploded view of the fuel pump

Key to Fig 2:1   1 Diaphragm and rod assembly
2 Diaphragm spring   3 Oil seal retainer   4 Oil seal
5 Pump body   6 Rocker arm pin   7 Rocker arm pin retainers
8 Gaskets   9 Heat insulator   10 Rocker arm spring
11 Spacing washers   12 Rocker arm link   13 Rocker arm
14 Inlet valve   15 Outlet valve   16 Valve gaskets
17 Upper cover   18 Upper cover screws   19 Filter screen
20 Bowl gasket   21 Filter bowl   22 Retaining clip

Note that owing to the high level at which the pump is situated the diaphragm spring is considerably stronger than that fitted to pumps on other Vauxhall engines and it is essential for the correct replacement part to be used. Examine the diaphragm for hardness or cracks. Diaphragm, rod and components are serviced as an assembly.

Ensure that all parts are clean and reassemble as follows, referring to **FIG 2:1**:

1 Fit a new oil seal 4 and retainer 3. Stake the boss lightly at four points to secure the retainer.

2 Assemble in the body 5 the rocker arm 13, link 12 with a spacing washer 11 each side, together with the rocker arm spring 10. Insert the rocker arm pin 6 and secure with two new retainers 7.

3 Place the diaphragm spring 2 in the pump body and assemble the diaphragm and pullrod assembly with the

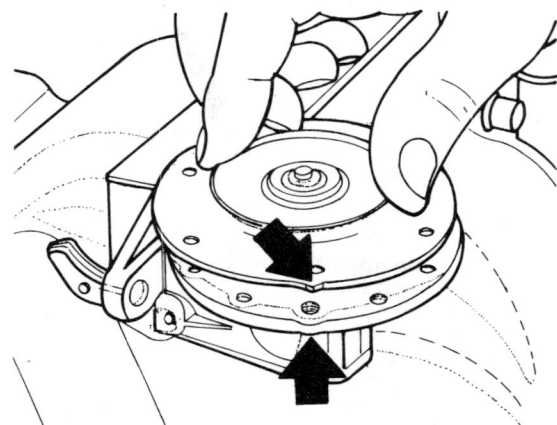

FIG 2:2   Refitting pump diaphragm. The assembly is turned through 90 deg. to align the tab with the lug on the body as indicated by arrows

2 Referring to **FIG 2:1** mark across the flanges of the upper cover 17 and pump body 5 to ensure correct reassembly.

3 Remove the screws 18 and lockwashers and separate the upper cover from the body.

4 Release the diaphragm assembly 1 by pressing down and turning through 90 deg.

5 Do not remove the rocker arm unless parts need renewal. It is removed by removing the pin retainers 7 and driving out the pin 6. This will release the spring 10, spacing washers 11, link 12 and rocker arm 13.

6 If the oil seal 4 needs renewal, remove the staking round the retainer 3 and withdraw seal and retainer using a draw-bolt and sleeve.

7 The valves 14 and 15 are staked into the upper cover. If defective they should be prised out and discarded.

2:4   Reassembling pump

Before reassembly, inspect all parts for wear, and renew as necessary. Alternatively, a replacement pump may be fitted. Only slight wear is permissible on the eccentric contact face of the rocker arm. Inspect the rocker arm spring for damage or weakness and check the diaphragm spring with figures given in Technical Data.

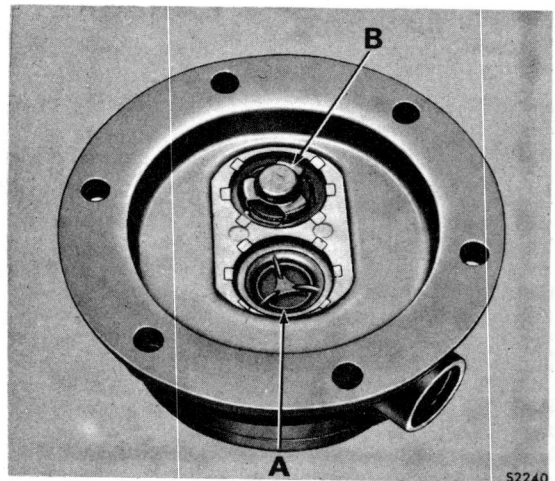

FIG 2:3   Installed position of pump valves. Each valve should be staked at six points

Key to Fig 2:3   A Outlet valve   B Inlet valve

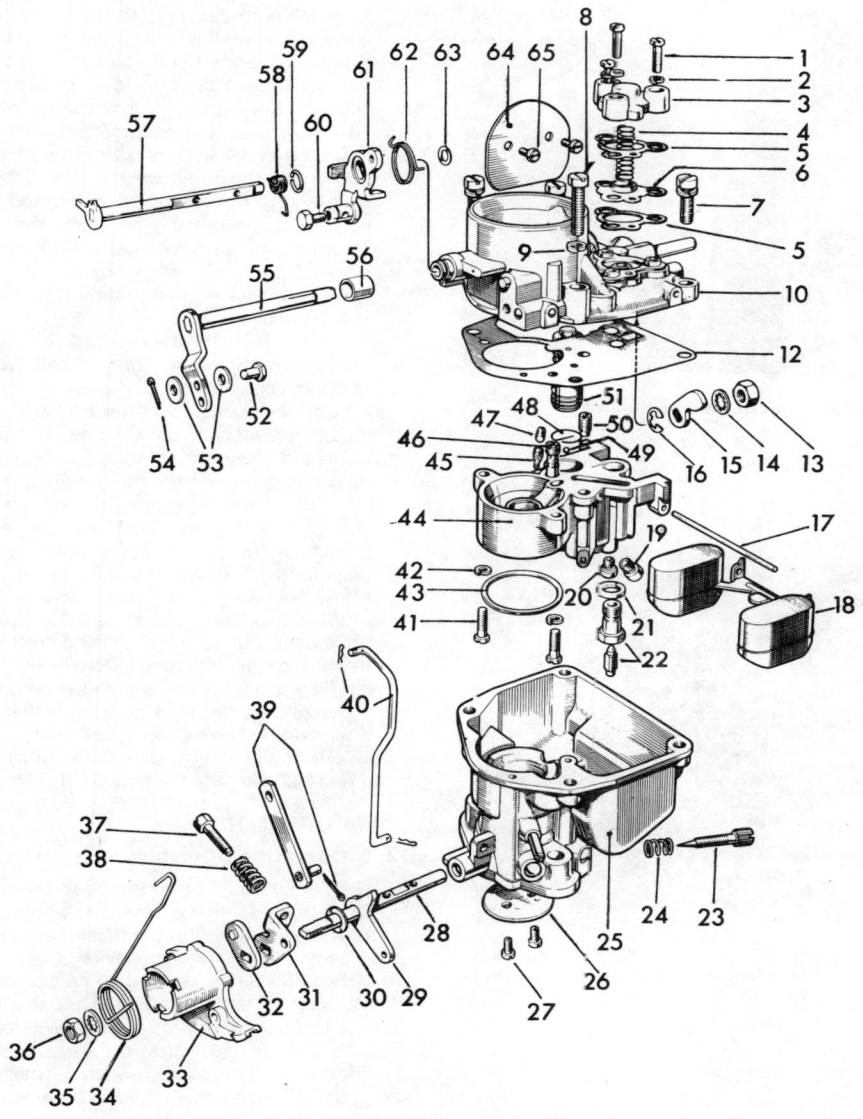

FIG 2:4   An exploded view of the Zenith 36IV carburetter

Key to Fig 2:4   1 Economy valve cover screws   2 Lockwasher   3 Economy valve cover   4 Diaphragm spring
5 Gaskets   6 Economy valve diaphragm   7/8 Float chamber cover screws   9 Lockwasher   10 Float chamber cover
12 Gasket   13 Pump lever nut   14 Lockwasher   15 Pump lever   16 Retaining ring   17 Float arm pivot   18 Floats
19 Main jet   20 Compensating jet   21 Needle seating washer   22 Needle and seating   23 Volume control screw
24 Spring   25 Main body   26 Throttle flap   27 Screws   28 Throttle spindle   29 Floating lever   30 Plain washer
31 Throttle stop   32 Inner lever   33 Cam type throttle lever   34 Return spring   35 Lockwasher   36 Nut
37 Stop screw   38 Spring   39 Throttle/pump link and splitpin   40 Throttle/choke interconnecting rod and pins
41 Emulsion block screw   42 Lockwasher   43 Sealing ring   44 Emulsion block   45 Pump jet   46 Pump discharge valve
47 Pump jet plug   48 Pump inlet circlip   49 Pump inlet ball   50 Slow-running jet   51 Pump piston   52 Pump link pin
53 Plain washers   54 Splitpin   55 Pump spindle and lever   56 Spacing collar   57 Choke spindle and pin
58 Choke spindle spring   59 Circlip   60 Cable connecting screw   61 Choke control lever   62 Choke lever spring
63 Choke spindle washer   64 Choke flap   65 Screws

FIG 2:5   Slow-running adjustment

Key to Fig 2:5   1 Mixture volume control screw
2 Throttle stop screw

FIG 2:6   Emulsion block of Zenith 36 IV carburetter showing double choke. Arrows indicate securing screws and float needle valve

FIG 2:7   The float chamber must be inverted and the distance from the gasket to the top of each float measured as shown. Dimension A should be 1.20 to 1.24 inch

small tab on the diaphragm at right angles to the location lug cast on the body. Then press down against the spring and rotate the diaphragm assembly through 90 deg. to engage the pullrod slots with the link and to align the tab with the lug as shown in **FIG 2:2**.

4 Fit a new gasket in each of the valve recesses in the upper cover 17 and install the two valve assemblies, noting that the outlet valve A in **FIG 2:3** is fitted with its spring to the top of the pump and is in the recess nearest to the outlet port, while the inlet valve B is installed the reverse way up. Press in the valves using a piece of tubing $\frac{9}{16}$ inch inside dia. and $\frac{11}{16}$ inch outside dia. Secure by staking the metal at six places round each hole as shown.

5 Fit the filter screen 19, bowl gasket 20 and bowl 21 and tighten the thumb nut on the bail 22. Assemble the upper cover as follows:

(a) Push the rocker arm towards the pump until the diaphragm is level with the body flange face.

(b) Place the pump upper cover in position so that the marks made across the flanges are in line.

(c) Fit the cover attaching screws and washers and tighten till the screw heads just contact the washers.

(d) Operate the rocker arm several times to align the diaphragm. Then with the arm fully depressed, tighten the screws diagonally and evenly.

(e) When installing the pump ensure that a new gasket is fitted each side of the heat insulator.

In the absence of specialized testing equipment the pump flow can be checked with the pump installed in the car. Disconnect the feed pipe from the carburetter and turn the engine a few times with the starter. Petrol should gush out. If it does not, remove the other end of the pipe and test again in case the pipe itself is blocked.

CARBURETTER

2:5 Operating principles

The Zenith 36 IV carburetter, shown in exploded form in **FIG 2:4**, is of the downdraught double choke tube type, incorporating a throttle-operated acceleration pump and a diaphragm type economy device. Carburetters fitted to 1600 and 2000 engines are identical except for jet settings. Carburetters fitted to cars with automatic transmission have an additional throttle control lever for the downshift throttle linkage (see **Chapter 6a**).

The carburetter comprises three main castings, the main body 25 with integral float chamber and main choke tube, the float chamber cover 10 and the emulsion block 44. Integral with the emulsion block is an extension of the main choke tube surrounding an inner choke tube and main discharge orifice as can also be seen in **FIG 2:6**.

In the base of the emulsion block are the main jet 19 and the compensating jet 20. In the top of the block are the slow-running jet 50 and the acceleration pump discharge valve 46. The slow-running jet communicates with a discharge hole below the throttle flap, the volume of mixture for slow-running being adjusted by the control screw 23. The acceleration pump is supplied with fuel through the ball check valve 49.

The economy valve diaphragm 6 is controlled by manifold depression. At steady speeds on part throttle, depression is high and the valve opens to supply extra air to the emulsion block. At full throttle and high speeds, the reduced manifold depression allows the valve to close, thus providing a richer mixture. This allows a smaller main jet to be used, thus reducing fuel consumption.

The strangler or choke is manually operated. It is interconnected with the throttle to provide a fast idling setting during the warming-up period. The choke flap is offset on its spindle and spring-loaded so that it is partly opened by engine suction as soon as the engine starts.

2:6 Routine maintenance, tuning for slow running

Jet cleaning and the checking of float level both involve partial dismantling of the carburetter and are therefore described in **Section 2:7**.

Before setting the slow-running adjustment note that air leaks, incorrect petrol level, partly closed choke flap, fouled sparking plugs or incorrect ignition timing will make satisfactory adjustment impossible. The engine must also be run until warmed up to the normal working temperature. On cars with manual gearboxes, idling speed should be 650 to 700 rev/min. On cars with automatic transmission, the adjustment must be carried out with the transmission in drive or reverse. The handbrake must be fully applied and care must be taken not to speed up the engine unduly, otherwise the car will move.

Referring to **FIG 2:5**, the slow-running adjustment is carried out with the mixture volume control screw 1 in conjunction with the throttle stop screw 2. Adjust the throttle stop screw to give a fairly fast idling speed. Unscrew the volume control screw until the engine begins to 'hunt' then screw it in until the engine runs evenly. By this time the engine may be running too fast, so unscrew the throttle stop until a suitable speed is obtained. This in turn may richen the mixture enough for the engine to 'hunt' again, calling for further adjustment of the volume control screw. Both adjustments should be carried out slowly and no attempt should be made to obtain a slower idling speed than 650 rev/min.

2:7 Dismantling

The carburetter should not be removed from the engine unless a complete overhaul is contemplated. Access to jets is obtained by removal of the float chamber cover and emulsion block. To remove the jets, referring to **FIG 2:4**:
1 Disconnect the pump link 39 from the lever 55. Disconnect the lower end of the choke rod 40 from the throttle floating lever 29. Unhook the throttle return spring 34 from the notch in the bracket.
2 Remove the float chamber cover screws 7 and 8 and lift off the cover 10. The main jet 19 and compensating jet 20 are now accessible.
3 The emulsion block 44 is secured by two screws 41 and by the needle seating 22. For access to the latter, withdraw the float arm pivot 17 to release the floats 18 and the needle valve. The two screws and needle seating are indicated by arrows in **FIG 2:6**. Take care when removing the emulsion block as the pump piston 51 will drop out if the block is inverted. The slow-running jet 50 and the pump discharge valve 46 are now accessible.
4 The pump jet 45 can be removed from the emulsion block after removing the pump jet plug 47 from the side of the block.
FIG 2:7 shows the method of checking float level.

FIG 2:8 Choke flap spring should be located in first notch on lever

FIG 2:9 Acceleration pump inlet ball and circlip

Key to Fig 2:9   1 Circlip   2 Ball

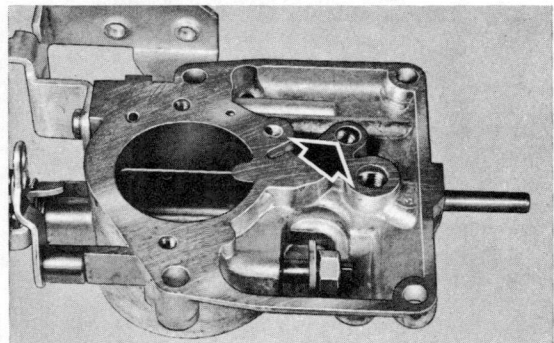

FIG 2:10 Part-throttle bleed passage indicated by arrow is threaded but no screw is fitted

The float chamber cover is removed as previously described. Invert the cover so that the needle valve is closed. With the cover gasket in position, the dimension A should be 1.20 to 1.24 inch. Slight adjustments to the level can be made by carefully bending the float arm tag which contacts the needle valve.

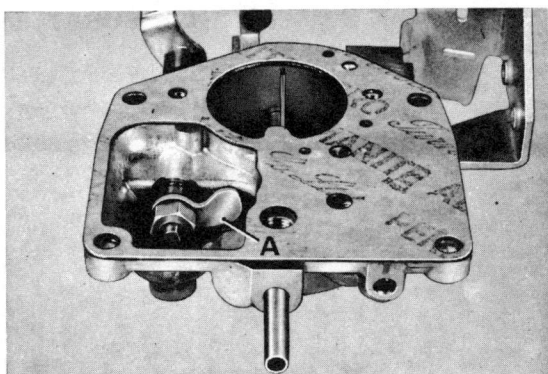

FIG 2:11 Before fitting emulsion block the pump lever **A** must be located as shown

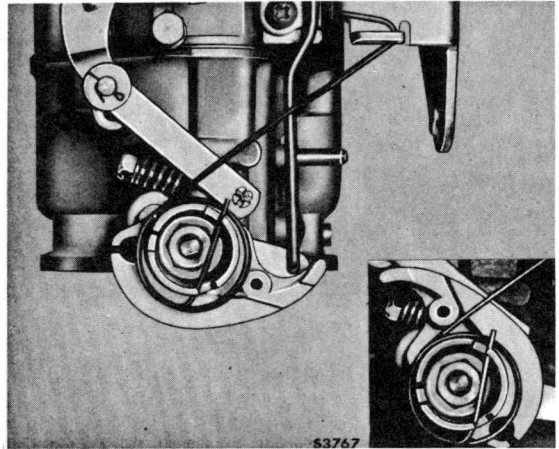

FIG 2:12 Throttle control lever return spring must be located as shown. Inset shows position of lever for LHD

2:8 Reassembly

Before reassembling the carburetter, jets and all drillings and passages should be cleaned by blowing out with compressed air. Do not use wire prickers to clean jets as this will enlarge their effective diameter. Check the jet sizes according to the figures given in Technical Data. After a considerable mileage the flow of fuel will itself enlarge the jet orifices. Actual sizes can only be checked by means of a flow meter, so that it is generally advisable to renew jets. All gaskets should be renewed, together with the economy valve diaphragm if this shows signs of hardening or splitting. Unless the carburetter is in a very bad condition, the purchase of a 'reconset', a reconditioning set containing all the jets and gaskets normally required, is the most satisfactory method of overhaul. Reassembly of the carburetter is generally a reversal of the dismantling procedure, but the following points should be noted:

If the choke flap spindle has been removed, locate the flap return spring in the first notch on the lever as shown

in FIG 2:8. Ensure that the choke operates correctly. It should close fully when the operating lever is moved to the closed position and return to the fully open position when the lever is released. Next hold the operating lever in the closed position and check that the choke flap can be opened by light finger pressure but returns to the closed position when released.

Before fitting the emulsion block, ensure that the pump inlet ball 2 and circlip 1 are installed in the pump cylinder as shown in FIG 2:9. Note that the part throttle air bleed passage, indicated by arrow in FIG 2:10, is threaded but no screw is fitted. Ensure that the pump lever A is located as shown in FIG 2:11 and that the pump piston is installed in its cylinder with its spring towards the float chamber cover. Ensure that both the pump jet and the pump jet plug, items 45 and 47 in FIG 2:4 are in position.

After installing the floats, check the float level as described in the previous Section. Ensure that the sealing ring round the outer choke tube in the float chamber casting is not defective as this would allow fuel to leak from the float chamber.

If the complete carburetter has been removed from the engine, fit a new gasket each side of the heat insulator between the carburetter and manifold. Do not overtighten the nuts securing the carburetter. Locate the throttle control lever return spring as shown in FIG 2:12. The acceleration pump link should always be connected to the upper hole in the lever as shown in FIG 2:12, the pump stroke setting being the same for summer or winter.

2:9 Accelerator and throttle linkage

FIG 2:13 shows the layout of the accelerator and throttle control linkage. The cam type throttle control lever 1 is cable operated. The inner cable 2 is connected to the accelerator pedal shaft lever 5 and retained by a spring clip 4. The pedal and shaft position is predetermined by a stop plate and buffer 6 on the shaft lever. Adjustment is provided by means of a threaded sleeve 3 and two nuts on the outer cable.

When the stop plate buffer is against the dash panel and the throttle lever is in the closed position, adjust the nuts on the threaded sleeve to provide a small amount of slack in the cable. Tighten the nuts against the cable mounting bracket and check for full opening and closing of the throttle.

For adjustment of the throttle and downshift linkage on cars with automatic transmission, reference should be made to **Chapter 6a**.

2:10 Air cleaner maintenance

The combined air cleaner and intake silencer is shown in FIG 2:14. The type shown on the left is fitted to the 2000 engine, that on the right to the 1600. The cleaner is attached to the carburetter intake by a rubber insulating sleeve 4 and contains a detachable pleated paper element 1. For crankcase ventilation the breather pipe 2 connects with the camshaft housing, while a branch pipe 3 connects directly with the inlet manifold, thus providing crankcase ventilation at low engine speeds, i.e. high manifold depression.

The element can be withdrawn after removing the screw or nut from the centre of the cleaner and lifting off the cover in the case of the 2000 engine or the cleaner shell on the 1600. Clean the element by lightly tapping

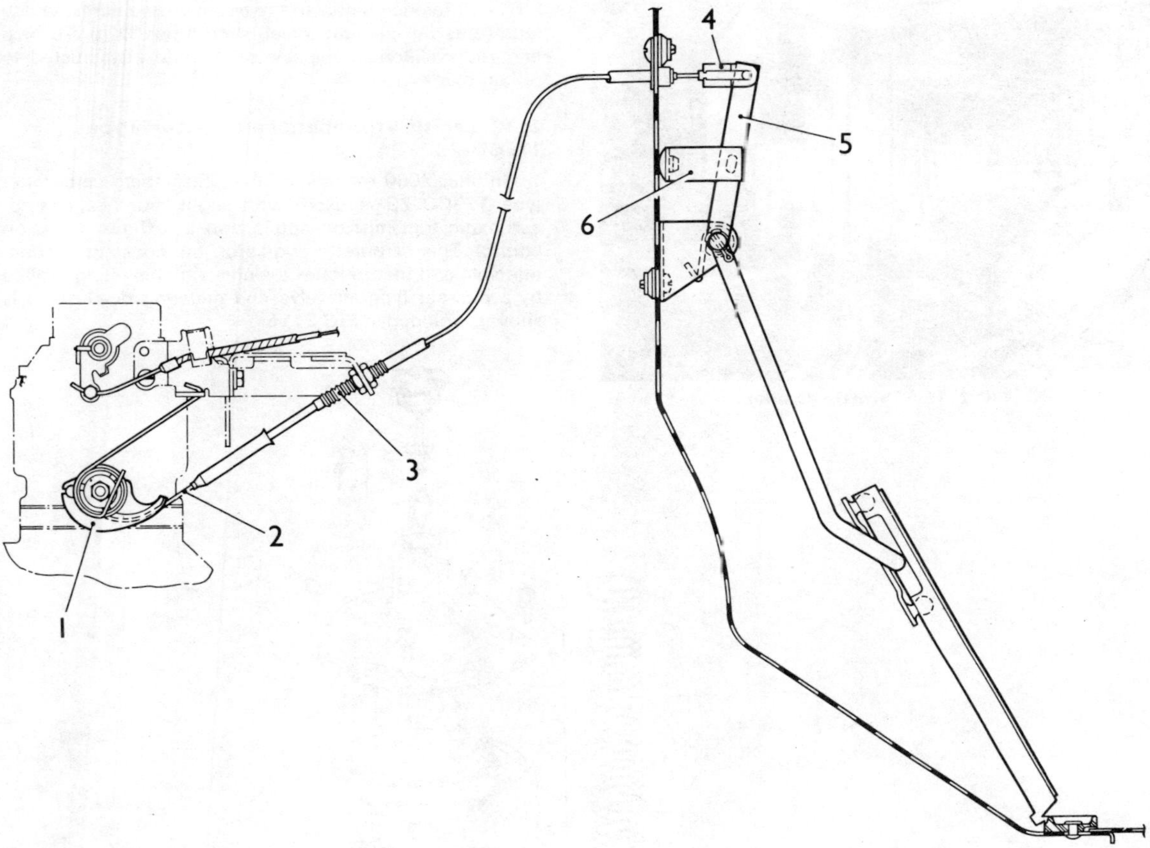

FIG 2:13 Accelerator and throttle linkage

Key to Fig 2:13   1 Throttle lever   2 Inner cable   3 Threaded sleeve   4 Spring clip   5 Pedal shaft lever   6 Stop plate and buffer

the end surfaces. **Do not attempt to clean by washing, brushing or blowing with compressed air.**

When reassembling ensure that the gaskets for the element are correctly fitted, one located on the bottom plate of the cleaner, the other in the cover or shell above the element.

2:11 Throttle damper. Borg-Warner transmission

On cars fitted with Borg-Warner automatic transmission a throttle damper is fitted as shown in **FIG 2:15** in order to slow up the last part of the throttle movement to its closed position. It should not be necessary to adjust the original setting, but if it is required proceed as follows:

Check engine idle speed and adjust if necessary. Stop the engine and hold the throttle slightly open so that the throttle lever just contacts the damper plunger, then measure the distance A between the lever and the damper housing. Allow the throttle to return to its idling position and again measure the distance A.

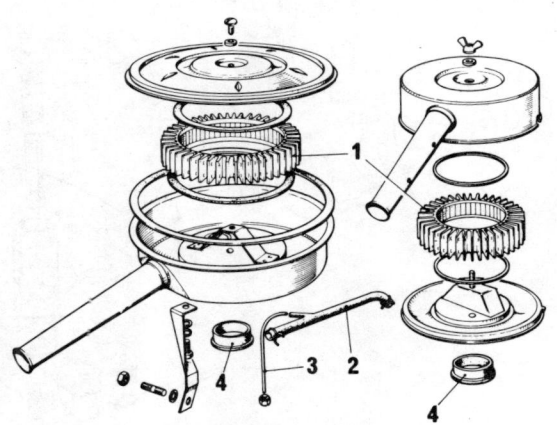

FIG 2:14   Air cleaners (left) for 2000 and (right) 1600 engines

Key to Fig 2:14   1 Element   2 Breather hose
3 Branch pipe   4 Sleeve

FIG 2:15   Throttle damper

The difference between the two measurements, which represents the plunger travel, should be .12 to .16 inch and the position of the damper should be adjusted to obtain this.

2:12 Zenith/Stromberg carburetter. Type 175CD-2S

On later 2000 models a Zenith/Stromberg carburetter type 175CD-2S is used, with slight modifications for automatic transmission application or exhaust emission control. This carburetter works on the constant vacuum principle and incorporates a single variable jet controlled by a plunger type air valve and metering needle and is shown exploded in **FIG 2:16**.

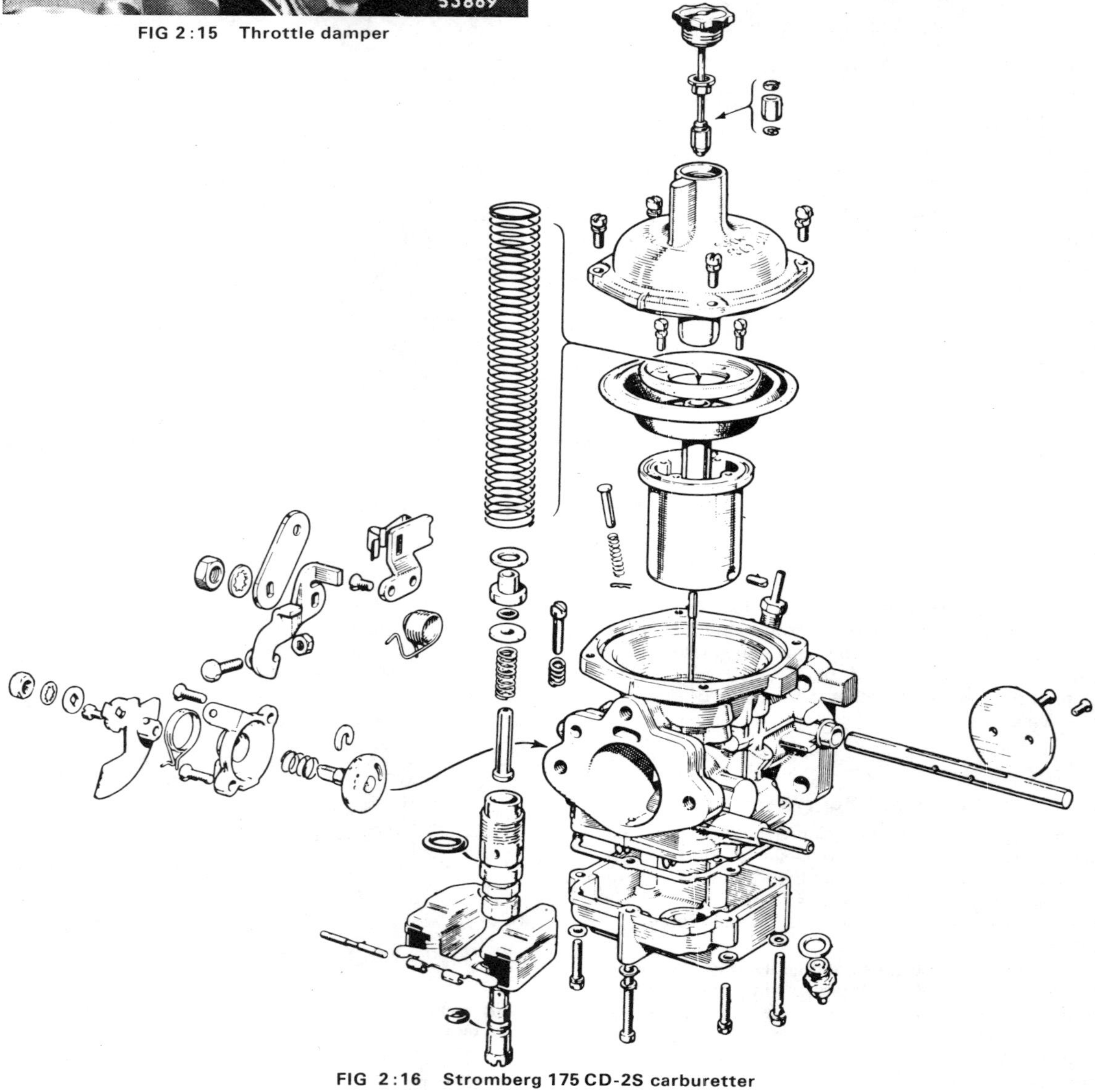

FIG 2:16   Stromberg 175 CD-2S carburetter

Cold starting is assisted by a disc-type enrichment device as shown in **FIG 2:17** and on some carburetters a temperature compensator is incorporated whose function is to eliminate minor variations in mixture strength due to temperature fluctuations. This assembly is pre-set and no adjustment is permissible.

Cold starting:

The cold-start device consists of a disc, rotated by the choke control, in which a number of holes are drilled and which permit fuel to flow from the float chamber to the mixing chamber when the choke control is operated. It will be seen that the number of holes in communication, and therefore the quantity of fuel, varies according to the extent by which the choke control is pulled out. In this manner the degree of mixture enrichment can be progressively varied to suit the conditions.

The choke control cable also operates the fast idle cam 3 attached to the cold-start device spindle 2. This cam contacts the adjusting screw 4 on the throttle stop plate and so ensures the required amount of throttle opening for a fast idle when the engine is cold.

A spring-loaded two-position stop 1 determines the movement of the fast idle cam. When the stop is fully in and the pin at right angles to its groove the degree of enrichment should be adequate for temperatures down to —18°C. For operation in lower ambient temperatures the stop should be turned to the fully raised position and the pin engaged in its groove to allow full travel of the cold start device.

Idling adjustment:

If it is desired to reset the idling after dismantling, insert a .002 inch feeler gauge between the carburetter bore and the pad on the underside of the air valve to the left of the needle. Screw in the jet adjuster underneath the body until the jet just contacts the air valve and the feeler is released. From this point, unscrew the adjuster two turns.

Start the engine and allow it to reach normal operating temperature, then adjust the throttle stop screw, to obtain an idling speed of approximately 700 rev/min. Next turn the jet adjuster as necessary to obtain the smoothest running of the engine, noting that if this causes a change in engine speed it should be restored by use of the throttle stop screw.

This setting can be checked by lifting the air valve about $\frac{1}{16}$ inch and observing the engine speed. This should rise slightly and then slow down. If the speed rises and stays up the mixture is too rich. If the engine tends to stall it is too weak. On early carburetters a spring loaded pin is provided to lift the air valve, on later models a thin screwdriver may be used.

Fast idle:

To ensure correct fast idle, adjust the stop screw 1 in **FIG 2:18** as follows:

With the fast idle cam 2 against the stop 3 and with stop pin 4 in the vertical location, adjust the screw until a .8 mm drill can be inserted between the throttle flap and the carburetter bore.

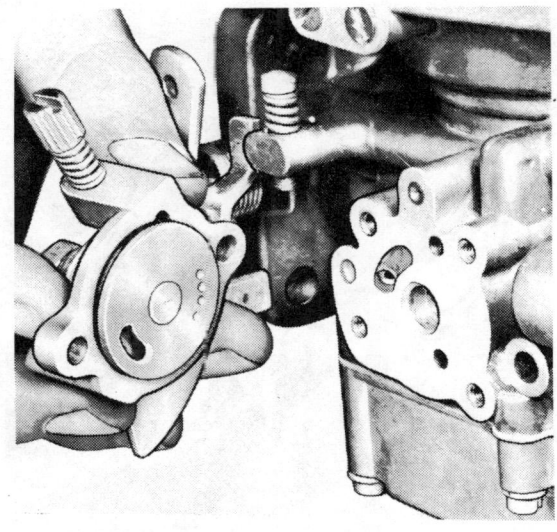

FIG 2:17   Cold start device

Key to Fig 2:17   1 Two-position stop   2 Choke spindle
3 Fast idle cam   4 Fast idle adjusting screw

Jet centralization:

Efficient operation of the carburetter depends upon free movement of the air valve assembly. This can easily be checked by removing the hydraulic damper, lifting the air valve and noting its free fall on to the bridge of the carburetter bore. If the fall is not free, or if the carburetter has been dismantled, it will be necessary to centralize the jet to ensure that the needle is not binding.

With the air cleaner and damper removed, lift the air valve and screw in the jet adjuster until the jet can be seen

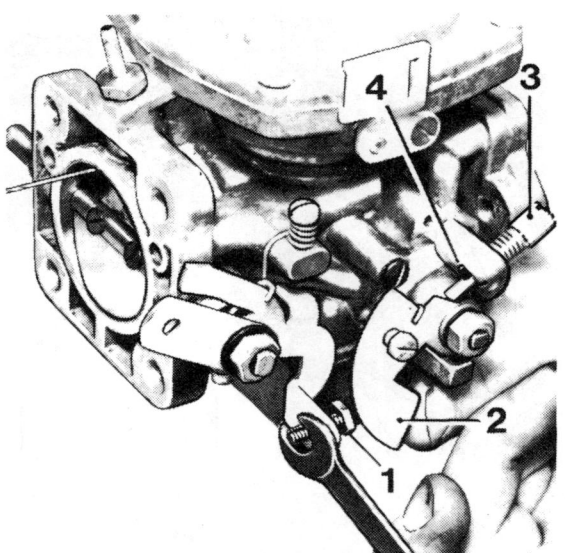

FIG 2:18 Fast idle adjustment showing position of .8 mm drill

Key to Fig 2:18 1 Adjusting screw 2 Fast idle cam
3 Two position stop 4 Stop pin

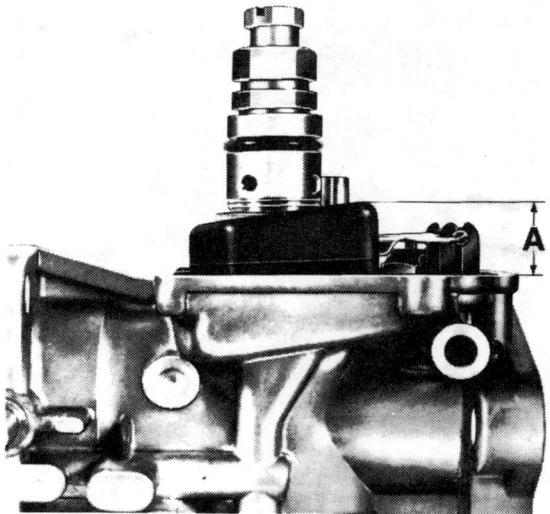

FIG 2:19 Checking float level A=15.5 to 16.5 mm

projecting into the carburetter bore. With a spanner slacken the jet bush retainer to release the bush holding the jet and allow the air valve to fall so that the needle passes through the jet orifice and centralizes it. If necessary the air valve may be pushed down with a pencil. Slowly tighten the bush retainer, at the same time checking that the needle remains free in the orifice.

Float level:

This must be checked with the carburetter removed from the engine and held in the inverted position and float chamber removed as shown in **FIG 2:19**. The float chamber can be removed without disturbing the jet bush.

With the needle valve on its seating, measure the dimension A between the highest point on the float and the face of the carburetter body. This should be between 15.5 and 16.5 mm and any correction should be made by bending the tag which contacts the end of the needle.

Hydraulic damper:

A periodic inspection should be made to ensure that the oil level in the hollow stem of the air valve is maintained about $\frac{1}{4}$ inch below the top. Engine oil is used for this.

2:13 Zenith/Stromberg carburetter 175CD-2ST

This is similar to the 175CD-2S previously described, except that it has a water heated automatic mixture enrichment device instead of the manually operated disc unit, and is fitted to cars with GM automatic transmission.

Automatic cold-start device:

This is shown in **FIG 2:20** and functions in the following manner:

If the accelerator pedal is depressed and released when the engine is cold, the thermostat lever 3 and the fast idle cam 5 will take up a rich position dependent on ambient temperature. The tapered needle 4 is lifted off its seat and fuel is allowed to pass into the mixing chamber.

When the engine fires, the vacuum from the inlet manifold is introduced behind the piston 1 and it moves against the spring. At the same time the vacuum kick rod 2 moves the thermostat lever position and so provides a weaker mixture while retaining a fast idle.

If the accelerator pedal is depressed before the engine has reached operating temperature, the vacuum behind the piston will fall and allow the spring to move the piston outwards. This will move the needle to a higher position and provide a richer mixture under open throttle conditions.

When normal temperature has been reached the thermostat allows the lever to seat the needle and closes off any extra fuel and the fast idle cam takes up its normal running position.

If this device has been dismantled, the correct setting for the thermostat is indicated by a dot on the rim of the housing which must line up with the marks on the choke body and heat insulator.

2:14 Zenith/Stromberg carburetter 175CD-2SETV

This type of carburetter is similar to that described in **Section 2:13** with certain modifications which, in conjunction with a specially calibrated distributor, assist in reducing the emission of hydrocarbons and carbon monoxide. It is designed to comply with Code 636 (European Exhaust Emission Control).

The tapered metering needle is mounted in the air valve with a bias towards the depression holes in the valve face. The jet/needle relationship is set in manufacture and must not be disturbed.

Fuel vapour from the float chamber is vented by a valve, operated by the throttle linkage, to the engine intake system at all speeds above idling when it is vented externally. The screw operating the valve is set and must not be disturbed.

Adjustment:

As mentioned earlier the jet/needle relationship is pre-set and the only adjustment of the carburetter is normally by the throttle stop screw.

During the running-in period the engine will run on a slightly weaker mixture and the idle trimming screw, see **FIG 2:21** is initially set just off its seat. This screw provides a very limited control of the mixture at idle.

Should the idling deteriorate during the running-in period, this screw can be rotated in a clockwise direction until smooth idling is restored.

2:15 Twin carburetters

All VX4/90 engines used with synchromesh transmission, and early engines with automatic transmission, are equipped with twin Zenith Stromberg 175CD-2S

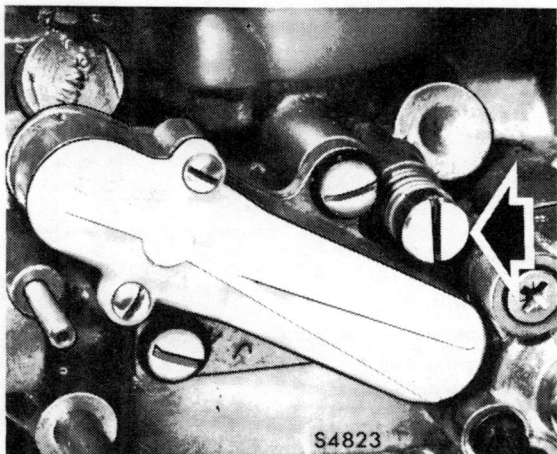

FIG 2:21   Idle trimming screw

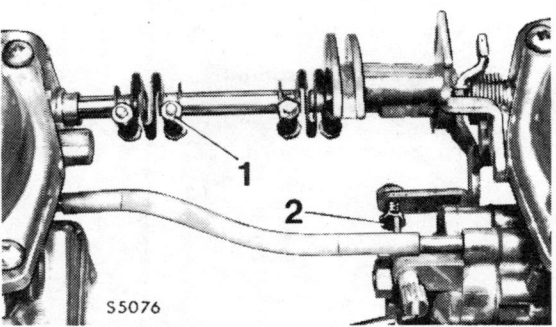

FIG 2:22   Twin carburetter couplings

Key to Fig 2:22   1 Clamp bolt   2 Stop screw

carburetters, similar to the unit already described in **Section 2:12** except for the following:

The disc-type cold start device is incorporated in the front carburetter only and is interconnected with the rear carburetter by means of a pipe.

The two throttle spindles are coupled by means of a rod and two spring couplings as shown in **FIG 2:22**.

To synchronize the throttles and adjust the idling, remove the air cleaner and make a preliminary setting of both jet adjusters as described in **Section 2:12**.

Slacken the clamp bolt on the rear throttle coupling 1 and check that the rear throttle spindle rotates freely in the coupling. Check also that the throttle cable does not hold the abutment lever away from the stop screw 2.

Run the engine up to normal working temperature and adjust the throttle stop screw on each carburetter to give an idling speed of about 750 rev/min with the air intake to each carburetter the same when checked with an air flow balancer.

The final mixture setting to obtain smooth idling is made by turning each jet adjuster the same amount. If this should bring the idle speed away from the specified figure the throttle stop screws should be reset and the air flow rebalanced.

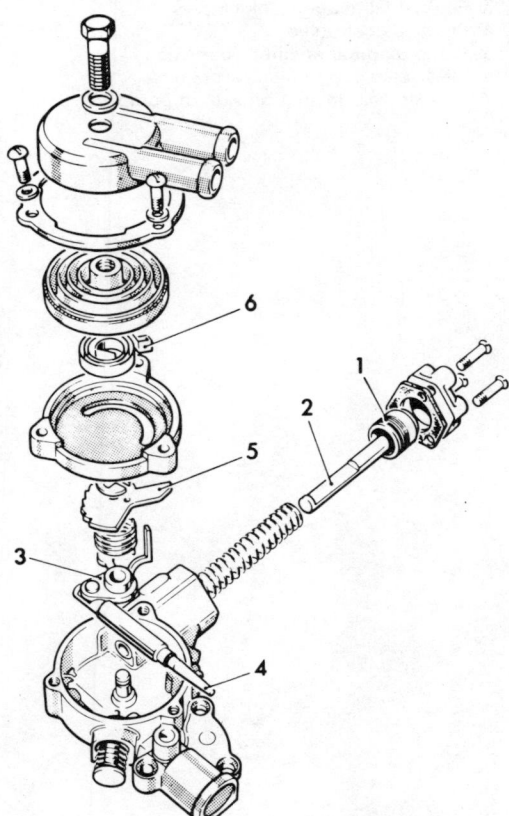

FIG 2:20   Automatic cold start device 175 CD-2ST

Key to Fig 2:20   1 Piston   2 Vacuum kick rod
3 Thermostat lever   4 Tapered needle   5 Fast idle cam
6 Thermostat

Twin 175CD-2ST:

These are used on later cars with automatic transmission and are similar to the single units previously described. Each carburetter has an automatic cold start device.

The servicing procedure already described is applicable to these installations, except that the clearance between the fast idle plunger and the base circle of the cam should be .035 inch (.9 mm).

The specification for all twin carburetters will be found in Technical Data.

2:16 Fault diagnosis

(a) Leakage or insufficient fuel delivered

1 Air vent in tank blocked
2 Petrol pipes blocked
3 Air leaks at pipe connections
4 Pump or carburetter filters blocked
5 Pump gaskets faulty
6 Pump diaphragm defective
7 Pump valves sticking or seating badly
8 Weak, broken or incorrect type diaphragm spring
9 Fuel vaporizing in pipelines due to heat

(b) Excessive fuel consumption

1 Carburetter needs adjusting
2 Fuel leakage
3 Sticking controls or choke device

4 Dirty air cleaner element
5 Excessive engine temperature
6 Brakes binding
7 Tyres under-inflated
8 Idling speed too high
9 Car overloaded

(c) Idling speed too high

1 Rich fuel mixture
2 Carburetter controls sticking
3 Slow running screws incorrectly adjusted
4 Worn throttle valve or spindle
5 Ignition too far advanced

(d) Noisy fuel pump

1 Loose mountings
2 Air leaks on suction side and at diaphragm
3 Obstruction in fuel pipe
4 Clogged pump filter

(e) No fuel delivery

1 Float needle stuck
2 Vent in tank blocked
3 Faulty fuel gauge (tank empty)
4 Pipeline obstructed
5 Pump diaphragm stiff or damaged
6 Inlet valve in pump stuck open
7 Bad air leak on suction side of pump

CHAPTER 3

THE IGNITION SYSTEM

Polarity of electrical circuits

All cars covered by this manual have an electrical system with negative earth. It is essential that replacement units should be of the same polarity as the system on the car. This affects the polarity of the generator or alternator and the connections on the battery and ignition coil, as well as certain accessories.

3 : 1 Distributor. Automatic timing controls

The Delco-Remy D.300 distributor is mounted on the cylinder block and driven from the auxiliary shaft as can be seen in **FIGS 1 : 2** and **1 : 31** in **Chapter 1**. The distributor is shown in exploded form in **FIG 3 : 1**. Three securing bolts pass through the base flange 10 and also through the top flange of the oil pump. The holes in the distributor flange are slotted to allow for variation of ignition timing. The mainshaft 4 is skew driven from the auxiliary shaft and revolves at the same speed, i.e. half crankshaft speed. The direction of rotation is anticlockwise viewed from the top of the distributor.

The disc-shaped rotor 2, which is also shown in **FIG 3 : 4**, is secured to the cam assembly 3 by two screws and located by dowels.

Referring to **FIG 3 : 1**, it will be seen that the centrifugal advance mechanism is located above the contact breaker. The mainshaft plate 20 is fixed to the mainshaft 4 but the cam assembly 3 can be rotated in relation to the shaft by the action of the advance weights 21 and springs 22. The vacuum advance mechanism is below the contact breaker. The contact breaker plate 8 can be rotated in relation to the distributor base by the vacuum control unit 16 and the link 15.

The two systems of automatic timing control are supplementary and both must be kept in good order to ensure the full range of ignition advance necessary.
1 In the centrifugal control any increase in engine speed throws the weights 21 outwards against the pull of the springs 22, turning the cam anticlockwise and thus advancing the ignition.
2 In the case of the vacuum control, any increase in manifold depression moves the contact breaker plate clockwise, thus also advancing the ignition.

It will be seen that each system has the effect of advancing the ignition under certain conditions. While the centrifugal control is governed entirely by engine speed, the vacuum control only advances the ignition when the engine is under light load. If the engine is pulling

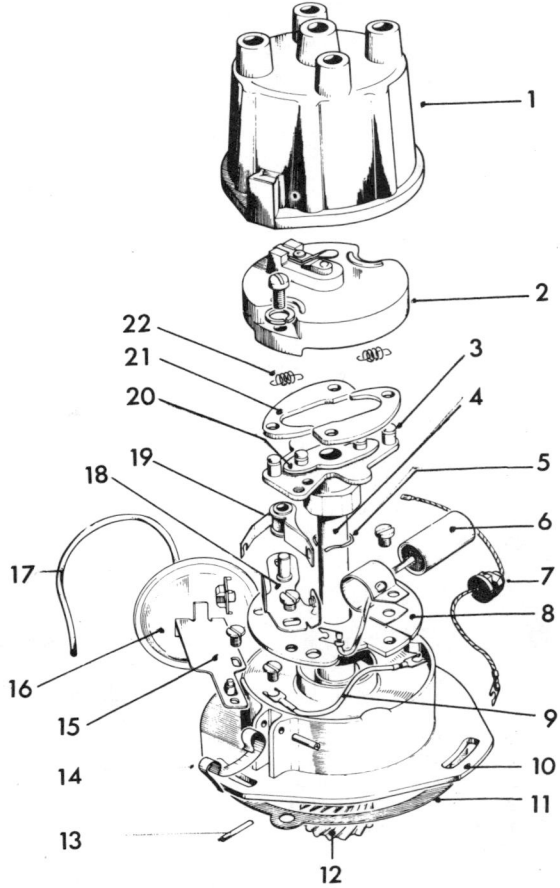

FIG 3:1 An exploded view of the Delco-Remy D.300 distributor

Key to Fig 3:1   1 Distributor cap   2 Rotor
3 Cam assembly   4 Mainshaft   5 Circlip
6 Capacitor   7 LT lead   8 Contact breaker plate
9 Earth lead   10 Base flange   11 Gasket
12 Drive gear   13 Pin   14 Spring clip
15 Vacuum control link   16 Vacuum control unit
17 Vacuum pipe   18 Fixed contact   19 Moving contact
20 Mainshaft plate   21 Advance weights   22 Advance weight springs

hard or accelerating, manifold depression will be less and the ignition will automatically be retarded.

3:2 Distributor maintenance, contact point adjustment

Referring to **FIG 3:1**, remove the distributor cap 1 by easing away the two retaining clips 14. To remove the rotor 2, remove the two screws securing it to the cam assembly 3. This will facilitate access to the contact points 18 and 19.

Apply a few drops of engine oil through the hole marked OIL in the contact breaker plate 8 to lubricate the felt pad. Lightly smear the cam faces with petroleum jelly

The contact points should be clean and free from pitting. They should be cleaned with a fine grade of oilstone but their faces must be kept flat and parallel. Badly pitted points should be renewed. To adjust the points, turn the engine until one of the distributor cams is centralized on the moving contact rubbing block. Referring to **FIG 3:2**, slacken the screws 1 and 2, insert a screwdriver in the slot 3 and move the fixed contact plate until the required gap is obtained. This should be .020 inch except where new contacts have been fitted, in which case the gap should be increased to .022 inch to allow for initial bedding down of the rubbing block. Tighten the two screws 1 and 2 and recheck the gap. After adjusting the contacts, check the ignition timing as described in **Section 3:7**.

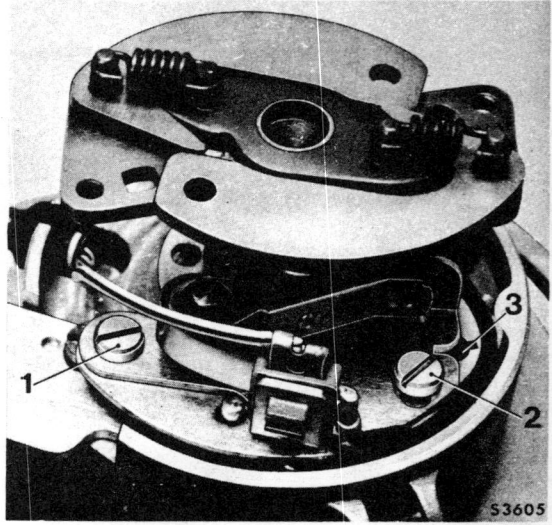

FIG 3:2 Distributor with rotor removed for access to contact points

Key to Fig 3:2   1 and 2 Screws   3 Screwdriver slot for adjustment

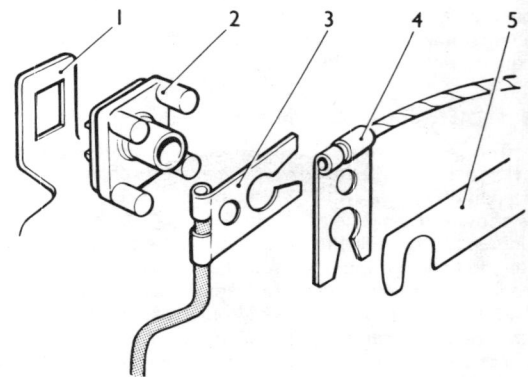

FIG 3:3 Location of leads and contact breaker spring

Key to Fig 3:3   1 Contact breaker plate   2 Insulator
3 Capacitor wire   4 LT wire   5 Contact spring

To renew the contacts:

1 Remove the distributor cap and rotor as previously described.

2 Remove the moving contact by easing the spring 5 (see **FIG 3:3**) clear of the insulator 2 and withdrawing the contact from the pivot.

3 Remove the fixed contact by removing the two screws 1 and 2 in **FIG 3:2**.

4 Refitting is a reversal of the removal procedure but before installing contacts, referring to **FIG 3:3**, locate the insulator 2 in the tab of the contact breaker plate 1. Apply a spot of engine oil to the moving contact pivot. Lightly smear the cam with the recommended lubricant. Assemble the capacitor wire 3 and LT wire 4 to the insulator followed by the contact spring 5. Adjust the contact gap as already described.

Before refitting the rotor, check that dimension A in **FIG 3:5** is 1.38 to 1.44 inch to ensure adequate contact spring pressure. **FIG 3:4** shows the round and square dowels on the underside of the rotor which must be engaged in the round and square holes respectively in the cam assembly. Tighten the two securing screws evenly.

Before refitting the distributor cap wipe it inside and out with a clean dry cloth. Examine the carbon button for wear and the segments for burning. Examine the cap for cracks or 'tracking' indicated by black lines caused by electrical leakage between the segments. An electrical check for tracking can be carried out as follows:

1 Detach a sparking plug HT lead from the cap

2 Insert the coil HT lead in its place

3 Flick open the contact points

4 Repeat with the coil HT lead in the opposite plug HT socket in the cap

5 Tracking between any two segments will be indicated by sparking inside the cap.

3:3 Distributor removal

To remove the complete distributor proceed as follows:

1 Disconnect both battery leads.

2 Disconnect the LT lead (white/black) from the coil. Mark the HT leads and remove them from the distributor cap.

3 Disconnect the suction pipe from the distributor vacuum unit.

4 Remove the three bolts securing the distributor flange to the oil pump flange and crankcase and withdraw the distributor.

3:4 Dismantling

FIG 3:1 shows the component parts of the distributor. To dismantle the distributor after it has been removed from the engine as described in the previous Section proceed as follows:

1 Remove the cap 1 after easing back the spring clips 14.

2 Remove the two screws and spring washers securing the rotor 2 and lift off the rotor.

3 Unhook the advance weight springs 22 and remove the advance weights 21.

4 If it is not intended to remove the mainshaft, remove the contact points 18 and 19 as described in **Section 3:2**.

If further dismantling is required, proceed as follows:

1 To remove the mainshaft 4, rest the drive gear 12 on a block of wood to prevent damage to the teeth and drive

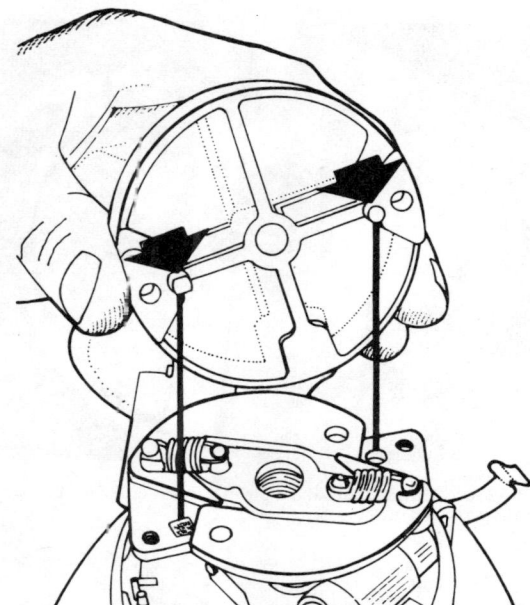

FIG 3:4 Distributor rotor. Arrows indicate round and square dowels which must be located in their respective holes in the cam assembly

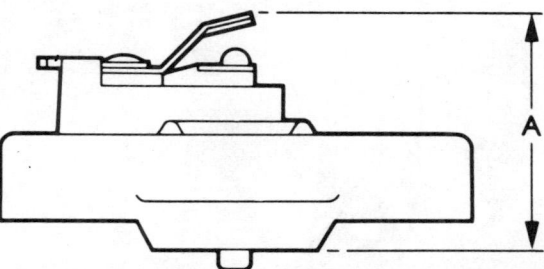

FIG 3:5 Rotor contact spring. Dimension A should be 1.38 to 1.44 inch

out the pin 13 with a suitable pin punch. Withdraw the mainshaft. The cam assembly 3 can now be removed from the mainshaft.

2 To remove the contact breaker plate 8, remove the contact points 18 and 19 and the capacitor 6. Remove the circlip 5, which is also shown in **FIG 3:6**. After withdrawing the contact breaker plate the vacuum unit 16 and the link 15 can be removed. Do not attempt to remove the mainshaft bushes as these are supplied with the base as a complete assembly.

3:5 Reassembly

Reassembly is a reversal of the dismantling procedure, but the following points should be noted:

1 If either the mainshaft, cam or any part of the centrifugal advance mechanism is being renewed, ensure that the

FIG 3:6 Contact breaker plate is retained by circlip indicated by arrow

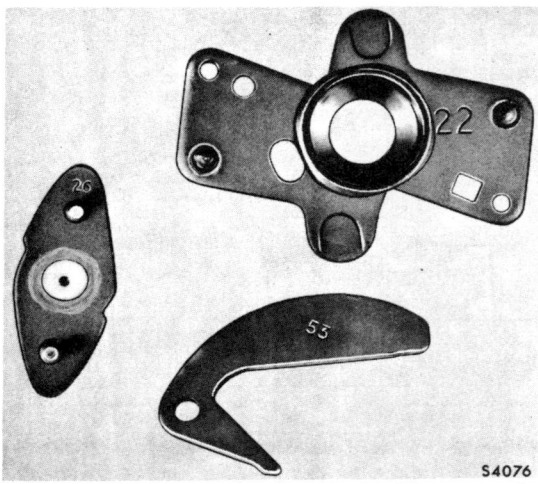

FIG 3:7 Identification numbers stamped on distributor parts, showing (left) mainshaft number on plate assembly, (top) cam assembly and (below) advance weight

correct replacements are fitted as these components differ according to the type of engine. **FIG 3:7** shows the position of indentification numbers which are as follows:

	2000 HC engine	Other engines
Mainshaft	26	36
Cam	22	20
Advance weights	53	Unmarked
Advance weight spring colour identification	Orange/blue	Orange/green

Always renew the advance weight springs.

2 Before fitting the cam to the mainshaft, pack the grooves in the upper end of the shaft with a recommended grease.

3 Before installing the contact breaker plate, soak the mainshaft felt in engine oil and engage the tongue in the slot in the base as shown in **FIG 3:8.** Lightly smear the link end of the vacuum control arm with grease.

4 Where a new mainshaft is being fitted, the drive gear must be positioned radially on the shaft so that the angle B in **FIG 3:9** (between the centre line of any tooth and the centre line of the pump drive slot) is 70 deg. It must also be positioned so that the end float A with the mainshaft assembled is .085 to .175 inch. The hole for the retaining pin is drilled with a $\frac{1}{8}$ inch drill. A new pin should always be used.

3:6 Refitting

Note that if the drive belt, auxiliary shaft or camshaft have been removed, the valve timing must be set as described in **Chapter 1, Section 1:7** before refitting the distributor to the engine.

Before installing the distributor, rotate the engine so that with the circular timing mark 3 on the camshaft pulley in the position shown in **FIG 3:10**, the crankshaft pulley mark 1 is exactly in line with the 9 deg. BTDC pointer as shown in the inset. With the engine set in this manner No.

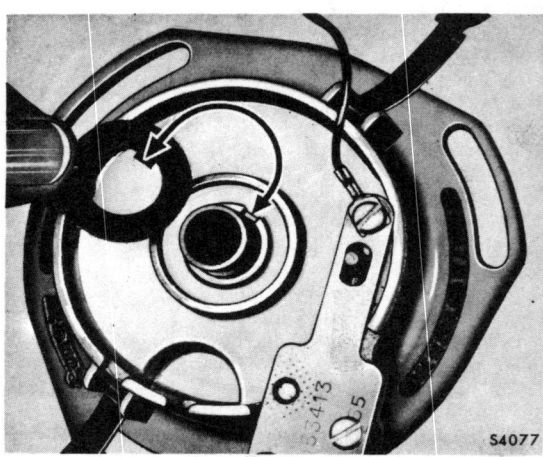

FIG 3:8 Arrow indicates location of tongue in distributor mainshaft felt. Illustration also shows vacuum advance arm

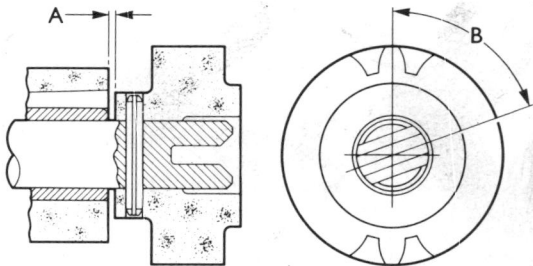

FIG 3:9 Position of gear on new mainshaft before drilling hole for pin, showing (A) end float and (B) angle of 70 deg. between centre line of tooth and centre line of drive slot

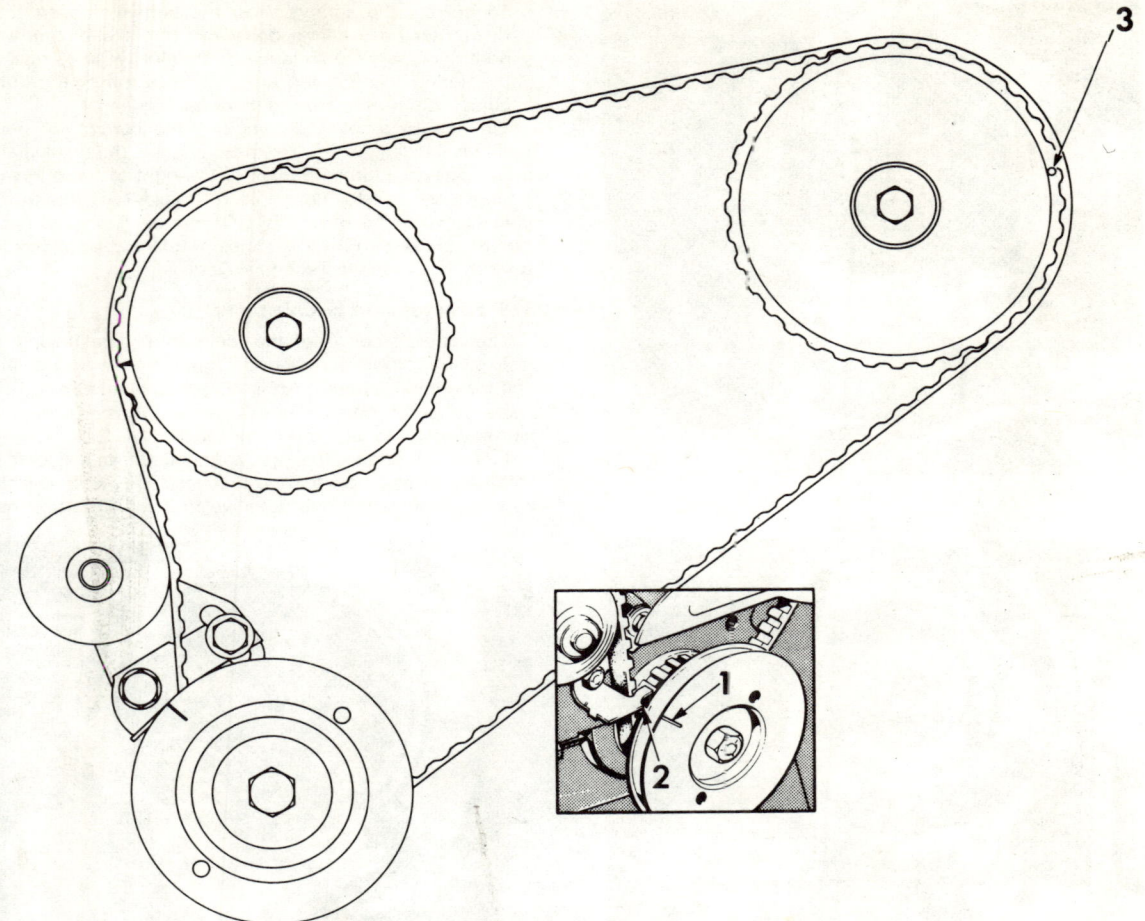

FIG 3:10 Ignition timing diagram. With marks set in this position No. 1 piston is on compression stroke

Key to Fig 3:10   1 Crankshaft pulley mark   2 Crankcase 9 deg. BTDC pointer   3 Circular timing mark on camshaft pulley

1 piston will be on the compression stroke. Lubricate the distributor drive gear with graphited oil. Proceed as follows:

1 **FIG 3:11** shows the position which the distributor and rotor will take up after installation, with the vacuum control towards the fuel pump, securing bolts approximately central in the base slots and the rotor in the position indicated.

2 Before installing the distributor however, hold it in the installed position and rotate the oil pump so that its tongue, is in line with the slot in the distributor shaft, as shown in **FIG 3:12**.

3 Install the base gasket with its adhesive side to the oil pump flange (early engines only).

4 To allow for the movement of the distributor mainshaft during engagement of the helical gears, turn the rotor anticlockwise to the position shown in **FIG 3:13**, then insert the distributor. The rotor should then take up the position shown in **FIG 3:11**. If it takes up a different

position or if the distributor cannot be fully inserted, remove the distributor completely and recheck the positions of the engine timing marks and the oil pump tongue.

5 Turn the distributor body clockwise until the contacts are just opening and then tighten the three bolts securing the distributor.

6 Refit the distributor cap and connect HT and LT leads and battery.

7 The ignition timing has been set with sufficient accuracy for the engine to be started, but if possible a final check should be made by the method described in the next Section.

3:7 Ignition timing

The most accurate method of checking the ignition timing is by means of a stroboscopic timing light. This produces a flash at the precise moment at which the

FIG 3:11   Distributor installed position

FIG 3:12   Oil pump tongue position

spark occurs at the plug, showing the exact position of the timing marks at that instant. It is used as follows:

1 Set the timing by the method described in the previous Section, so that the engine can be run.
2 Check the contact point gap as described in **Section 3:2**.
3 Connect the timing light to No. 1 sparking plug.
4 Run the engine at a speed not exceeding 500 rev/min for the 2000 HC engine or 525 rev/min for other engines. This will involve a reduction from the normal idling speed by adjusting the throttle stop, the purpose being to ensure that the centrifugal advance does not begin to operate. Direct the light on the crankshaft pulley timing mark which should have the appearance of being stationary and aligned with the 9 deg. BTDC pointer as shown in the inset to **FIG 3:10**. On those engines fitted with a front cover over the camshaft driving belt the two marks indicating TDC and 9 deg. BTDC are moulded on the cover. Where a third mark at 18 deg. BTDC is included, it should be ignored.

5 To correct the setting, stop the engine, loosen the distributor base flange bolts and turn the distributor body clockwise to advance or anticlockwise to retard the timing. Tighten the bolts, recheck the timing and adjust the throttle stop to its normal setting.

On a number of 1600 engines the correct ignition timing is 18 deg. BTDC. On these engines the crankshaft pulley has an additional mark to the right of the original timing mark and for timing at 18 deg. BTDC this must coincide with the 9 deg. BTDC pointer. A revised carburetter is used on these engines of which the specifications will be found in Technical Data.

3:8 Low tension circuit tests

The ignition coil is of the 'cold-start' type having a resistor interposed between the ignition switch and the coil for normal running. An additional connection to the starter solenoid short-circuits the resistor thus providing a higher voltage for starting purposes.

FIG 3:14 shows the coil connections and also the voltmeter connection for the first test. The white/black wire 1 connects the coil negative to the distributor, the

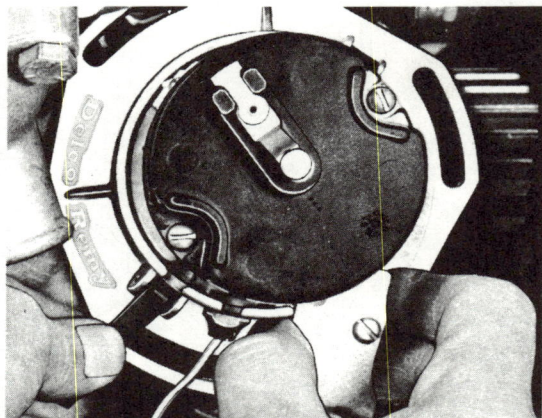

FIG 3:13 Inserting distributor. Rotor must be positioned as shown before inserting distributor to allow for rotation of mainshaft during engagement of skew gears

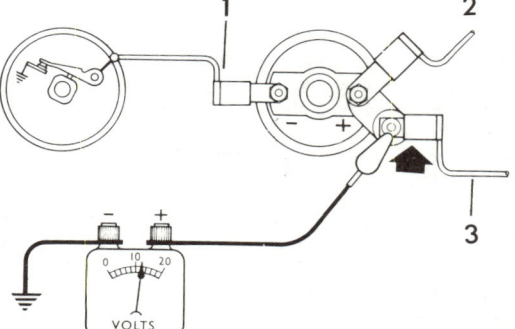

FIG 3:14   LT circuit test 1. Also showing indentification colours of coil connections

Key to Fig 3:14
1 White/black (to contact breaker)
2 White/blue (solenoid)
3 White (ignition switch)

white/blue wire 2 connects the coil positive to the solenoid while the white wire 3 connects the resistor to the ignition switch. Ensure that the battery is fully charged and carry out the following tests as rapidly as possible to prevent overheating of the resistor:

1 (**FIG 3:14**). With the ignition switched off, connect the positive lead of a test voltmeter to the white wire terminal on the coil and the negative lead to earth. Close the contact points and switch on the ignition. The voltmeter should read 11.5 to 12 volts. If no reading, check whether the fuel gauge registers. If the gauge does register, check the coil white wire. If the gauge does not register, check the ignition switch and multi-socket connector.

2 (**FIG 3:15**). Connect the voltmeter positive to white/blue wire terminal and negative to earth. Close the contact points and switch on ignition. The voltmeter should read 5 to 6 volts. If no reading, the resistor is open-circuited.

3 (**FIG 3:16**). Connect voltmeter positive to white/black wire terminal and negative to earth. Open the contact points and switch on ignition. The voltmeter should read 11.7 to 12 volts. If no reading, the coil primary winding is open-circuited or there is a shortcircuit in either the contact breaker connections or the capacitor.

4 (**FIG 3:16**). Connect the voltmeter as for previous test. Close the contact points and switch on the ignition. The voltmeter should read 0 to 0.2 volts. If over 0.2 volts, the contact points are dirty, the contact breaker plate and/or distributor housing earth faulty or the white/black wire open-circuited.

On certain later cars a neoprene cover is fitted over the ignition coil. In these cases the coil resistor is superseded by a length of resistance wire incorporated into the wiring harness between the ignition and starter switch and the coil starting feed wire.

To check starting supply to coil, disconnect the white wire from the coil and connect the positive lead of a voltmeter to the wire and the negative lead to earth. Turn the ignition switch to the start position and the reading should be at least 9 volts.

If, with the same test circuit, the switch is turned to 'ignition' the voltmeter reading should be 6 to 7 volts.

The procedure for checking the coil primary winding and contact breaker circuits is unchanged.

3:9 Sparking plugs. HT cables

The sparking plugs are of the special type shown in **FIG 3:17**. They have a long reach, 14 mm thread but have a $\frac{5}{8}$ inch AF hexagon and a taper seat which is used without a gasket. It is essential to use the special socket tool No. VR.2040 for removal and fitting of plugs. The tool is shown in **FIG 1:6** in **Chapter 1**. When tightening plugs it is essential for a torque wrench to be used in conjunction with the socket. The plugs should be tightened to 12 lb ft with clean dry threads.

For normal running conditions the AC.42.TS plug is specified. For high-speed running the AC.41.T model should be substituted. In all cases the plug gap should be set to .030 inch by bending the outer electrode only. Plugs can be cleaned and tested under working pressure on a machine used by service agents. Those which fail the test should be renewed.

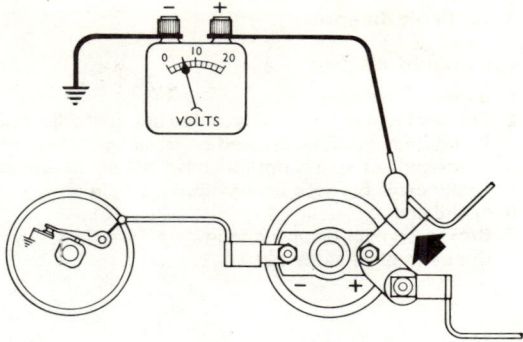

FIG 3:15   LT circuit test 2

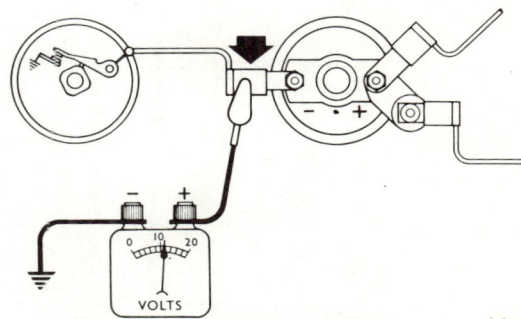

FIG 3:16   LT circuit tests 3 and 4

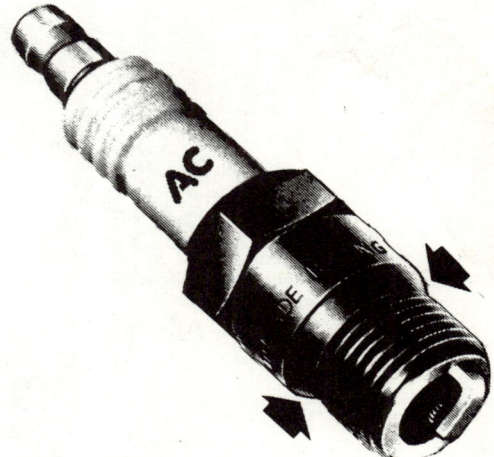

FIG 3:17   The special type sparking plug with tapered seat (arrowed)

HT cables should be examined for cracked and defective insulation. Cables normally fitted for UK are of the suppressor type with a non-metallic graphited core. This has a resistance of 4000 to 8000 ohms per foot of cable and its continuity can only be checked by means of an ohmmeter.

3:10 Fault diagnosis

(a) Engine will not fire

1 Battery discharged
2 Contact breaker points dirty, pitted or out of adjustment
3 Distributor cap dirty, cracked or 'tracking'
4 Rotor contact spring not touching carbon stud in cap
5 Faulty cable or loose connection in LT circuit
6 Faulty coil
7 Broken contact breaker spring
8 Contact points stuck open

(b) Engine cuts out when starter switch released

1 Open-circuit in 'cold-start' resistor on coil

(c) Engine misfires

1 Check 2, 3, 5, 7 in (a)
2 Weak contact spring
3 HT plug and coil leads defective
4 Loose sparking plug
5 Sparking plug insulation cracked
6 Sparking plug gap incorrect
7 Ignition timing too far advanced

CHAPTER 4

THE COOLING SYSTEM

4:1 Principles of system

The cooling system incorporates a water pump, fan, thermostat and radiator. **FIG 4:1** is an exploded view of the radiator components and shows the layout of the hose connections. The radiator is bolted to the two side panels 12 which are fitted with a detachable top shield. This arrangement is for convenience of manufacture, allowing models with six-cylinder engines (not covered by this manual) to utilize the same body shell. On the four-cylinder cars, removal of the radiator and top shield leaves a space which greatly facilitates engine removal and other operations.

The water pump, shown in exploded form in **FIG 4:2** is of the centrifugal type and is driven from the crankshaft by an endless belt which also drives the generator or alternator. The pump body 6 which is bolted to the cylinder block, houses a shaft and bearing assembly 1 secured by a locking ring 2. The bearing is packed with lubricant on assembly and periodic lubrication is unnecessary. A rotor 4 pressed on to the rear of the shaft operates inside the cylinder block. A flange pressed onto the front of the shaft carries the pulley and a four-bladed fan.

Water which has been cooled by the radiator is pumped through the water passages in the cylinder block and head. Warm water from the cylinder head passes through two ports in the cylinder head into the water jacket incorporated in the inlet manifold. In **Chapter 1,** the head is shown in **FIG 1:4** and the inlet manifold and its connections in **FIG 1:5**. The water jacket provides preheating of the inlet manifold, taking the place of a hotspot device. The latter would not be practicable owing to the position of inlet and exhaust manifolds on opposite sides of the head. As explained in **Chapter 1,** the purpose of this water jacket is to provide preheating of the inlet manifold, which is shown in **FIG 1:5** in the same Chapter.

To facilitate rapid warming-up of the engine, a thermostat is fitted. Referring back to **FIG 1:5**, the thermostat is located in the water jacket aperture 1 which carries the main return pipe to the radiator. During the warming-up period the thermostat valve is closed, preventing warm water from leaving the cylinder head by this outlet. Pressure is relieved however by means of a small diameter pipe connecting the aperture 5 (see **FIG 1:5**) with the water pump union (see **FIG 4:2**). As soon as the thermostat reaches working temperature its valve opens and water is allowed to flow through the main outlet and back to the radiator.

A pressure vent type radiator filler cap shown in **FIG 4:3** creates a pressurized cooling system which raises the boiling point of the coolant. The pressure valve 1

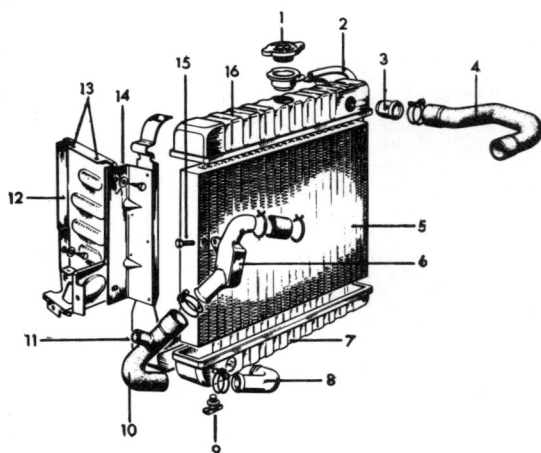

FIG 4:1   Radiator components and water connections

Key to Fig 4:1   1 Pressure filler cap   2 Overflow pipe
3 Inlet pipe   4 Radiator top hose (from thermostat)
5 Radiator core   6 Water pump inlet elbow   7 Bottom tank
8 Outlet pipe   9 Drain tap   10 Radiator bottom hose
11 Heater connection   12 Side panels   13 Bolt holes for
top shield   14 Strap assembly   15, Bolt, water pump elbow
to cylinder head   16 Top tank

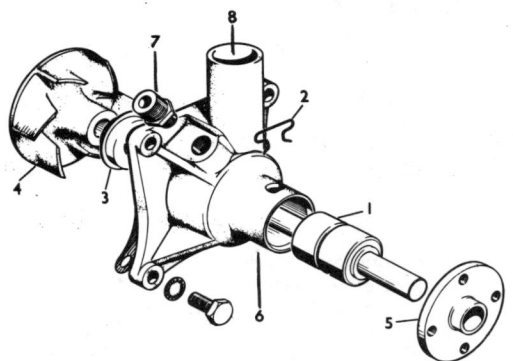

FIG 4:2   An exploded view of the water pump

Key to Fig 4:2   1 Shaft and bearing assembly   2 Spring
locking ring   3 Self-adjusting seal   4 Rotor
5 Pulley flange   6 Pump body   7 Bypass pipe union
8 Pump inlet

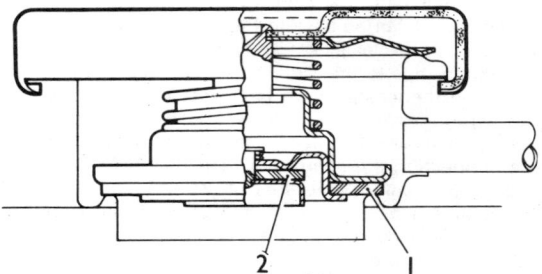

FIG 4:3   Pressure filler cap

Key to Fig 4:3   1 Pressure valve   2 Vacuum valve

allows steam and water to escape through the overflow pipe when the pressure exceeds the specified limit. As the engine cools down, any depression within the system is relieved by air drawn in through the vacuum valve 2. Pressure testing equipment is necessary for checking the correct functioning of the pressure valve, which should open at $13\frac{1}{2}$ to $17\frac{1}{2}$ lb/sq inch.

On later cars with GM automatic transmission an oil cooler is added to the bottom tank of the radiator. It is essential that if such a radiator is removed, the oil cooler pipes must be sealed to prevent the ingress of foreign matter and, after refitting, the fluid level in the transmission must be checked.

4:2 Maintenance, flushing, belt tension, antifreeze

Before draining the cooling system, the radiator filler cap must be removed. The heater control should also be set in the HOT position. **If possible, avoid removing the filler cap while the engine is at working temperature, which in a pressurized system can reach 125°C. Should it be necessary to remove the cap while the engine is hot, hold the cap with a large piece of rag. Turn the cap anticlockwise to the first detent position and wait a few moments for the pressure to be released before finally removing the cap. On no account must the cap be released in a single movement.**

There are two drain taps, one in the radiator bottom tank (see **FIG 4:1** item 9) the other at the rear lefthand side of the cylinder block. To drain the system, open both taps and ensure that they are clear. A tap can become blocked by sludge after a certain amount of water has run out. The car must be on level ground.

The radiator and engine water passages should be flushed from time to time to clear away clogging sediment. A service agent or radiator repair specialist will carry out this work by means of a special flushing gun. This introduces water and compressed air into the system and, by flushing in the reverse direction to the normal flow, more effectively removes deposits. The owner not possessing special equipment can devise methods of reverse flushing the system without pressure, but this will not be as effective as pressure flushing.

The repair of a damaged or leaking radiator should be entrusted to a specialist repairer. The latter will have facilities for flow testing, flushing and testing under pressure and will be able to advise whether the fitting of a replacement radiator will be more satisfactory than repair.

When refilling the cooling system add $\frac{1}{8}$ pint of Vauxhall corrosion preventative. Note that if antifreeze is used it must be of a type specially treated to mix with the corrosion preventative. The water level should be one inch below the bottom of the radiator filler neck.

To remove the radiator:
1 Disconnect both battery leads.
2 Drain the cooling system as previously described.
3 Disconnect top and bottom hoses from the radiator.
4 Remove the screws attaching the radiator to the side panels and lift away the radiator.
5 If required, remove the top shield, which is attached by two screws to each side panel.

If for any reason, as for instance when carrying out engine overhauls, the radiator has to be left unused for any length of time, it should not be allowed to dry out. It should be reverse flushed, the inlet and outlet pipes plugged and the radiator filled with water. Neglect of this precaution may cause sediment to harden and block the radiator.

Radiator hoses and heater hoses should be renewed if they show any signs of cracking or interior fouling. It is generally advisable to fit a complete new set of hoses when filling with antifreeze.

The fan belt drives the generator or alternator and water pump as well as the fan and its correct adjustment is important. A loose fan belt will slip and cause over-heating as well as reduced charging current. It will also wear rapidly. An overtightened belt will strain water pump and generator or alternator bearings. A broken fan belt means a complete failure of the charging system and virtually a complete failure of the cooling system, so that a replacement belt of the correct type is a most useful spare to carry. Referring to **FIG 4:4,** there should be $\frac{1}{2}$ inch free play when a load of 10 lb is applied midway between the fan and generator or alternator pulleys. To adjust, disconnect the battery and proceed as follows. Slacken the two pivot bolts at the top of the generator. These can be seen in **FIG 1:2** in **Chapter 1.** Slacken also the brace bolt in the slot shown in **FIG 1:1** and the nut securing the brace to the crankcase. Pivot the generator as necessary, tighten the bolts and nut and recheck the adjustment. When a new fan belt is fitted, tension should be rechecked after 1000 miles.

In winter and in cold climates the use of a suitable antifreeze mixture is preferable to draining the cooling system. Complete draining is difficult to ensure and when a heater is fitted this does not drain with the cooling system. Note that if a corrosion preventative is used the antifreeze must be of a type specially treated to mix with this. The degrees of protection afforded by antifreeze varies with the proportions used and the instructions of the makers of the antifreeze should be carefully followed. Before filling with antifreeze the radiator should be flushed and the radiator and heater hoses renewed. When topping up the radiator, use antifreeze mixture in the original proportions. Frequent topping up with plain water can reduce the strength of the mixture in the cooling system below the danger point.

FIG 4:4 Showing point at which fan belt tension should be checked

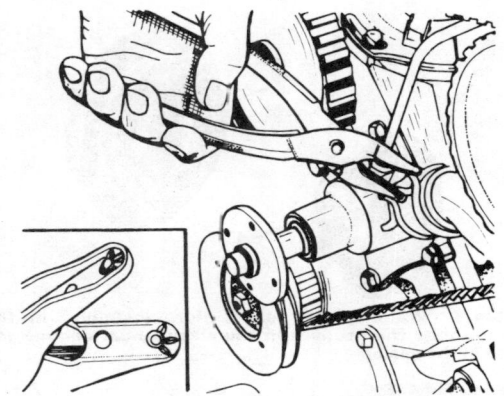

FIG 4:5 Using the special pliers No. UM.9 to release spring hose clips on water pump connection

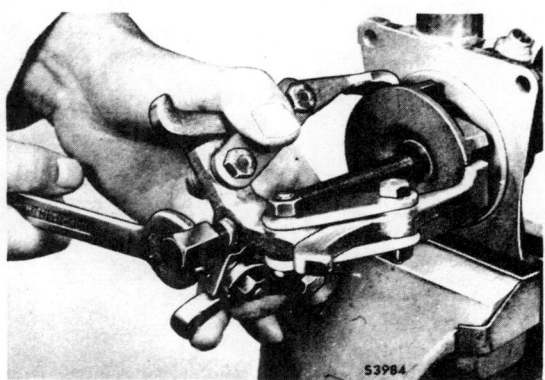

FIG 4:6 Three-legged puller used to withdraw water-pump rotor

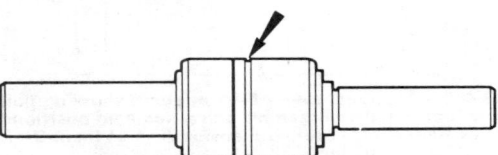

FIG 4:7 Water pump shaft and bearing assembly. The assembly must be pressed into the body so that the lock-ring groove indicated by arrow coincides with the groove in the body. The front of the shaft is identified by its larger diameter.

4:3 Water pump removal

To remove the water pump when the engine is in the car proceed as follows:

1 Disconnect both battery leads.
2 Drain the cooling system as described in the previous Section.
3 Slacken the fan belt as described in the previous Section and remove the belt.
4 Remove the four bolts from the front of the fan and withdraw the fan blades and fan pulley.
5 On late models where a camshaft drive belt cover is fitted, remove the cover as described in **Chapter 1.**

FIG 4 : 8 Water pump seal. Before installing in the pump body the grooves in the sleeve must engage the pips in the casing

Key to Fig 4 : 8   1 Grooves   2 Pips

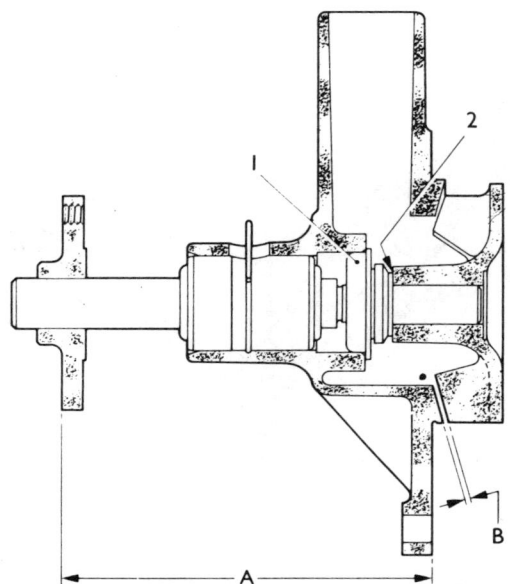

FIG 4 : 9 Sectional view of water pump showing points to be lubricated on assembly and assembled positions of pulley flange and rotor. Dimension A: 4.44 inch, Dimension B : .03 to .05 inch

Key to Fig 4 : 9   1 Periphery of seal   2 Thrust face

6 Disconnect the hose from the pump inlet as shown in **FIG 4 : 5.** Removal of hose clips is facilitated by the use of the special pliers No. UM.9 as illustrated. If it is found necessary to release the water pump inlet elbow, also shown at 6 in **FIG 4 : 1,** note that it is secured to the cylinder head by one bolt.

7 Disconnect the bypass pipe at the pump union.

8 Remove the four bolts and spring washers securing the pump to the cylinder block and withdraw the pump.

4:4 Water pump dismantling, reassembling and refitting

The water pump components are shown in exploded form in **FIG 4 : 2. FIG 4 : 9** is a sectional view of the pump. Referring to **FIG 4 : 2,** both the rotor 4 and the pulley

flange 5 are a press fit on the shaft 1. The rotor can be withdrawn using a three-legged puller as shown in **FIG 4 : 6.** The seal 3 can then be withdrawn. If the shaft and bearing assembly 1 is to be removed, first remove the locking ring 2 by squeezing the sides together. The shaft together with pulley flange 5 can then be pressed out of the pump body.

When reassembling the pump, the shaft and bearing must be pressed into the body so that the locking ring groove, indicated by the arrow in **FIG 4 : 7,** coincides with the groove in the pump body. The front of the shaft can be identified by its larger diameter. Before installing the seal in the body, ensure that it is correctly assembled. Referring to **FIG 4 : 8,** the grooves 1 in the sleeve must engage in the pips 2 in the casing.

When installing the seal shown at 1 in **FIG 4 : 9,** smear the thrust face 2 with rubber grease. The pulley flange must be pressed onto the shaft until the dimension A is 4.44 inch and the rotor must be pressed on until dimension B is .03 to .05 inch.

On later models an eight-bladed plastic fan is used with a revised pulley and flange. With this type of installation dimension A is 3.78 inch.

If several components of the water pump need renewal, it will be more satisfactory to fit a replacement pump, which is available on an exchange basis.

When installing the pump on the engine, note the following:

1 Ensure that the pump attaching faces are clean and free from burrs.

2 Smear jointing compound on each side of a new gasket.

3 Adjust the fan belt tension as described in **Section 4 : 2.**

4 After refilling the cooling system, check hose connections for leaks.

4 : 5 Thermostat removal and testing

A capsule type thermostat is fitted, two alternative makes being used. These are shown in **FIG 4 : 10.** The Western Thomson (left) opens upwards while the AC (right) opens downwards, but in other respects the two are similar. The thermostat is fitted in the inlet manifold water jacket aperture shown at 1 in **FIG 1 : 5** in **Chapter 1.** To remove the thermostat:

1 Drain the cooling system as previously described. If only the thermostat is to be removed, it is sufficient to drain off enough coolant to lower the level to below that of the manifold water jacket. Retain the coolant if antifreeze is used.

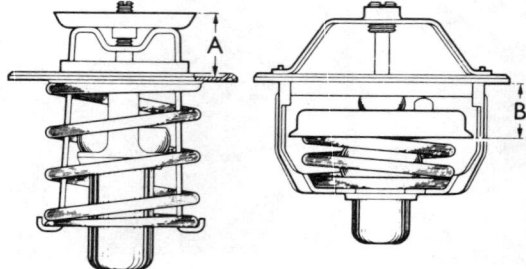

FIG 4 : 10 Thermostats. (Left) Western Thomson. (Right) AC. Fully open positions are shown at **A** and **B**

2 Remove the water outlet by removing the two bolts securing it to the manifold. Withdraw the thermostat and remove the gasket.

To check the working of the thermostat, suspend it and a thermometer in water, gradually heating the water and stirring to bring water and thermostat to the same temperature. Do not let either thermometer or thermostat touch the container or a false reading will be obtained. Note the temperature at which the thermostat starts to open and the temperature at which it is fully open, also the amount of valve opening as shown at A and B respectively in **FIG 4:10**. Specified temperatures and valve openings are given in Technical Data. If the thermostat is found to be defective it must be renewed. A thermostat which fails to open can cause serious over-heating. In an emergency it is safer to run the engine without a thermostat until a replacement can be obtained.

When refitting the thermostat, ensure that the aperture in the water jacket is clear. Refit the water outlet using a new gasket and after refilling the system check for leaks.

4:6 Fault diagnosis

(a) Internal water leakage

1 Faulty cylinder head gasket
2 Loose cylinder head bolts
3 Cracked cylinder head
4 Cracked cylinder wall
5 Leakage between water jacket and inlet manifold

(b) Poor circulation

1 Radiator core blocked
2 Engine water passages restricted
3 Low water level
4 Loose fan belt
5 Defective thermostat
6 Perished or collapsed radiator hoses

(c) Corrosion

1 Impurities in water
2 Infrequent draining and flushing

(d) Overheating

1 Check (b)
2 Sludge in crankcase
3 Faulty ignition timing
4 Low oil level in sump
5 Tight engine
6 Choked exhaust system
7 Binding brakes
8 Slipping clutch
9 Incorrect valve timing
10 Weak mixture
11 Radiator air passages or air flow to radiator restricted

NOTES

CHAPTER 5

THE CLUTCH

5:1 Construction and operation

The clutch is of the diaphragm spring type and is enclosed in a housing, shown in **FIG 5 : 7**. The front of the housing is attached to the crankcase while the rear end is bolted to the gearbox.

FIG 5 : 1 shows the principal components of the clutch, namely the flywheel with starter ring, the disc or driven plate, the pressure plate and cover assembly, the release bearing, clutch fork and operating cable.

The disc has riveted friction linings and drives the gearbox main drive pinion (first motion shaft) through a spring-loaded hub with internal splines. The disc is sandwiched between the rear surface of the flywheel and the pressure plate. The diaphragm spring is fitted between the pressure plate and cover, the plate being attached to the cover by three drive straps. The diaphragm spring is dished, and being located by fulcrum rings attached to the cover, exerts pressure at its outer edge on the pressure plate, thus transmitting the drive through the clutch disc to the gearbox.

The inner end of the clutch fork pivots on a ball stud pressed into the clutch housing and is held in position by a spring retainer. The fork jaw pins engage in the sleeve of the release bearing. The outer end of the fork projects through an aperture in the housing and is operated by a cable from the clutch pedal.

When the pedal is depressed the clutch fork moves forward and the release bearing exerts pressure on the centre of the diaphragm spring. The diaphragm spring is prevented from moving forward by the fulcrum ring so that its outer edge moves in the opposite direction. This releases the pressure on the pressure plate and at the same time, by means of three retractor clips, moves the pressure plate away from the clutch disc, thus completing the disengagement.

5:2 Routine maintenance

With the cable-type control, the clutch pedal does not give a reliable indication of the amount of free play at the clutch fork. This play is necessary to compensate for wear in the clutch linings. Insufficient play can cause clutch slip and a burnt out clutch. Excessive play will prevent the clutch disengaging properly, but this fault will make itself evident by difficulty in engaging the gears.

To adjust the cable, slacken the locknut shown in **FIG 5 : 5** and turn the adjusting nut until there is .20 inch free travel at the outer end of the fork. Tighten the locknut, operate the clutch pedal two or three times and recheck the adjustment. The nylon outer cable is graphited during assembly and must not be lubricated.

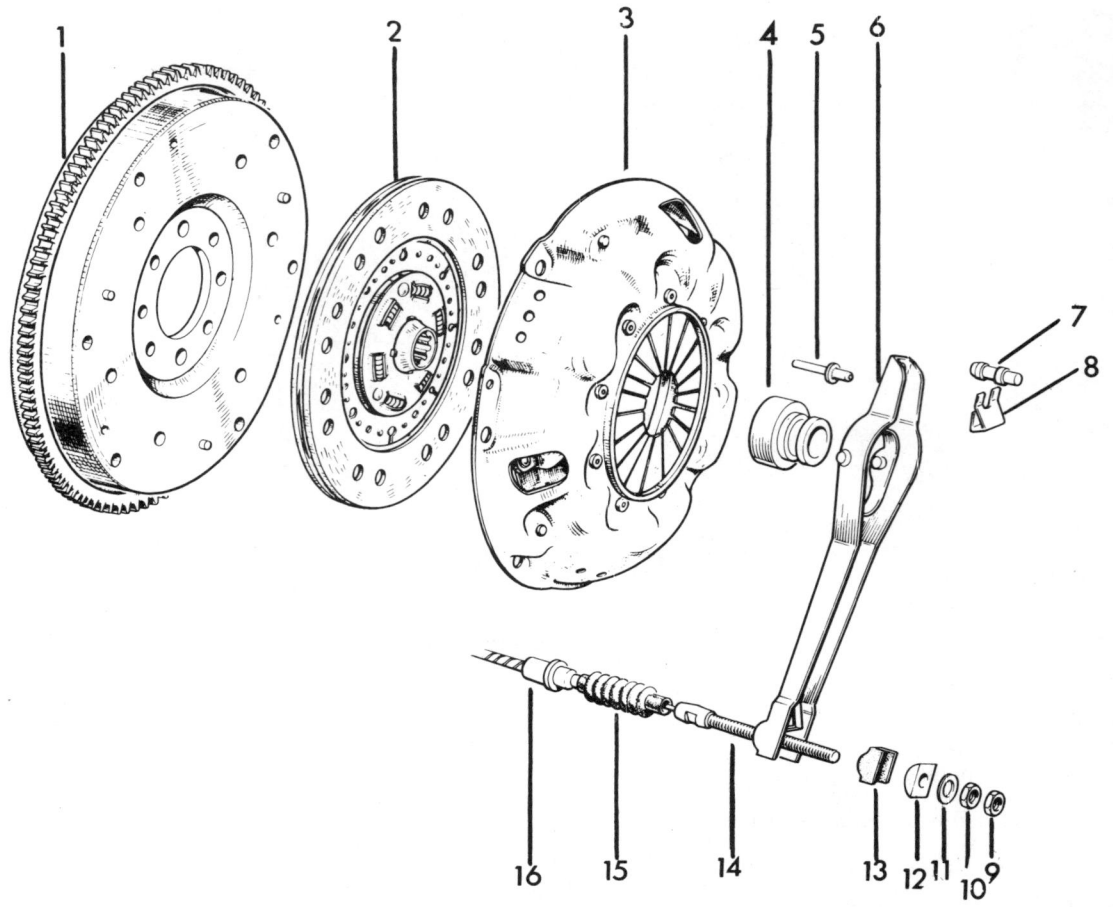

FIG 5:1   An exploded view of the flywheel and clutch components

Key to Fig 5:1   1 Flywheel with starter ring   2 Clutch disc (or driven plate)   3 Clutch cover, diaphragm and pressure plate assembly   4 Release bearing   5 Rivet retainer to fork   6 Clutch fork   7 Fork ballpin   8 Spring clip   9 Locknut   10 Adjusting nut   11 Washer   12 Pressure pad   13 Insulator   14 Inner cable end   15 Boot   16 Outer cable

5:3 Clutch pedal and cable

The pendant type clutch pedal has nylon bushes and is mounted on a common shaft with the brake pedal as shown in **FIG 5:2**. Each end of the shaft has a spring pin 1 or a splitpin to retain the shaft in the support bracket. A rubber stop 2 is located on a lug integral with the support bracket. The clutch pedal can be removed leaving the support bracket in position. The method is shown in **FIG 5:3**, in which the assembly has been removed from the car for the purpose of illustration only. Proceed as follows:

1 Disconnect the inner cable from the clutch pedal and the master cylinder pushrod from the brake pedal by removing the clevis pin spring clips and withdrawing the clevis pins.

2 Remove the spring clip or splitpin from the clutch pedal side of the pedal shaft and withdraw the shaft towards the offside sufficiently to release both pedals.

3 Remove the handbrake lever on righthand drive models and remove the brake pedal so that the clutch pedal can be withdrawn through the slot (indicated by arrow) in the support bracket.

4 When reinstalling the pedals, lubricate the pedal shaft bushes with a recommended grease. Ensure that the rubber pedal stop is not dislodged when installing the clutch pedal.

If necessary, the pedals and support bracket can be removed as an assembly complete with clutch cable. Disconnect the clutch inner cable from the clutch fork. Remove the brake master cylinder (see **Chapter 10**) and servo where fitted, also the handbrake lever. The four nuts securing the support bracket to the dash panel are in the engine compartment and are indicated by arrows in **FIG 5:4. When refitting the support bracket, care must be taken not to trap any of the adjacent electrical cables on the front of the dash panel, or** those running to the fuse block on the rear of the panel. The fuse block cover can be seen at the lower righthand corner of **FIG 5:4**.

To renew the clutch cable assembly:

1 Referring to **FIG 5:5,** remove the locknut and nut from the clutch fork end of the cable.

2 Referring to **FIG 5:6,** remove the anchor nut 2 from the pedal end of the outer cable, together with the washers as shown. The inner and outer cables can now be withdrawn as an assembly.

3 When installing the new cable, ensure that the insulating washers 1 are located on each side of the pedal support bracket as shown. **Before tightening the anchor nut 2, ensure that the adjacent electrical cables on both sides of the dash panel, are not trapped.**

4 When reconnecting the lower end of the cable to the clutch fork, locate the insulator 1 (in **FIG 5:5**) in the clutch fork, followed by the pressure pad 2 and the washer. The long end of the fork return spring must be located in the lower hole in the bracket on the gearbox casing. Ensure that the end of the boot 3 is located in the groove in the outer cable.

5 Adjust the clutch fork free travel as described in **Section 5:2.**

5:4 Clutch removal and dismantling

For removal of the clutch, the gearbox must first be removed from the car as described in **Chapter 6.** On cars

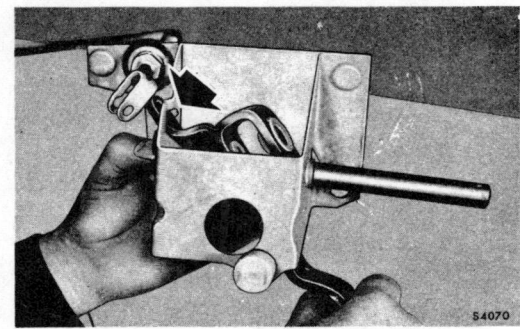

FIG 5:3 Removal of clutch pedal. Arrow indicates aperture in support bracket. Bracket removed from car for the purpose of illustration only

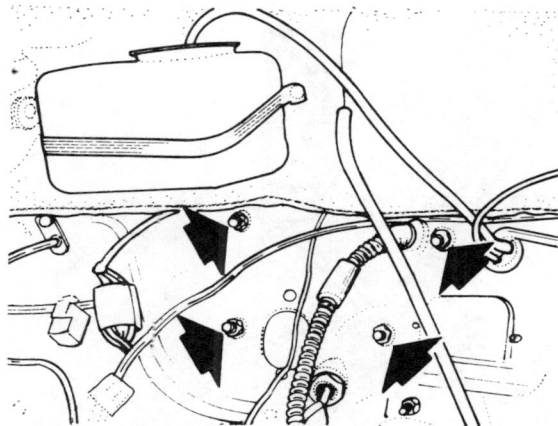

FIG 5:4 Pedal support bracket nuts (arrowed) in engine compartment.

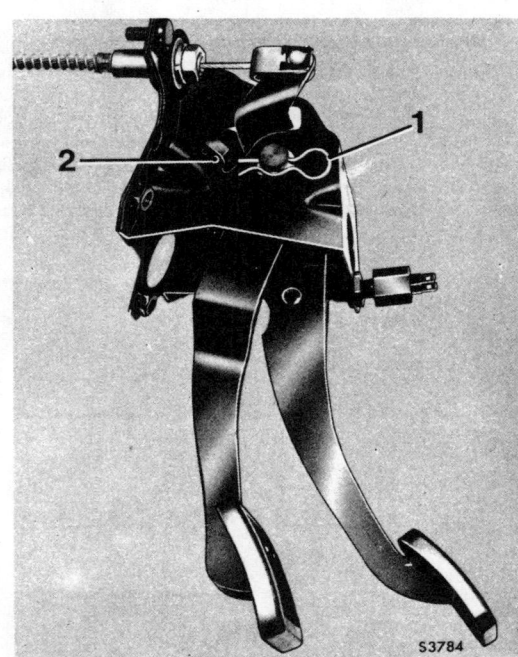

FIG 5:2 Clutch and brake pedals and support bracket
Key to Fig 5:2   1 Spring pin   2 Clutch pedal rubber stop
On some cars a splitpin is fitted in place of the spring pin

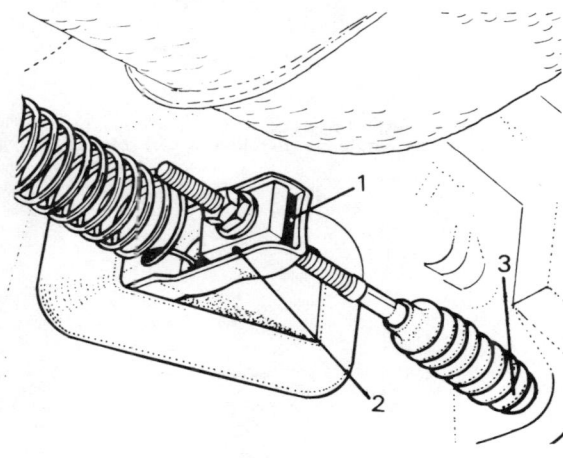

FIG 5:5   Clutch fork and cable

Key to Fig 5:5   1 Insulator   2 Pressure pad   3 Boot

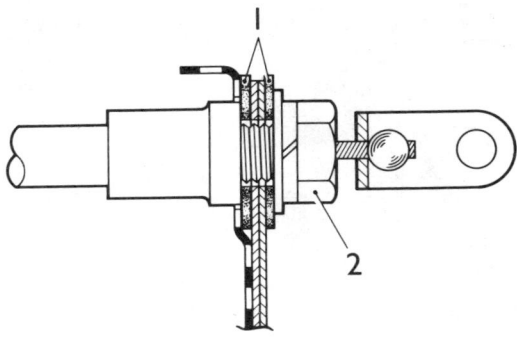

FIG 5:6   Clutch cable fitting to support bracket

Key to Fig 5:6   1 Insulating washers   2 Anchor nut

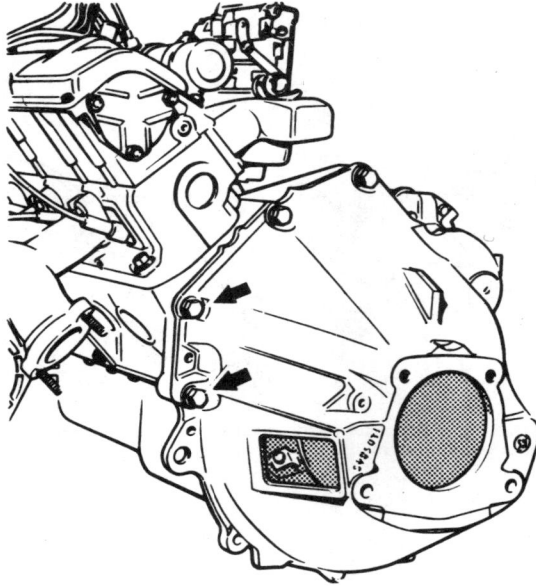

FIG 5:7   For method of access to clutch housing bolts
(arrowed) when engine is installed in car, refer to text

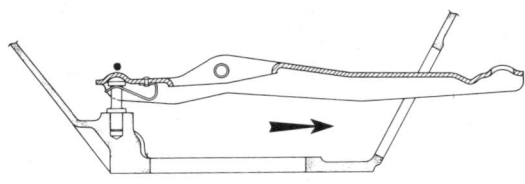

FIG 5:8   Clutch fork is removed from ball by pulling in
direction of arrow

fitted with overdrive, see note in **Chapter 6** before commencing preliminary operations.

After removal of the gearbox, the clutch and clutch
housing (bellhousing) remain attached to the engine as
shown in **FIG 5:7**. If the engine is also to be removed
for overhaul, the engine, clutch and clutch housing will
be lifted out as a unit as described in **Section 1:3**, in
Chapter 1. Whichever method is used, the clutch
housing can be disconnected from the engine after
removing the housing bolts. If the engine remains in the
car, proceed as follows:

1 Disconnect the clutch cable from the fork.
2 To gain access to the two bolts arrowed in **FIG 5:7**,
   disconnect the exhaust pipe from the manifold.
   Support the engine by a jack under the sump, using
   a block of wood to prevent damage to the sump.
   Remove the righthand front engine mounting bracket
   and ease the engine over to the righthand side.
3 Lower the engine sufficiently to allow the clutch
   housing to be withdrawn from the dowel at each side
   of the crankcase. The housing can then be removed.
   Before proceeding to dismantle the clutch, mark the
   clutch cover to flywheel relationship. Unscrew the clutch
   cover attaching bolts evenly, slackening each a turn at a
   time until the spring pressure has been released and the
   clutch assembly can be removed.

If the engine is not being dismantled the flywheel need
not be removed, but the starter ring should be examined
and the flywheel checked for security of fixture on the
crankshaft flange. The rear surface of the flywheel acts as
a friction surface for the clutch, so that it should be
examined for scoring or pitting. For flywheel removal
reference should be made to **Section 1:10** in **Chapter 1**.

5:5 Clutch inspection and reconditioning

Referring to **FIG 5:1** for the components of the clutch,
examine the friction face of the flywheel as described in
the previous Section. Inspect the clutch disc. Check for
worn hub splines and broken or weak damper springs.
Examine the friction linings for excessive wear, loose
rivets, cracks or discolouration. The polished glaze is
normal and does not affect the ability to transmit power,
but the linings should be light in colour with the grain

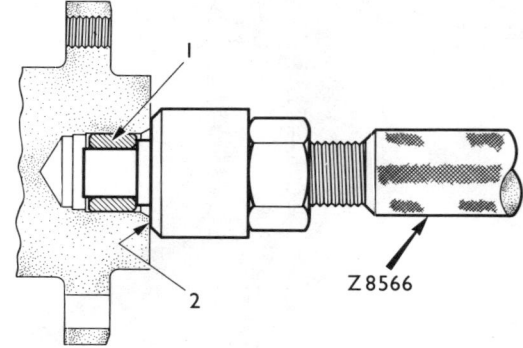

FIG 5:9   Installing spigot bush (pilot bush) using
special tool No. **Z.8566**

Key to Fig 5:9   1 Bush   2 Crankshaft

of the material clearly visible through the glaze. Evidence of oil on the linings is seen in a much darker colour which obliterates the grain. This condition can cause both clutch slip and clutch drag. No attempt should be made to reline the disc as it is serviced as a complete assembly.

Next examine the pressure plate and cover assembly. There must be no scoring or pitting on the friction surface of the pressure plate. Excessive wear or scoring of the centre portion of the diaphragm spring indicates a defective release bearing. The cover, pressure plate and diaphragm spring are serviced as a complete assembly and should not be dismantled.

Examine the fork and release bearing, which remain attached to the clutch housing. To remove the fork and bearing, pull the fork in the direction shown by the arrow in **FIG 5:8.** Do not wash or degrease the bearing. If the fork ball is worn, remove it by tapping the ball shank out of the housing, using a suitable drift under the ball head. When installing a new ball, use a soft hammer to avoid damaging the ball end. Lubricate the ball with a recommended grease.

Check the main drive spigot bearing (pilot bush) in the crankshaft flange for wear or slackness. To renew, remove the worn bush by means of the special tool No. Z.8527. Assemble the new bush on the installer tool No. Z.8566 as shown in **FIG 5:9,** and turn the adjusting nut until the pilot projects slightly through the bush 1. The pilot is used for the correct sizing of the bush bore and must therefore be free from burrs. Drive the bush into the crankshaft until the installer sleeve contacts the shaft 2. Withdraw the pilot by screwing down the nut. The bush is oil-impregnated and does not require lubrication on assembly.

5:6 Reassembling, refitting, plate alignment

When installing the clutch, note the following:
1 Ensure that the clutch disc is located so that the side marked FLYWHEEL is towards the flywheel.
2 Before tightening the clutch cover bolts in the flywheel, the clutch disc must be aligned so that the main drive pinion (first motion shaft) will enter the clutch disc hub and the crankshaft spigot bearing when the gearbox is refitted to the engine. For this purpose a spare main drive pinion is first inserted in the clutch disc hub.
3 Next tighten the clutch cover bolts evenly a turn at a time diagonally, finally tightening to a torque of 14 lb ft.
4 Refit the clutch fork and release bearing. The bearing must not be lubricated, but the fork ball should be lubricated with the recommended grease on assembly.
5 Refit the clutch housing to the crankcase. Ensure that the dowel on each side is correctly located before tightening the attaching bolts.

6 If the engine has been removed, refer to **Chapter 1** for installation instructions. If the engine has been left in the car, refit the engine mounting bracket and connect the exhaust pipe to the manifold.
7 Fit the clutch cable and adjust the clutch fork free travel as described in **Section 5:2.** Refit the gearbox according to instructions in **Chapter 6.**

5:7 Laycock clutch. VX4/90

The clutch which has been described in this chapter is of Borg and Beck manufacture. Later cars and VX4/90 are equipped with a Laycock clutch which is interchangeable with the former type provided the appropriate disc is used, *except* on VX4/90.

5:8 Fault diagnosis

(a) Clutch drag or spin

1 Excessive fork free travel
2 Oil or grease on linings
3 Flywheel not running true
4 Misalignment between engine and gearbox
5 Clutch disc binding on splines
6 Main drive pinion (first motion shaft) binding in spigot bearing
7 Clutch disc distorted
8 Cover or pressure plate distorted
9 Disc linings broken
10 Dirt or foreign matter in clutch

(b) Clutch fierce or judders

Check 2, 3, 4, 7 in (a)
1 Worn clutch linings
2 Pressure plate not parallel with flywheel face
3 Contact area of linings not evenly distributed
4 Bent main drive pinion (first motion shaft)
5 Faulty engine or gearbox mountings
6 Worn rear suspension arm bushes
7 Backlash in transmission

(c) Clutch slip

Check 2, 3, 4 in (a) and 1 in (b)
1 Insufficient fork free travel
2 Weak diaphragm spring

(d) Rattles and knocks

1 Broken damper springs in clutch disc hub
2 Defective pressure plate assembly or diaphragm
3 Badly worn splines in disc hub
4 Release bearing loose on fork
5 Worn or loose fork ball
6 Play in main drive spigot bearing
7 Loose flywheel

NOTES

CHAPTER 6

THE GEARBOX

6:1 Construction and operation

Threespeed column change or fourspeed floor change synchromesh gearboxes are optional on all models, the Laycock overdrive (see **Section 6:8**) being available as an optional extra with the fourspeed gearbox only. As an alternative to the synchromesh gearbox, cars with the 2000 engine may have the Borg Warner automatic transmission described separately in **Chapter 6a**.

The threespeed and fourspeed gearboxes, shown in section in **FIGS 6:1** and **6:2** respectively, are basically similar in design, having synchromesh on all forward speeds. The gearbox casing is fitted with a combined filler and oil level plug on the lefthand side. The bottom cover and the front and rear covers are detachable. The front end of the gearbox is secured to a separate clutch housing by four bolts, the lower two of which are inside the housing. On cars fitted with overdrive, an overdrive adaptor takes the place of the gearbox rear cover.

The main drive pinion or first motion shaft runs in a ballbearing in the gearbox front cover and in a spigot bearing in the rear end of the engine crankshaft. The mainshaft runs in needle rollers in the main drive pinion and in a ballbearing in the rear cover or adaptor. The one-piece laygear assembly runs on needle rollers on a

stationary layshaft below the mainshaft. The reverse pinion has bronze bushes and runs on a fixed shaft situated to the left of the layshaft.

Referring to **FIGS 6:1** and **6:2** it will be seen that the second- and third-speed synchromesh clutch and hub of the threespeed model is identical to the third- and fourth-speed clutch and hub of the fourspeed gearbox. In each case the assembly is moved forward to engage the higher gear and backward to engage the lower ratio.

In the threespeed gearbox the first-speed synchromesh clutch and hub assembly is moved forward to engage first gear. The clutch assembly also incorporates a straight-toothed reverse gear. On backward movement of the assembly this gear engages with the teeth of the reverse pinion, which is in constant mesh with the corresponding layshaft gear.

On the fourspeed gearbox the first- and second-speed synchromesh clutch and hub assembly is moved forward to engage second gear and rearward to engage first. It also carries a straight-toothed reverse gear, but in this case the reverse pinion is a sliding gear operated by a separate reverse striking fork, enabling it to slide into mesh with both the gear on the first and second synchromesh hub and the layshaft reverse gear.

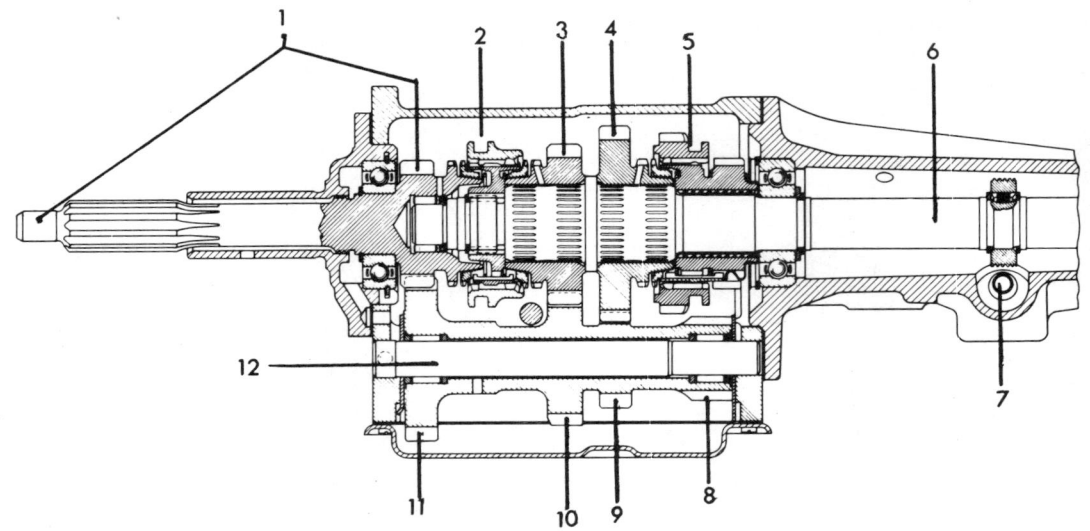

FIG 6:1   Sectional view of threespeed gearbox

Key to Fig 6:1   1 Main drive pinion (first motion shaft)   2 Second- and third-speed clutch and hub assembly
3 Mainshaft second-speed gear   4 Mainshaft first-speed gear   5 First-speed clutch and hub assembly and reverse gear
6 Mainshaft   7 Speedometer driven gear   8 Layshaft reverse gear   9 Layshaft first-speed gear   10 Layshaft second-speed
gear   11 Layshaft constant mesh or main drive gear   12 Layshaft

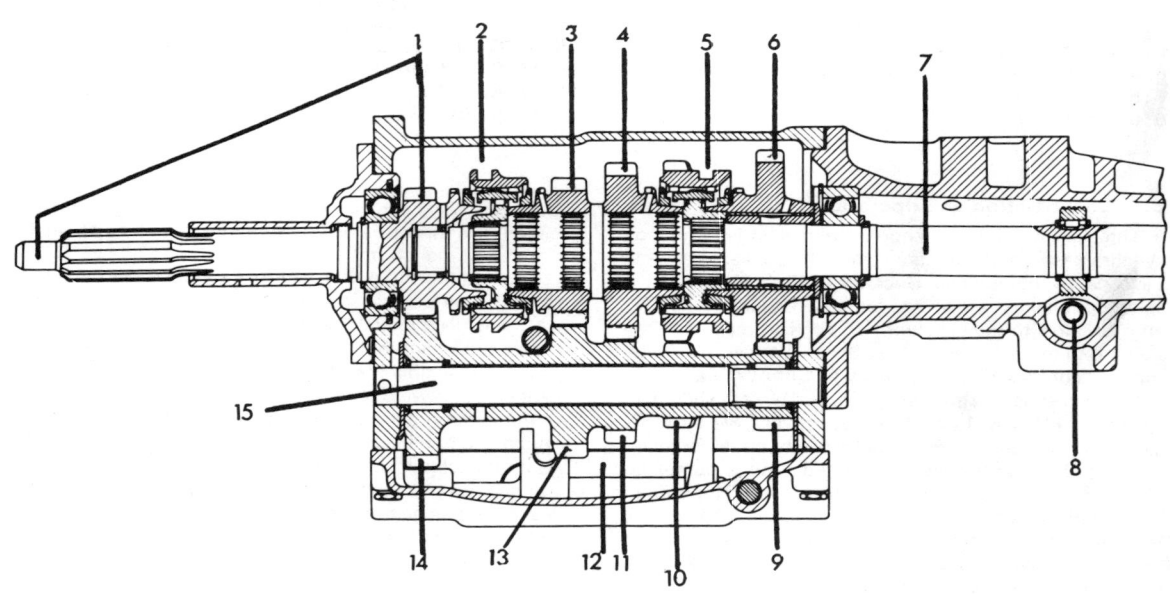

FIG 6:2   Sectional view of fourspeed gearbox

Key to Fig 6:2   1 Main drive pinion (first motion shaft)   2 Third- and fourth-speed clutch and hub assembly
3 Mainshaft third-speed gear   4 Mainshaft second-speed gear   5 First- and second-speed clutch and hub assembly and reverse
gear   6 Mainshaft first-speed gear   7 Mainshaft   8 Speedometer driven gear   9 Layshaft first-speed gear   10 Layshaft
reverse gear   11 Layshaft second-speed gear   12 Reverse striking rod   13 Layshaft third-speed gear   14 Layshaft
constant mesh or main drive gear   15 Layshaft

In the selector mechanism of the threespeed gearbox, two striking forks are secured to rods mounted longitudinally in the gearbox casing. The striking fork on the righthand side of the gearbox engages the second and third synchromesh clutch, while that on the lefthand engages the first-speed clutch and reverse gear. Each striking fork rod has slots in which a spring-loaded detent ball engages. Mounted transversely below the striking fork rods is the striking lever shaft, to which the two striking levers are attached by setscrews. The striking levers engage in slots in each of the striking fork rods. When the gearlever is operated, movement is conveyed by the linkage (see **Section 6:7**) to the striking lever shaft, which is moved transversely so that one of the striking levers engages in the slot in the striking fork rod. At the same time the hub of the other lever engages in a concave recess in the adjacent striking fork rod, preventing the rod from moving but allowing the striking lever shaft to be rotated. When the striking lever shaft is rotated the striking fork rod and fork move the clutch and hub assembly towards the selected gear.

The layout of the selector mechanism of the fourspeed gearbox is similar to that already described for the threespeed model, but the striking lever shaft extends through the lefthand side of the casing and is reduced in diameter to engage a baulk locking ball and spring. To engage reverse gear, the striking lever shaft has to be moved beyond the first- and second-speed position, overcoming the resistance of the baulk spring. At the same time the long end of the third- and fourth-speed striking lever engages the reverse shift fork in the bottom cover (see **FIG 6:18**) and the reverse striking fork slides the reverse pinion into mesh with both the mainshaft and layshaft reverse gears.

6:2 Maintenance, oil seal renewal

A combined oil level and filler plug is fitted on the lefthand side of the gearbox casing. Clean away all dirt from around the plug before removal. The oil should be level with the bottom of the filler hole. Top up if necessary with the recommended grade of oil.

The gearbox rear cover oil seal can be renewed with the gearbox in position as follows:

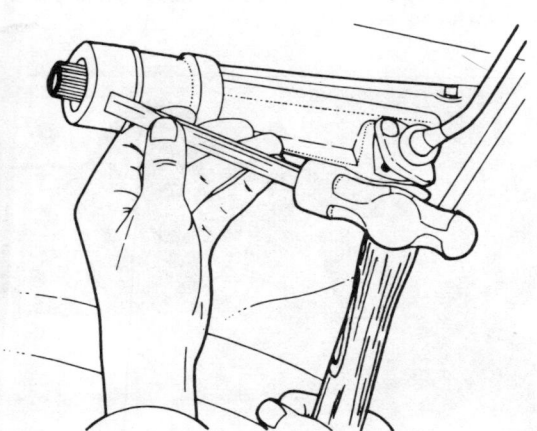

FIG 6:3   Rear cover oil seal removal

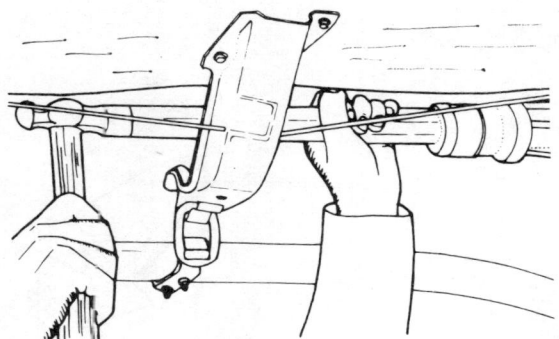

FIG 6:4   Rear cover oil seal installation

1 Place a tray to catch the oil from the gearbox rear cover. Remove the propeller shaft as described in **Chapter 7**.
2 Drive off the old oil seal using a sharp drift applied alternately each side of the seal outer casing as shown in **FIG 6:3**.
3 Soak the new oil seal in a recommended gearbox lubricant then drive it home on the end of the rear cover, using a tubular drift as shown in **FIG 6:4**.
4 Install the propeller shaft. Run the engine for a few minutes to circulate the oil from the gearbox casing into the rear cover. Stop the engine and top up the gearbox with a recommended lubricant.
5 The procedure for renewal of the oil seal on overdrive, where fitted, follows similar lines, but Remover No. 7657 and Adaptor No. CBW.46 should be used for removal. If the work is carried out immediately after a long run, note that the oil in the overdrive casing will be hot enough to burn the skin.

6:3 Gearbox removal

The gearbox must in all cases be removed as a separate component, leaving the engine and clutch in position. On cars fitted with overdrive, however, gearbox and overdrive are removed as a unit. Before starting preliminary operations for gearbox removal on overdrive cars, reference should be made to **Section 6:10**. On all cars gearbox removal is carried out as follows:

1 Disconnect the battery. Raise and firmly support the car or work over a pit.
2 On gearboxes fitted with a drain plug, the oil can be drained at this stage. **On cars fitted with overdrive, note that after a long run the oil will be hot enough to burn the skin and suitable precautions should be taken.**
3 Remove the propeller shaft (see **Chapter 7**) and insert a spare sliding sleeve in the rear end of the gearbox or overdrive to prevent loss of oil. Disconnect the speedometer cable from the gearbox or overdrive. On overdrive models disconnect the wiring from the overdrive switch on the gearbox, from the inhibitor switch on the overdrive adaptor and from the solenoid on the overdrive.
4 Disconnect the gearchange linkage from the gearbox as follows:

FIG 6:5   Rear engine mounting

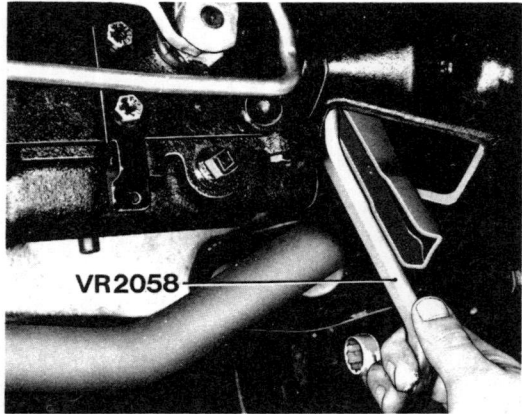

FIG 6:6   Access to lower bolts securing gearbox to clutch housing is through clutch fork slots. Wrench No. VR.2058 is shown

(a) On cars with threespeed gearboxes, disconnect the cross-shaft 7 in **FIG 6:19** from the gearbox coupling.

(b) On cars with fourspeed gearboxes, referring to **FIG 6:24,** remove the screws securing the gearlever sleeve to the body floor panel. Disconnect the selector bar 7 and the control rod 5 from the carrier 1. Remove the two bracket bolts, accessible from inside the car, and lift off the gearlever and carrier assembly. Retain the spacer fitted between the carrier and the gearbox rear cover.

5 Take the weight of the engine by a jack under the sump, using a block of wood to prevent damage to the sump. Remove the nut securing the engine rear mounting to the crossmember (see **FIG 6:5**). Remove the four bolts securing the crossmember to the underbody sidemembers. Raise the rear of the engine sufficiently to allow removal of the crossmember.

6 Support the weight of the gearbox and remove the four bolts securing it to the clutch housing (bellhousing). The lower two bolts are inside the housing but are accessible through the clutch fork slots, using the

special spanner No. VR.2058 as shown in **FIG 6:6**. Withdraw the gearbox, supporting its weight until the main drive pinion (first motion shaft) is clear of the clutch disc.

6:4 Dismantling

Complete dismantling and reassembly of the gearbox entails the use of a hydraulic press, so that part of the work at least must be carried out by a service agent. If extensive repairs are needed it may be better to fit a replacement box. The components however can be removed for inspection as follows:

1 Remove the gearbox bottom cover and drain the oil. On cars fitted with overdrive, remove the overdrive from the adaptor as described in **Section 6:10.**

2 On fourspeed gearboxes remove the remainder of the gearchange linkage from the gearbox.

3 Further operations will be facilitated if the gearbox is bolted to a piece of angle iron, shaped and secured in a vice as shown in **FIG 6:7**.

4 Referring to **FIGS 6:1** and **6:2** remove the speedometer driven gear (not applicable on cars with overdrive).

5 Remove the bolts securing the rear cover or overdrive adaptor and turn the cover or adaptor to expose the rear end of the layshaft. Drive out the layshaft from rear to front using a brass drift. Retain the locking ball at the front end of the shaft. Lift out the laygear assembly with its two rows of needle rollers (51 rollers in all) and the two thrust washers.

6 On fourspeed gearboxes, remove the reverse baulk locking ball and spring housing (see **FIG 6:8**).

7 The striking levers are secured to the striking lever shaft by spring pins. To ensure pins clearing striking fork rods when being removed, position the shaft so that a striking lever engages the slot in a fork rod, then drive out the pin in the striking lever on the opposite end of the shaft sufficiently to release the lever from the shaft. Remove the other striking lever in a similar manner (see **FIG 6:9**). On threespeed gearboxes, striking levers and shaft are matched assemblies. To enable the levers to be refitted to their respective ends of the shaft, mark the levers and shaft with a spot of paint before removal. Withdraw the shaft and levers.

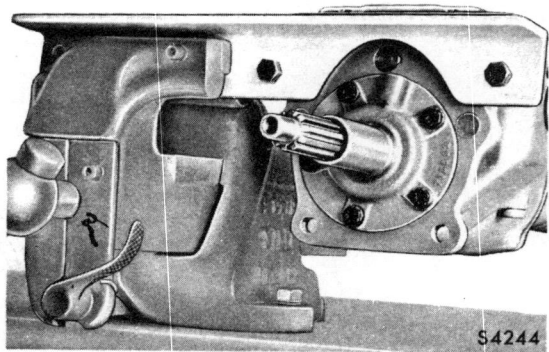

FIG 6:7   Gearbox inverted and secured in vice using a shaped piece of angle iron

8 Drive out the striking fork retaining pins only sufficiently to release the forks on their rods. If the pins are driven out completely they may jam on the gearbox casing. On the threespeed gearbox, engage reverse gear so as to support the rear end of the fork rod when driving out the pin.

9 Remove the retaining screws and the striking fork detent balls and springs. These will be found on each side of the gearbox casing as shown in **FIG 6:10.**

10 Rotate the rear cover or overdrive adaptor to allow access to the rear ends of the fork rods. Using a brass drift, drive the rods out from rear to front. The rod end covers will be driven out with the rods. Withdraw the striking forks.

11 The reverse pinion must be removed before the mainshaft can be withdrawn. The reverse pinion shaft is withdrawn using Remover No. Z.8547 or a suitable alternative puller.

12 Remove the bolts securing the gearbox front cover and remove the main drive pinion (first motion shaft) front cover and bearing as an assembly. Withdraw the mainshaft and rear cover or overdrive adaptor as an assembly.

6:5 Reassembly

Reassembly is a reversal of the instructions given for dismantling, but the following points should be noted:

1 Ensure that all parts are clean and oilways clear.

2 Lightly smear the counter bore in the main drive pinion with petroleum jelly and fit the 24 needle rollers, followed by the spacer. The main drive pinion rollers are shorter than those used for the layshaft gear. Use only sufficient petroleum jelly to hold the rollers, as a surplus may block the oilways.

3 Assemble the needle rollers in the layshaft gear, also using petroleum jelly to hold them in place. There are 25 rollers at the rear end and 26 at the front, with a spacer at either side of the rollers at each end.

4 Lightly smear the front face of the rear cover or overdrive adaptor with grease. Assemble the top speed clutch to the hub on the mainshaft so that the striking fork groove is towards the front, as shown in **FIG 6:11.** Insert the mainshaft and cover assembly into the gearbox casing but do not fit the cover bolts or adaptor bolts at this stage.

FIG 6:8 Reverse baulk locking ball and spring housing on fourspeed gearbox

5 Locate a steel ball with a spot of grease in the drilling in the reverse pinion shaft. Assemble the reverse pinion to the shaft with the chamfered ends of the teeth to the front. On fourspeed gearboxes ensure that the spacer is located between the rear face of the pinion and the gearbox casing. Insert the shaft,

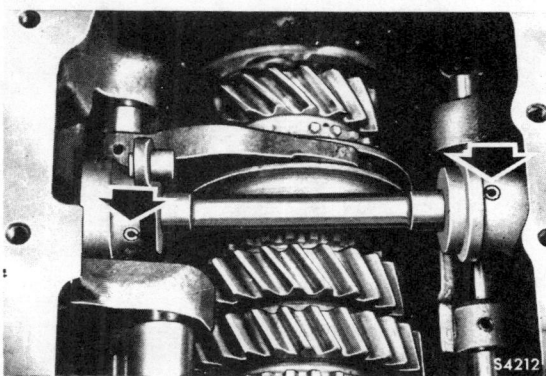

FIG 6:9 Spring pins securing striking levers to striking lever shaft

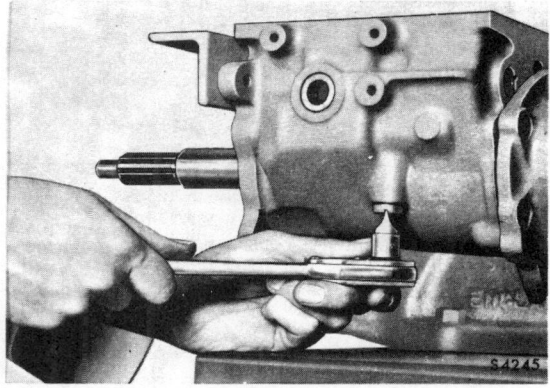

FIG 6:10 Striking fork rod locking balls and springs are retained by a screw at each side of gearbox casing

FIG 6:11 Top speed clutch must be assembled to hub as shown prior to installing mainshaft

FIG 6:12 Location of bracket for overdrive inhibitor switch on adaptor bolts

FIG 6:13 Slots in top speed synchronizing ring must be aligned with hub sliding keys when installing main drive pinion

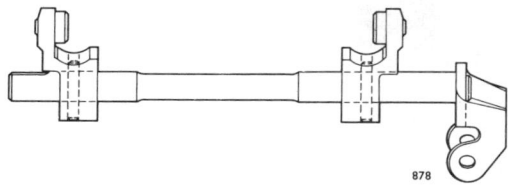

FIG 6:14 Position of striking levers on striking lever shaft in threespeed gearbox

FIG 6:13. Using new copper washers, install and tighten the front cover bolts.

8 Place the striking forks in position so that the recessed portion on each is towards the front of the gearbox. Note that on top speed forks the legs are of equal length. Insert each striking fork rod from the front of the casing. On threespeed gearboxes engage reverse to support the rear end of the rod when installing the first and reverse fork retaining pin. On fourspeed gearboxes the first and second shift fork is assembled to the rod so that the jaw of the fork is to the front of the casing. Secure the forks with new spring pins.

9 Insert the fork rod end covers, open ends first, in the front face of the casing and drive home until flush.

10 Fit a new striking lever shaft oil seal. Smear the lip of the seal with oil and install the seal with the lip towards the inside of the gearbox. Using a suitable drift, drive the seal home until it contacts the abutment face in the casing.

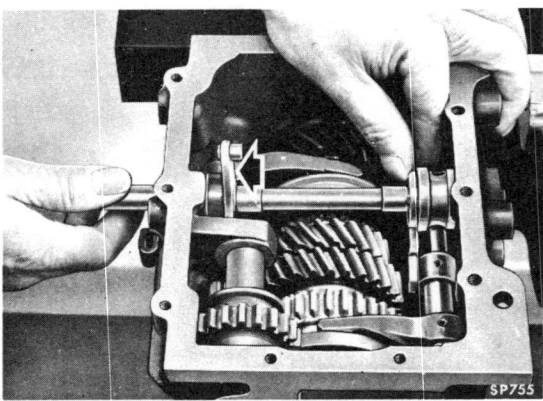

FIG 6:15 On the fourspeed gearbox the long side of the third- and fourth-speed striking lever (arrowed) must be to the bottom of the casing. The striking lever shaft must be located with setscrew hole towards the front of the casing

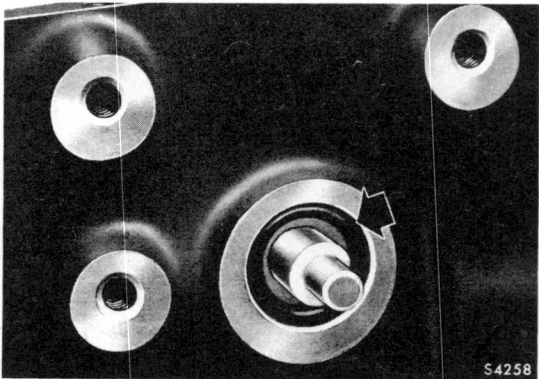

FIG 6:16 On a fourspeed gearbox fit the O-ring in the casing counterbore before fitting the reverse stop housing

lining up the ball with the recess in the casing and drive the shaft home with a brass drift.

6 Rotate the rear cover or overdrive adaptor to its normal position. Fit the securing bolts but do not fully tighten at this stage. On cars with overdrive, ensure that the bracket for the inhibitor switch is fitted as shown in **FIG 6:12.**

7 Lightly smear the front cover face with grease and fit a new gasket. Carefully insert the main drive pinion into the casing so that the front end of the mainshaft enters the spacer and needle rollers in the pinion. Turn the top speed synchronizing ring so that the hub sliding keys engage the slots in the ring as shown in

11 Assemble the striking lever shaft and striking levers as follows:

(a) On threespeed gearboxes the levers must be located on the lever shaft as shown in **FIG 6:14** and the shaft located so that the external yoke is inclined to the front and will be facing downwards when the gearbox is installed (see also item 8 in **FIG 6:19**).

(b) On fourspeed gearboxes, the long side of the third and fourth striking lever must be to the bottom of the casing as shown in **FIG 6:15** and the striking lever shaft located so that the control rod coupling setscrew hole in the shaft is towards the front of the casing. Insert a new O-ring in the casing counterbore as shown in **FIG 6:16**. Assemble the reverse stop housing to the casing. Insert the reverse baulk locking ball and spring, install the fibre washer and special screw and tighten securely.

12 Install the layshaft gear assembly as follows:

(a) Smear the thrust washers with petroleum jelly and place them on the thrust faces of the casing with their indented faces towards the gear. Position the front washer with its tab in the slot in the casing and the rear washer with its flat edge parallel to the bottom face of the casing as shown in **FIG 6:17**.

(b) Locate the steel ball with a spot of grease in the drilling in the layshaft.

(c) Install the layshaft gear assembly in the gearbox, ensuring that the thrust washers remain in position. Insert the layshaft, lining up the ball with the recess in the casing front face. Drive the layshaft home with a brass drift until it is flush with the casing.

13 Tighten the rear cover or overdrive adaptor bolts.

14 On fourspeed gearboxes ensure that the reverse striking fork 1 in **FIG 6:18** is located on the rod in the bottom cover with the retaining pin hole offset to front of cover and the shift fork 2 with the jaw towards the centre of the cover. Install the rod end covers open side first.

15 Fit the bottom cover to the gearbox. On fourspeed gearboxes ensure that the reverse striking fork engages in the groove in the reverse pinion.

16 Install the striking fork rod locking balls and springs, fit the fibre washers and special screws and tighten securely. This operation will be easier with the gearbox the right way up.

17 Ensure that the speedometer driven gear thrust pad is located in the rear cover before installing gear and housing. Fit the housing, which is eccentric to allow for differing sizes of gear teeth, with the flat located as described in Technical Data.

18 Check for correct selection of all gears.

19 On cars with overdrive, fit the overdrive unit to the adaptor as described in **Section 6:10**.

6:6 Refitting

Installation of the gearbox is a reversal of the removal procedure. The following points however should be noted:

1 Check that the breather in the top of the gearbox rear cover is clean and that its cap can be rotated freely.

2 Inject $\frac{1}{8}$ of a pint of recommended lubricant into the rear cover, smear the oil seal and felt with oil and insert a spare sliding sleeve to prevent leakage during installation.

FIG 6:17 Layshaft gear thrust washers must be fitted with indented face towards gear. Front washer tab locates in slot in casing and rear washer is installed with flat edge positioned as shown

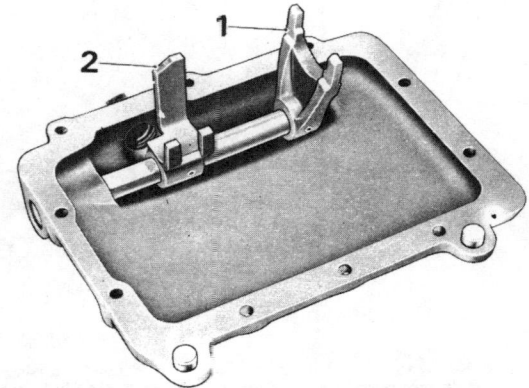

FIG 6:18 Bottom cover of fourspeed gearbox showing correct locations of reverse striking fork (1) and shift fork (2)

3 Before fitting the gearbox to the engine, check the clutch release bearing for wear. Check that the mating faces of the gearbox and clutch housing are clean and free from burrs.

4 Lightly smear the main drive pinion splines and front cover sleeve with a recommended grease.

5 **Do not allow the weight of the gearbox to hang on the clutch disc until the spigot is fully home in the spigot bearing in the crankshaft flange.** In the case of cars with overdrive, where the gearbox and overdrive are installed as a unit, the use of a jack or hoist is recommended in order to support the considerable weight involved.

6 Connect the gearbox to the clutch housing, using spanner No. VR.2058 for tightening the lower two bolts. Access to these is obtained through the clutch fork aperture as shown in **FIG 6:6**.

7 Refit and adjust the gearchange linkage as described in **Section 6:7**.

8 Refit the propeller shaft as described in **Chapter 7**.

9 On cars with overdrive connect the electrical wiring and carry out final checks as described in **Section 6:9**.

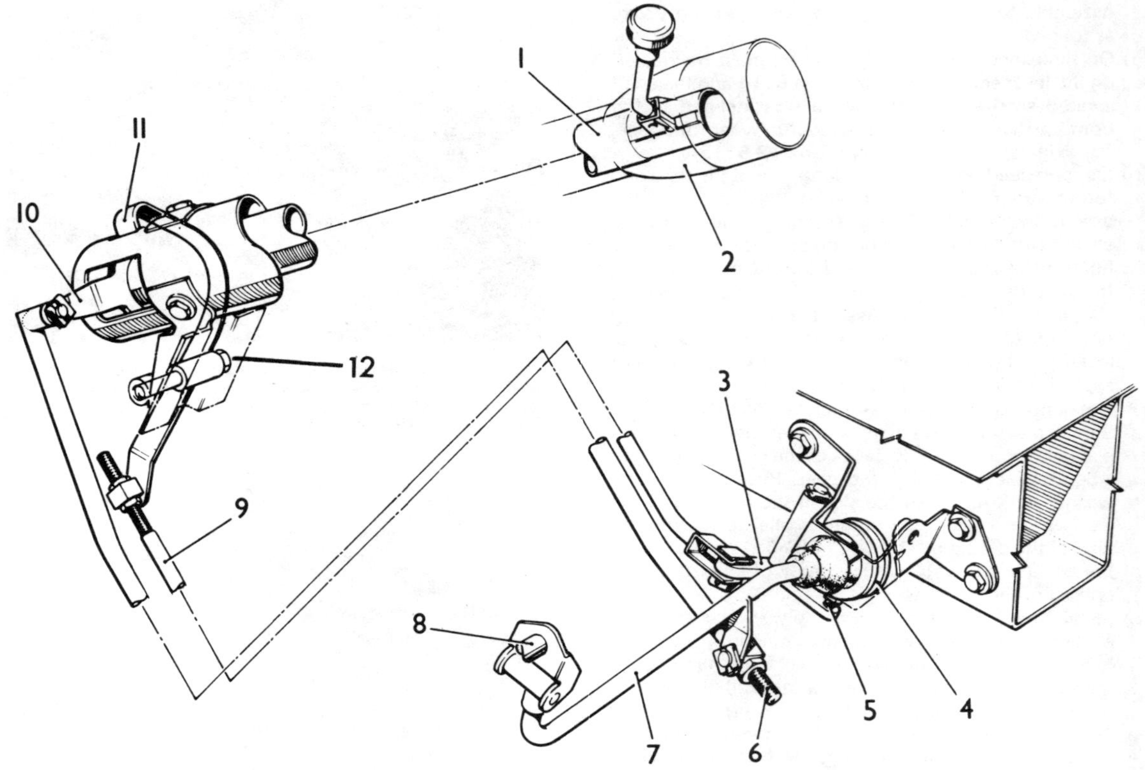

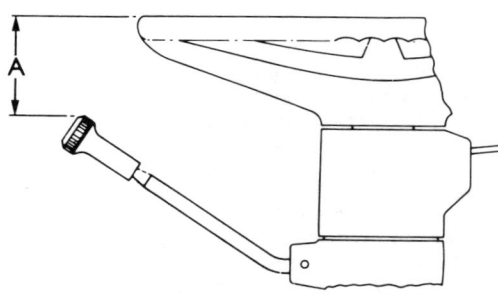

FIG 6:19 Gearchange linkage of threespeed gearbox

Key to Fig 6:19   1 Control tube   2 Lever housing   3 Bellcrank lever   4 Grooved collar   5 Bellcrank pin
6 Gearshift control rod   7 Cross-shaft   8 Gearbox striking lever shaft   9 Selector control rod   10 Changespeed lever
11 Selector lever   12 Selector lever pivot bolt

FIG 6:20 Threespeed gearlever height. Dimension A should be 3.30 inch when lever is in second and third-speed plane

10 Refill the gearbox with a recommended oil. Run the engine for a few minutes, recheck the oil level and top up if necessary.

6:7 Gearchange servicing and adjustment

Cars with threespeed gearboxes are fitted with a column gearchange while those with fourspeed gear-boxes have a remote control floor change.

FIG 6:19 shows the layout of the column change linkage. The lever is mounted in a housing 2 which is free to move radially on the steering (outer) column. The inner end of the gearlever engages a control tube 1 which is keyed to the lever housing but free to move independ-ently of the housing in an endwise direction. Attached to the lower end of the control tube is a changespeed lever 10. A selector lever 11 pivots on a bracket at the lower end of the steering column. The upper end of the the lever is forked to engage the boss of the changespeed lever.

Mounted between the gearbox and the underbody sidemember is a cross-shaft 7, carried in a bushed bracket and coupled to the gearbox striking lever shaft 8, which is also shown in FIG 6:14. A bellcrank lever 3 is mounted on the cross-shaft support bracket and incor-porates a pin 5 which engages in a grooved collar 4 on the cross-shaft. An adjustable rod 9 connects the selector lever on the steering column to the bellcrank lever, and an adjustable control rod 6 couples the control tube changespeed lever to a lever on the cross-shaft.

Up and down movement of the gearlever causes end-wise movement of the control tube, which in turn operates the bellcrank lever through the selector lever and rod. The bellcrank lever moves the cross-shaft and the gearbox striking lever shaft in an endwise direction, so that one of the striking levers engages the appropriate striking fork rod. Radial movement of the gearlever causes the cross-shaft and gearbox striking lever shaft to rotate, so moving the striking fork into the engaged position.

There are two adjustments for the gearchange linkage. With the gearlever in the second and third gear plane, the distance A in **FIG 6 : 20** should be 3.30 inch. This can be corrected if necessary by adjusting the selector rod at the adjuster B shown in **FIG 6 : 21**. Lengthening the rod will lower the position of the lever.

When in neutral, the radial position of the gearlever should be 5 deg. above the horizontal as shown at A in **FIG 6 : 22**. Correct if necessary by adjusting the gear shift control rod adjuster B shown in **FIG 6 : 23**. Lengthening the rod will raise the position of the gearlever.

The steering column gearlever is retained in its housing by a spring pin, a plain washer being installed on each side of the lever to prevent vibration. Referring to **FIG 6 : 19,** the gear selector lever 11 can be lifted out of engagement with the lower end of the control tube 1 after removing the pivot bolt 12 and disconnecting the selector rod 9. When refitting the selector lever ensure that the slipper is in place before installing the lever on the control tube. It should be noted that the (outer) steering column, control tube and steering shaft (inner column) are only serviced as a complete assembly. Details are given in **Chapter 9**. To renew the bearing or the boot on the cross-shaft 7, the cross-shaft bracket must be removed from the body sidemember. After removing the plain washer from inside the boot, the bearing can be pushed out of the boot. The boot can then be withdrawn from the bracket. To prevent the pin 5 on the bellcrank lever 3 from bottoming in the groove of the collar 4, adjust the pin so that it projects $\frac{1}{2}$ inch from the face of the bellcrank.

FIG 6 : 24 shows the layout of the gearchange linkage on the fourspeed gearbox. The central gearlever is located on top of an inverted U-shaped carrier 1 by a through-bolt 2. The carrier pivots on bushes pressed into the carrier and a bracket 3 bolted to the top of the gearbox rear cover, or in the case of cars with overdrive, on the overdrive adaptor. The outer leg of the carrier extends downwards and is connected by the control rod 5 to the gearbox striking lever shaft coupling 6 (see also **FIG 6 : 14**). The spherical end of the gearlever engages the carrier bracket pivot shaft 4 and is loaded by a spring and pad through the centre of the shaft. A selector bar 7 pivots on a fulcrum bracket 8 which is integral with the gearbox casing, and connects the carrier bracket shaft to the gearbox striking lever shaft coupling.

Sideways movement of the gearlever causes the selector bar to pivot on its fulcrum bracket, so that the gearbox striking lever shaft moves in an endwise direction, bringing one of the striking levers into engagement with the appropriate striking fork rod. Forward or rearward movement of the gearlever causes the gearbox striking lever shaft to rotate, moving the striking fork into the engaged position.

FIG 6 : 25 shows the control rod (see item 5 in **FIG 6 : 24**). To ensure full engagement of the gears the dimension A must be 1.35 inch and the dimension B between hole centres 8.90 inch. For removal of the gearlever and carrier assembly, remove the screws securing

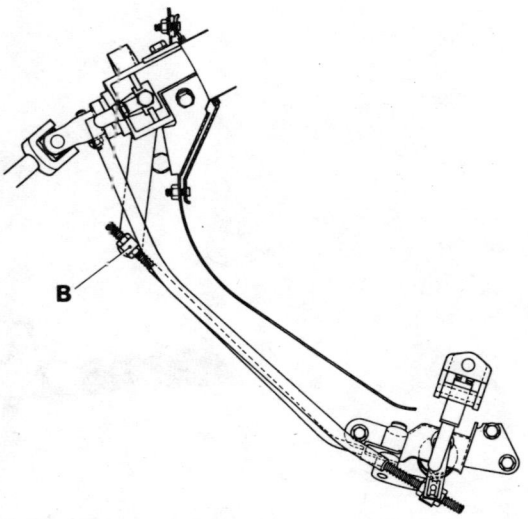

FIG 6:21 Threespeed gearlever height is controlled by adjustment of selector rod at B. Lengthening the rod will lower the gearlever

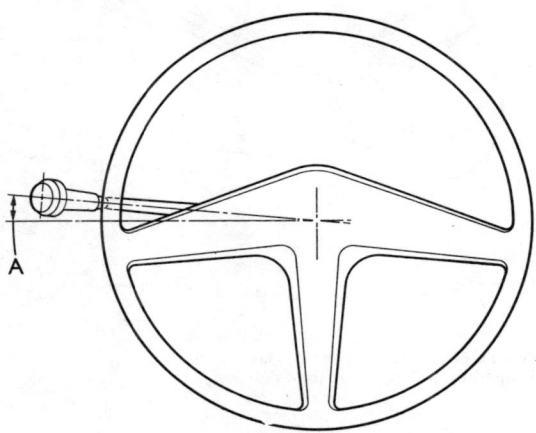

FIG 6:22 Threespeed gearlever should be 5 deg. above horizontal position when in neutral as shown at A

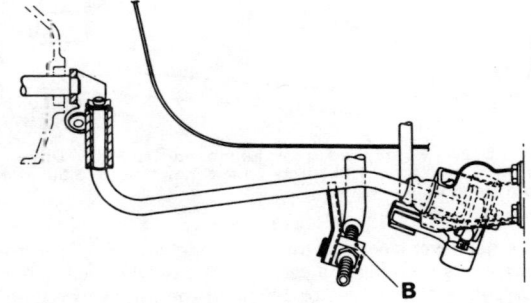

FIG 6:23 Radial position of threespeed gearlever is controlled by adjustment of the gear shift control rod at B. Lengthening the rod will raise the gearlever

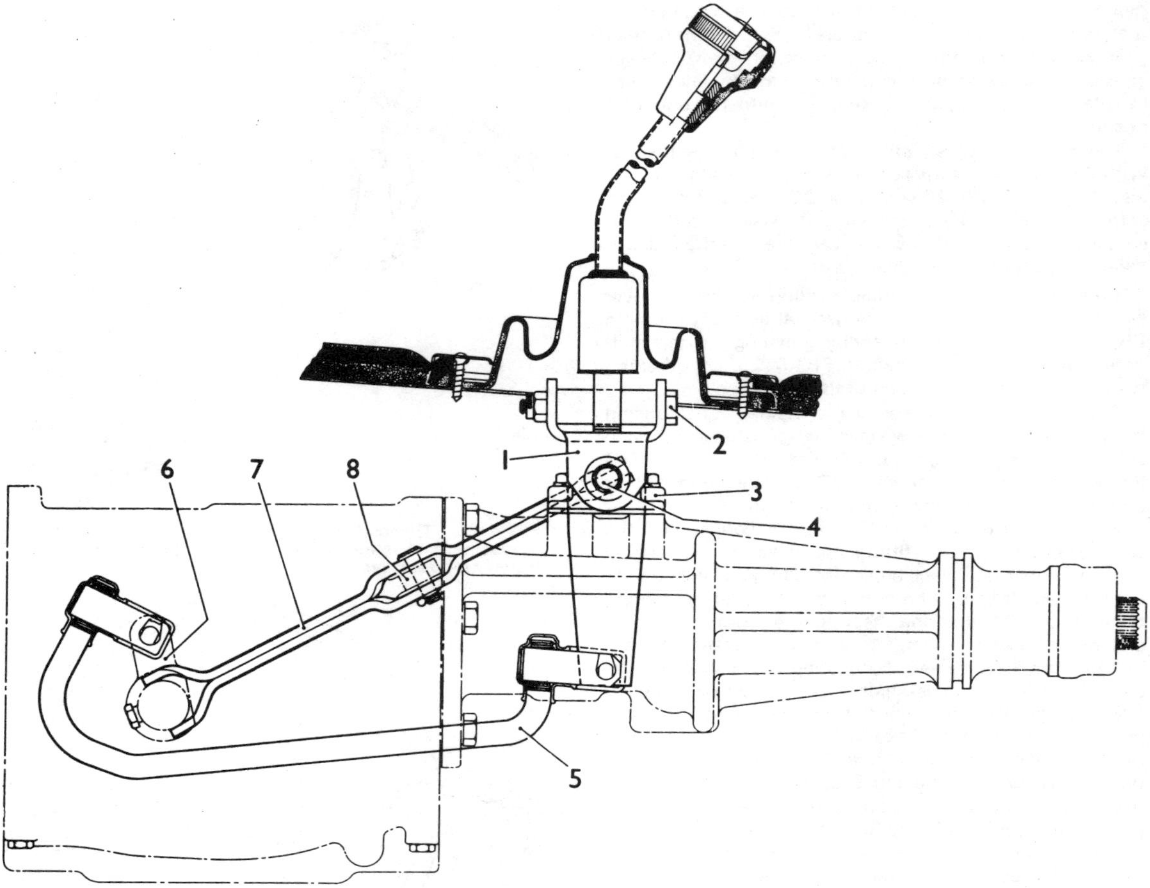

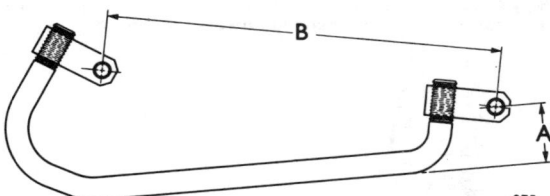

FIG 6 : 24   Fourspeed gearchange linkage

Key to Fig 6 : 24   1 Carrier   2 Through bolt   3 Carrier bracket   4 Carrier bracket pivot   5 Control rod
6 Gearbox striking lever shaft coupling   7 Selector bar   8 Fulcrum bracket

FIG 6 : 25   Fourspeed gearchange control rod. Dimension A must be 1.35 inch and dimension B 8.90 inch between hole centres

the gearlever sleeve to the floor panel and withdraw the two bolts securing the carrier to the gearbox rear cover. Disconnect the selector bar and control rod from the carrier and lift off the carrier and gearlever. Retain the spacer which is fitted between the carrier and the gearbox cover.

6 : 8 Overdrive description

A Laycock type J overdrive shown in part-section in **FIG 6 : 26**, is available as an extra on cars fitted with fourspeed gearboxes. The overdrive, having a ratio of 0.778:1, is controlled by a switch incorporated in the gearlever knob and can be engaged in conjunction with third and top gears only. Engagement of overdrive in first, second or reverse is prevented by an inhibitor switch.

The overdrive is bolted to an adaptor which takes the place of the gearbox rear cover. The overdrive incorporates an epicyclic gear train controlled by a hydraulically operated cone clutch. The hydraulic system is pressurized by a plunger type pump operated by an eccentric on the gearbox mainshaft which extends into the overdrive. The pressure requirements of the system are controlled by a relief valve which incorporates a dashpot, providing progressive increase and decrease of pressure for smooth engagement and disengagement of the overdrive. Engagement and disengagement are controlled by a solenoid valve. Wired in series with the solenoid coil are the overdrive switch, incorporated in the gearlever knob, and the inhibitor switch which is mounted on a bracket on the adaptor and is mechanically operated by the gearchange linkage.

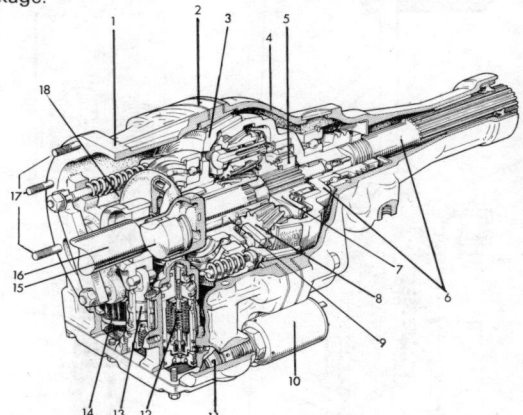

FIG 6:26 Part-sectioned view of Laycock type J overdrive (lefthand front view)

Key to Fig 6:26   1 Main casing   2 Brake ring 3 Cone clutch   4 Rear casing   5 One-way clutch 6 Annulus and output shaft   7 Planet carrier   8 Planet wheels   9 Sunwheel   10 Solenoid   11 Solenoid valve 12 Relief valve   13 Pump   14 Pressure filter 15 Operating piston   16 Gearbox mainshaft   17 Studs for adaptor   18 Clutch springs

Referring to **FIG 6:27,** when the overdrive switch is in the normal or direct drive position, the solenoid valve 1 is closed and oil is delivered from the pump 2 via the pressure filter 3 and operating cylinders 4 to the relief valve 5. Oil passes through the passage 6 to the mainshaft for the lubrication of the running gear and excess pressure is relieved through the valve spill port 7. Under these conditions the clutch springs maintain the cone clutch in contact with the annulus of the epicyclic gear train and the train is locked. Forward drive is thus transmitted through the one-way clutch to the output shaft, thus relieving the load on the cone clutch. Overrun or reverse torque is taken through the cone clutch, without which the one-way clutch would permit a freewheeling condition.

FIG 6:28 shows the conditions when the overdrive switch is in the closed or overdrive position. The solenoid valve 1 opens and oil at residual pressure enters passage 2 to the bottom of the dashpot piston 3. The resultant compression of the dashpot and relief valve springs 4 and 5 increases the system pressure which acts on the operating pistons 6. With forward movement of the pistons, the outer friction lining of the cone clutch contacts the stationary brake ring and locks the sunwheel of the epicyclic train. The planet carrier is splined to the gearbox mainshaft and driven by it, so that the planet wheels orbit round the sunwheel and rotate the annulus and output shaft at a greater speed than the planet carrier and mainshaft, thus providing the overdrive.

Oil for the operation of the hydraulic system of the overdrive and for the lubrication of its moving parts is

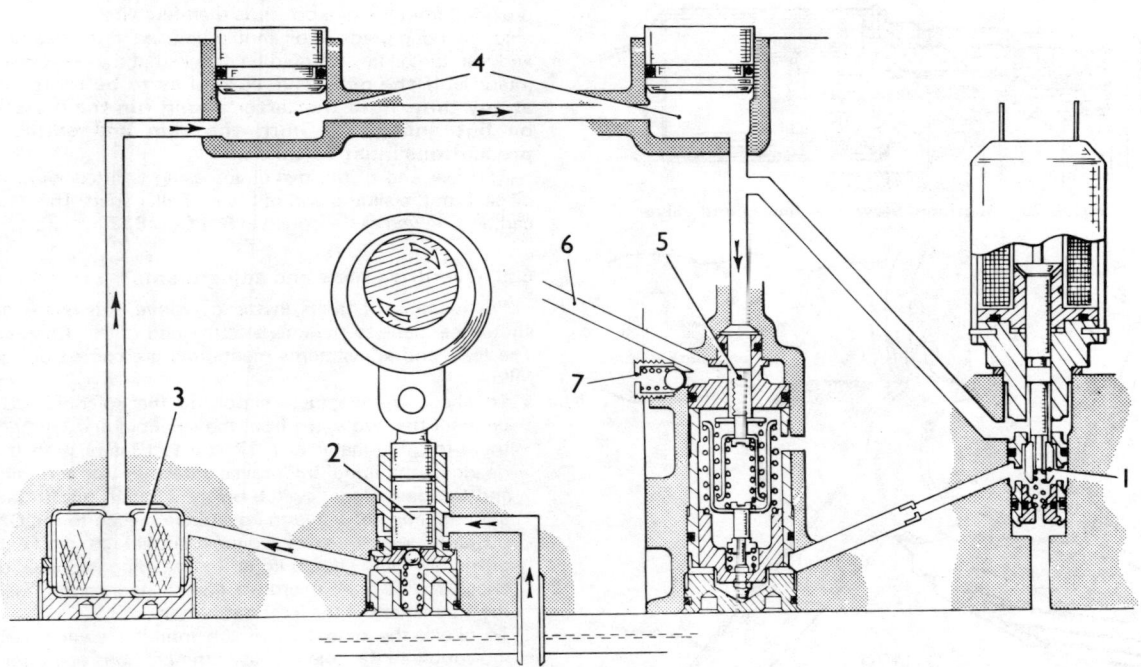

FIG 6:27   Diagram showing overdrive hydraulic system in direct drive

Key to Fig 6:27   1 Solenoid valve   2 Pump   3 Pressure filter   4 Operating cylinders   5 Relief valve 6 Passage   7 Valve spill port

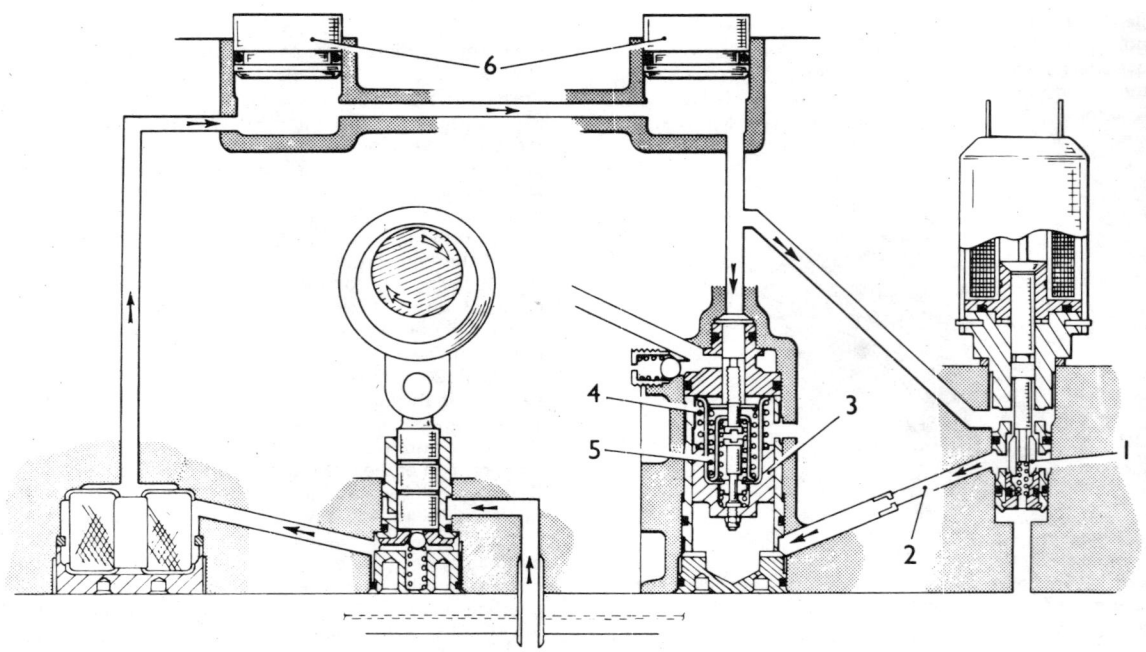

FIG 6 : 28   Diagram showing overdrive hydraulic system when overdrive engaged

Key to Fig 6 : 28   1 Solenoid valve   2 Passage   3 Dashpot piston   4/5 Relief valve springs   6 Operating pistons

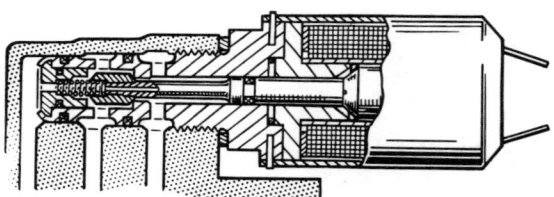

FIG 6 : 29   Sectional view of solenoid and valve

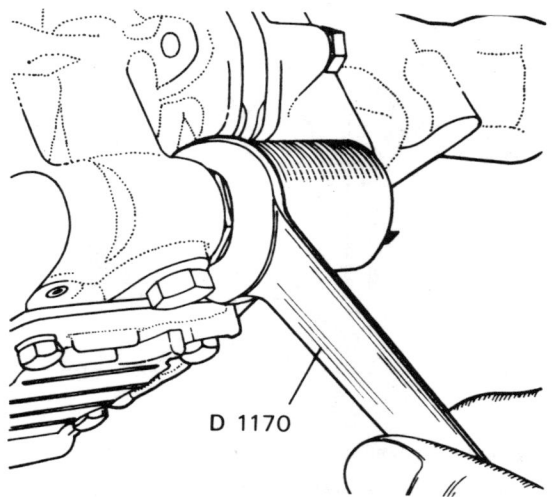

FIG 6 : 30   Solenoid removal

provided from the gearbox. It is therefore vital that only a recommended grade of oil should be used in the gearbox and that the oil level should be checked at the prescribed intervals. **If the overdrive sump has to be removed at any time, note that after a long run the oil will be hot enough to burn the skin and suitable precautions must be taken.**

The rear end of the overdrive casing is fitted with an oil seal for the sliding end of the propeller shaft. This seal can be renewed as described in **Section 6 : 2.**

6 : 9 Overdrive tests and adjustments

For location of faults in the overdrive unit reference should be made to the charts at the end of this Chapter. The tests and adjustments mentioned are carried out as follows:

1 To check the electrical supply to the solenoid, disconnect the two wires from the solenoid and connect them to a voltmeter or a 12 volt test lamp. With the gearlever in neutral but moved sideways into the third and top gear plane, switch on the ignition but do not start the engine. Move the overdrive switch to the ON position, when battery voltage should be recorded or the test lamp should light. If no reading is obtained, check No. 2 fuse, overdrive switch and wiring, also the adjustment of the inhibitor switch.

2 To check the operation of the inhibitor switch, test the supply to the solenoid as in the previous operation. Then with the ignition and overdrive switch still in the ON positions, move the gearlever over to the first and second gear position, when no voltage should be recorded. Operation of the inhibitor switch can be

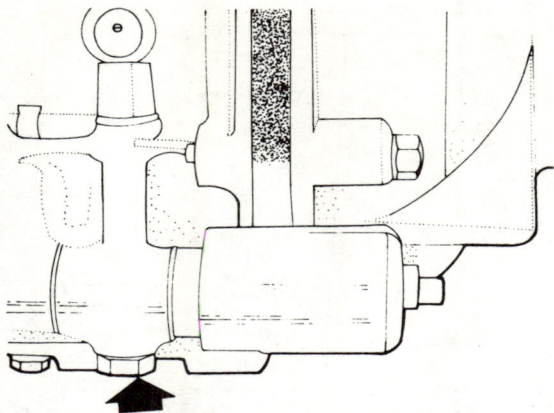

FIG 6:31 Showing position of hydraulic test plug

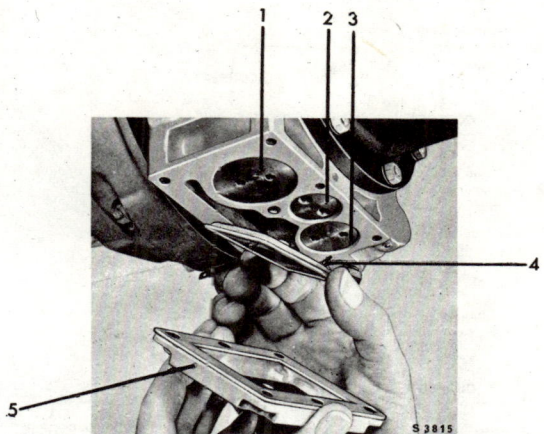

FIG 6:32 Overdrive sump, suction filter and plugs, viewed from the righthand side

adjusted by slackening the retaining screws and repositioning the switch.

3 The combined solenoid and hydraulic valve is a self-contained sealed unit which is screwed into the over-drive main casing. The solenoid has a single coil which is completely waterproof (see **FIG 6:29**). After disconnecting the wires, the solenoid and valve can be removed using Wrench No. D.1170 as shown in **FIG 6:30**. Do not attempt to remove by gripping the cylindrical body of the solenoid. A small quantity of oil will drain when the solenoid is withdrawn. Check the solenoid coil with a 12 volt battery and ammeter, when the current consumption should be approximately 2 amps and movement of the valve should be audible. If the solenoid is faulty or the valve seized, the complete assembly must be renewed. When installing the solenoid and valve renew the O-rings in addition to the body washer.

As a general rule, servicing of the remainder of the overdrive unit will be entrusted to a service agent. If however, the necessary test equipment is available, the hydraulic pressure test can be carried out. After removing the plug adjacent to the solenoid, as shown in **FIG 6:31**, screw in the Adaptor L.188-2 and connect the Gauge and Hose V.188. The rear wheels must then be raised clear of the floor, with the car firmly supported and the front wheels chocked. Start the engine, engage top gear and run in direct drive at a speed equivalent to about 25 mile/hr. A maximum pressure reading of 20 lb/sq in should be obtained, this being the residual pressure. Engage the overdrive and check that the operating pressure gives a reading between 300 to 340 lb/sq in. Then disengage overdrive and check the time taken to return to residual pressure. This should not exceed 3 seconds.

If the operating pressure is incorrect, further checks are indicated in the fault location chart, involving removal and inspection of the relief valve, pump non-return valve and body and the pressure filter. These three items are accessible after removal of the overdrive sump and gauze suction filter as shown in **FIG 6:32. After a long run the oil will be hot enough to burn the skin, therefore suitable precautions must be taken.** Each

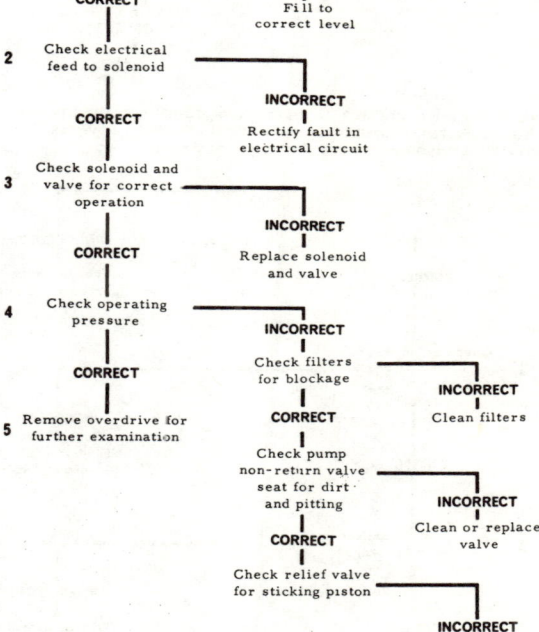

FIG 6:33 Procedure if overdrive does not engage

of the three components is secured by a circular plug, which is screwed into the casing and secured by peening. A special Wrench No. L.354, of the peg type, is used for unscrewing the plugs. Access to the control orifice is obtained after removal of the relief valve. The orifice

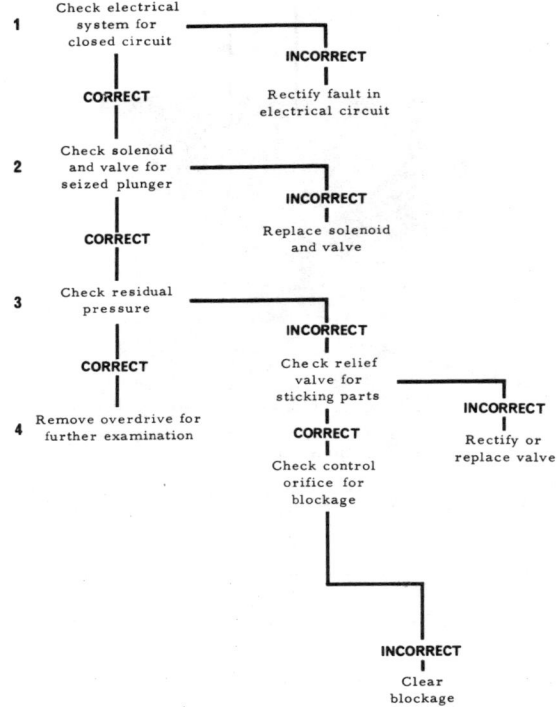

FIG 6:34 Procedure if overdrive does not disengage. This calls for immediate attention. Do not reverse the car otherwise extensive damage may be caused

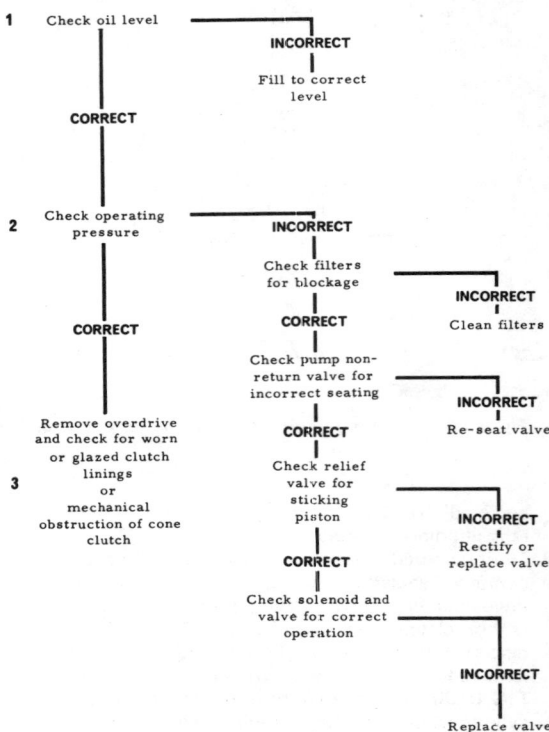

FIG 6:35 Procedure if overdrive slips when engaging

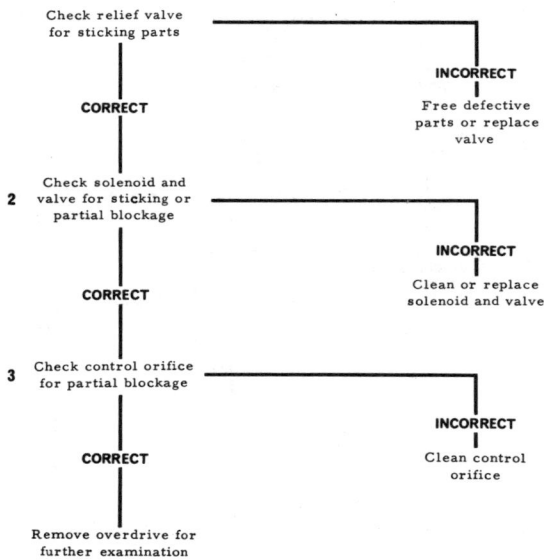

FIG 6:36 Procedure if overdrive disengagement slow, and/or freewheeling on overrun

should be blown out with compressed air. Wire must not be used for this purpose as the drilling in the orifice is accurately calibrated.

6:10 Overdrive removal and refitting

Dismantling of the overdrive is best entrusted to a service agent. The overdrive can be removed from the car as follows:

1 Before commencing preliminary operations, it should be noted that if the overdrive was disengaged during acceleration, the splines in the planet carrier and in the one-way clutch may remain torsionally loaded on the gearbox mainshaft. This will prevent withdrawal of the mainshaft and will thus make it impossible to separate gearbox and overdrive. The car should therefore be driven in third or top gear and overdrive engaged. Then, with the clutch pedal depressed, the overdrive should be disengaged and not used again before commencing removal operations. If for any reason the car cannot be driven, refer to Operation 4.

2 Where a gearbox drain plug is fitted, drain the oil from the gearbox and overdrive. **Note that after a long run the oil in the overdrive will be hot enough to burn the skin and suitable precautions must be taken.** Remove the gearbox and overdrive as described in **Section 6:3**. If no drain plug is fitted remove the gearbox bottom cover to drain the oil.

3 Remove the bolts securing the overdrive casing to the adaptor and remove the overdrive.

4 If the gearbox and overdrive have been removed from the car without the correct procedure of disengagement being carried out as in Operation 1, any torsional load on the gearbox mainshaft and overdrive splines

can be released by pressurizing the overdrive hydraulic system and at the same time energizing the solenoid. Invert the gearbox and overdrive and replace the hydraulic test plug shown in **FIG 6:31** by a grease nipple adaptor plug. This can be made from a $\frac{3}{8}$ inch 16 threads/inch bolt $\frac{3}{8}$ inch long, suitably drilled and tapped to take a grease nipple. The bolt must not exceed the length stated or the solenoid threads could be damaged. The plug copper washer should be used on the adaptor. A high-pressure oil gun is then applied to the grease nipple, using clean gearbox oil only, while current from a 12 volt battery is applied to the two solenoid terminals.

Refitting of the overdrive is a reversal of the removal procedure but the following points should be noted:

1 The eccentric for the overdrive pump is located on the gearbox mainshaft by a circlip. Before fitting the overdrive to the gearbox, turn the gearbox mainshaft until the peak of the eccentric is in the lowest position. This will of course be facing upwards while the gearbox is inverted on the bench. Placing the eccentric in this position will facilitate engagement of the pump strap in the overdrive unit.

2 After attaching the overdrive to the adaptor on the gearbox, the gearbox and overdrive are installed as a unit in the car as described in **Section 6:6**. Install the propeller shaft as described in **Chapter 7**.

3 Electrical connections for the overdrive are shown in the accessory wiring diagram in the Appendix.

4 Fill the gearbox and overdrive unit with a recommended grade of oil and after running the engine for a short period check the level at the gearbox filler plug. The total oil capacity of gearbox and overdrive is 3 pints.

6:11 Modified four-speed gearchange linkage

On later cars a modified gearchange linkage is used as shown in **FIG 6:37**.

The linkage consists of a gear shift upper lever (11) pinned to a finger (2) which pivots in an intermediate lever (1). The intermediate lever pivots on a bush (8) pressed into a carrier bracket (7), which is bolted to the transmission rear cover. The outer leg of the intermediate lever is extended downwards and is connected to the quadrant-shaped striking lever shaft coupling (6) by a control rod (5). The spherical end of the finger engages in the intermediate lever pivot shaft (10) which runs in the carrier bracket bush, and is loaded by a spring and pad (9) in the centre of the shaft. A selector bar (4) engages a grooved adjuster (3) in the lever pivot shaft and connects the pivot shaft to the striking lever shaft coupling. The selector bar pivots on a shouldered bolt attached to a lug on the transmission casing.

Forward or rearward movement of the upper lever is transmitted through the intermediate lever to the control rod. Sideways movement of the upper lever is transmitted through the finger and intermediate lever pivot shaft to the selector bar.

Accidental selection of reverse gear is prevented by a cable-operated stepped abutment contacting a corresponding step on the intermediate lever. This cable passes up through the centre of the gearchange lever and is connected to a lifting collar at the top of the lever.

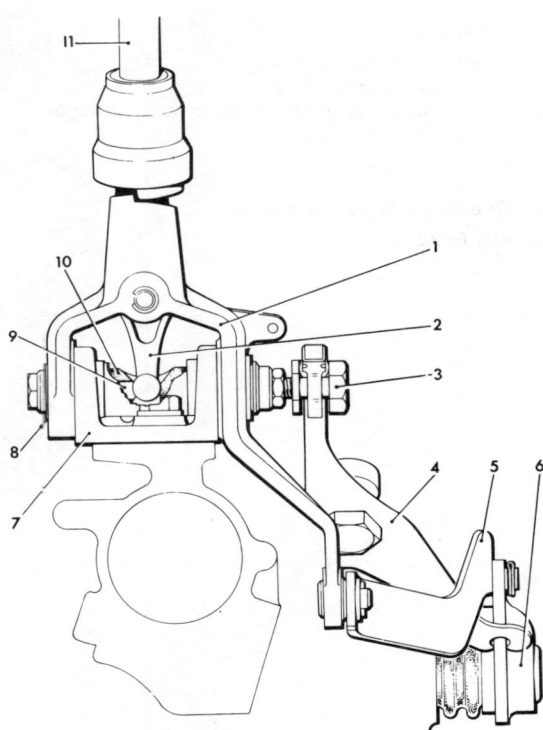

FIG 6:37   Modified four-speed gearchange

Key to Fig 6:37   1 Intermediate lever   2 Finger   3 Adjuster   4 Selector bar   5 Control bush   6 Coupling   7 Carrier   8 Bush   9 Spring and pad   10 Intermediate lever pivot shaft   11 Gearchange lever

Cable renewal requires the removal of the gearchange lever assembly.

On overdrive models the knob on the gearchange lever includes the overdrive switch, and may be unscrewed after prizing off the top of the knob and disconnecting the wires from the switch.

6:12 Fault diagnosis

(a) Jumping out of gear

1 Broken spring behind locking ball in selector rod
2 Excessively worn groove in selector rod
3 Worn coupling dogs
4 Fork to selector rod spring pin loose

(b) Noisy gearbox

1 Insufficient oil
2 Incorrect grade of oil
3 Worn or damaged bearings
4 Excessive end play in layshaft gear
5 Worn or damaged gear teeth

(c) Difficulty in engaging gear

1 Clutch drag (see **Chapter 5**)
2 Worn synchromesh cones
3 Incorrectly adjusted or worn gearchange linkage

(d) Oil leaks

1 Damaged joint washers
2 Worn or damaged oil seals
3 Front, rear or bottom covers loose or faces damaged

(e) Overdrive does not engage

See **FIG 6:33**

(f) Overdrive does not disengage

See **FIG 6:34**

(g) Overdrive slips when engaging

See **FIG 6:35**

(h) Overdrive disengagement slow, and/or freewheeling on overrun

See **FIG 6:36**

CHAPTER 6a

AUTOMATIC TRANSMISSION

6a:1 Borg-Warner automatic transmission

The Borg-Warner 35 fully automatic transmission is available as an alternative to the manual gearbox on cars fitted with the 2000 engine. FIG 6a:1 is a sectional view of the transmission, which consists of a fluid torque converter coupled to a hydraulically operated planetary gear set.

The hydraulic converter, shown diagrammatically in FIG 6a:2 transmits or disconnects the drive from the engine according to engine speed and provides a smooth take-off from standstill. It is also capable of multiplying the engine torque at an infinitely variable ratio between 2:1 and 1:1 in each of the three forward speeds provided by the planetary gears. The converter consists of the impeller 3, which forms part of the converter case, the latter being driven from the engine crankshaft by means of the flexplate, the turbine 1, which has no mechanical connection with the impeller but which is splined to the input shaft of the planetary gears, and the stator 2, situated between the impeller and the turbine and mounted on a one-way clutch.

When the engine is started, the impeller is rotated and the oil flows from the impeller to the turbine, and returns to the impeller through the stator. The curvature of the vanes is designed so that when the impeller and turbine are rotating at differing speeds the angle of flow from the turbine is changed by the stator vanes to assist in driving

the impeller. Under these conditions torque multiplication varies from 2:1 when the turbine is stalled to 1:1 when the turbine reaches 90 per cent of the speed of the impeller. When impeller and turbine speeds are nearly the same, the oil flow angle from the turbine is such that the stator freewheels and is driven in the same direction as the turbine and the impeller. Under these conditions the converter becomes a fluid flywheel or coupling and there is no torque multiplication.

FIG 6a:3 shows the planetary gear set. This consists of two sun gears, forward and reverse, two sets of planet pinions, a planet carrier and the ring gear and output shaft. It is controlled by the two brake bands and two multi-disc clutches, all operated through hydraulic pressure generated by an oil pump and regulated by valves and a centrifugal governor.

Five operating ranges are provided and are selected by the floor-mounted selector lever. The ranges are indicated by the letters on the indicator plate at the side of the lever in the following order:

L — Lock-up, for increased engine braking
D — Drive, for all normal driving
N — Neutral and starting
R — Reverse
P — Parking and starting

A two-stage stop, actuated by a spring-loaded push button in the lever grip, prevents unintentional selection

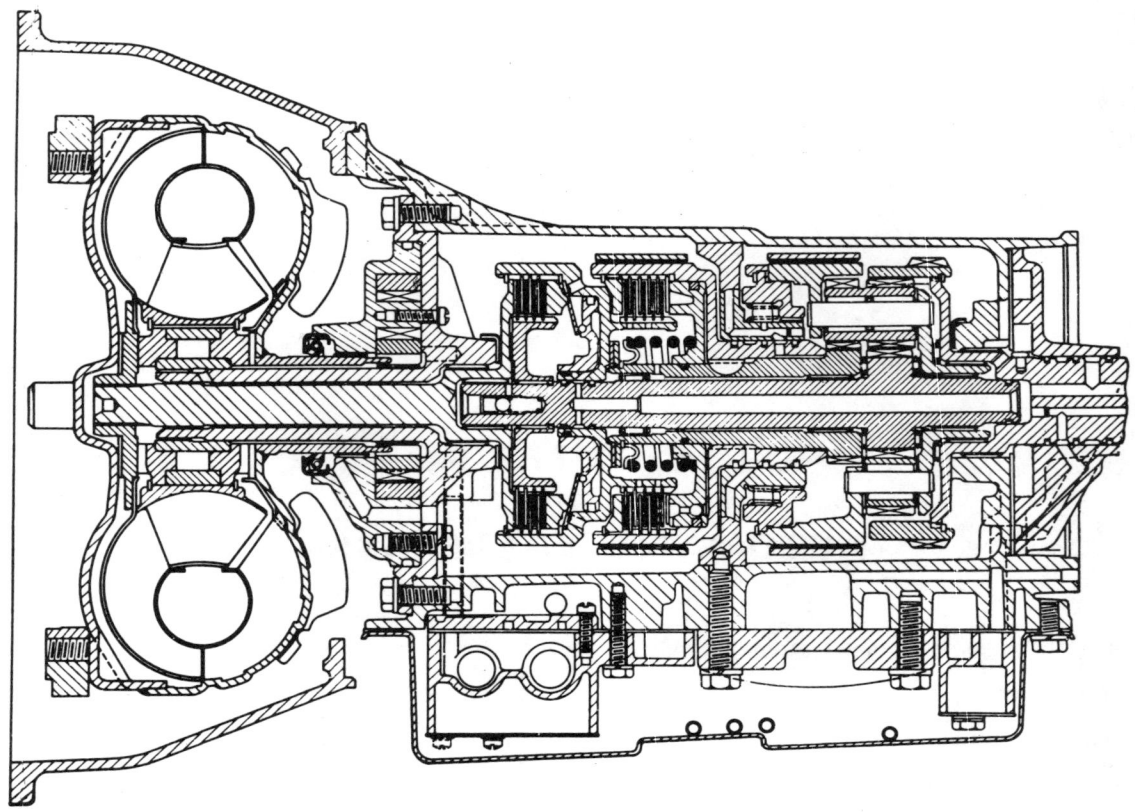

FIG 6a:1 Sectional view of Borg-Warner Model 35 automatic transmission. Victor models have starter ring attachments differing from that shown

of L, R and P. Partial depression of the button is necessary before L or R can be selected, while full depression, against increased spring pressure, is required for the selection of P.

To prevent accidental engagement of the starter whilst the transmission is in gear, an inhibitor switch is fitted ensuring that the starter is only operative when the selector lever is on the P or N positions.

Selector lever in P position:

No torque is transmitted from the engine and the transmission output shaft is mechanically locked by a pawl engaging in a ring gear on the planetary gear set. Do not engage the P position while the car is in motion.

Selector lever in N position:

In neutral the output shaft is unlocked and no torque is transmitted from the engine. The parking brake must be applied if the car is at rest.

Selector lever in D position:

In this position, which is used for all normal driving, the transmission starts in first speed and automatically upshifts to second and third. The road speed at which the upshift occurs depends on the amount the accelerator is depressed. Normal application of the accelerator

controls the timing of the gearshift through a throttle valve incorporated in the transmission. If rapid acceleration is required and the accelerator is fully depressed the detent is brought into operation enabling a higher road speed to be reached before the upshift occurs, as is shown in the shift speed table at the end of this Section. Downshifts are also effected at higher road speeds at full throttle, but to prevent overspeeding of the engine the detent does not operate at speeds over 50 mile/hr for a third to second downshift or above 28 mile/hr for a second to first downshift. When ascending long steep hills it may be advisable to select the L range to assist in engine cooling.

Selector lever in L position:

In this position the transmission remains locked in first-speed irrespective of road speed or accelerator position. If L range is selected when the car is travelling at over 5 mile/hr in the D range, an immediate downshift is made to second and the transmission is locked in this speed to provide moderate engine braking. Reducing the road speed to below 5 mile/hr gives an automatic downshift to first. At full throttle the downshift to first will be made at speeds up to 28 mile/hr. Road speed should not exceed 55 mile/hr in L range. Also, L range should not be selected when travelling at more than 50 mile/hr on normal roads or above 10 mile/hr on slippery roads as this may result in a skid.

Selector lever in R position:

This position must not be selected while the car is moving forward. By moving the lever between R and D whilst applying light throttle, the car may be rocked out of mud, sand or snow.

Engine tuning:

Idling adjustment must be carried out with the selector lever in D range or Reverse. Ensure that the parking brake is applied and take care not to speed the engine unduly, otherwise the car will move. Adjust to obtain the smoothest idling with minimum creep.

Towing:

If it is necessary to tow the car, first check the oil level in the transmission (see **Section 6a:2**) and top it up if required. The car may then be towed up to 10 miles at not more than 30 mile/hr. Check the oil level again after towing. For longer towing distances or with a faulty transmission, the propeller shaft must be removed or the rear wheels lifted clear of the ground. It is not possible on this model to engage any of the gear ranges for starting the engine by towing or pushing.

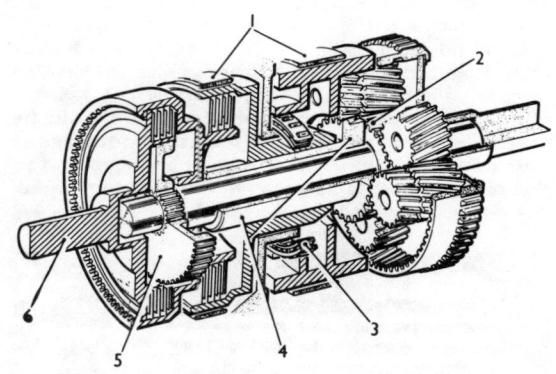

FIG 6a:2 The torque converter

Key to Fig 6a:2   1 Turbine   2 Stator   3 Impeller

engine idling in P range as previously described. **The level must be rechecked as soon as the transmission reaches normal operating temperature.**

The transmission s cooled by air entering through slots in the front of the case and passing through grilles at the bottom of the converter housing. Every 12,000 miles, or more frequently under bad conditions, check that the slots, grilles and oil pan (see **FIG 6a:4**) are free from mud and dust.

Shift speed table (mile/hr):

Selector Lever Position	Accelerator Position	Upshifts			Downshifts		
		1st to 2nd	2nd to 3rd		3rd to 2nd	3rd to 1st	2nd to 1st
D range	Minimum throttle	8–10	12–22		—	4–6	—
	Maximum throttle	30–37	53–60		Below 50	Below 28	—
L range	Minimum throttle	—	—		—	—	5
	Maximum throttle	—	—		—	—	Below 28

6a:2 Maintenance

Periodic changes of the transmission oil are not recommended but the oil level should be checked every 6000 miles or every three months. The dipstick is in the transmission filler pipe at the righthand rear of the engine. The car must be on a level surface and the oil warmed up to normal working temperature by a run of about five miles. Do not attempt to warm up by running the engine with the car stationary as this can lead to overheating of the transmission. Select the P range and let the engine run at idling speed for two minutes. With the engine still idling, remove and wipe the dipstick with non-fluffy rag or paper, insert and withdraw immediately. If the oil level is low, top up to the FULL mark. **Do not overfill.** Use a clean funnel with a fine mesh gauze filter. It is essential to use the recommended oil. No additives may be used.

If the oil pan is drained for any reason, note that after a run the oil will be hot enough to cause serious burns, therefore suitable precautions must be taken.

If the oil level has to be checked with the transmission cold, as for example after repairs to the unit, the level must be at least $\frac{3}{8}$ inch below the FULL mark with the

FIG 6a:3 Clutches and planetary gear set

Key to Fig 6a:3   1 Front and rear brake bands
2 Forward sun gear   3 One-way clutch   4 Reverse sun gear
5 Front clutch hub   6 Input shaft

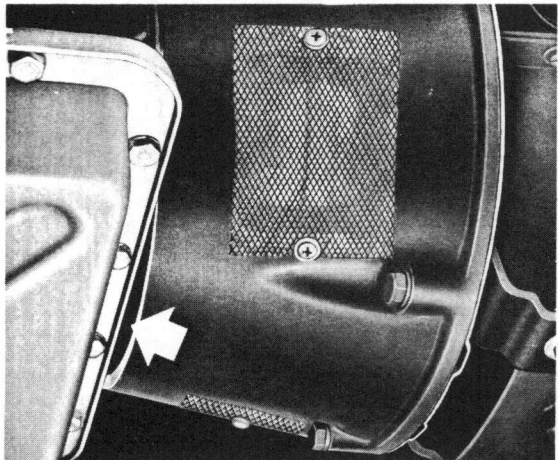

FIG 6a:4 The cooling grilles and lower slot (arrowed) must be kept clear

Additional cooling is provided by an oil cooler, mounted behind the front end panel as shown in **FIG 6a:5.** Oil passes from the converter outlet through a long pipe to the oil cooler. After circulating through the cooler the oil returns through a second pipe to a union at the rear of the converter.

6a:3 Adjustments

In the event of faults developing in the transmission, it will be best to entrust the work of repair to a service agent having the necessary equipment and facilities. However, it is possible to carry out adjustments to the external linkages which will in any case be necessary if the owner fits a replacement unit as described in **Section 6a:5.** An accurate pressure gauge and tachometer are essential for tests.

The following instructions cover the checking and adjustment of the downshift and throttle valve linkage, damper, manual linkage and starter inhibitor switch.

Checking the operation of the downshift and throttle valve cable necessitates running the engine at increased speed whilst the D range is engaged and the car stationary. **Hence for safety reasons an assistant should be seated in the car to ensure that the footbrake is fully depressed whilst the drive is engaged and to prevent accidental release of the parking brake.** It is also essential that the accelerator to throttle linkage

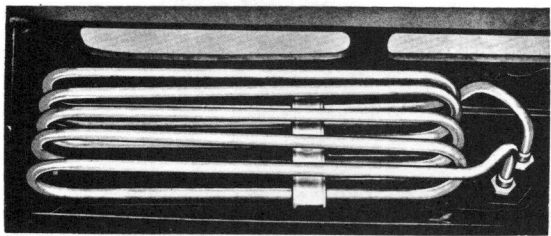

FIG 6a:5 Transmission oil cooler

is correctly adjusted before any adjustment is made to the valve cable, to ensure full throttle opening at the carburetter. Instructions will be found in **Section 2:9** in **Chapter 2.** After the throttle linkage has been set operations are as follows:

1 Referring to **FIG 6a:6,** ensure that the linkrod is adjusted so that dimension A is 6.20 inches.
2 Check the oil level in the transmission.
3 Connect a pressure gauge to the transmission line pressure check point. Connect a tachometer to the engine. Ensuring that the parking brake is fully applied, start the engine.
4 Place the selector lever in the D position. Adjust the engine speed to obtain smooth idling consistent with minimum creep.
5 Note the reading on the pressure gauge, which should be between 50 and 65 lb/sq in. If the pressure is not within these limits, adjust the valve cable by means of the outer cable adjuster shown in **FIG 6a:6.** If the required pressure is still not obtained, the valve body assembly should be removed and the downshift and throttle valves checked. This work should be entrusted to a service agent.
6 Increase the engine speed by 500 rev/min. The line pressure should rise by 20 lb/sq in over the figure obtained at the end of the previous operation. If necessary, adjust the cable. Tightening the cable increases the pressure, slackening the cable reduces pressure.

To prevent stalling the engine, a throttle damper is fitted as shown in **FIG 6a:7,** its function being to cushion the throttle during the last part of its travel to the closed position. Before making any adjustment to the damper setting, ensure that engine idling is correctly adjusted (see **Section 2:6** in **Chapter 2**).

Hold the throttle partially open so that the throttle stop lever just contacts the damper plunger and measure the distance A between the lever and the dashpot diaphragm housing. Allow the throttle to return to the idling position and again measure the distance A. The difference between the two dimensions represents the amount of plunger travel, which should be .12 to .16 inch. If necessary, slacken the locknut and adjust the position of the damper to obtain correct plunger travel.

FIG 6a:8 shows details of the selector lever linkage adjustment. The adjustment when set correctly ensures that there is sufficient clearance between the pin and the ends of the slot in the clevis so that movement of the engine and transmission assembly is not transmitted to the floor-mounted selector lever. Adjustment is carried out as follows:

1 Disconnect the selector rod clevis from the selector lever.
2 Move the selector lever to the P position and the front selector lever fully rearwards to the park position.
3 Adjust the clevis as required to align the lower pip 1 with the selector lever notch 2.
4 After adjustment, lubricate the clevis slot and pin with Keenol grease and locate the boot over the end of the selector lever.

A fault in the starter inhibitor switch should first be sought in the wiring. The switch has four terminals, two for the starter inhibitor which protrude outwards radially and two angled at 45 deg. for reverse lamps. These terminals are numbered for identification as shown in **FIG 6a:9**. The wiring can be checked by disconnecting all wires from the switch and joining together the wires of each circuit. If the wiring is serviceable it should then be possible to operate the starter, and with the ignition switched on the reverse lamps should light. If the fault is not in the wiring, check the manual linkage adjustment as previously described, then check the switch adjustment as follows:

1 Apply the parking brake and chock the front wheels, as the car may move if the engine is inadvertently started with the selector lever in the L, D or R positions.
2 Place the selector lever in the L or D position.
3 Slacken the locknut using the special spanner VR.2025 and fully unscrew the switch from the transmission case as shown in **FIG 6a:10**.
4 Connect a small bulb and battery across the reverse lamp terminals.
5 Screw the switch into the transmission until the test lamp just goes out. Mark the position of the switch relative to the transmission case at this point.
6 Connect the test lamp across the starter inhibitor terminals and screw the switch in further until the test lamp just lights. Again mark the position of the switch.

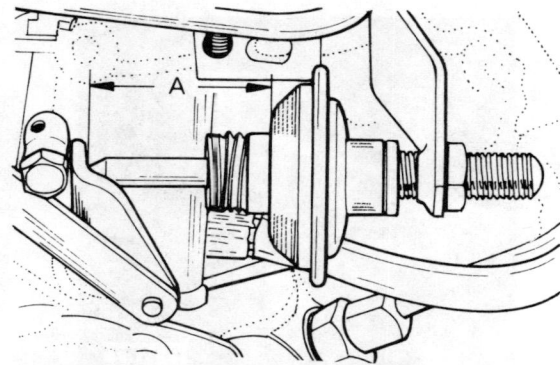

FIG 6a:7 Throttle damper setting. **A** shows check measurement between lever and diaphragm housing

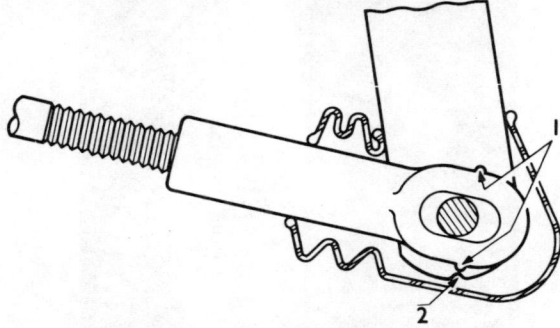

FIG 6a:8 Selector lever linkage adjustment

Key to Fig 6a:8   1 Pips on clevis   2 Notch in lever

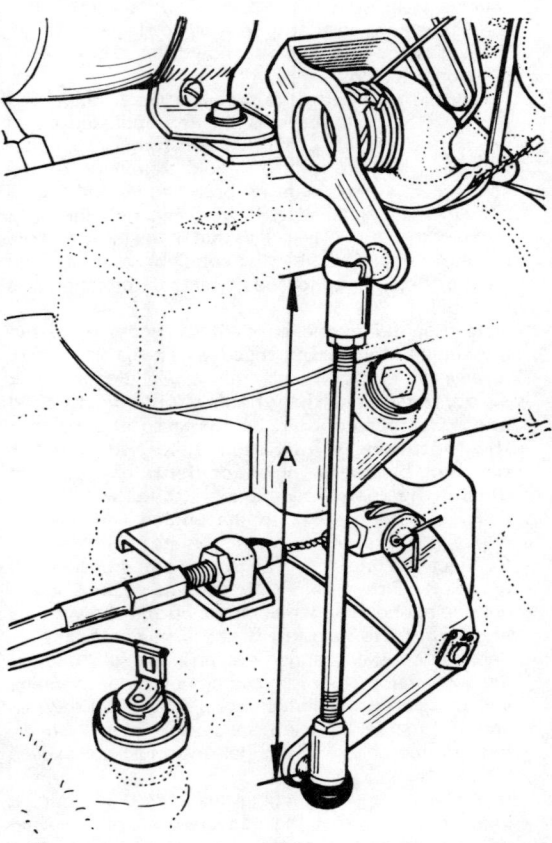

FIG 6a:6 Downshift and throttle valve cable linkage. Dimension **A** should be 6.20 inches

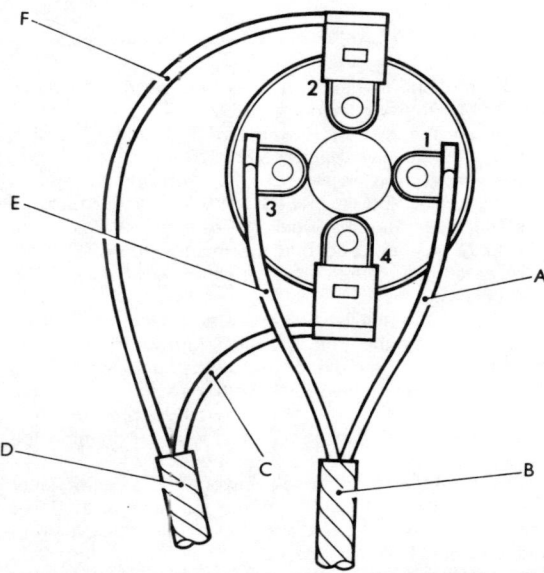

FIG 6a:9 Starter inhibitor switch terminal identification and colour code

Key to Fig 6a:9   1, 3 Starter inhibitor terminals
2, 4 Reverse lamp terminals   **A** White-yellow   **B** Inhibitor
switch harness   **D** Reverse lamp harness   **E** White-red
C Green-brown   **F** Green

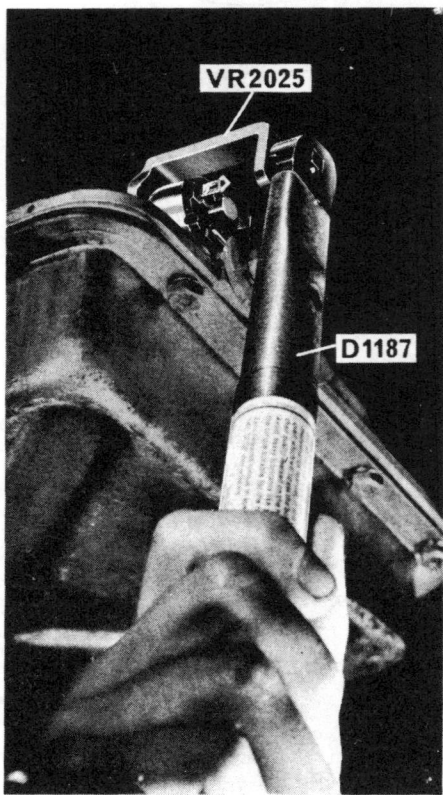

FIG 6a:10   Adjustment of inhibitor switch

7 Unscrew the switch until it is in a position midway between the two marks made.

8 Tighten the switch locknut to a torque of 6 lb ft using the special spanner VR.2025.

9 Reconnect the wires to the appropriate switch terminals as shown in **FIG 6a:9** and verify that the starter operates only when the selector lever is in the P or N position, and that the reverse lamps, if fitted, operate only when the selector lever is in the R position.

If the switch still fails to operate correctly it must be removed, since the unit is sealed and cannot be dismantled. Before removing the switch ensure that the surrounding area is clean. Whilst the switch is removed, seal the aperture in the transmission to prevent entry of dirt. The switch can be removed without draining the transmission oil.

FIG 6a:11 is a sectional view of the selector lever mechanism. Access to the mounting screws of the lever and housing is obtained after removing the lever grip and console. Hold the grip cap 5 whilst the grip 3 is unscrewed, otherwise damage may be caused to the press button 4. After disconnecting the clevis at the lower end of the lever and removing the screws, the lever and the housing 7 can be withdrawn from inside the car. After removing the boot 1, removal of the lever pivot bolt and pushrod nut, washer and pad 6 will

enable the lever to be detached from the housing.

When reassembling, lubricate the pushrod bushes 2 and pivot bushes with Keenol grease. The flats formed at the upper end of the pushrod must be positioned so that they are parallel to the sides of the selector housing when tightening the pad nut. Adjust the selector lever linkage as previously described.

6a:4 Road tests

It has already been stated that the owner can undertake little in the way of repairs to the automatic transmission. The carrying out of the following standard road test procedure, however, will enable an adequate report of any faults to be given to a service agent. In all cases the stated road test procedure should be carried out completely as there may be more than one fault. Before commencing the tests, check the oil level and ensure that the transmission is free from leaks. Also check the downshift and throttle cable adjustment as previously described.

1 Check the starter operation by ensuring that it will operate only with the selector lever in the P or N positions, and that the reverse lamps, when fitted, operate only with the lever in the R position.

2 Test the transmission engagement. With the brakes applied and the engine at idling speed, move the selector lever from N to D position, then from N to the L position, and lastly from N to the R position. Transmission engagement should be felt in each position selected.

3 Check the converter stall speed in the L range and reverse. The stall speed is the maximum speed at which the engine can drive the torque converter impeller while the turbine is held stationary. As the stall speed is dependent on both engine and torque converter characteristics, it will vary with the condition of the engine as well as that of the transmission. It follows, therefore, that the condition of the engine must be determined for the correct interpretation of a low stall speed.

4 Note that during the check it is necessary to run the engine at increased speed whilst the L range or reverse is engaged and the car stationary. **For safety reasons all the wheels should be chocked and extra care should be taken to ensure that the footbrake is fully depressed and that the parking brake is not accidentally released during the test.** Operations are as follows.

5 Connect a tachometer to the engine and place it where it can easily be read from the driver's seat. Connect a pressure gauge to the transmission pressure check point. With the engine and transmission at operating temperature, **chock the wheels and apply the parking brake and footbrake.**

6 Select either the L range or reverse and fully depress the accelerator. Note the readings on the tachometer and pressure gauge which should be 2000 rev/min and 150 to 160 lb/sq in respectively. To avoid overheating, the period of the stall test must not exceed 10 seconds.

7 If the stall speed is higher than 2200 rev/min, it indicates either that the converter is not receiving the required oil supply or that slip is occurring in the clutches of the transmission. If the stall speed is between 1400 and 1900 rev/min the engine requires

tuning. If the stall speed is under 1000 rev/min the torque converter must be renewed.

8 Below standard acceleration in third speed above 30 mile/hr, combined with a substantially reduced maximum speed, indicates that the stator one-way clutch has locked in the engaged position. The stator will then not rotate with the turbine impeller and consequently the fluid flywheel phase of the converter cannot occur. Excessive overheating of the transmission will take place, although the stall speed remains normal. If the converter is faulty, the unit must be renewed since it cannot be dismantled.

9 Test for upshift operation at minimum throttle. With the transmission at normal operating temperature, select the D range. Release the brakes and accelerate with minimum throttle opening. Check for 1 to 2 and 2 to 3 upshifts according to the table in **Section 6a:1**. At minimum throttle opening the upshifts may be difficult to detect. Confirmation that the transmission is in third-speed may be obtained by selecting L range, when a 3 to 2 downshift may be felt.

10 Test the shifts at full throttle. Stop the car and select the D range. Retain the transmission in this range for the following operations.

11 Accelerate at full throttle and check for 1 to 2 and 2 to 3 upshifts according to the table in **Section 6a:1**.

12 Travelling at 51 to 56 mile/hr in third-speed, accelerate at full throttle. The car should continue to accelerate in third-speed and should not downshift to second.

13 At a speed approaching 50 mile/hr in third-speed, accelerate at full throttle. The transmission should downshift to second-speed.

14 At a speed approaching 28 mile/hr in third-speed, accelerate at full throttle. The transmission should downshift to first-speed.

15 At 45 mile/hr in third speed, on a dry road, release the accelerator and select L range. Check for a 3 to 2 downshift and engine braking. With the accelerator released, check for a 2 to 1 downshift and increased engine braking.

16 Test the operation of the clutches. Stop the car and, with L range still engaged, release the brakes. Using full throttle, accelerate to 20 mile/hr. Check that there is no front clutch slip or squawk from the transmission and that no upshift takes place.

17 Stop the car and select reverse. Release the brakes and reverse the car, using full throttle if possible. Check that there is no rear clutch slip or squawk from the transmission.

18 Test the operation of the parking pawl. Using the brakes, stop the car on a gradient facing downhill and select Park. Release the brakes and check that the pawl will hold the car. Re-apply the brakes before disengaging Park. Check that the selector lever is held in the P position by the spring-loaded catch. Repeat the check with the car facing uphill.

6a:5 Transmission removal

Owing to the weight of the transmission assembly (over 120 lb) removal or installation should not be attempted without the use of a suitable hoist and cradle. It will also be necessary to raise and safely support the car or work over a pit. Proceed as follows:

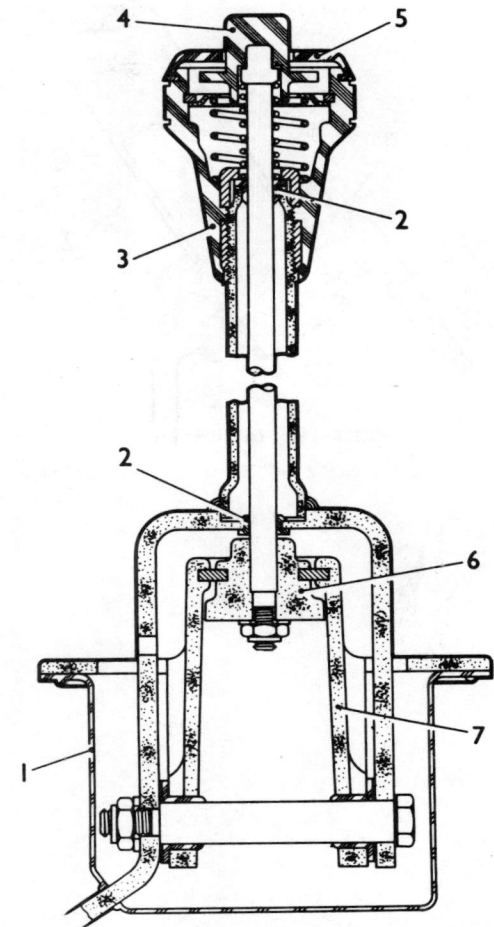

FIG 6a:11   Sectional view of selector lever assembly

Key to Fig 6a:11   1 Boot   2 Pushrod bushes
3 Lever grip   4 Push button   5 Grip cap   6 Pad
7 Housing

1 Disconnect both battery cables.

2 Remove the front tunnel trim assembly and disconnect the wire to the selector lever indicator lamp.

3 Disconnect the selector rod clevis from the selector lever. The lever with housing and console remains on the car.

4 Disconnect the downshift and throttle valve cable from the throttle linkage on the cylinder head.

5 Remove the heater outlet duct to provide access to the converter housing top bolts. Due to the close proximity of these bolts to the floor panel it will be found that although the bolts can be slackened they cannot be removed. To increase the distance between the top bolts and the floor panel, disconnect the exhaust pipe from the manifold and remove the bolt securing the engine righthand front support bracket to the mounting.

6 Unless working over a pit, raise and firmly support the car.

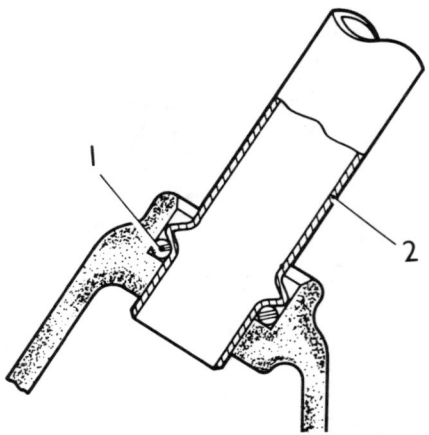

FIG 6a:12 Oil filler pipe

Key to Fig 6a:12   1 O-ring   2 Pipe

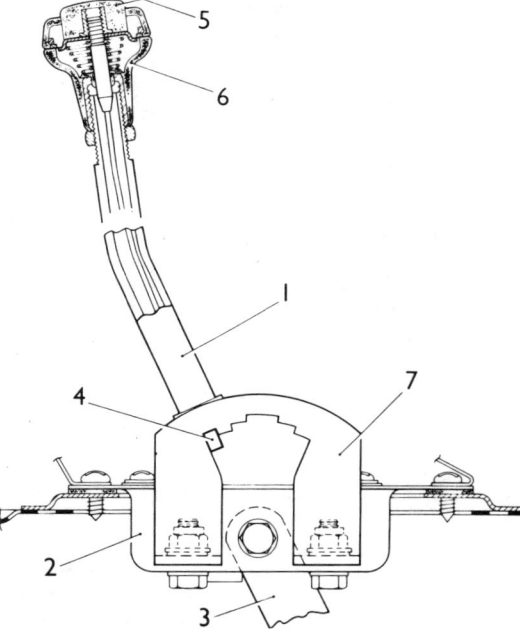

FIG 6a:13 Selector lever and mounting

Key to Fig 6a:13   1 Lever   2 Housing   3 Lower lever
4 Plunger   5 Push button   6 Grip   7 Selector plate

7 Drain the oil from the transmission. **After a long run the oil will be hot enough to cause serious burns, therefore suitable precautions must be taken.**

8 Disconnect the oil cooler pipes and remove the oil filler pipe. Before disconnecting the pipes ensure that the surrounding surface is clean. Afterwards seal the apertures to prevent entry of dirt.

9 Disconnect the speedometer cable and the wires to the starter inhibitor switch.

10 Remove the converter housing front cover.
11 Remove the propeller shaft.
12 Support the engine under the rear of the sump.
13 Remove the engine rear mounting crossmember.
14 Position a cradle under the transmission and support the assembly.
15 Lower the rear end of the transmission.
16 Remove the bottom bolt securing the starter to the crankcase, and move the starter upward and forward as far as possible.
17 Remove the bolts securing the torque converter to the flexplate.
18 Remove the engine righthand front support bracket. Ease the engine over to the righthand side until there is sufficient clearance for removal of the top bolts securing the converter housing to the crankcase. The use of Wrench No. VR.2068 is recommended for this purpose.
19 Remove the remaining bolts securing the converter housing and withdraw the transmission. To ensure that the torque converter moves with the transmission during withdrawal and does not fall out whilst the transmission is being handled, it is recommended that two flat steel strips are bolted to the converter housing, using the same holes as are used for the front cover upper securing bolts.

6a:6 Refitting transmission

Installation of the transmission is a reversal of the removal procedure, but the following points should be noted:

1 If the flexplate has been removed from the crankshaft, ensure that it is refitted with the distance pieces 1 and 2 positioned as shown in **FIG 1:35** in **Chapter 1** and that the bolts are tightened to a torque of 26 lb ft.

2 On later models, plain washers are used under the heads of the bolts securing the converter to the flexplate. Washers can be fitted on earlier models provided longer bolts are used.

3 Before installing the transmission, assemble the two steel strips (see **Section 6a:5**) to the converter housing to retain the torque converter during the operation.

4 Ensure that the painted balance marks on the torque converter rim and the rear of the flexplate are as closely aligned as possible. Tighten the converter to flexplate bolts to a torque of 30 lb ft.

5 Ensure that the converter housing top bolts are started in their threads before the engine rear mounting crossmember is installed. Finally tighten all the converter housing bolts to a torque of 10 lb ft.

6 Refit the oil cooler pipes and the transmission filler pipe. The latter is a push fit in the transmission case. Referring to **FIG 6a:12,** ensure that a new O-ring 1 is fitted to form a seal between the pipe 2 and the case.

7 Refit the remaining components in the reverse order to that of removal. Refill the transmission with the recommended oil. Refit the downshift and throttle cable and adjust as described in **Section 6a:3**.

8 Test the operation of the transmission as described in **Section 6a:4** and as soon as it reaches working temperature check the oil level as described in **Section 6a:2**.

6a:7 GM automatic transmission

At the end of 1969 the transmission described in the early part of this chapter was superseded by the GM automatic transmission. Like the Borg-Warner 35 it uses a fluid torque convertor and a threespeed planetary gear set, with selection by means of a floor mounted selector lever and quadrant with six positions: P, R, N, D, I and L. A two-stage stop actuated by a spring-loaded button in the selector lever grip prevents accidental selection of L, I, R or P. Partial depression of the button is necessary before I or R can be selected and full depression against increased spring resistance is required before selecting L or P.

The action of the transmission when P, R, N and D are selected is the same as that described earlier, but in I (Intermediate) the transmission has the same starting ratio as Drive range, but is prevented from shifting above second gear. This range should not be selected at speeds above 60 miles/hour (97 km/hour) to prevent overspeeding the engine. When I is selected the transmission will immediately shift into second gear and remain there until the car's speed or the throttle position is changed to obtain first gear operation as in D range.

When L (low) range is selected the transmission will shift to and remain in first gear regardless of speed or throttle position. This range should not be selected above 35 mile/hour (56 km/hour).

If the transmission is working satisfactorily, the vehicle may be towed at speeds up to 30 mile/hour for distances up to 30 miles. For longer distances, higher speeds or if the transmission is damaged the propeller shaft should be removed or the vehicle towed on its front wheels.

It is not possible to start the engine by towing or pushing.

6a:8 Maintenance

Transmission fluid:

Check the transmission fluid level every 6000 miles. The oil pan should be drained and the oil strainer renewed every 24,000 miles unless the vehicle is subject to hard driving or high temperature operating conditions, when the intervals should be 12,000 miles. The automatic transmission must be filled with Dexron Automatic Transmission Fluid, or any fluid to the same specification. Note that no additives or compounds may be used in the transmission without grave risk of damage.

Checking fluid level:

The automatic transmission is designed to operate with the fluid level at the 'FULL' mark at normal operating temperature, 180°F. This temperature will only be reached after approximately fifteen miles of driving. With the transmission at operating temperature proceed to check the fluid level as follows. Clean the area around the dipstick and start the engine with the control lever in the 'Park' position. Do not race the engine. Move the control lever through each position on the quadrant and return the lever to the 'Park' position. Immediately, check the fluid level on the dipstick with the engine idling and the vehicle on level ground. Add fluid if necessary, up to the 'FULL' mark.

If the vehicle cannot be driven sufficiently to bring the fluid up to normal operating temperature, the fluid level

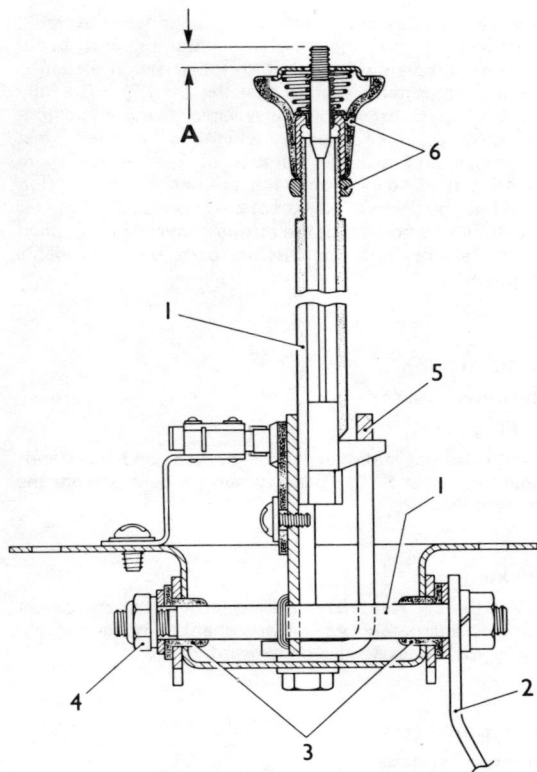

6a:14 Selector lever assembly

Key to Fig 6a:14 1 Lever 2 Lower lever 3 Bushes 4 Nut 5 Selector plate 6 Locking ring and grip **A**=.26 inch

may be checked at room temperature (70°F) as just described but, when a reading is made, the fluid level should be $\frac{1}{4}$ inch below the 'ADD' mark on the dipstick. When the transmission reaches the normal operating temperature the fluid level will then be at the level of the 'FULL' mark due to normal thermal expansion of the transmission fluid.

Do not overfill the transmission. Approximately one pint of fluid is sufficient to raise the level from 'ADD' to 'FULL'.

Renewing oil strainer:

Raise the car to provide access to the underside and support it in a safe manner. Have a container ready to catch the transmission fluid. Remove the oil pan and gasket then remove the oil strainer and gasket. Install a new oil strainer assembly and gasket. Thoroughly clean the oil pan with petrol or paraffin and dry off before replacing it, using a new gasket. Lower the car and refill the transmission as described previously.

6a:9 Faulty performance

Those tests and adjustments which can be made by a reasonably competent owner are given in **Sections 6a:10** and **6a:12**. More serious performance faults which require pressure take-off points to be opened and pressure measurements taken to diagnose the fault, adjustment of the governor or clutches and band, partial or complete dismantling to replace worn or failed internal components dictate that the services of a fully equipped specialist should be enlisted. Quite apart from the specialised knowledge which is required, test equipment and a large number of special tools are essential. It is advised that the automatic transmission should not be dismantled except by a Service Station.

It should be noted that the torque converter is supplied as an assembly only, no internal parts being available separately.

6a : 10 Testing

Stationary tests:

Parking pawl:

With the car stationary on a gradient and the handbrake off, select P. The parking pawl should prevent the car from moving.

'Rocking':

With the car stationary apply slight throttle and select D and R alternately. As the gearchanges occur the car should 'rock' backwards and forwards.

Operational tests:

Governor speeds:

The following table gives the approximate speeds at which gearchanges normally occur at the specified throttle settings. Select D and, by testing on a level road, check the actual speeds at which gearchanges occur.

Change	Throttle	Road speed (mile/hr)
1 to 2	Light	12 to 14
2 to 3	Light	16 to 18
1 to 2	Full	42 to 47
2 to 3	Full	56 to 61
1 to 2	'Kick-down' held	40 to 46
2 to 3	'Kick-down' held	65 to 71
3 to 2	Light	14 to 16
2 to 1	Light	12 to 13

'Kick-down' is normally available up to approximately 58 mile/hr for the 3 to 2 change and approximately 34 mile/hr for the 2 to 1 change on all models.

Engine braking:

While driving at about 55 mile/hr in D, release the throttle and select I. This should result in rapid deceleration and increased engine speed. While driving at about 35 mile/hr in D, release the throttle and select L. Again, rapid deceleration and increased engine speed should result.

6a : 11 Fault diagnosis

This section contains a list of faults which may occur in the automatic transmission, followed by a list of possible causes. Although the owner will be in a position to deal with only a few of these himself, the list will assist him to consult knowledgeably with the specialist he selects to carry out the repairs. Before any attempt is made at diagnosis the fluid level must be checked as described in **Section 6a : 8** and the selector and governor linkages correctly adjusted as described in **Sections 6a : 12** and **6a : 13**.

Fault	Possible cause
No drive in any selector position	1, 2, 3, 4, 5, 6
No drive in D or I	7
No gearchange at any speed	16, 17, 18
Gearchange only at full throttle	11, 12, 15
Gearchange only at part throttle	13, 14
No light throttle 3 to 2 gearchange at low speeds	19
Upchange only from 1 to 2	20
Slipping 1 to 2 gearchange	21, 22, 23
Slipping 2 to 3 gearchange	24, 25, 26
Abrupt 1 to 2 gearchange	22, 27
Abrupt 2 to 3 gearchange	27
Abrupt 3 to 2 'kick-down' at high speed	28
Abrupt 3 to 2 no-throttle gearchange	29
'Flare' on high speed 'kick-down'	21, 24
'Flare' on low speed 'kick-down'	21, 24, 30
No 'kick-down'	14
No engine braking in L	31, 33
No engine braking in I	33
No parking lock in P	32, 33

Key to Possible causes:
1 Low fluid level.
2 Clogged strainer.
3 Inner manual valve disconnected.
4 Input shaft broken.
5 Pressure regulator malfunction.
6 Failed pump.
7 Sprag clutch faulty or installed backwards.
8 Leak in pump suction circuit.
9 Internal leak in pressure circuit.
10 Priming valve stuck.
11 Broken or disconnected vacuum line.
12 Engine or accessory vacuum system leak.
13 Detent pressure regulator valve stuck.
14 Detent cable broken or improperly adjusted.
15 Failed vacuum modulator.
16 Governor valves stuck.
17 1 to 2 change valve stuck in downchanged position.
18 Bad leak in governor pressure passage
19 3 to 2 gearchange valve stuck
20 2 to 3 gearchange valve stuck.
21 Low fluid pressure
22 1 to 2 accumulator valve stuck
23 Leaking second clutch piston seals or ball stuck open.
24 Band adjustment loose.
25 Leaking third clutch piston seals or ball stuck open.
26 Worn input shaft bush.
27 High fluid pressure.
28 High speed downchange timing valve stuck open.
29 Low speed downchange timing valve stuck open.
30 High speed downchange timing valve stuck closed.
31 Manual low control valve stuck.
32 Faulty parking pawl, gear or lock actuator spring.
33 Selector linkage improperly adjusted.

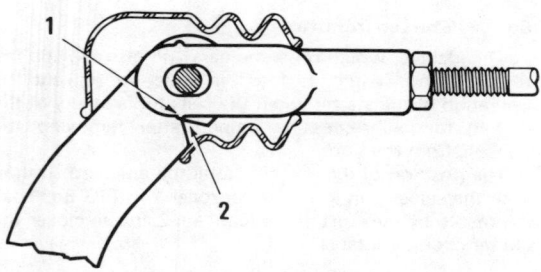

FIG 6a:15   Linkage adjustment

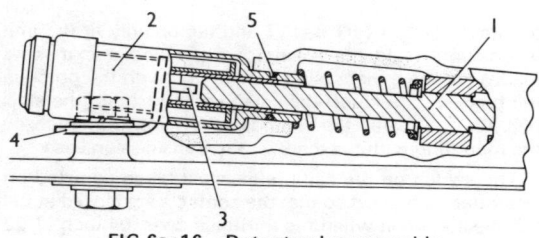

FIG 6a:16   Detent valve assembly

Key to Fig 6a:16   1 Valve   2 Solenoid   3 Plunger
4 Bracket   5 Rubber O-ring

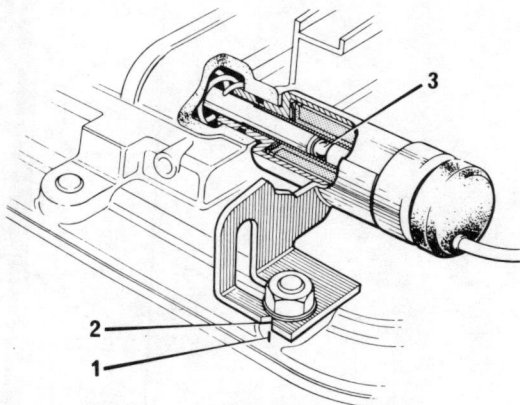

FIG 6a:17   Detent valve installation

Key to Fig 6a:17   1 Locating mark   2 Notch   3 Steel
ball .25 inch diameter

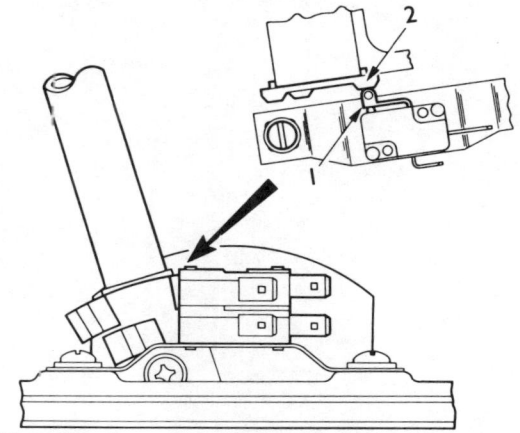

FIG 6a:18   Starter inhibitor and reverse lamp switch

Key to Fig 6a:18   1 Upper roller   2 Rear cam

6a:12 Selector lever and linkage

Referring to **FIG 6a:13,** the selector lever 1 pivots in a housing 2 screwed to the transmission tunnel and its lower lever 3 is connected to the transmission selector lever by an adjustable rod. A plunger 4, actuated by a spring-loaded push button 5 in the lever grip 6 engages in the selector plate 7 and prevents accidental selection of L, I, R and P. A starter inhibitor and reverse lamp switch is mounted on the lever housing.

A sectional view of the selector lever mechanism is given in **FIG 6a:14.** Dismantling is undertaken by withdrawing the selector lever and pivot shaft 1 from the housing after removing the lower lever 2 and prising out the pivot shaft bushes 3. When reassembling place the selector lever and pivot shaft into the housing and fit the bushes. Tighten the lower lever nut, then pre-load the selector lever by tightening the pivot shaft self-locking nut 4. Position the selector plate 5 to give .08 to .10 inch clearance with the selector lever over its full travel. With the selector lever in P and the plunger raised to its full extent screw the locking ring and grip 6 on to the lever until dimension A is .26 inch (6.6 mm) then tighten the locking ring. Screw the button onto the plunger until it just contacts the retainer and then back off by at least one half turn, so that the narrowest portion of the button is parallel to the centre line of the vehicle. Clip the cap onto the retainer in this position.

To adjust the linkage, set the selector in the P position and the transmission selector lever also in Park. Set the adjuster so that the pip 1 in **FIG 6a:15** is aligned with the lever notch 2. This adjustment ensures that the clevis pin is in the centre of the slot so that movement of the engine transmission assembly is not transmitted to the selector lever. After adjustment, lubricate the clevis pin with Duckhams Keenol (GM.4550-M) and refit the boot over the end of the lever.

6a:13 Detent valve

This component, whose purpose is to cause the transmission to shift to a lower gear when the accelerator pedal is fully depressed, i.e. 'kick-down', is shown in **FIG 6a:16.** It is controlled by a switch mounted on the carburetter and operated by the throttle lever.

The solenoid 2 is a push fit in the transmission casing and is secured by the bracket 4 to one of the oil pan bolts. The rubber O ring 5 acts as an oil seal. The valve 1 is pulled into position by the solenoid which contains two windings, 'pull-in' and 'hold-in'. The pull-in winding is switched off by contacts operated through the plunger 3 moved by the detent valve.

After removal for any reason, the solenoid must be set to allow .25 inch (6.35 mm) clearance for movement of the valve. Place a .25 inch steel ball inside the solenoid as shown at 3 in **FIG 6a : 17** and temporarily fit the unit in position. Hold the solenoid in position and make a mark 1 on the transmission case in line with the notch in the bracket 2. Take off the solenoid and extract the steel ball, then re-install the solenoid and align the notch on the mounting with the mark on the transmission case.

The switch on the carburetter must be so adjusted on its mounting bracket so that the contacts are closed at full throttle and open when the throttle stop is .04 inch (1.02 mm) from its abutment on the carburetter body.

6a : 14 Starter inhibitor

This device, which on some cars will also include the reverse lamp switch, is fitted in order to prevent the operation of the starter when the selector is in any of the driving ranges. Access is gained after removing the console from the floor.

The position of the switch should be adjusted so that, with the selector in P, the upper roller 1 in **FIG 6a : 18** is depressed by the crest of the rear cam 2 and so closes the starter circuit contacts.

CHAPTER 7

PROPELLER SHAFT, REAR AXLE, REAR SUSPENSION

7:1 Description of layout

The open tubular propeller shaft incorporates two universal joints of the trunnion and needle roller type as shown in **FIG 7:1.** The universal joints are packed with grease on assembly and periodic lubrication is not required. The yoke of the front universal joint carries an internally splined sleeve which can slide on the splined mainshaft of the gearbox (or output shaft in case of cars fitted with overdrive or automatic transmission) thus compensating for movement of the rear axle. The rear universal joint is bolted to a flange attached to the pinion shaft of the rear axle.

The rear axle is of the semi-floating type with a hypoid final drive enclosed in a one-piece axle housing with detachable rear cover. The rear suspension is of the four-link coil spring type, with longitudinal upper and lower arms and a Panhard rod. The layout is shown in **FIG 7:10** and described in detail in **Section 7:8**.

7:2 Dismantling and servicing universal joints

Two makes of propeller shaft are used, namely Hardy Spicer and BRD, identified by the name cast on the propeller shaft yoke. Replacement shafts, yokes and complete bearing assemblies are interchangeable and the following instructions apply to both makes.

To remove the propeller shaft:

1 Have ready a spare sliding sleeve to insert in the rear cover of the gearbox (or overdrive or automatic transmission where fitted) to prevent oil loss.

2 Mark the relationship between the rear universal joint flange 7 in **FIG 7:1** and the rear axle pinion shaft flange with quick-drying paint. Remove the locking nuts and bolts securing the flanges.

3 After withdrawing the sliding sleeve from the gearbox protect the outer ground surface of the sleeve by binding with tape to prevent damage. Burrs or scratches on this surface may cause premature wear to the rear cover bush and oil seal.

To dismantle the universal joints, referring to **FIG 7:1**, clean all dirt and paint from around the snap rings 8. Mark the yokes 1 and 7 and the shaft 2 with paint to ensure reassembly in the same relationship. Tap the end of one of the bearings 3 with a brass drift to relieve the pressure on the snap ring 8 which can then be removed using circlip pliers. Hold the shaft in the left hand with

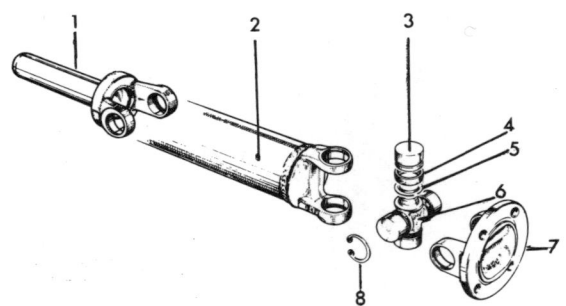

FIG 7:1 Propeller shaft and universal joint components

Key to Fig 7:1   1 Sliding sleeve and yoke   2 Propeller shaft   3 Bearing   4 Oil seal   5 Retainer   6 Trunnion   7 Yoke bolted to pinion coupling flange   8 Snap ring

the bearing to be removed uppermost and tap the yoke downwards with a lead or copper hammer. Reaction should jar out the bearing upwards. When it projects enough to be gripped, invert the joint and pull the bearing cup out downwards so that the needle rollers come out with it.

Remove the opposite snap ring and bearing, then the yoke can be detached from the trunnion 6. Remove the other two bearings and dismantle the other universal joint in the same way. An alternative method of dismantling is to use the special tool D.1093. Note that the trunnion 6, bearings 3 and oil seals 5 are serviced only as an assembly. If the yoke bores are worn, note that a complete propeller shaft can be supplied on an exchange basis.

When reassembling universal joints, coat the needle rollers with petroleum jelly to hold them in the races. Ensure that each bearing is one-third filled with the recommended grease before assembly, as no grease nipples are fitted. Tap home the races using a flat faced drift slightly smaller in diameter than the yoke bore and ensure that the snap rings seat correctly. Any excess grease exuding from the hole of the fourth journal, after three bearings have been installed, should be removed before the fourth bearing is fitted. When installing the propeller shaft, note that the heads of the rear flange coupling bolts are towards the propeller shaft. Tighten the nuts securely. Run the engine for a few minutes to circulate oil from the gearbox casing into the rear cover. Stop the engine and top up the gearbox with the recommended oil.

7:3 Description and construction of axle

FIG 7:2 is an exploded view of the rear axle components. The axle housing consists of a cast differential carrier with pressed-in tubular assemblies, to the ends of which are welded the axle shaft bearing housings (see **FIG 7:7**) which also provide attachment for the brake backplates. The suspension upper and lower arm mountings are welded to the tubular assemblies, the righthand upper arm bracket also providing the attachment point for the Panhard rod.

The differential case or cage incorporates two differential pinions and side gears and is bolted to the hypoid gear. The differential and hypoid gear assembly is carried by two taper roller bearings secured to the housing by caps and bolts. Lateral location of the assembly and preload of the bearings are controlled by graded spacers and shims.

The hypoid pinion is overhung mounted in the axle housing in two preloaded taper roller bearings and is located in correct mesh with the hypoid gear by spacers and shims between the front face of the rear bearing outer race and the housing. A spring-loaded oil seal is pressed into the front of the axle housing and operates

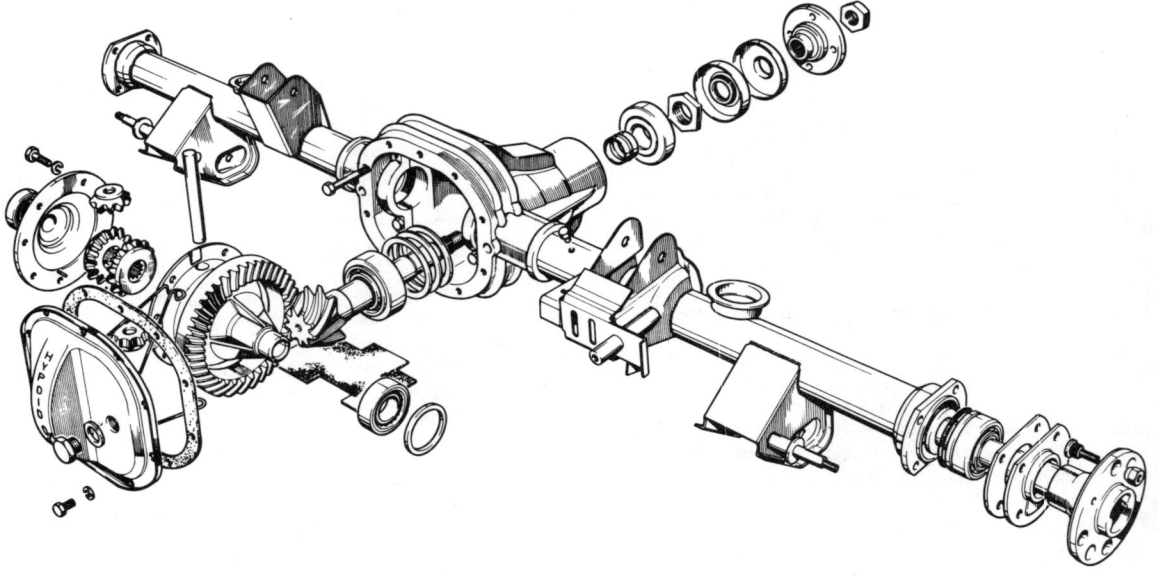

FIG 7:2   Exploded view of rear axle components

directly on the pinion shaft.

To prevent oil leakage from the axle into the hubs and brakes each hub bearing embodies inner and outer oil seals, a description of which will be found in **Section 7:7**.

Complete dismantling of the rear axle and differential is not recommended as the work of reassembly entails the use of special jigs and equipment. The work should therefore be entrusted to a service agent. Complete replacement axles are available on an exchange basis. Procedure for removal and installation of axle are given in **Sections 7:5** and **7:6**.

7:4 Lubrication. Servicing parts without axle removal

The hypoid rear axle requires special hypoid gear oil for its satisfactory operation and the manufacturer's recommendations must be followed in this respect. The combined oil level and filler plug is on the axle housing rear cover. Clean all dirt from around the plug before removing it. The oil level should be at the bottom of the filler plug hole, checked with the car unladen and on level ground. In other circumstances it is possible to put in far too much oil and the surplus may find its way past the seals and into the brakes.

The following operations can if required be carried out without removing the axle from the car: removal and refitting of axle shafts, hub bearings and oil seals (see **Section 7:7**), also renewal of pinion shaft oil seal.

To renew the pinion shaft oil seal proceed as follows:
1 If the axle is not to be removed, disconnect the rear end of the propeller shaft only (see **Section 7:2**) and tie it up to a suitable component to prevent the front sliding sleeve from disengaging from the gearbox.
2 Tap back the staking on the coupling flange nut and remove the nut using a suitable socket wrench and the holding bar Z.8307 as shown in **FIG 7:3**. A substitute for this tool can be devised from a piece of flat bar with two holes to bolt to two adjacent holes in the coupling flange and a cutaway to clear the socket of the spanner used, but it is essential for the flange to be firmly held as the specified torque for this nut is 75 lb ft.
3 Mark the position of the coupling flange in relation

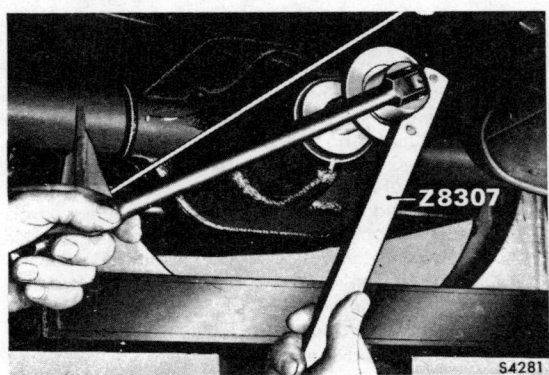

FIG 7:3   Pinion shaft nut removal

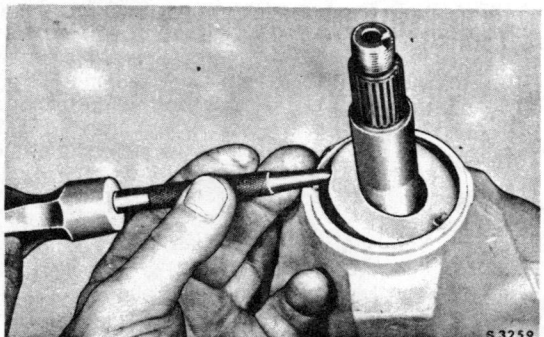

FIG 7:4   Removing pinion shaft oil seal

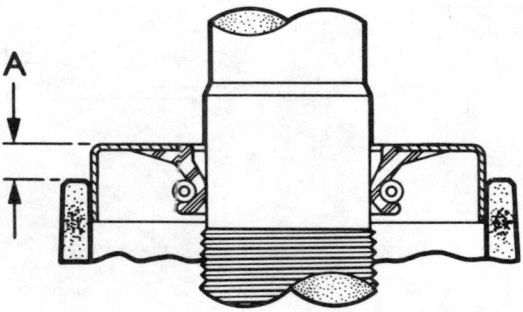

FIG 7:5   Pinion shaft oil seal installation. Dimension **A** should be .19 inch

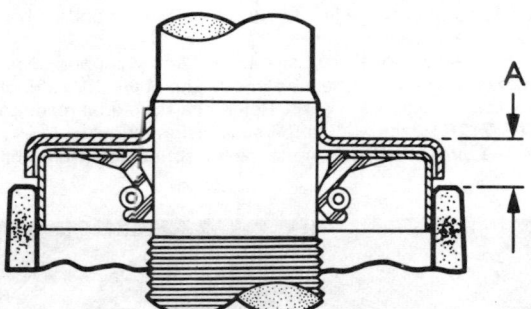

FIG 7:6   Pinion shaft dust shield installation. Dimension **A** should be .36 inch

to the pinion shaft and withdraw the flange, using a suitable puller if necessary.
4 Prise off the dust shield shown in **FIG 7:6.** Pierce the oil seal with a punch as shown in **FIG 7:4** and remove it from the axle housing.
5 Clean the seal bore of the axle housing. Oil the shaft and the lip of the new seal, and using Installer VR.2053 drive in the seal with the open end first until dimension A in **FIG 7:5** is .19 inch. See **Section 7:12** for later type axles.

6 Drive a new dust shield on to the shaft until dimension A in **FIG 7:6** is .36 inch.

7 Ensure that the marks on the coupling flange and pinion shaft are in line. Fit the flange, and holding it with the holding bar described in operation 2, tighten the nut to a torque of 75 lb ft.

8 Top up the axle as described at the beginning of this Section and couple up the propeller shaft as described in **Section 7:2.**

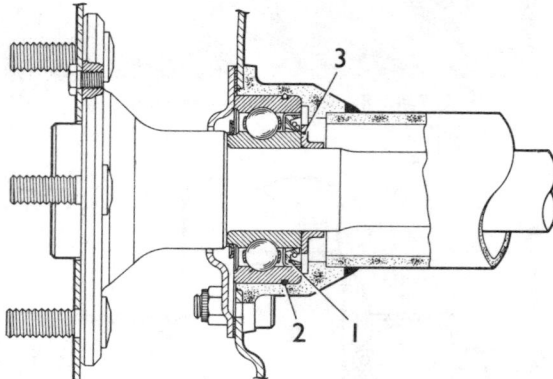

FIG 7:7   Axle shaft and hub bearings

Key to Fig 7:7   1 Lip-type oil seal   2 Oil sealing ring
3 Flanged ring

7:5 Axle removal

Removal of the rear axle is only likely to be called for if a replacement unit is to be fitted. As already stated, dismantling of the axle and differential is best undertaken by a service agent.

For axle removal the car must be firmly supported on stands located on the underbody members forward of the lower suspension arms. Reference should be made to **FIG 7:10** which shows the suspension layout.

The propeller shaft must be disconnected from the

FIG 7:8   Removing axle shaft bearing retainer nuts

FIG 7:9   Removing axle shaft and bearing assembly, using a slide-hammer and adaptor fitted·to wheel studs

rear axle and tied up to a suitable component to prevent the front sliding sleeve being disconnected from the gearbox. Alternatively the propeller shaft can be removed from the car as described in **Section 7:2**. It will also be necessary to disconnect the hydraulic brake hose (see **Chapter 10** for precautions to be observed) and to disconnect the handbrake cable by removing the clevis pin securing it to the equalizer lever on the axle. The weight of the axle is taken on jacks or a hoist. The upper and lower suspension arms, Panhard rod, dampers and springs are then disconnected as described in **Sections 7:9, 7:10** and **7:11.**

7:6 Refitting axle

Refitting the rear axle entails a reversal of the removal procedure, but the following points should be noted:
1 Referring to **FIG 7:10**, the weight of the car must be on the rear springs before finally tightening the mounting nuts of the upper arms 1 and lower arms 2 to a torque of 38 lb ft. Panhard rod and spring mounting bolts and nuts are tightened to 24 lb ft.
2 Bleed the braking system (see **Chapter 10**), reconnect the handbrake cable and adjust the brakes.
3 Connect or refit the propeller shaft (see **Section 7:2**).
4 Check the oil level in the rear axle (see **Section 7:4**).

7:7 Axle shafts, hub bearings and oil seals

FIG 7:7 shows a rear hub in section. The axle shaft is supported by a ballbearing embodying a lip type oil seal 1 and an oil sealing ring 2. On saloon models the bearing is retained on the axle shaft by a pressed-on flange ring 3. On estate cars a larger diameter bearing is used and is retained on the shaft by a shrunk-on ring. If the bearing and the oil seal 1 have to be renewed on either model the work of removal and refitting the retainer and bearing can be more easily carried out by a service agent. The same applies to the work of pressing out and renewing hub flange bolts.

To remove an axle shaft proceed as follows:
1 Raise and support the vehicle.
2 Remove the road wheel and release the handbrake.
3 Remove the bolt securing the brake drum to the axle shaft flange and withdraw the drum. It may be necessary

to slacken off the brake shoe adjuster for this purpose.

4 Remove the nuts securing the axle shaft bearing retainer plate. The nuts are accessible through holes in the flange as shown in **FIG 7:8**.

5 Withdraw the axle shaft and bearing assembly by pulling the flange. If the bearing is tight in the housing, a slide hammer and an adaptor fitted to the wheel bolts should be used, as shown in **FIG 7:9**. Do not use levers, otherwise the flange plate may be distorted.

When installing the axle shaft note the following points:

1 Check that the oil drain hole in the brake flange plate is clear and that the cutaway in the bearing retainer plate gasket lines up with the drain hole.

2 Fit a new sealing ring (item 2 in **FIG 7:7**) in the groove in the periphery of the bearing and lubricate the ring and the bearing housing to facilitate entry.

3 Coat the shaft from the bearing to the splined end with oil to prevent rust.

4 On saloon cars tighten the bearing retainer plate nuts to 12 lb ft.

5 Check the oil level in the axle as described in **Section 7:4**.

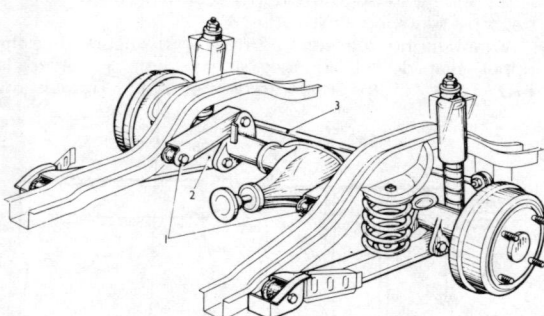

FIG 7:10   Rear axle and suspension layout

Key to Fig 7:10   1 Suspension upper arms   2 Suspension lower arms   3 Panhard rod

7:8 Description of rear suspension system

FIG 7:10 shows the layout of the rear suspension. The rear axle is coupled to the underbody members by two upper arms 1 and two lower arms 2. These four arms are parallel and are rubber bushed to pivot on mounting brackets on the underbody members and on the axle casing. Lateral stability is provided by a Panhard rod 3, the ends of which are also rubber bushed. The rod is fitted between a mounting bracket on the underbody lefthand sidemember and the righthand upper arm mounting bracket on the axle. Coil springs are fitted between mountings on the underbody sidemembers and mountings on the suspension lower arms. Double acting telescopic dampers (see **Section 7:11**) are fitted between the underbody and the suspension lower arm mounting bracket on the axle housing.

7:9 Rear spring removal and refitting

If weakness of the rear springs is suspected, check the

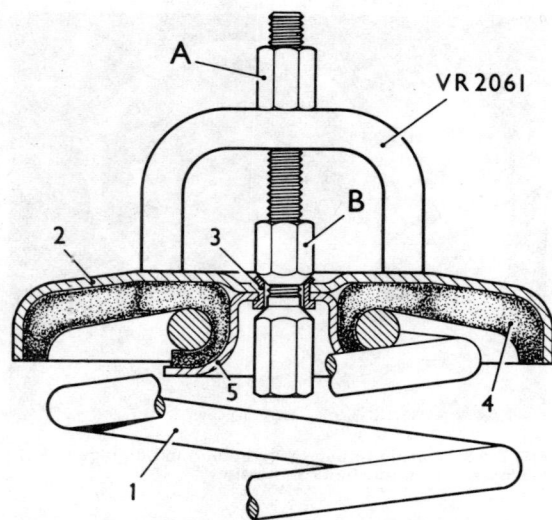

FIG 7:11 Spring assembly components showing expander VR.2061 in use

Key to Fig 7:11   1 Spring   2 Upper seat   3 Bush   4 Insulator   5 Retainer   **A/B** Expander nuts

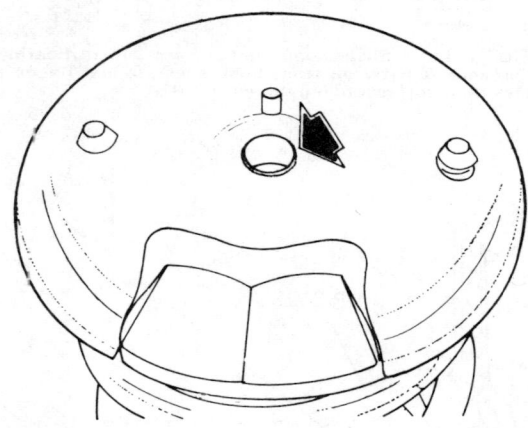

FIG 7:12   Spring upper seat showing peened bush (arrowed)

rear standing height. This must be measured with the car standing on a level floor at kerb weight, that is unladen but with a full petrol tank or equivalent weight placed on the tank. All tyre pressures must be correct. Bounce the rear end of the car, then allow it to settle and measure the vertical height from the floor to the centre of the lower arm front mounting bolt. Take this measurement on both sides of the car. If the measurements are outside the limits given in Technical Data, check the front standing height (see **Chapter 8**) to determine whether rear height is being influenced by the condition of the front springs, before renewing the rear springs.

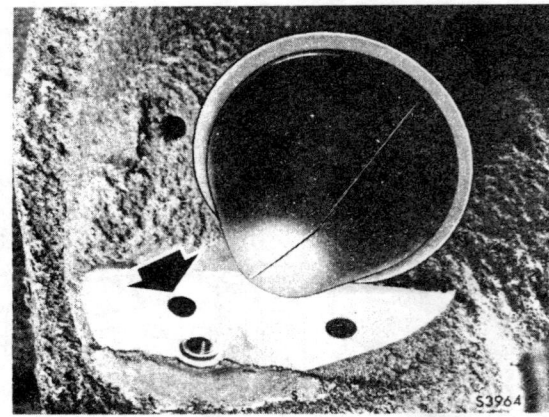

FIG 7:13 Spring upper seat dowel must engage in hole (arrowed) in underbody mounting

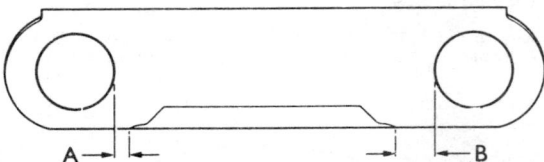

FIG 7:14 Suspension upper arm identification. Distance **A** between front bush aperture and flange is less than corresponding dimension **B** at rear

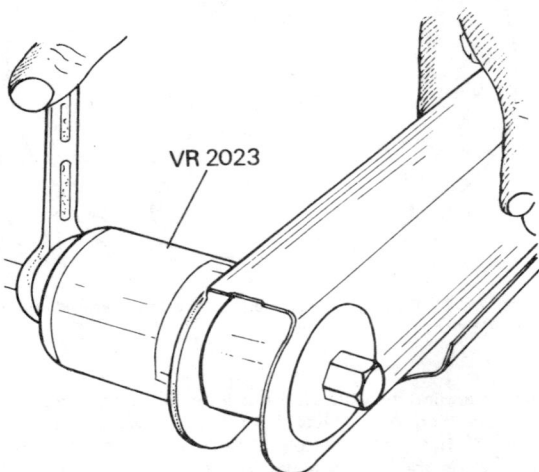

FIG 7:15 Withdrawing upper arm bush. Remover and installer VR.2023 is also used for lower arm bushes

Referring to **FIG 7:11,** a rear spring assembly consists of a coil spring 1, upper seat 2, rubber insulator 4 and retainer 5, held together by the peening of a bush 3. The upper seat is located by a dowel and bolted to a mounting on the underbody sidemember, while the lower end of the spring is secured through a retainer to

the suspension lower arm. Note that the righthand spring is always longer than the left and is therefore not interchangeable. There is a range of eight different springs to suit various models and the vehicle identification number should always be quoted when ordering replacements.

To renew a rear spring:

1 Support the rear of the car firmly on stands placed under the body members, at the same time supporting the rear axle on a jack.
2 Remove the rear wheel.
3 Disconnect the lower end of the rear damper by removing the bottom nut (see **Section 7:11**).
4 Disconnect the spring from the bottom mounting on the suspension lower arm.
5 Lower the axle as far as possible without straining the brake hose. Remove the spring upper mounting bolt and withdraw the spring.

If the spring or the insulator are to be renewed, punch out the peened bush (arrowed in **FIG 7:12**) securing the components of the spring assembly. To reassemble, referring to **FIG 7:11**, assemble a new bush 3, retainer 5, spring 1, insulator 4 and upper seat 2 to the special expander tool VR.2061. Tighten the nut 'A' until the bush is protruding through the upper seat, then peen over the bush by screwing down nut 'B'.

When fitting the spring to the car, ensure that the upper seat dowel engages in the hole (arrowed in **FIG 7:13**) in the underbody mounting. Tighten the

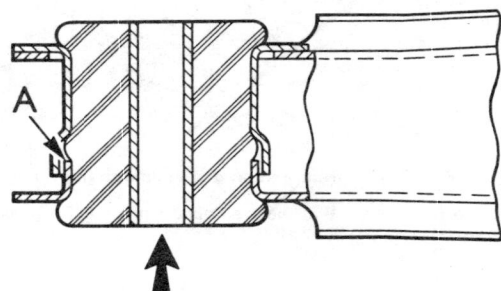

FIG 7:16 Arrow indicates direction in which upper and lower arm bushes must be installed. If installed from the opposite direction the flange **A** will damage bush

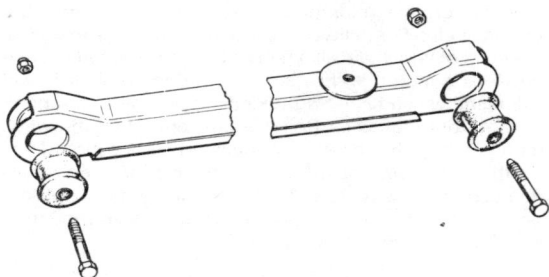

FIG 7:17 Suspension lower arm. The spring lower mounting is nearer to the rear end of the arm

upper mounting bolt and lower mounting nut to 24 lb ft with clean dry threads.

7:10 Rear suspension arms and Panhard rod

The suspension upper arms are rubber bushed at each end. The arms are clamped between brackets on the underbody sidemembers and on the axle housing. The upper arms can be removed irrespective of the position of the axle in relation to the body, so that it is only necessary to remove the bolts and nuts from the ends of the arms. **FIG 7:14** shows the method of identifying front and rear ends of the arms.

To renew the upper arm bushes, use the remover and installer, Tool No. VR.2023 as shown in **FIG 7:15**. Note that the bush fitted in the front end of the arm is softer than that fitted to the rear end. The front end bush bears the number 45 while the rear end bush bears the number 60 on one end face. After smearing the new bush with liquid soap, install in the direction shown by the arrow in **FIG 7:16**, otherwise the edge of flange 'A' will damage the bush. When refitting to the car, ensure that the front end of the arm with the bush marked 45 is fitted to the underbody bracket. Allow the weight of the car to be taken on the rear springs before tightening the arm mounting bolt nuts to 24 lb ft.

To remove the suspension lower arms:

1 Support the rear of the body firmly on stands.
2 Support the rear axle on a jack or hoist. Remove the road wheel.
3 Disconnect the bottom mountings of the spring and the damper. Lower the axle as far as possible without straining the brake hose.
4 Remove the bolts from the front and rear ends of the lower arm and withdraw the arm.
5 Renewal of lower arm bushes is carried out in the same manner as that described for upper arm bushes. The front bush is marked 45 and the rear bush 60. The rear end of the arm can be identified by the spring bottom mounting as shown in **FIG 7:17**.

The Panhard rod, shown in **FIG 7:18**, is fitted between a mounting bracket on the underbody lefthand side-member and the righthand upper arm mounting bracket on the rear axle, its purpose being to provide lateral stability in the suspension. The end of the rod which is attached to the axle has a sleeved rubber bush, whereas the other end is secured to the underbody through two tapered rubber bushes.

To remove the rod, support the body firmly on stands and position the axle with a jack or hoist so that the rod is horizontal. This will facilitate installation. Remove the bolt from the rod underbody mounting and the nut and bolt from the rod axle mounting and withdraw the rod. Renew the rod bushes if necessary and examine the rod for damage. When refitting, tighten the bolt and the nut to 24 lb ft with clean dry threads.

7:11 Rear dampers

The double-acting dampers have a rubber bushed stud fixing to the underbody and a rubber bushed eye attachment to the suspension lower arm mounting bracket on the axle housing. If the car is raised to facilitate damper removal, the axle must also be supported to prevent the dampers becoming fully extended. Remove

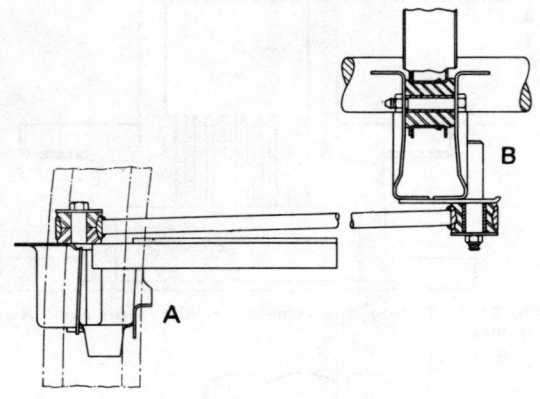

FIG 7:18   Panhard rod as viewed from below

Key to Fig 7:18   **A** Mounting bracket on lefthand underbody sidemember   **B** Righthand upper arm mounting
bracket on rear axle

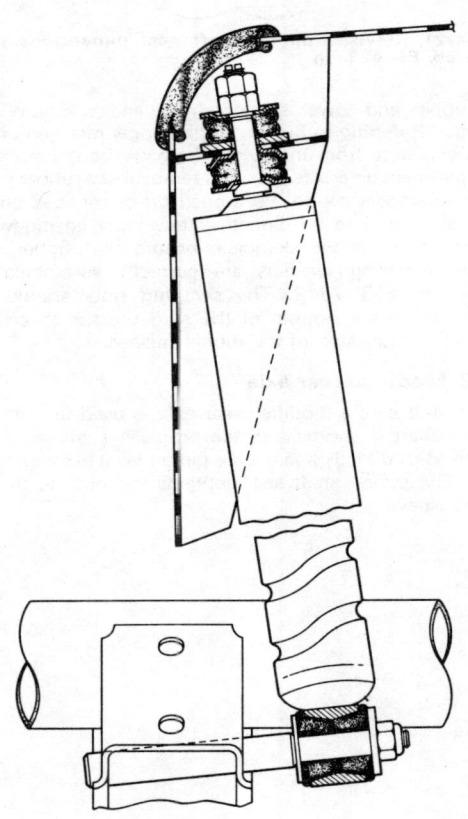

FIG 7:19   Rear damper showing rubber plug inside luggage boot covering top fixing

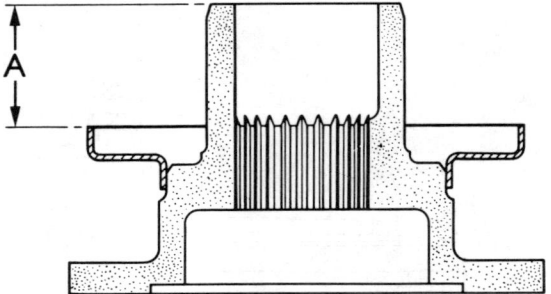

FIG 7:20 Fitting dust shield to later type axle. A= .70 inch

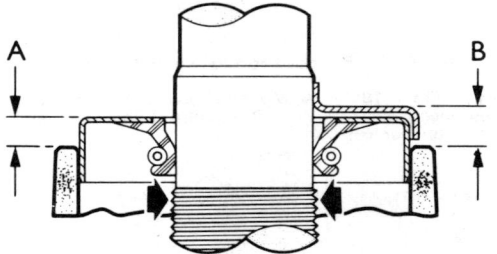

FIG 7:21 Revised pinion shaft seal dimensions. A= .26 inch, B=.42 inch

the upper and lower securing nuts and withdraw the damper. Referring to **FIG 7:19,** the upper mounting nuts are accessible from inside the luggage boot (or cargo compartment on estate car) after removal of a rubber plug.

The dampers cannot be topped up or serviced and if they are found to be defective they must be renewed. When installing the dampers, ensure that upper and lower mounting washers are correctly assembled as shown in **FIG 7:19.** The securing nuts should be tightened to the bottom of the stud threads to ensure correct compression of the rubber bushes.

7:12 Modified rear axle

On later cars a modified rear axle is used in that the pinion shaft is shorter and the propeller shaft coupling flange seats directly against the pinion front bearing inner race. The pinion shaft seal contacts the outside of the flange sleeve.

The method of fitting the dust shield on these later axles is shown in **FIG 7:20.**

Before the short pinion shaft was introduced some later cars used a modified pinion shaft seal which caused a changed specification from that given earlier (see **Section 7:4**).

When installing this type of seal, smear the periphery of the seal casing with jointing compound and locate the seal in the axle housing so that dimension A in **FIG 7:21** is increased to .26 inch to avoid fouling the threads on the pinion shaft.

The dust shield must be located so that dimension B is .42 inch.

7:13 Fault diagnosis

(a) Noisy axle

1 Insufficient or incorrect lubricant
2 Worn bearings
3 Worn gears

(b) Excessive backlash

1 Worn gears or bearings
2 Worn axle shaft splines
3 Worn universal joint or loose coupling flange bolts
4 Loose or broken wheel studs

(c) Oil leakage

1 Defective hub oil seals
2 Defective pinion shaft oil seal

(d) Vibration

1 Propeller shaft out of balance
2 Worn universal joint bearings

(e) Rattles

1 Worn damper bushes
2 Damper securing nuts loose
3 Defective upper spring seat insulator
4 Worn suspension arm bushes
5 Worn Panhard rod bushes

(f) 'Settling'

1 Weak or broken coil spring(s)
2 Incorrect springs fitted (see **Section 7:9**)

CHAPTER 8

FRONT SUSPENSION AND HUBS

8:1 Description of system

The independent front suspension is of the short and long arm type with coil springs and is shown in **FIG 8:1**. The wishbone type upper arms and single lower arms are rubber bushed at their inner ends and pivot on fulcrum bolts attached to a crossmember bolted to the engine side rails. At the outer ends of upper and lower arms, ball joints carry the steering knuckles (or stub axles). The coil springs and telescopic dampers are fitted between the crossmember and the lower arms. Adjustable control rods are bolted to the lower arms and rubber mounted in the crossmember braces. Bump stops which contact the upper arms are retained in brackets on the crossmember, while rebound is controlled by the dampers. A stabilizer bar (or anti-roll bar) is mounted in front of the crossmember and linked to the lower arms (see **FIG 8:17**). Reference to **FIG 8:1** will show that up and down movement is controlled by the coil springs and dampers, while fore and aft rigidity is provided by the triangulated upper arms and the control rods attached to the lower arms. The stabilizer limits the relative movement between the two sides of the suspension and thus reduces tendency to roll.

8:2 Routine maintenance, lubrication points

There are only four points which require lubrication on the front suspension system, these being the upper and lower suspension arm ball joints, two grease nipples being placed on each side of the car. Inject sufficient lubricant of the recommended grade to ensure that the rubber boots are filled, but do not over-lubricate as this will damage the rubber boots. On disc brake models the utmost care must be taken not to allow grease to find its way on to the discs or friction pads. Lubrication of the front hub bearings is dealt with in the next Section.

8:3 Front hub bearings and seals

The front hub bearings are of the taper roller type and are packed with grease during assembly to the hub. The grease is retained by a steel grease cap on the outer side of the hub and by a spring-loaded lip type oil seal at the inner end of the hub. **FIG 8:2** shows disc brake and drum brake types of hub in section. It is essential that only the recommended grease is used and that only the rollers are lubricated. The hub itself must not be packed with grease.

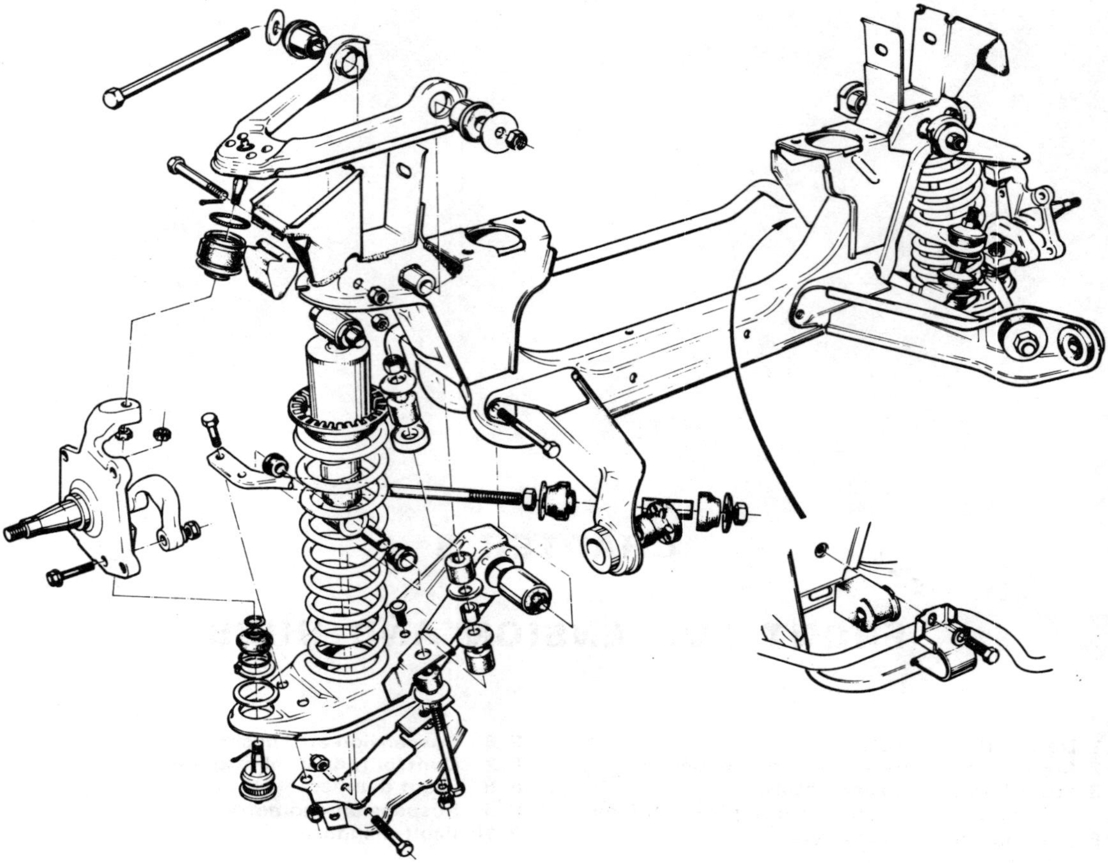

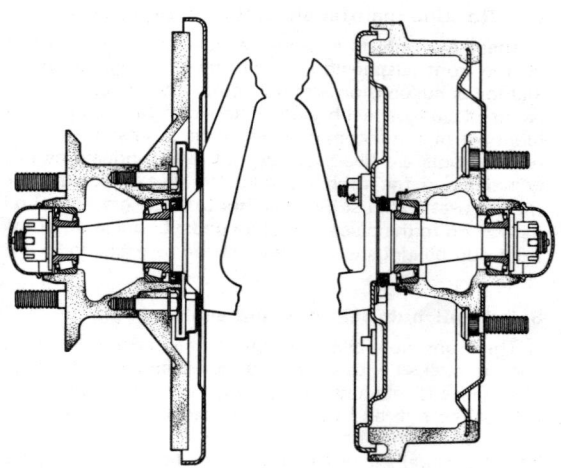

FIG 8:1 An exploded view of the front suspension as seen from lefthand rear

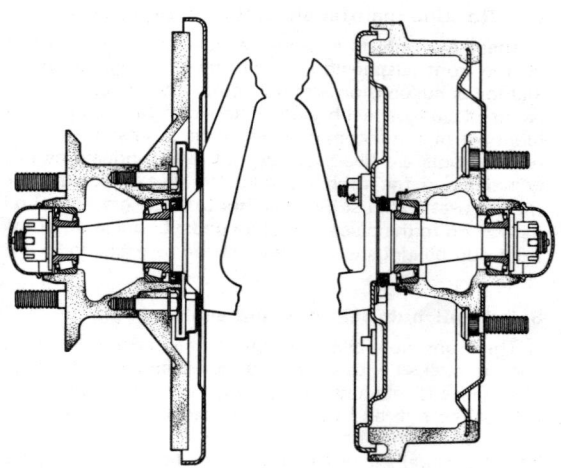

FIG 8:2 Sectional view of front hubs with (left) disc brakes and (right) drum brakes

Check for slackness in the hub bearings by rocking the front wheel as shown in **FIG 8:3.** If only slight play is perceptible, adjust the bearings as follows:

1 Remove the wheel disc and the hub grease cap.
2 Remove and discard the splitpin, then tighten the hub nut using a tubular box spanner with an 8 inch tommy bar.
3 Slacken the nut and remove the tommy bar, then gripping the spanner by hand only, retighten the nut.
4 Insert a new splitpin, turning the nut **back** if necessary to align the splitpin hole.
5 Refit the grease cap and wheel disc.

If the preliminary check shows excessive slackness or roughness in the bearings, or if there is any sign of contamination of the grease by water or grit, it is essential to remove the hub for examination of the bearings as follows:

1 Remove the wheel.
2 (Drum brakes) Slacken brake shoe adjustment. (Disc brakes) Remove the caliper as described in **Chapter 10.**
3 Remove the grease cap, splitpin, hub nut and keyed washer.

4 Remove the hub complete with drum or disc.

To remove the outer races of the inner and outer bearings drive them out of the hub using a drift from the opposite end. The oil seal will be driven out with the inner bearing outer race. On disc brake models care must be taken not to damage the surfaces of the discs during this operation. If it is desired to remove the disc, mark its position relative to the hub with a dab of paint and undo the four bolts with tab washers at the back of the hub. For general notes on inspection and cleaning of bearings reference should be made to Hints on Maintenance in the Appendix.

Examine the wheel bolts and if these have damaged threads or are loose in the hub flange new ones should be fitted. This work can be more conveniently carried out by a service agent using a hydraulic press.

To reassemble and install the hub:

1 Assemble the bearing outer races, wide end first, squarely into the hub and ensure that each race is fully home against the shoulder as shown in **FIG 8:2**.
2 Pack the inner bearing inner race and rollers with the recommended grease and install in the hub. Do not pack the hub itself with grease.
3 Press the oil seal on to the hub.
4 Fit the drum or disc to the hub. (Disc brakes) Fit new tab washers to the disc bolts. Tighten and lock each bolt with one tab.
5 Pack the outer bearing inner race with grease. Refit the hub, outer bearing, keyed washer and hub nut. Adjust the bearings as previously described.
6 (Drum brakes) Adjust the brakes. (Disc brakes) Before installing the caliper refer to **Chapter 10**.

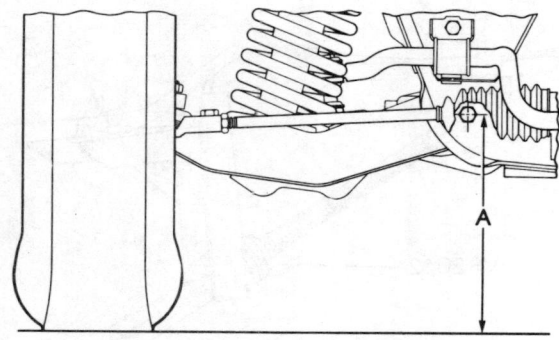
FIG 8:4 Front standing height check

8:4 Checking, removing and refitting front springs

If weakness of the front springs is suspected, check the front standing height as shown in **FIG 8:4**. This must be measured with the car standing on a level floor and at kerb weight, that is unladen but with a full petrol tank or equivalent weight placed on the tank. All tyre pressures must be correct. Bounce the front of the car then allow it to settle and measure the height from the floor to the centre of each lower fulcrum bolt (dimension A in **FIG 8:4**). If the results are outside the limits given in Technical Data, check the rear standing height as described in **Chapter 7, Section 7:9** to determine whether the front height is being influenced by the condition of the rear springs, before renewing the front springs.

To remove a front spring, proceed as follows:

1 Support the car firmly under the body. Care must be taken to ensure the safety of the operator when working underneath the car.
2 Remove the road wheel.
3 Remove the four nuts indicated by arrows in **FIG 8:5**. Detach the control rod from the lower suspension arm (see **FIG 8:15**). Slacken the suspension arm fulcrum bolts and disconnect both stabilizer bar link bolts (see **FIG 8:17**)

FIG 8:3 Checking play in front hub bearings

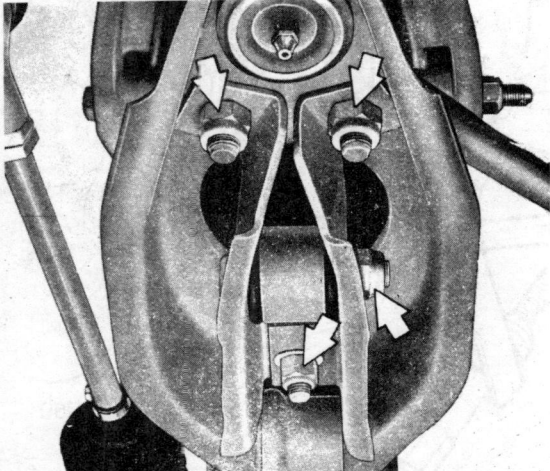
FIG 8:5 Front spring or damper removal. The four nuts (arrowed) must be removed before fitting spring compressor

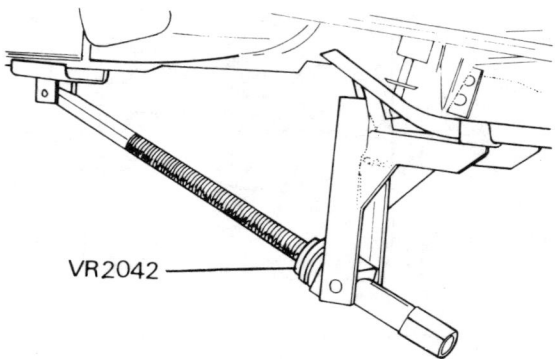

FIG 8:6 Method of using the special Spring Compressor VR.2042 for front spring or damper removal

4 Using the special spring compressor VR.2042, compress the spring as shown in FIG 8:6.
5 Remove the damper brackets and lower mounting bolt.
6 Using the special ball joint remover JWP.362, release the lower arm ball joint from the steering knuckle. Before fitting the tool it is advisable to remove the splitpin and unscrew the nut sufficiently to protect the end of the thread.
7 Attach the Spring Keep VR.2060 over six coils of the spring, ensuring that the longer keep is positioned on the side nearest the lower arm ball joint as shown in FIG 8:7. This will curve the spring and facilitate removal and installation.

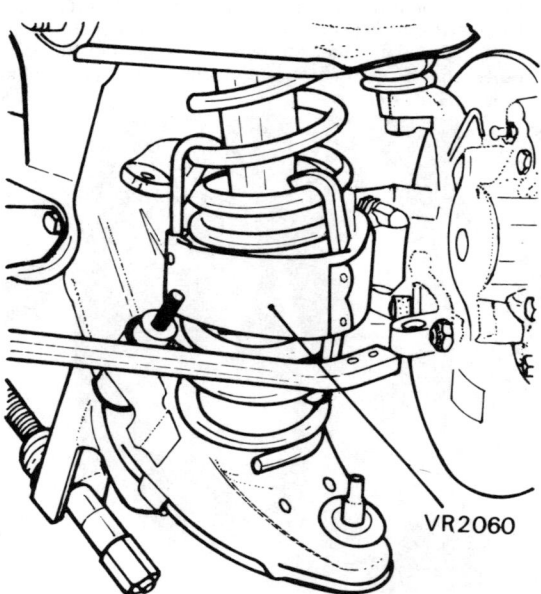

FIG 8:7 Front spring removal. Method of fitting Spring Keep VR.2060 so as to bend the coil spring

8 Release the spring compressor slowly and withdraw the spring.
   Springs differ in length according to model and the Chassis numbers should always be quoted when ordering replacements. Where springs differ in length, note that the longer spring is always fitted to the lefthand side.
   Refitting of springs follows a reversal of the foregoing procedure but the following points should be noted:
1 If new springs are fitted, the Spring Keep VR.2060 must be transferred to the new spring, using the Pre-compressor VR.2065 or a suitable alternative for compressing both the old and the new spring. Ensure that the longer keep is positioned in relation to the spring coils as shown in FIG 8:8.

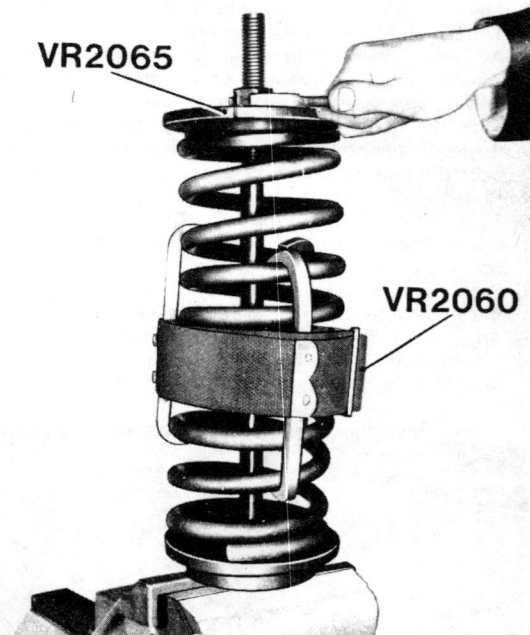

FIG 8:8 Using Spring Precompressor VR.2065 for transfer of spring keeps to new spring

2 Ensure that the spring is correctly located on the lower seat.
3 Ensure that the rubber boot is correctly located.
4 Ensure that the mating tapers are clean and free from grease before fitting the ball joint. Tighten the ball joint stud nut to 33 lb ft. Tighten further where necessary to align splitpin hole.
5 Lower the car to the ground and tighten the lower arm fulcrum bolt to 38 lb ft in the case of early models with plain rubber bushes, or to 68 lb ft on later cars with sleeve bushes.

8:5 Suspension arm ball joints

The ball joints at the outer ends of the upper and lower suspension arms can be checked as follows. Support the car under the suspension lower arms and rock the wheel holding each joint in turn. If there is any perceptible slackness in a joint it should be renewed.

The joints have seatings which are internally loaded by a neoprene pressure ring and must not be compressed in a vice for assessment of wear. **FIGS 8:9** and **8:10** are sectional views of upper arm and lower arm ball joints respectively.

To renew an upper arm ball joint proceed as follows:

1 Remove the suspension upper arm as described in **Section 8:6.**
2 Production ball joints are riveted to the upper arm as shown in **FIGS 8:9** and **8:13.** Replacement joints are secured by nuts and bolts. Drill and chisel off the rivet heads of the old joint and drill out the holes in the arm to $\frac{5}{16}$ inch dia.
3 Bolt the new joint to the arm and tighten the nuts to a torque of 22 lb ft with clean dry threads.
4 Refit the arm as described in **Section 8:6.**

The lower arm ball joint is secured in the arm by a circlip and a special washer. It can be renewed without removal of the lower arm as follows:

1 Support the car under the lower damper mounting bolt bracket, setting it firmly in the vee of an axle stand. Care must be taken to ensure the safety of the operator when working underneath the car.
2 Remove the road wheel.
3 Release the lower arm ball joint from the steering knuckle after removing the splitpin and nut, using the remover JWP.362.
4 Slacken the upper arm fulcrum bolt and wedge the upper arm in the raised position.
5 Remove the circlip and the special washer.

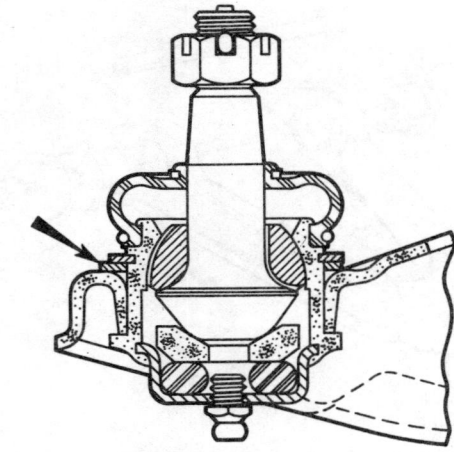

FIG 8:10 Suspension lower arm ball joint. Arrow shows special washer

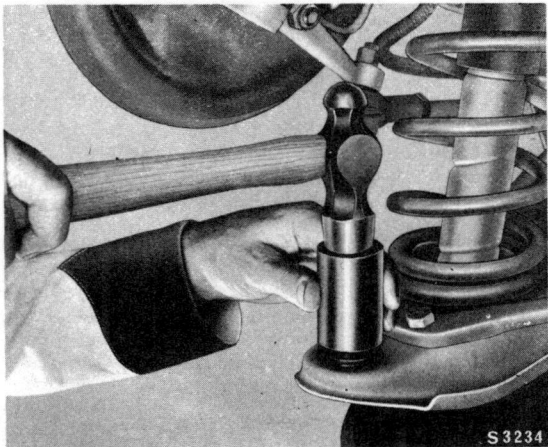

FIG 8:11 Removing lower arm ball joint

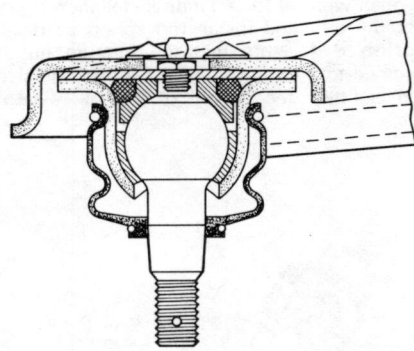

FIG 8:9 Suspension upper arm ball joint

6 Using a suitable piece of tube, drive out the old joint as shown in **FIG 8:11.** Engage the splines of the new joint with those in the arm and drive the joint home.
7 Locate the special washer with the flat in the position shown in **FIG 8:12** and with the concave side upwards and install a new circlip.
8 Assemble the ball joint to the steering knuckle and tighten the nut to a torque of 33 lb ft with clean dry threads. Where necessary tighten further to align the splitpin hole. Secure with a new splitpin.
9 Refit the road wheel and lower the car to the ground.
10 Tighten the upper arm fulcrum nut to a torque of 57 lb ft with clean dry threads. It is essential for the weight of the car to be carried on the tyres before tightening the nut, otherwise the rubber bushes will be strained.

FIG 8:12 Lower arm ball joint showing location of special washer

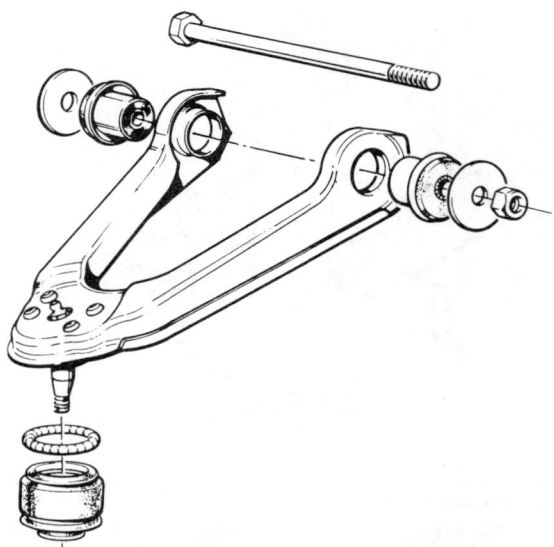

FIG 8:13 Suspension upper arm showing fulcrum bolt and bushes

8:6 Suspension arm bushes

The wishbone type upper arms are rubber bushed and secured to the front axle crossmember by long fulcrum bolts and nuts as shown in **FIG 8:13**. To remove the upper arms proceed as follows:

1 Support the car under the lower damper mounting bolt bracket, setting it in the vee of an axle stand. Remove the road wheel.
2 Disconnect the upper arm ball joint from the steering knuckle using the remover JWP.362. Before fitting the tool remove the splitpin and unscrew the nut sufficiently to protect the end of the thread.

3 Remove the fulcrum bolt and withdraw the arm.

To renew upper arm bushes, remove the old bushes and install the new ones using the remover and installer tool No. VR.2023 in the same manner as described for rear suspension bushes in **Chapter 7**.

When refitting the upper arm, ensure that the rubber boot is in good condition and correctly located and that the mating tapers of the ball joint are clean and free from grease. Tighten the ball joint stud nut to a torque of 33 lb ft. Where necessary tighten further to align the splitpin hole. Secure with a new splitpin. Retighten the upper arm fulcrum bolt to a torque of 57 lb ft with the weight of the car on the tyres.

The inner end of the suspension lower arm (see **FIG 8:14**) is rubber bushed on early models or sleeve bushed on later cars, and clamped between flanges on the front axle crossmember. To renew the bushes proceed as follows:

1 Remove the front spring as described in **Section 8:4** taking particular note of precautions for the safety of the operator when working underneath the car.
2 Remove the fulcrum bolt and nut and withdraw the arm.
3 On early type rubber bushes, cut off the flange of the bush with a sharp knife to prevent distortion of the arm during removal of the bush.
4 Remove the bush using the remover and installer tool No. VR.2023 as described for rear suspension bushes in **Chapter 7**.
5 Only the sleeve type bush is supplied and this is installed using the same tool as for removal. Smear the bush with oil to facilitate installation.
6 Refit the arm and install the spring as described in **Section 8:4**. Note that the fulcrum nut must be tightened to a torque of 68 lb ft when the sleeve type bush is fitted, the weight of the car resting on the tyres.

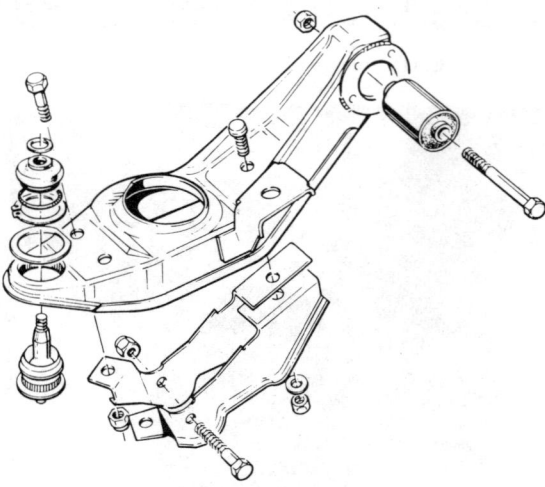

FIG 8:14 Suspension lower arm (later type with sleeve bush)

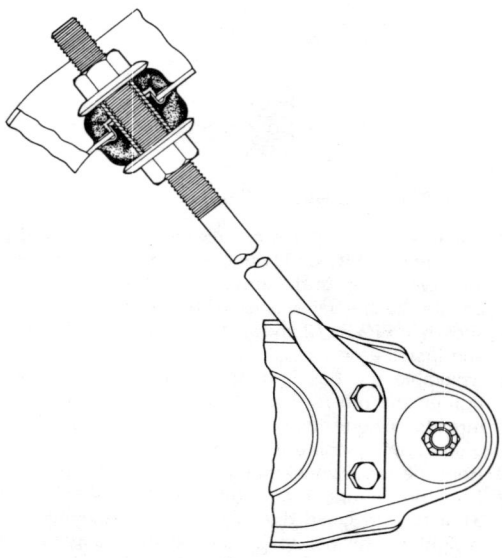

FIG 8:15 Control rod

8:7 Control rods. Stabilizer bar

An adjustable control rod is fitted between each front suspension lower arm and a brace attached to the front axle crossmember. In addition to providing fore and aft stability for the lower arms, the control rods (see **FIG 8:15**) provide a means of adjusting the castor angle (see **Section 8:9**).

Removal and refitting of the control rods is facilitated by supporting the car under the suspension lower arms. During installation, ensure that the bush sleeve is installed and the insulator incorporating the boss is fitted to the front of the crossmember brace as shown in **FIG 8:16**. Tighten the control rod to lower arm nuts to 38 lb ft with clean dry threads and adjust the castor angle as described in **Section 8:9**.

The stabilizer bar (or anti-roll bar) shown in **FIG 8:17** is rubber mounted in straps bolted to the crossmember. Each end of the bar is attached through rubber bushes and a link bolt and nut to a bracket on the suspension lower arms. When refitting the bar, ensure that the bushes, cups, spacer and plain washer are located as shown in **FIG 8:17**. Tighten the link bolt nut to the bottom of the thread.

8:8 Front dampers

The double-acting telescopic dampers are secured through rubber bushed eye mountings to the front axle crossmember and brackets bolted to the lower arms. Suspension rebound (and therefore spring extension) is controlled by the dampers. It is thus important to note that no attempt must be made to remove the damper upper mounting bolt when the front wheels are off the floor unless either the car is supported under the suspension lower arm or the spring compressor VR.2042 is in position. To remove the dampers, proceed as follows:

1 Support the car firmly under the body. Care must be taken to ensure the safety of the operator when working underneath the car.
2 Remove the nuts indicated by arrows in **FIG 8:5**.
3 Compress the spring using the spring compressor VR.2042 as shown in **FIG 8:6**.
4 Remove the damper lower mounting bolt and brackets, then remove the upper mounting bolt and withdraw the damper.

The dampers are not adjustable and no provision is made for topping up. If the dampers are defective they must be renewed. The upper bushed eye mounting is not serviced separately from the damper, but the lower bushes can be renewed if necessary. These are fitted by hand. When installing damper, loosely assemble the lower mounting bolt and brackets to the eye bushes before engaging the upper mounting. Tighten the upper mounting nut to 38 lb ft and the lower mounting bolt nut to 57 lb ft with clean dry threads in each case.

8:9 Suspension geometry

Although affecting the steering, castor angle, camber and steering pivot inclination are controlled by components of the front suspension and are therefore dealt with in the present Chapter. Toe-in and toe-out on turns are covered in **Chapter 9, Section 9:7**.

FIG 8:16   Installing control rod bushes

Professional equipments for checking suspension and steering geometry are unlikely to be available to the owner, and in view of the accuracy called for the work should preferably be carried out by a service agent.

Whatever type of measuring equipment is used, however, the car must be on a level floor and tyre pressures, front and rear standing height, front hub bearings and suspension joints must all be in order.

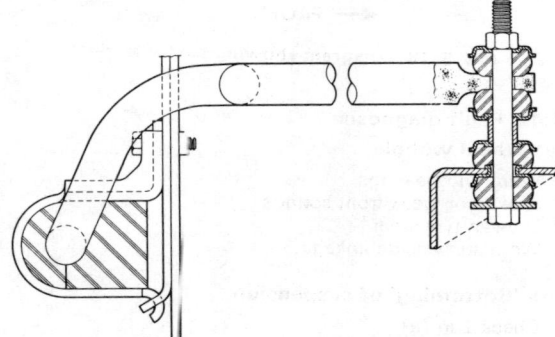

FIG 8:17   Stabilizer bar showing location of bushes, cups, spacer and plain washer

FIG 8:18 shows castor angle, which can be adjusted by means of the control rod front nut shown in **FIG 8:15**. To increase the castor the control rod must be lengthened. To decrease, the rod must be shortened. The rear nut is then tightened to 47 lb ft and the castor angle rechecked. After adjusting castor angle, the toe-in must be checked and if necessary adjusted as described in **Chapter 9**. The necessary dimensions for both will be found in Technical Data

FIG 8:19 shows camber and steering pivot (or king-pin) inclination. These should be checked in accordance with figures given in Technical Data. These angles are not adjustable. If camber angle is below the low limit and steering pivot inclination is correspondingly greater, or if camber angle is above the high limit and steering pivot inclination correspondingly less, this will indicate distorted suspension arms or crossmember. If, however, steering pivot inclination is within the specified limits but camber angle is outside the limits, this indicates a distorted steering knuckle.

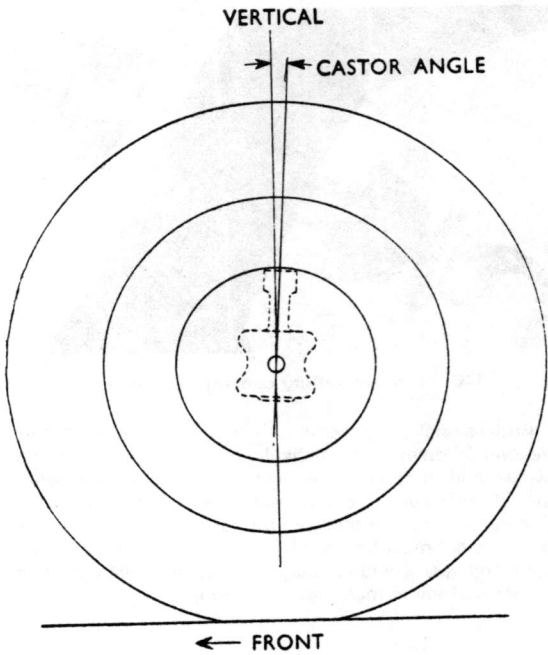

FIG 8:18   Diagram showing castor angle

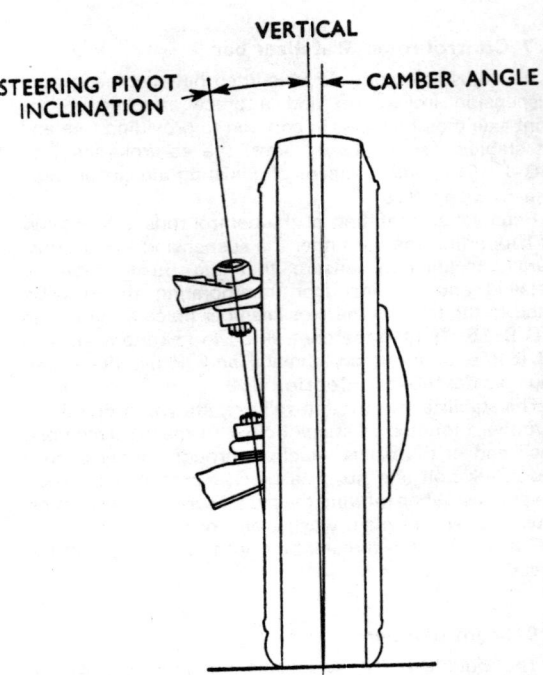

FIG 8:19   Diagram showing camber angle and steering pivot inclination

8:10 Fault diagnosis

(a) Wheel wobble

1 Worn hub bearings
2 Broken or weak front springs
3 Uneven tyre wear
4 Worn suspension linkage

(b) 'Bottoming' of suspension

1 Check 2 in (a)
2 Bump stop rubbers worn or missing
3 Dampers defective

(c) Heavy steering

1 Lack of lubricant in ball joints
2 Wrong suspension geometry
3 Front tyres under-inflated

(d) Excessive tyre wear

1 Check 4 in (a); 3 in (b); and 2 in (c)

(e) Rattles

1 Check 2 in (a)
2 Worn ball joints or defective suspension bushes
3 Damper bushes defective or bolts loose
4 Control rod mountings loose or bushes worn
5 Stabilizer bar mountings loose or bushes worn

(f) Excessive rolling

1 Check 5 in (e)

CHAPTER 9

THE STEERING GEAR

9:1 Operating principles and construction

FIG 9:1 shows the layout of the steering gear and steering column. The rack and pinion type steering gear 5 is secured to the front axle crossmember by three bolts and nuts. A tie rod 2 is connected to each end of the rack by a ball joint enclosed in a concertina type rubber boot 4. The outer end of each tie rod is threaded into a ball joint 1 attached to the steering arm. Steering lock is controlled by the inner ball joints contacting the steering gear housing. Two makes of rack and pinion gear are fitted, Burman and Cam Gears Ltd. These are interchangeable as complete assemblies only.

The steering column is specially designed to minimize injury to the driver in the event of a collision. At its lower end the column is connected to the steering gear by a universally jointed intermediate shaft, so that if the front suspension is forced back there is less tendency for the column to be driven back into the car. Secondly, in the event of frontal impact still being transmitted axially to the column, the latter is designed to telescope for approximately 8 inches at a controlled rate. The column is rigidly attached to the dash panel (bulkhead) by the mounting 10 but the bracket 14 on the instrument panel is designed to break away on impact.

The following is a more detailed description. Still referring to FIG 9:1, a flange secured to the pinion shaft 6 of the rack and pinion gear is connected by means of the flexible coupling 7 to the intermediate shaft 8. The upper end of this shaft incorporates a universal coupling 9 which connects it to the steering shaft (or inner column) 13.

The energy absorbing steering column comprises an outer jacket (or outer column) 11, a gear control tube 12 and the steering shaft (or inner column) 13. The outer jacket has a mesh section which compresses when sufficient force is applied to either end of the column. The gear control tube 12, which is fitted to all cars whether fitted with a column change or not, is fabricated from three tubes arranged so that one section telescopes into another, each section being retained by plastic injections. The steering shaft 13 is in two sections which are telescoped and have flats to take the steering load, the assembly being held together by plastic injections. The bracket 14 has three pads secured by plastic injections which will shear on impact. Instructions for removal, inspection for damage, and installation of the steering column are given in Section 9:8.

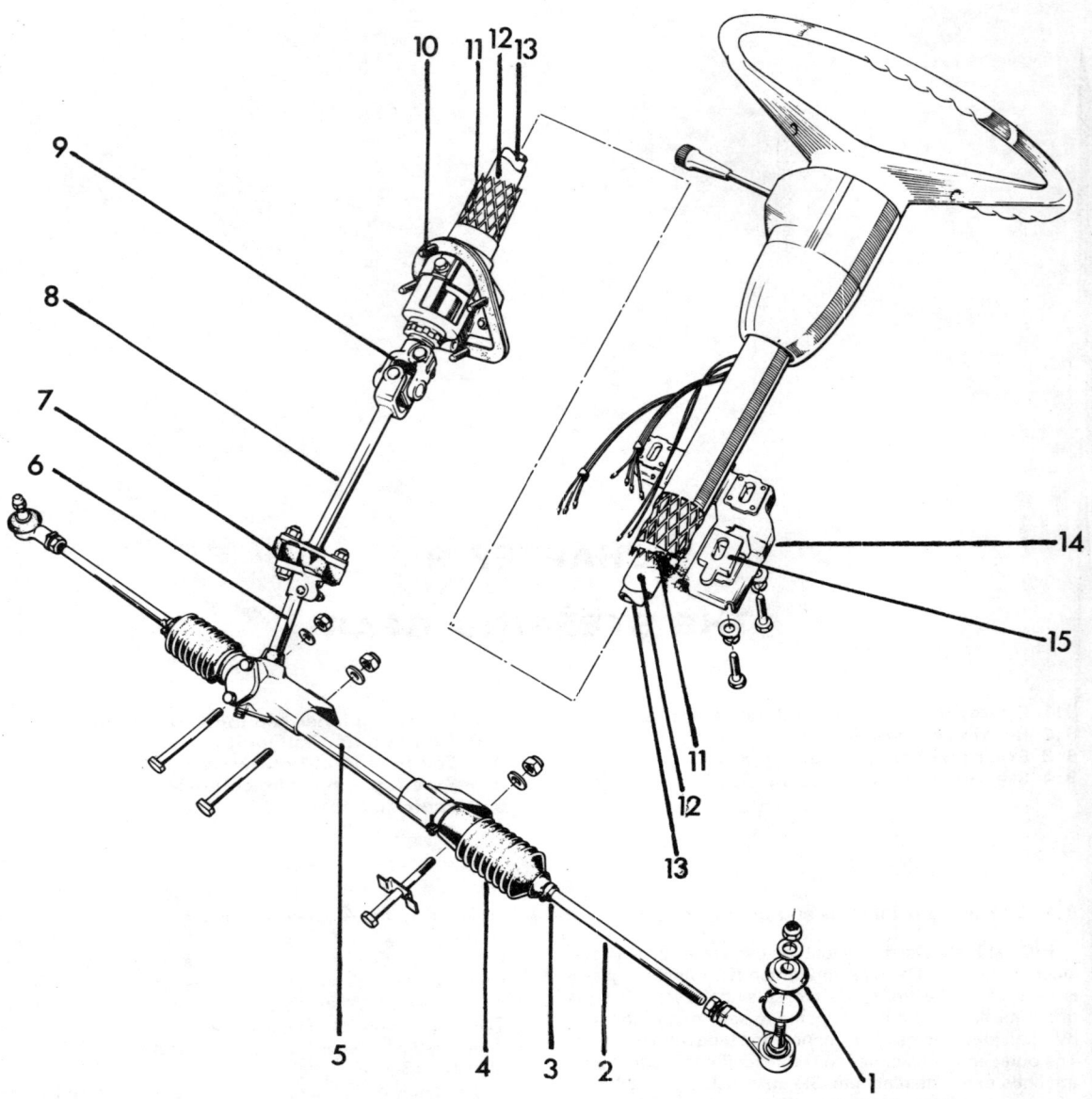

FIG 9:1 Layout of rack and pinion steering and energy absorbing steering column

Key to Fig 9:1   1 Tie rod outer ball joint   2 Tie rod   3 Boot clip   4 Rubber boot   5 Rack and pinion housing
6 Pinion shaft   7 Flexible coupling   8 Intermediate shaft   9 Universal joint   10 Dash panel mounting   11 Outer jacket
with mesh section   12 Telescopic gear control tube   13 Telescopic steering shaft   14 Mounting bracket to instrument panel
15 Wedge

9:2 Routine maintenance

There are no grease nipples on the steering gear or
its connections. Maintenance is confined to a renewal
of the rubber boots on the rack and pinion gear should
the boots become defective, in which case the gear will be
refilled with oil. This operation is described in **Section 9:5.**
The inner ball joints are enclosed by these boots and do
not require separate lubrication. The tie rod outer ball

joints are lubricated on assembly and the checking of
these components is described in **Section 9:6.**

Dismantling of the rack and pinion steering gear is
not recommended. If the gear develops defects it
should be renewed. Instructions for removal and refitting
are given in **Sections 9:3** and **9:4.** Renewal of the
inner ball joints calls for precise drilling operations and
the owner is not advised to attempt this work.

9:3 Steering gear removal

To remove the rack and pinion steering gear for the purpose of fitting a replacement unit or for renewal of the concertina type rubber boots, proceed as follows:

1 Remove the cotter from the flexible coupling (item 7 in **FIG 9:1**) using the extractor Z.8563 as shown in **FIG 9:2**.
2 Detach the tie rod outer ball joints (item 1 in **FIG 9:1**) from the steering arms using the claw-type extractor JWP.362.
3 Remove the three nuts and bolts securing the steering gear to the front axle crossmember and withdraw the steering gear complete with tie rods.

9:4 Steering gear installation

Refit the rack and pinion gear as follows:

1 Secure the steering gear to the front axle crossmember and tighten the three nuts and bolts to a torque of 19 lb ft with clean dry threads.
2 After ensuring that the mating tapers are clean and free from grease, attach the outer ball joints to the steering arms and tighten the nuts to 24 lb ft.
3 Tighten the flexible coupling cotter nut to a torque of 7 lb ft. Check that the nuts on the four bolts securing the flexible coupling to the intermediate shaft are tightened to 12 lb ft.
4 Check and if necessary adjust toe-in according to instructions given in **Section 9:7**.

9:5 Renewing inner ball joint rubber boots

Renewal of the inner ball joints involves precise drilling operations and the owner is not advised to attempt this work. The rubber boots (item 4 in **FIG 9:1**) should however be renewed if either or both is found to be defective. The boots not only protect the inner ball joints but are essential to retain the oil in the rack and pinion housing and to prevent entry of grit. Renewal is carried out as follows:

1 Remove the steering gear as described in **Section 9:3**, but before removing the outer ball joints from the steering arms, slacken the locknuts at the end of each tie rod leaving them in contact with the shakeproof washer and only finger tight. This will greatly facilitate subsequent removal of the ball joints from the tie rod.
2 Remove the ball joints from the steering arms using extractor JWP.362 as shown in **FIG 9:3**.
3 To facilitate reassembly, mark the position of the locknut on each tie rod with paint or count the number of threads visible. These should be approximately the same on each tie rod.
4 Unscrew the ball joints and remove the shakeproof washers and the locknuts. Release the four boot clips and remove the boots.
5 Ensure that all oil is drained from the steering gear housing.
6 Fit a new rubber boot at the end opposite to the pinion shaft. Locate the boot clips so that their screws are accessible when the unit is mounted in the car.
7 Refill the steering gear by pouring in $\frac{1}{4}$ pint of the recommended oil at the pinion end as shown in **FIG 9:4**. The specified quantity of oil **must not be exceeded**.
8 Fit a new boot to the pinion end, also ensuring that

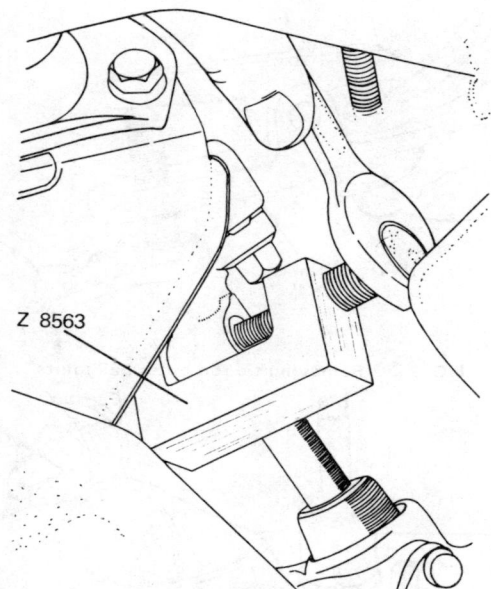

FIG 9:2   Removing cotter from flexible coupling using extractor Z.8563

the boot clips are so positioned that their screws will be accessible when the unit is fitted on the car.
9 Screw the tie rod locknuts back into their marked positions. Fit new shakeproof washers and screw on the ball joints, leaving the locknuts finger tight at this stage.
10 Install the steering gear as described in the previous Section, but after attaching the ball joints to the steering arm and tightening the nuts to 24 lb ft, tighten the tie rod locknuts securely, holding the ball joint with a spanner on the flats provided.
11 Check and if necessary adjust the toe-in as described in **Section 9:7**.

9:6 Tie rod outer ball joints

The tie rod outer ball joints are of the spring-loaded type with nylon seatings and it is therefore possible to move the socket up and down in line with the stud against the compression of the spring when a load is applied. Check by attempting to move the joint up and down by hand. If any free movement can be felt at the joint without applying pressure, this indicates wear or a broken spring and the joint must be renewed. Proceed as follows:

1 Slacken the locknut on the tie rod, leaving it in contact with the shakeproof washer and only finger tight.
2 Slacken the ball joint stud nut sufficiently to protect the end of the thread and release the ball joint from the steering arm using the extractor JWP.362 as shown in **FIG 9:3**. Remove the nut.
3 Unscrew the ball joint from the tie rod, holding the locknut in position to facilitate adjustment on reassembly. Remove and discard the shakeproof washer.
4 Fit a new shakeproof washer and screw the new ball joint on to the tie rod until it contacts the washer. Ensure that the mating tapers are clean and free from grease, attach the ball joint to the steering arm and tighten the nut to 24 lb with clean dry threads.

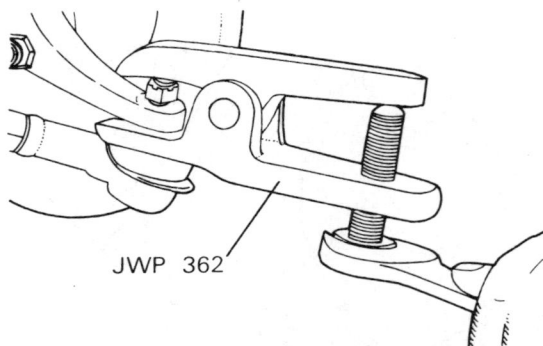

FIG 9:3 Removing tie rod outer ball joints

JWP 362

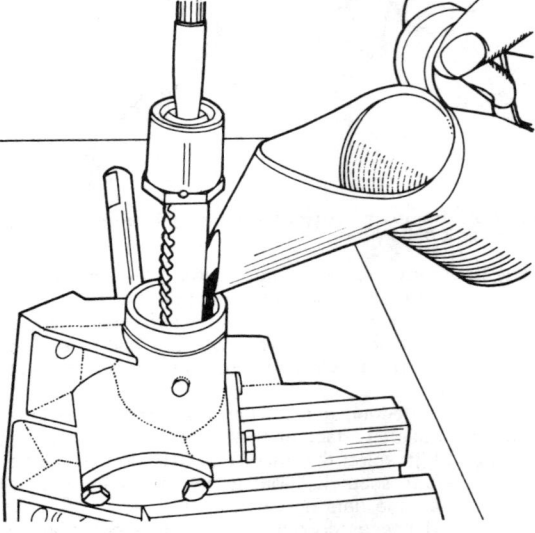

FIG 9:4 Refilling steering gear

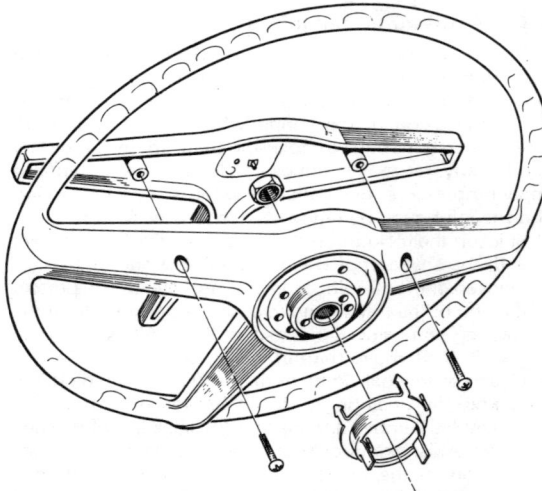

FIG 9:5 Steering wheel showing screws securing medallion, steering wheel nut and direction indicator cancelling sleeve

5 Hold the ball joint by means of a spanner on the flats provided and tighten the locknut.
6 Check and if necessary adjust the toe-in as described in **Section 9:7**.

9:7 Toe-in. Toe-out on turns

Castor angle, camber and steering pivot inclination, although affecting steering, are determined by the condition and adjustment of the front suspension and have therefore been dealt with in the previous Chapter.

Toe-in is the adjustment of the front wheels when the car is stationary so that they are either parallel or point inwards by a small amount at the front, to counteract the tendency for them to turn outwards when the car is moving. Toe-in is expressed as the difference between the distances between the wheel rims measured at the front and back of the front wheels at wheel centre height. On the cars covered by this manual there should be between .06 inch toe-in to .03 inch toe-out. The measurement can be accurately checked by a service agent using specialized equipment which is unlikely to be available to the owner. However, the following method can be used:

1 The car must be on a level floor, with the wheels in the straight-ahead position. Front tyre pressures must be identical.
2 Measure the distance between the front wheel rims at the front at wheel centre height.
3 Roll the car forward half a revolution of the wheels and measure the distance between the backs of the front wheel rims at wheel centre height. This measurement minus the first measurement gives the amount of toe-in.
4 If necessary, adjust toe-in as follows:
(a) Slacken the retaining clips on the rubber boots on the steering gear to prevent them being twisted when the tie rods are turned.
(b) Slacken each outer ball joint locknut and adjust the length of the tie rods equally to obtain the specified toe-in. Both rods have righthand threads. The rods must be adjusted by an equal amount, that is the same amount of thread will be visible each end.
(c) Tighten the locknuts, holding each ball joint by means of a spanner on the flats provided.
(d) Recheck the toe-in.

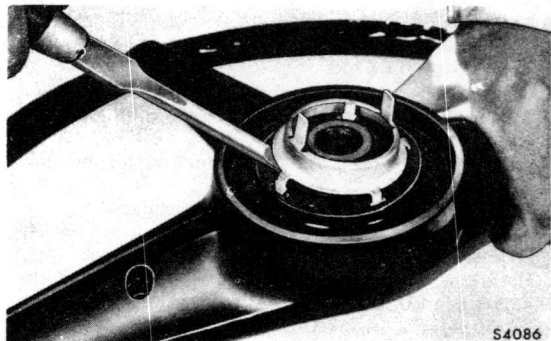

S4086

FIG 9:6 Removing cancelling sleeve

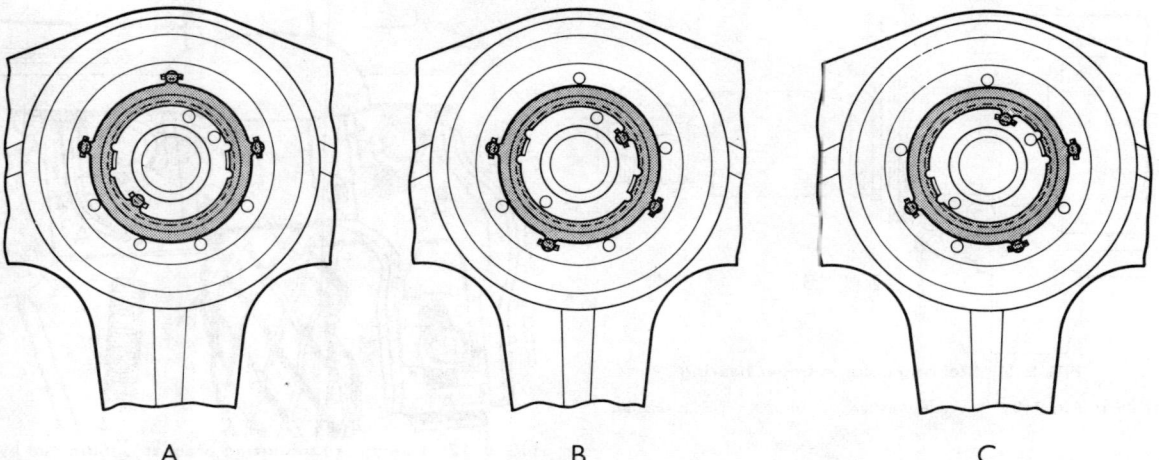

A   B   C

FIG 9:7   Showing position of cancelling sleeve on (A) cars without steering column lock; (B) righthand drive cars with steering column lock, and (C) lefthand drive cars with steering column lock

(e) Tighten the boot clips on the steering gear, positioning them so that their screws are readily accessible.

Toe-out on turns is a measurement which is not adjustable, being controlled by the shape of the steering arms. Its purpose is to enable the wheels to be turned so that the inside front wheel can follow a path with a smaller radius than the outside wheel (the Ackerman principle). It is not easy to check without specialized equipment, being expressed in degrees. On cars covered by this manual, when the outside wheel is turned 19 deg. from the straight-ahead position the inside wheel should be at 20 deg. If toe-out on turns is found to be incorrect it indicates that the steering arms are distorted and must be renewed.

9:8 Steering wheel and column

To remove the steering wheel, first remove the two small screws securing the medallion. These are accessible from underneath the steering wheel spokes as shown in **FIG 9:5**. The wheel is a push fit on the splined steering shaft (or inner column) and can be withdrawn after removing the centre nut. The indicator cancelling sleeve is a press fit on the steering wheel hub. Replacement steering wheels do not include the sleeve, so the old one may be prised off as shown in **FIG 9:6**. When fitting the sleeve, reference should be made to **FIG 9:7**, which shows the correct position of the sleeve on (A) cars without steering column lock, (B) righthand drive cars with steering column lock and (C) lefthand drive cars with steering column lock.

When installing the steering wheel ensure that the internal and external splines are clean and free from grease. Fit the wheel so that the spokes are in the form of a letter T when the wheels are in the straight-ahead position. **The wheel should be pushed on to the splines by hand pressures only. On no account must a hammer be used or the plastic inserts in the steering shaft may be damaged.** Tighten the steering wheel nut to a torque of 57 lb ft with clean dry threads.

The steering column canopy is secured to the steering column by two screws accessible from the underside of the canopy. The canopy can be removed or installed without removal of the steering wheel as shown in **FIG 9:8**.

The upper end of the steering shaft is supported by a double row ballbearing shown in section in **FIG 9:9**. Preload is maintained on the bearing by a wave washer 1 and shims 2 assembled between the bearing top race and a flat washer 3 and retained by a circlip 4. The upper bearing preload can be checked as follows:

1 Remove the steering wheel as previously described.
2 Grip the end of the steering shaft with the fingers and test for side play.
3 If side play is apparent, remove the circlip 4, flat washer 3 and install shims 2 as required until side play is just eliminated.

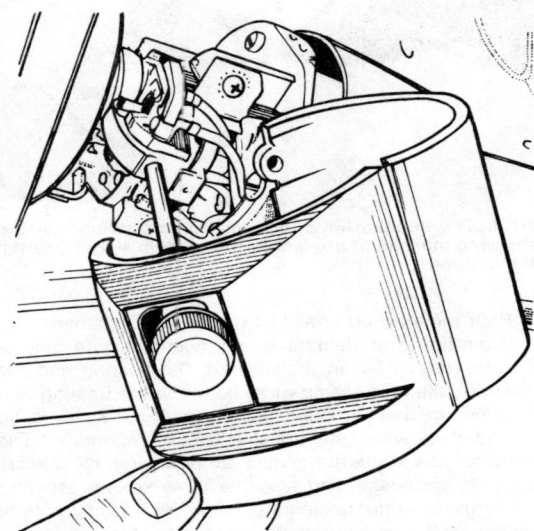

FIG 9:8   Removing steering column canopy

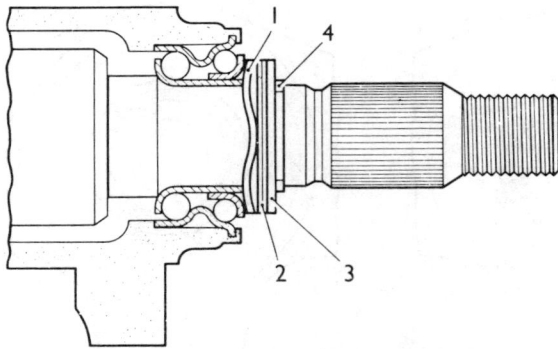

FIG 9:9   Steering column upper bearing

Key to Fig 9:9   1 Wave washer   2 Shims   3 Flat washer   4 Circlip

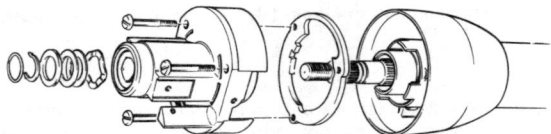

FIG 9:10   Exploded view of steering column upper bearing and housing

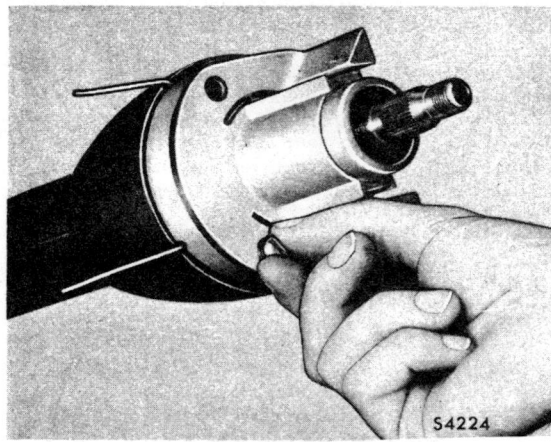

FIG 9:11   Installation of column upper bearing housing showing method of preventing plate from slipping down the column

4 Refit the steering wheel as previously described.

If the fitting of shims does not eliminate side-play or if roughness is felt in the bearing, the bearing and the steering column housing must be renewed. Bearing and housing are not supplied separately. **FIG 9:10** is an exploded view of the housing and components. The housing can be withdrawn after removing the circlip, washers and shims and also the three screws securing the housing to the retaining plate. If the housing is tight on the shaft, it must be removed by means of the special remover VR.2064. **On no account must either the**

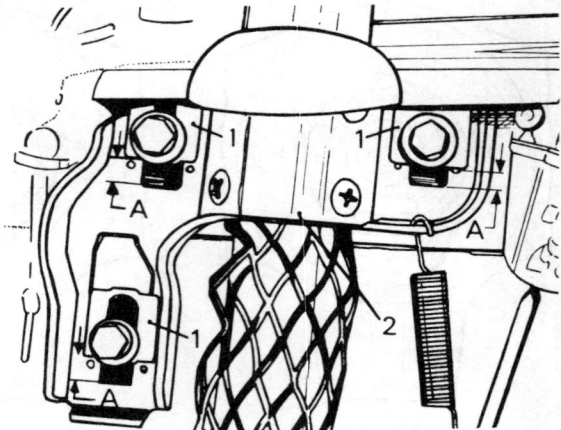

FIG 9:12   Damage to mounting bracket is indicated by gaps **A** between pads 1 and brackets 2

housing or the shaft be hammered or levered, as this can damage the plastic injections and render the shaft unserviceable. Only the upper bearing and housing assembly, shims, washers and circlip are serviced separately from the steering column. If any other parts are unserviceable no attempt should be made to dismantle the column, but the complete column assembly should be renewed.

When installing the upper housing, difficulty may be found in starting the three securing screws owing to the retaining plate slipping down the column. If this occurs, the plate may be located using pieces of wire with hooked ends inserted between the housing and the outer column as shown in **FIG 9:11**.

The steering column and mounting bracket can be checked for damage without being removed from the car. Referring to **FIG 9:12**, damage to the mounting bracket is indicated if gaps 'A' are observed between the pads 1 and the bracket 2. If gaps exist, the plastic injections securing the pads to the bracket have sheared, allowing the bracket to move forwards and the steering column to collapse.

Referring to **FIG 9:13**, damage to the steering column is indicated by bulging or bending of the outer jacket mesh section. The mesh is slightly corrugated during manufacture and collapsing will only have taken place if the overall length of the mesh section 'A' is less than 9.70 inches. If the mesh section has begun to collapse, the plastic injections in the gear control tube and the steering shaft will also have sheared and the column assembly must be renewed.

The steering intermediate shaft, shown in **FIG 9:14**, connects the steering shaft to the pinion shaft on the steering gear. The upper end of the intermediate shaft incorporates a universal coupling. On early models the coupling is secured to the steering shaft by a cotter, while on later models it is splined to the steering shaft and secured by a clamp bolt and nut. At the lower end of the intermediate shaft is a flexible coupling, the lower flange of which is secured to the pinion shaft by a cotter. The extractor Z.8563 should be used to remove the cotter from the flexible coupling (see **FIG 9:2**) and also the universal coupling cotter on earlier models. Slide the shaft downwards until the universal coupling is clear of the steering shaft and then withdraw. If the couplings do not slide on the steering shaft or pinion shaft, do not strike with a hammer as this may damage the plastic injections in the steering shaft. Instead the couplings should be eased by twisting the intermediate shaft while the steering wheel is held.

If a new flexible coupling is used, this is supplied held together by a retention band as shown in **FIG 9:15**. In transferring the original coupling to a new intermediate shaft, a hose clip should be assembled around the coupling as shown in **FIG 9:16** before removing the bolts. This will stress the rubber and facilitate installation. After assembling the flexible coupling to the intermediate shaft, tighten the nuts to 12 lb ft and remove the retention band or hose clip. With the steering wheel and the road wheels in the straight-ahead position, install the cotters or clamp bolt and cotter from the top, installing the universal coupling first. Tighten the cotter nut or nuts to 7 lb ft and the clamp bolt nut on later models to 14 lb ft.

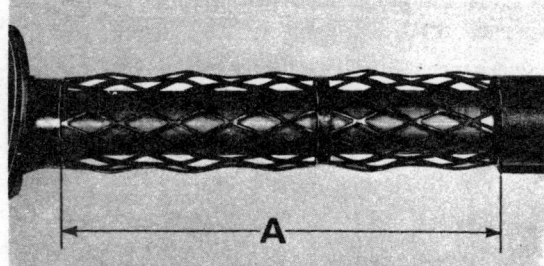

FIG 9:13 Damage to steering column is indicated if the length of mesh section **A** is less than 9.70 inches

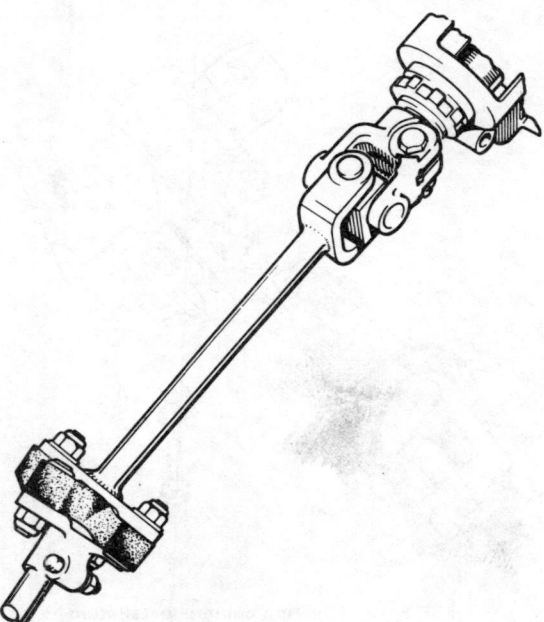

FIG 9:14 Steering intermediate shaft showing flexible coupling and universal coupling

FIG 9:15 Replacement steering column flexible coupling is supplied with retention band (arrowed) to be removed after fitting coupling

FIG 9:16 Using hose clip in place of retention band when transferring original coupling to new shaft

To remove the steering column assembly complete with steering wheel, proceed as follows:
1 Remove the steering intermediate shaft and coupling as previously described.
2 On column change models, referring to **FIG 9:17**, disconnect the control rod 5 from the changespeed lever 3 and detach the selector lever 1 from the bracket 4 on the steering column.
3 On all models remove the nuts 2 (**FIG 9:17**) securing the cover panel (item 10 in **FIG 9:1**) to the dash panel.
4 Where a steering column lock is fitted, remove the centre instrument panel and partially withdraw the instrument head assembly to gain access to the ignition and starter switch wiring connector.
5 Remove the steering column finisher and harness cover, and disconnect the combined switch and horn push wiring at the connector.
6 Disconnect the column upper mounting bracket (**FIG 9:1**, item 14) from the instrument panel by

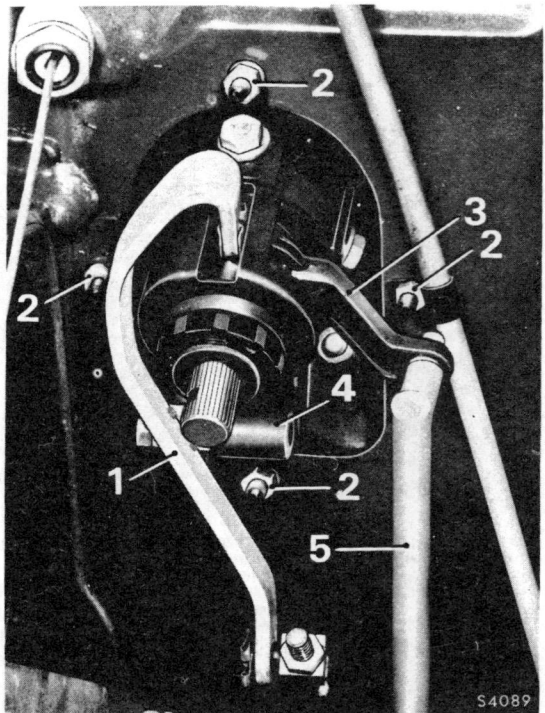

FIG 9:17 Steering column removal

Key to Fig 9:17 1 Selector lever 2 Cover panel
securing nuts 3 Changespeed lever 4 Bracket
5 Control rod

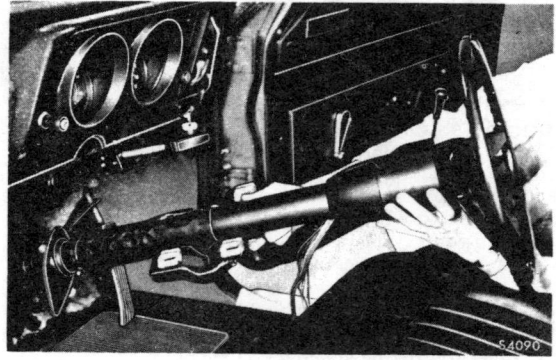

FIG 9:18 Removing steering column assembly

removing the three screws (**FIG 9:19,** items 2 and 4).
Withdraw the steering column from inside the car as
shown in **FIG 9:18**. Retain the wedge from the upper
bracket.

7 Handle the steering column assembly with care to
avoid damage to plastic injections. These can shear if
the column is dropped or knocked, rendering the
assembly unserviceable.

When refitting the steering column the following
sequence of operations should be adhered to:

1 Referring to **FIG 9:19,** locate the cover panel studs 1
in the dash panel.
2 Screw the two bolts 2 home finger tight.
3 Fit the nuts to the studs 1 and tighten fully.
4 Tighten the bolts 2 to 17 lb ft.
5 Insert wedge 3 as far as possible between the mounting
bracket lower pad and the instrument panel using
finger pressure only.
6 Insert the bolt 4 and tighten to 17 lb ft.

Assembly of the remaining components is a reversal of
the dismantling procedure.

9:9 Fault diagnosis

(Reference should also be made to **Section 8:10**
describing suspension faults, as these can often affect
steering).

(a) Wheel wobble

1 Unbalanced wheels and tyres
2 Slack steering connections
3 Incorrect steering geometry
4 Excessive play in steering gear
5 Steering gear loose on crossmember
6 Worn hub bearings

(b) Wander

1 Check 2, 3, 4 and 5 in (a)
2 Front and rear wheels not in line
3 Uneven tyre pressures
4 Uneven tyre wear
5 Defective dampers
6 Weak spring

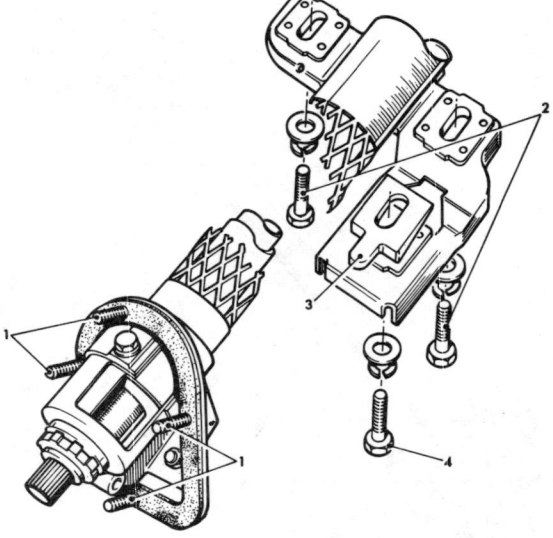

FIG 9:19 Steering column installation

Key to Fig 9:19 1 Cover panel studs 2, 4 Upper
bracket securing bolts 3 Wedge

(c) Heavy steering

1 Check 3 in (a)
2 Very low tyre pressures
3 Lack of oil in steering gear
4 Tie rod or suspension ball joints tight
5 Wheels out of track
6 Steering column out of line or strained
7 Steering shaft bent
8 Steering shaft bearings tight

(d) Lost motion

1 Play in intermediate shaft couplings
2 Couplings loose on steering shaft or pinion shaft
3 Loose steering wheel

4 Steering gear loose on crossmember
5 Play in steering gear (rack and pinion)
6 Worn tie rod ball joints
7 Worn suspension ball joints
8 Sheared plastic injections in steering column

(e) Irregular front tyre wear

1 Excessive toe-in produces feathered edges on inner side of tread
2 Toe-out produces similar effects on outer side of tread
3 Excessive positive camber causes wear on outer side of tread
4 Negative camber causes more wear on inner side of tread

NOTES

CHAPTER 10

THE BRAKING SYSTEM

The standard equipment on cars and estate cars with the 1600 engine consists of hydraulically operated drum brakes front and rear. All models fitted with the 2000 engine have disc brakes on the front wheels with a vacuum-operated servo to assist the hydraulic operation of all four brakes. Disc front brakes and servo are available as an optional extra on 1600 models. The rear drum brakes are the same on all models. The first part of this Chapter deals with drum brakes and with components which are common to all models. The second part deals with disc brakes and servo.

DRUM BRAKES

10:1 Layout of drum brakes

The master cylinder is of the centre valve type with integral fluid reservoir. The cylinder is operated by a non-adjustable captive type pushrod from the pendant type brake pedal. The hydraulic system operates front and rear brakes. The front brakes (see **FIG 10:2**) are of the two-leading-shoe type, with a single-ended cylinder and cam adjuster for each shoe. The rear brakes (see **FIG 10:3**) are of the leading-and-trailing-shoe type, with a floating single-ended cylinder and expanding adjuster for each pair of shoes. The handbrake operates the rear brake shoes by mechanical linkage.

10:2 Routine maintenance, brake shoe adjustment

The combined master cylinder and fluid reservoir is under the bonnet on the driver's side and has a screw-type filler cap. Clean the cap before removal and top up to about $\frac{3}{8}$ inch below the top of the filler with Castrol Girling Brake and Clutch Fluid (Crimson) or Lockheed Super 105 Brake Fluid. It is essential that only the recommended fluid is used. Do not use containers which have been used for mineral oils or other liquids as contamination can affect the rubber seals in the system and cause complete brake failure. If frequent topping up is necessary, check the hydraulic system for leaks.

Excessive pedal travel indicates the need for brake shoe adjustment. The hydraulic system provides equalized pressure on all four brakes, but each shoe must be adjusted as near as possible to its drum in order to avoid lost movement. Each front brake has two adjusters and each rear brake has a single adjuster operating on both shoes.

When carrying out brake adjustments the handbrake must be in the off position and the car should be on a level floor. Jack up each wheel in turn to adjust its brake, chocking one of the other wheels to prevent rolling. All four wheels must receive attention. **FIG 10:1** shows the

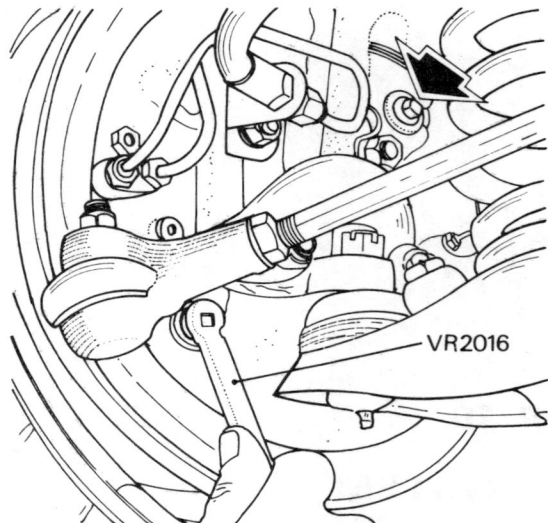

FIG 10:1 Adjusting a front brake lower shoe. The arrow indicates adjuster for upper shoe. Rear brakes have a single adjuster

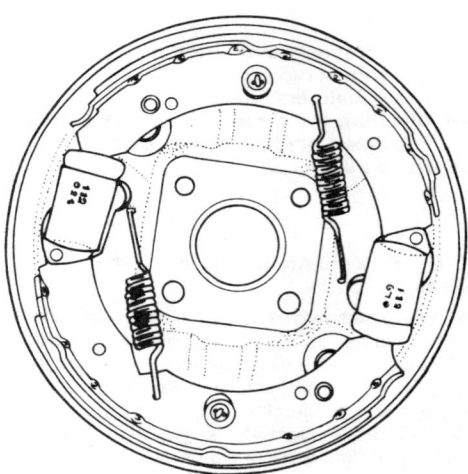

FIG 10:2 Front brake assembly showing correct location of shoes and springs

method of adjusting a front brake, using the special Girling Brake Spanner (Vauxhall Part No. VR.2016). Rotate each adjuster clockwise as viewed from the inside of the wheel until the shoe is hard on, then slacken off until the brake is just free. Check that all brakes are free. The rear brakes are adjusted in a similar manner except that there is only one adjuster on each brake, situated near the upper edge of the brake backplate. If the adjusters are found to be very stiff they should be slackened right off and the threads lubricated with the recommended grease.

Normally, adjustment of the brake shoes will automatically take up the handbrake adjustment, but if there is still excessive travel of the hand lever, or if the cables have been renewed, reference should be made to **Section 10:10** for method of adjustment.

10:3 Removing master cylinder

1 Disconnect the master cylinder pipe at the four-way connector. Drain the master cylinder by operating the brake pedal, then disconnect the pipe from the master cylinder.
2 Detach the pushrod clevis pin from the brake pedal.
3 Remove the two bolts and nuts securing the master cylinder to the panel and lift away the cylinder.

10:4 Dismantling brakes. Note on flexible hoses

To remove the brake shoes:
1 Jack up and remove the road wheels. In the case of the rear brakes the handbrake must be in the off position.
2 Remove the brake drums. The drums are located by the wheel bolts and secured to the hubs by single bolts. In the case of front brakes remove the hubs as described in **Chapter 8**.
3 Note that front drums are machined as an assembly with the hubs and must not be interchanged or renewed individually. Do not handle the inside of the drums or the brake shoe linings as oil or grease is detrimental to braking surfaces. Blow out the accumulation of dust with compressed air. Ensure that the brake pedal is not depressed when the drums are off.
4 Slacken the brake adjusters fully.
5 Remove the front brake shoes (see **FIG 10:2**) by prising the trailing end of each shoe in turn out of the slot in the end of the cylinder. Tie a length of wire round each cylinder and piston to prevent the pistons being forced out if the footbrake is applied while the shoes are removed.
6 To remove the rear brake shoes, compress the slotted spring clip in the centre of each shoe and slide the clip off the steady pin (see **FIG 10:3**). Prise the leading shoe out of the adjuster and withdraw both shoes and springs. Tie a length of wire round the brake cylinder and piston.

When removing brake hoses, not the following points:
1 To minimize fluid loss when a hose is disconnected, the air vent in the master cylinder filler cap should be temporarily sealed.
2 Hoses must not be twisted or permanent damage will result. Always unscrew the union nuts on the metal pipes first. Hold the hexagon on the flexible hose with a second spanner as a precaution against its turning when removing the hose locknut at a bracket.
3 Blocked, chafed or perished brake hoses must be renewed. The metal brake pipes (Bundy tubes) should also be examined periodically and if they show signs of corrosion or damage they must be renewed.

10:5 Servicing hydraulic internals

The following instructions apply to the servicing of the internal parts of all hydraulic components. Absolute cleanliness is essential. Any traces of grit can damage highly polished bores or seals. Brake fluid or Girling cleaning fluid should be used for cleaning internal parts as petrol and other solvents will cause damage to rubber cups and seals. Rubber seals are available in kit form so that when master and brake cylinders are dismantled it is best to fit new seals throughout. Alternatively, complete cylinders are available as exchange units. Wet all internal parts with clean brake fluid during reassembly. Be very careful not to turn back the lips of piston seals when installing them in cylinder bores.

10:6 Servicing master and wheel cylinders

To dismantle the master cylinder (see **FIG 10:4**):
1 Ease the boot 4 off the end of the cylinder 7.
2 Withdraw the circlip 2 and remove the pushrod 1, retainer washer 3 and boot as an assembly.
3 Withdraw the piston and valve assembly 8 to 15 from the cylinder. The assembly can usually be dislodged by a vigorous shake of the cylinder, otherwise it can be blown out by means of compressed air.
4 A spring retainer 10 is held in position on the spigot end of the piston 8 by a tab engaging in a shoulder on the piston. Prise up the tab as shown in **FIG 10:5** and remove the spring retainer, spring and valve assembly from the piston.
5 Release the valve stem 14 from the spring retainer by compressing the spring 11 and moving in the direction of the slotted hole in the retainer.
6 Withdraw the valve stem from the valve spacer 12 taking care not to lose or damage the spring shim washer 13.
7 Carefully ease off the valve seal 15 from the valve stem and the piston seal 9 from the piston.
8 Thoroughly clean all parts with Girling Cleaning Fluid.
9 Examine the cylinder bore and piston for ridges and scores. If there is any doubt regarding the condition of the bore a new cylinder should be installed.
10 Both rubber seals should be renewed. If the old seals show signs of swelling due to mineral oil contamination the rest of the brake system should be checked and flushed out with Girling Cleaning Fluid.

To remove and dismantle the front brake cylinders (see **FIG 10:6**).
1 If master cylinder is not also to be removed, temporarily seal the air vent in the cap.
2 Remove the brake shoes as described in **Section 10:4**.
3 Detach the pipes from the brake cylinder (see note on brake hoses in **Section 10:14**). Remove the cylinder from the backplate, taking care of the sealing ring.
4 Referring to **FIG 10:6**, remove the rubber boot 8.
5 Withdraw the piston 6, the seal 5 and the spring 4 from the cylinder 3.
6 Remove the bleed nipple 1 (from rear cylinder only).
7 Clean, inspect and renew parts as described for the master cylinder.

To remove and dismantle the rear brake cylinders:
1 If master cylinder is not also to be removed, temporarily seal the air vent in the cap.
2 Remove the brake shoes as described in **Section 10:4**.
3 Disconnect the handbrake cable from the brake shoe lever.
4 Detach the brake hose pipe from the cylinder and seal the end of the pipe (see note on hoses in **Section 10:4**).

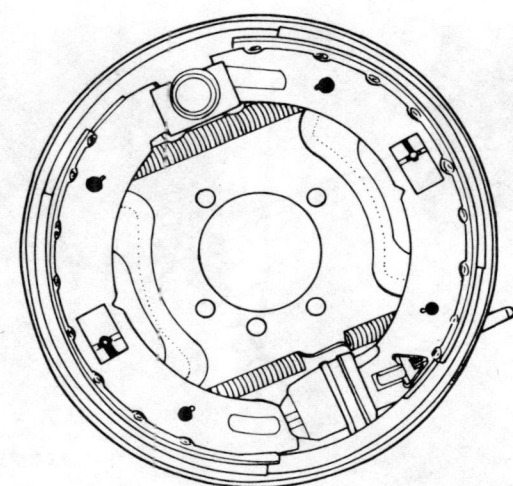

FIG 10:3 Rear brake assembly showing correct location of shoes and springs

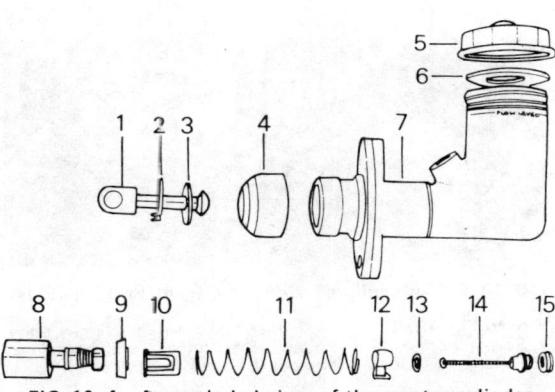

FIG 10:4 An exploded view of the master cylinder

Key to Fig 10 4   1 Pushrod   2 Circlip
3 Retainer washer   4 Boot   5 Filler cap   6 Gasket
7 Cylinder body   8 Piston   9 Piston seal
10 Spring washer   11 Spring   12 Valve spacer
13 Spring shim washer   14 Valve stem   15 Valve seal

5 Remove the external boot (item 7 in **FIG 10:9**) from the cylinder boss and the handbrake shoe lever 5.
6 Referring to **FIG 10:7**, use the Expander D.1148 to depress the spring plate tags 1 sufficiently to disengage them from the slots in the retaining plate 2. Hold the plate in this position by inserting a piece of thin rod between the plates as shown.
7 Prise out the retaining plate as shown in **FIG 10:8**. Remove the distance washer and spring plate and withdraw the cylinder.
8 Referring to **FIG 10:9**, withdraw the handbrake shoe lever 5. Remove the boot clip 1 and internal boot 2.

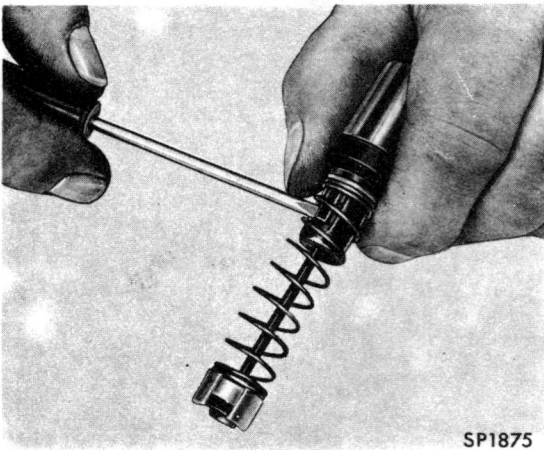

FIG 10:5 Prising tab of master cylinder spring retainer out of spigot end of piston

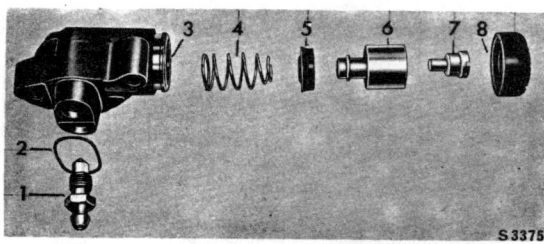

FIG 10:6 An exploded view of a front brake cylinder

Key to Fig 10:6 1 Bleed nipple (rear cylinder only)
2 Sealing ring   3 Cylinder   4 Spring   5 Piston seal
6 Piston   7 Brake shoe guide   8 Boot

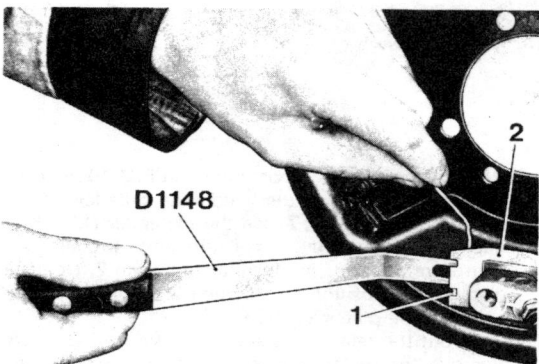

FIG 10:7 Rear brake cylinder removal. Using Expander D.1148 to depress spring plate tags 1 to disengage them from slots in retaining plate 2

9 Withdraw the piston 3 and piston seal 4 from the cylinder 11. Remove the bleed screw 6.

10 Clean, inspect and renew parts as previously described for the master cylinder.

10:7 Reassembly. Brake shoe linings

When reassembling the master cylinder, note the following:

1 Referring to **FIG 10:10**, assemble the new valve seal 1 to the valve stem 2 and ensure that the spring shim washer 3 is fitted with its concave face towards the valve spacer 4 (see **FIG 10:4** items 12 to 15).

2 Fit a new piston seal on the piston as shown in **FIG 10:11**.

3 Assemble the spring with a new spring retainer to the valve stem and engage the end of the valve stem in the retainer. Locate the retainer over the end of the piston and bend the retainer tab into the recess in the piston as indicated by arrow in **FIG 10:11**. Reference should also be made to **FIG 10:4**.

4 Smear the piston and mouth of the cylinder with clean brake fluid and insert the assembly into the cylinder bore, easing the seal in carefully to ensure the lip is not bent back or damaged. Neglect of this precaution may result in serious leakage.

5 After installing the pushrod and retainer washer, ensure that the circlip fully engages the groove in the cylinder.

When assembling front and rear brake cylinders, ensure that the new seal is fitted with the larger diameter towards the inner end of the piston. In the case of front brake cylinders note that the small end of the spring locates on the inner end of the piston. Similar precautions must be observed when inserting the piston as described in operations 4 and 5 for the master cylinder.

When installing front brake cylinders, fit a new sealing ring (item 2 in **FIG 10:6**) round the pipe union boss before fitting the cylinder to the backplate. When installing rear brake cylinders, apply a thin film of Keenol grease to both sides of the backplate where the cylinder slides, to ensure that the latter remains floating and distributes pressure equally to both shoes. A little of the same lubricant should be applied to the handbrake shoe lever fulcrum pin. Referring to **FIG 10:12**, locate the cylinder in the backplate with the shoe lever in position and install the spring plate 1 and distance washer 2 so that the closed end of each is towards the shoe lever. Press in the retaining plate (item 9 in **FIG 10:9**) until the tags on the spring plate engage the slots in the end of the retaining plate. Assemble the external boot 7 over the cylinder boss and shoe lever. In the case of both front and rear brakes refit the brake shoes as described later in this Section and bleed the brakes as described in **Section 10:8**.

Brakes should be relined if the linings show signs of excessive wear, if they are contaminated with oil or brake fluid or if new drums are fitted. It is advised that brake shoes with linings ready fitted and supplied on an exchange basis should be employed. Only genuine makers' replacements should be used, which should be fitted in complete sets otherwise uneven braking will result. Do not handle linings or drums with greasy fingers.

When renewing linings on account of oil or fluid contamination the source of such contamination must be traced and the fault rectified. Oval or scored brake drums can be machined provided they will still be within the limits given in the Technical Data Section. Front drums must be machined on their individual hubs to maintain concentricity.

When installing brake shoes apply a thin film of Keenol grease on the shoe contact pads. Remove wire if used to retain pistons in brake cylinders. On front brakes locate the brake shoes and springs as shown in **FIG 10:2**, ensuring that the longer hook of each return spring is fitted to the brake backplate. In the case of rear brake shoes, ensure that the support plate 1 and clip 2 are fitted to the leading shoe as shown in **FIG 10:13** before installing the shoes. **FIG 10:3** shows the correct locations for rear brake shoe springs. Adjust the brake shoes as described in **Section 10:2**.

FIG 10:14 shows the component parts of the rear brake adjuster. If the brake shoes are removed or if difficulty has been found in adjusting the brake, withdraw the two tappets and unscrew the adjusting screw. Clean all parts including the housing bores and smear with Keenol grease before reassembly.

10:8 Bleeding the system

This will be necessary if air has entered the hydraulic system owing to leakage or low fluid level or when any of the pipelines have been disconnected. The presence of air in the system usually produces symptoms of a 'spongy' brake pedal and loss of braking power. In bleeding the brakes the pedal has to be operated, expelled fluid has to be watched for air bubbles and at the same time the reservoir must be kept topped up, so that an assistant is essential. Proceed as follows:

1 Slacken off the four front brake shoe adjusters to the limit by turning anticlockwise. Turn the two rear brake shoe adjusters clockwise until the shoes contact the drums. These operations reduce the capacity of the brake cylinders to the minimum.

2 Ensure that all hydraulic connections are secure and that the reservoir has been topped up. Use only Castrol/Girling Brake and Clutch Fluid (Crimson) or Lockheed Super 105 Brake Fluid. Unsuitable fluids, or the use of vessels contaminated with mineral oils, petrol or similar solvents can cause serious brake trouble. Note also that the reservoir on the master cylinder must be kept topped up throughout the process, or more air will enter the system and a fresh start will have to be made.

3 Bleed the brakes in the following order: lefthand rear, lefthand front then righthand front. There is no bleed screw for the righthand rear brake.

4 Remove the rubber cap from the bleed screw on the first brake. If no cap is fitted, clean the screw first. Fit a rubber or plastic tube over the bleed screw and immerse the free end in a small quantity of brake fluid in a clean glass jar. Unscrew the bleed screw a part of a turn only. Operate the brake pedal giving one sharp application to the limit of its travel followed by three short rapid strokes through the last third of pedal movement. Pause when the pedal is right back to allow the master cylinder to refill and repeat the sequence until fluid is seen to emerge from the bleed tube free of air bubbles. Then on a downward stroke of the pedal tighten the bleed screw.

5 Repeat with the other two brakes, still ensuring that the reservoir is kept topped up.

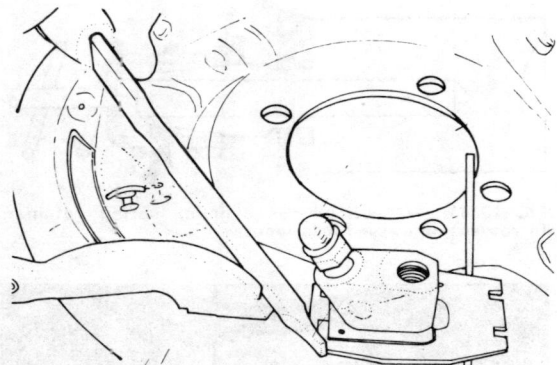

FIG 10:8 Rear brake cylinder removal. Prising out retaining plate

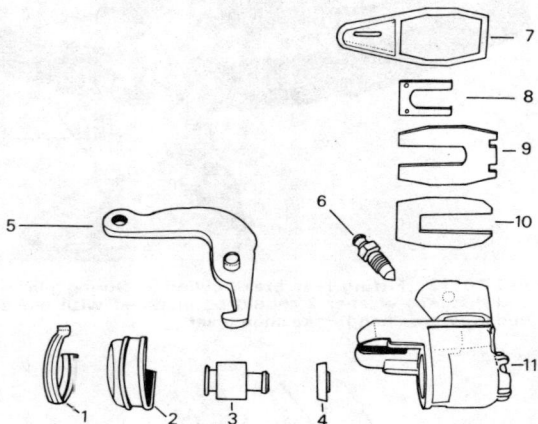

FIG 10:9 An exploded view of a rear brake cylinder

Key to Fig 10:9   1 Boot clip   2 Boot (internal)
3 Piston   4 Piston seal   5 Handbrake shoe lever
6 Bleed screw (lefthand brake only)   7 Boot (external)
8 Distance washer   9 Retaining plate   10 Spring plate
11 Cylinder body

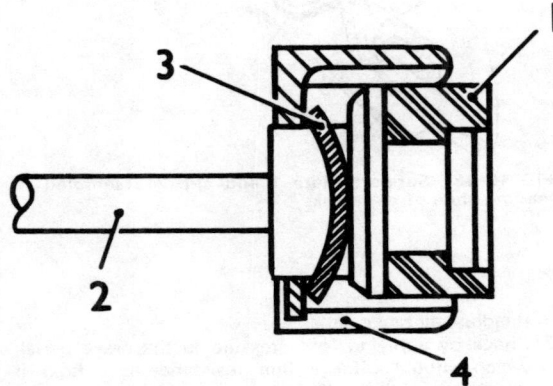

FIG 10:10 Sectional view of master cylinder valve

Key to Fig 10:10   1 Valve seal   2 Valve stem
3 Spring shim washer   4 Valve spacer

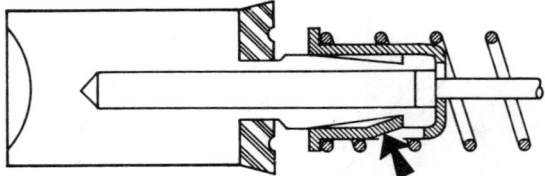

FIG 10:11 Tab of master cylinder spring retainer (arrowed) depressed into recess

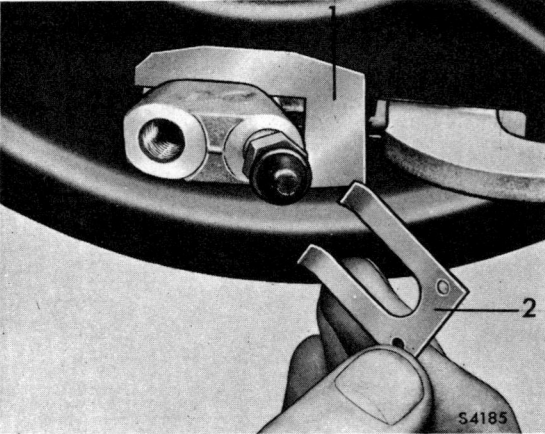

FIG 10:12 Fitting rear brake cylinder. Spring plate 1 and distance washer 2 should be installed with closed ends towards handbrake shoe lever

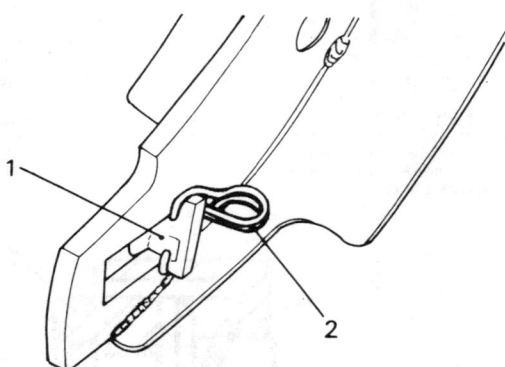

FIG 10:13 Support plate 1 and clip 2 assembled to leading shoe of rear brake

6 Readjust all brake shoes.
7 Check by applying foot pressure to the brake pedal, which should offer a firm resistance and hold it indefinitely. If the pedal feels 'spongy' there is still air in the system. If the pedal sinks gradually there is a leakage. In either case the trouble must be located and the system bled once more.

10:9 Brake pedal

The pendant type brake pedal is mounted on a common shaft with the clutch pedal (see **Chapter 5, Section 5:3**). Both pedals are nylon bushed and the shaft is carried in nylon bushes in the pedal support bolted to the dash panel or bulkhead. The pedals and shaft are retained by a spring pin at each end of the shaft. (On some cars a split-pin is fitted at the clutch pedal end of the shaft). To remove the brake pedal only, remove the spring pin from the brake pedal end of the shaft and withdraw the shaft sufficiently to release the pedal. Disconnect the master cylinder push-rod clevis and withdraw the pedal. Note that on cars fitted with automatic transmission a spacer is assembled on the pedal shaft in place of the clutch pedal. If necessary the two pedals and support bracket can be removed as an assembly. For instructions and illustrations reference should be made to **Chapter 5, Section 5:3**.

10:10 Handbrake

The twist-release handbrake control is secured to the underside of the instrument panel and to the dash panel. The control can be removed as an assembly complete with cable, after disconnecting the clevis from the front lever (on the engine side rail) and removing the nut securing the lower end of the control housing to the dash panel. Access to the bolts securing the handbrake control housing bracket to the instrument panel can be obtained by removing the steering column finisher. The pawls and spring can be removed after withdrawing the control from the housing.

When reassembling the handbrake, fit the pawls and spring into the housing as shown in **FIG 10:15** before installing the control rod and cable. Tighten the nut at the lower end of the housing before tightening the bolts securing the housing bracket to the instrument panel. Lubricate the clevis with Keenol grease.

The handbrake front cable can be renewed without removing the control from the car. Disconnect the clevis from the front lever on the engine side rail. Withdraw the control rod until its guide pin is clear of the housing mounting bracket, then turn the rod 180 deg. to release the cable. Do not remove the rod completely otherwise the pawls will be displaced. Before installing lubricate the cable and clevis with Keenol grease and ensure that the pawls and spring are located correctly in the control.

The handbrake rear cable is connected to the handbrake front lever by a slotted clevis and attached to the equalizer lever on the rear axle through a threaded adjuster. When installing the cable, lubricate the guides and clevises with Keenol grease. Note that the cable should run above the engine rear mounting crossmember on all models except on righthand drive cars fitted with automatic transmission, where it should run underneath the crossmember.

Normally the handbrake is automatically adjusted by the action of adjusting the rear brake shoes, but if there is still excessive travel of the handbrake lever, or if either or both of the cables have been renewed, adjustment should be carried out as follows. **FIG 10:16** shows the brake equalizer lever and cable adjustment on the rear axle. Slacken the locknut 2, and rotate the sleeve 1 until the clevises at the outer ends of the brake rods are just free to rotate, then tighten the locknut. If the handbrake is found to operate one rear brake more than the other, the equalizer lever is at fault. The latter should be dismantled and its pivot and all clevises lubricated with Keenol grease. Renew the equalizer lever spring if it is weak or broken.

DISC BRAKES

10:11 Disc brakes, description of layout

Self-adjusting disc brakes on the front wheels, with a servo assisted hydraulic system, are fitted to all cars having the 2000 engine, and are optional equipment on cars with the 1600 engine. The rear brakes are of the drum type and are the same as on the drum brake models already described, but have the additional benefit of servo assisted operation. Brake pedal details and handbrake operation are similar on all models.

The master cylinder is of similar design but has a larger bore and its integral reservoir has an extension to provide greater capacity. The vacuum servo unit, shown in **FIG 10:17**, is installed between the brake pedal and the master cylinder.

The brake discs are bolted to the front hubs and the calipers are attached to the steering knuckles. Each caliper has two hydraulic pistons operating the friction pads. Details of discs and calipers are given in **Section 10:13**.

10:12 Vacuum servo unit

The suspended vacuum type servo (see **FIG 10:17**) is installed between the brake pedal and the master cylinder. The unit has a renewable air filter (**FIG 10:18**) and a non-return valve (**FIG 10:19**) which is connected by a hose to the engine induction manifold (see **FIG 1:5** in **Chapter 1**). When the brake pedal is depressed, the servo makes use of engine manifold depression to increase the pressure exerted by the master cylinder, thus providing more powerful application of all four brakes.

If any internal failure occurs in the servo unit, or the non-adjustable pushrod setting is incorrect, a replacement unit must be fitted. The only component parts serviced are the air filter, the non-return valve, the pushrod seal and plate assembly and the boot or dust cover.

To gain access to the filter, withdraw the dust cover at the rear of the servo unit and the filter retainer from the end of the housing. The parts are shown in **FIG 10:18**. Withdraw the filter and cut it to remove. If necessary, also cut the replacement filter to install. When installing, ensure that the filter retainer is assembled to the end of the housing and that the dust cover engages its retaining flange.

The non-return valve, shown in **FIGS 10:17** and **10:19**, is retained by tags in the servo body and is removed by turning anticlockwise a quarter of a turn with a spanner. When installing the non-return valve, a new O-ring must be fitted without using grease or jointing compound. To ensure the correct run for the hose, the valve must be installed in position B as shown in **FIG 10:19** (position A is for lefthand drive cars only).

To remove and refit the vacuum servo unit, proceed as follows: Seal the vent hole in the master cylinder to minimize fluid loss. Disconnect the pipe from the master cylinder and remove the cylinder. Before removing the servo, check the projection of the servo pushrod as shown at A in **FIG 10:20**. The rod should project .095 to .100 inch from the front face of the servo unit body, with

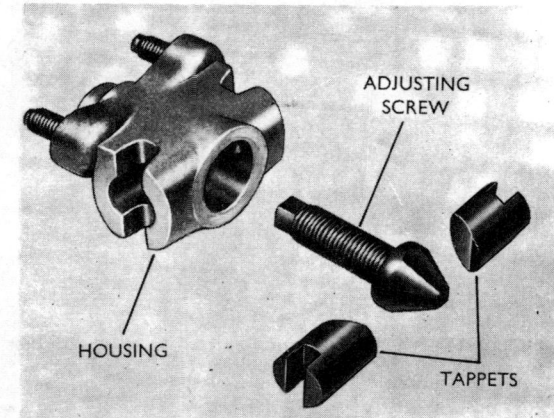

FIG 10:14   Rear brake adjuster components

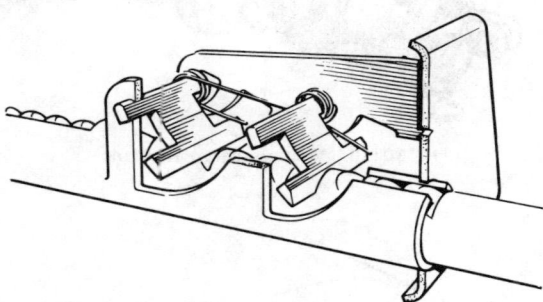

FIG 10:15   Handbrake pawls and spring must be assembled as shown before installing control rod and cable

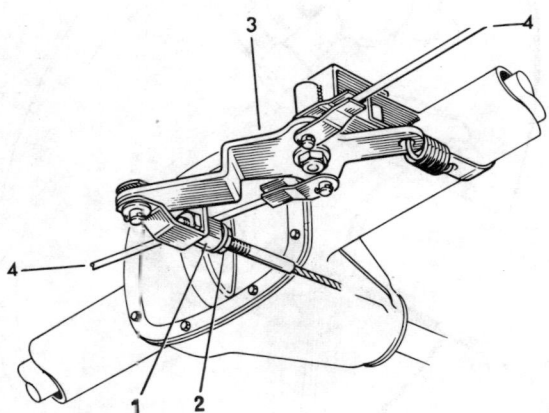

FIG 10:16   Handbrake equalizing lever and cable adjustment
Key to Fig 10:16   1 Sleeve   2 Locknut
3 Equalizer lever   4 Brake rods

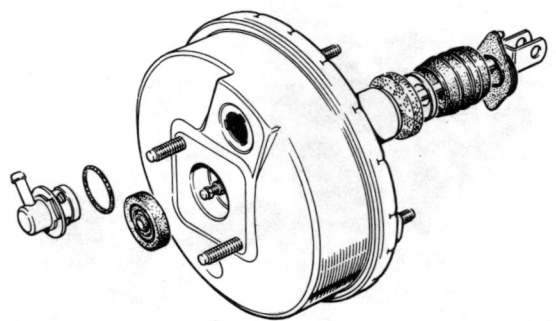

FIG 10:17 Vacuum servo unit fitted to cars with disc brakes

FIG 10:18 Vacuum servo air filter

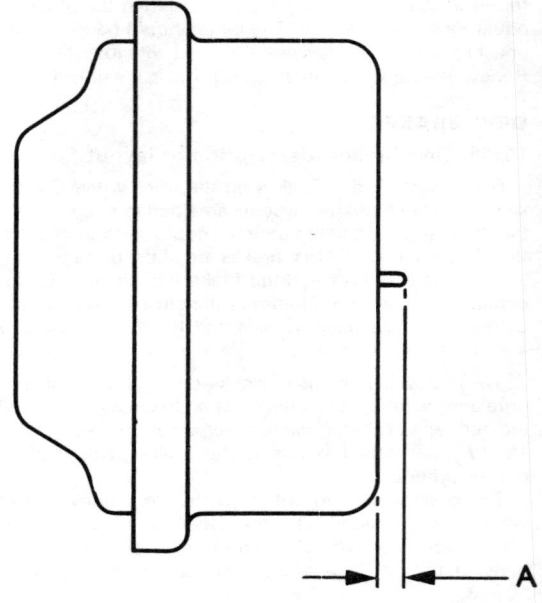

FIG 10:20 Checking projection of servo pushrod. Dimension A to be be .095 to .100 inch

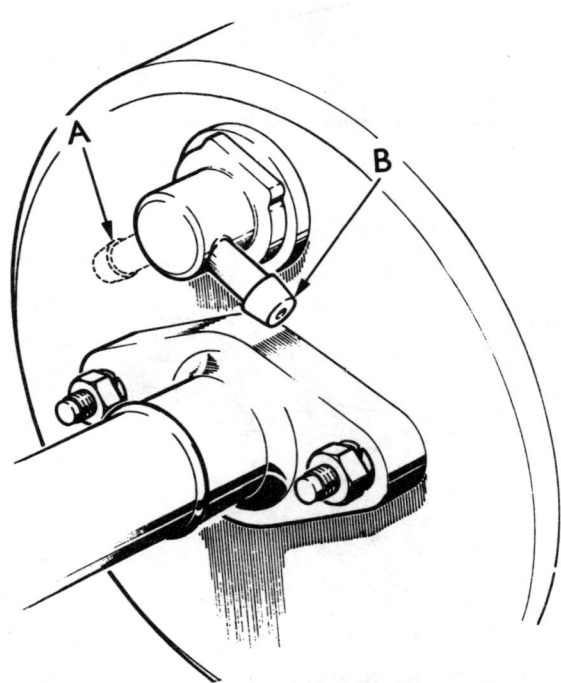

FIG 10:19 Vacuum servo non-return valve. Valve to be fitted in position B for righthand drive cars

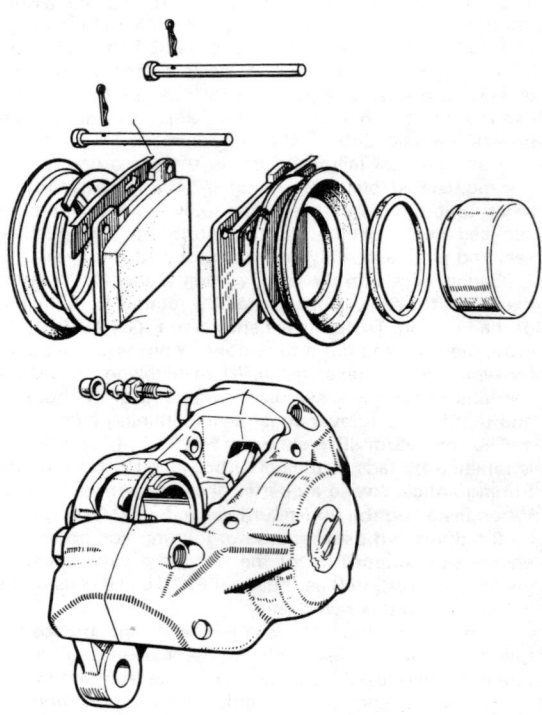

FIG 10:21 Exploded view of Girling disc brake caliper assembly. One piston is shown in its cylinder

vacuum introduced in the servo system and the servo in the off position. If the dimension is not within these limits a replacement servo unit must be fitted.

When installing the servo unit ensure that the pushrod grommet attaching pegs are fully engaged in the holes in the pedal support. Renew the vacuum hose if there is any doubt about its condition and ensure that all connections are tight. Refit the master cylinder and connect the hydraulic pipe. Unseal the vent hole in the cap and bleed the brakes as described in **Sections 10:8** and **10:14**.

10:13 Discs, calipers and pads

Each brake disc is attached to the front hub by four bolts with lockwashers. The disc and hub are shown in section in **FIG 8:2** in **Chapter 8**. Brake discs should be checked for run-out, preferably using a suitably mounted dial gauge. If such equipment is not available it may be possible to make the check using a fixed pointer and feeler gauges. The measurement is taken about $\frac{3}{4}$ inch from the outer edge of the disc. The hub nut should first be tightened to eliminate play. The maximum permissible run-out is .004 inch and if this measurement is exceeded the disc should be renewed. After completing the check, readjust the hub bearings. Excessive run-out will push the caliper pistons back into their bores, resulting in excessive pedal travel. Oil or grease must not be allowed to come into contact with the discs or brake pads.

Disc brake pads must be renewed when the friction material has worn to a thickness of $\frac{1}{16}$ inch or if they are contaminated by oil, grease or brake fluid. In cases of contamination the source of leakage must be traced and cured. Two makes of calipers and pads are used, namely Girling and Lockheed. They are interchangeable only as complete assemblies and as they differ somewhat in construction the method of servicing each make will be separately described.

FIG 10:21 is an exploded view of the Girling caliper assembly. The caliper and disc shield are attached to the steering knuckle by bolts having a nylon insert in the threads as shown in **FIG 10:23**. Each half of the caliper assembly incorporates a cylinder with a groove for a sealing ring. The exposed end of each piston is protected by a rubber dust cover secured to the caliper body by a spring. In **FIG 10:21** one of the pistons is shown in position in its cylinder. The friction pads are held in the caliper body by retaining pins and spring clips. An anti-squeal shim is interposed between each pad and piston. Hydraulic pressure is applied equally to both cylinders and the brakes are self-adjusting.

To renew Girling brake pads:
1 Remove the road wheel.
2 Withdraw the spring clips from pad retaining pins and withdraw the pins. Details are shown in **FIG 10:21**.
3 Siphon off fluid from the master cylinder until the reservoir is half full to allow for displacement of fluid in the next operation.
4 Press each piston back into the caliper by applying light finger pressure to the pad.
5 Lift the friction pads and anti-squeal shims out of the caliper. Do not depress the brake pedal while the pads are removed.
6 Install the new friction pads and the anti-squeal shims with the arrows on the shims pointing in the

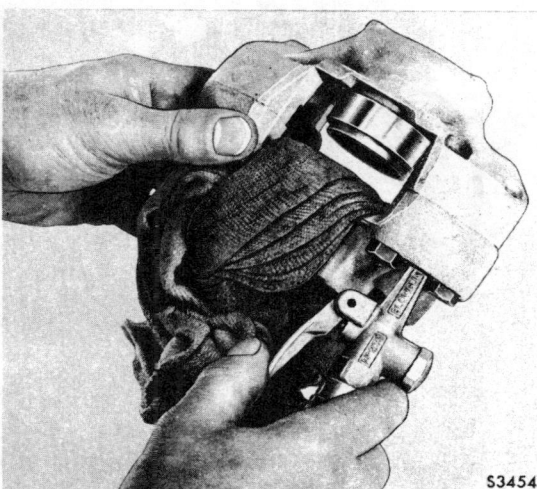

FIG 10:22 Removal of Girling caliper pistons. Restraining piston on inlet port side of caliper while ejecting other piston

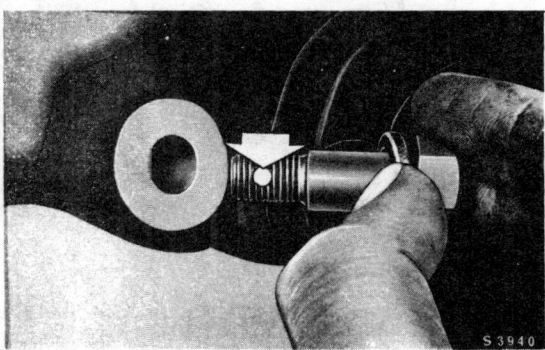

FIG 10:23 Bolts securing caliper to steering knuckle (Girling and Lockheed brakes) have nylon insertion and must not be re-used

direction of forward rotation of the disc. Install the pad retaining pins using new spring clips.
7 Depress the brake pedal two or three times to reposition the pistons in the caliper. Top up the master cylinder reservoir with the recommended fluid to within $\frac{3}{8}$ inch of the top.
8 Refit the road wheel.
To remove Girling calipers:
1 Remove the friction pads as already described.
2 Temporarily seal the vent hole in the master cylinder filler cap to minimize fluid loss.
3 Disconnect the brake pipe from the caliper.
4 Remove the bolts and lockwashers securing the caliper to the steering knuckle and withdraw the caliper. **The bolts clamping the two halves of the caliper together must not be disturbed.**
To renew fluid seals in Girling calipers:
1 Remove the caliper as already described. Clean the outside of the caliper.

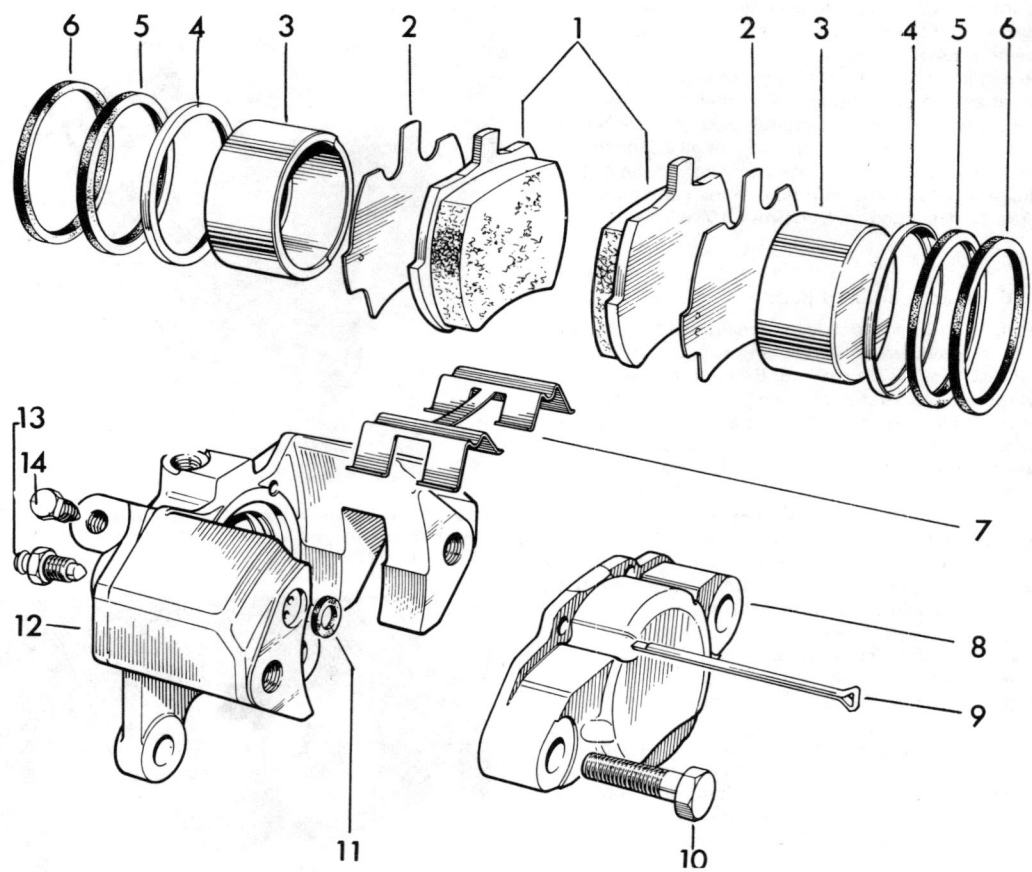

FIG 10:24   An exploded view of a Lockheed disc brake caliper assembly

Key to Fig 10:24   1 Friction pads   2 Anti-squeal shims   3 Pistons   4 Dust seal retainers   5 Dust seals (grooved)
6 Fluid seals (plain)   7 Pad restraining spring   8 Caliper (rim half)   9 Splitpins   10 Bolt securing caliper halves
11 Fluid channel seal   12 Caliper (mounting half)   13 Bleed screw   14 Plug

2 Remove the spring ring and dust cover from each half of the caliper (see **FIG 10:21**).

3 Retain the piston in the inlet port side of the caliper by binding a cloth round caliper and piston as shown in **FIG 10:22**. Apply compressed air to eject the other piston. **Keep fingers clear of pistons as compressed air will eject these forcibly.**

4 Untie the cloth and place it inside the caliper to act as a cushion while applying air pressure to the port to eject the second piston.

5 Using a small screwdriver remove the fluid seals, taking care not to damage the seal groove or bore.

6 Examine the bores and pistons for scuffing and corrosion. The bores from the seal recesses outwards may be cleaned with fine steel wool but care must be taken to remove any particles of steel wool afterwards.

7 Thoroughly flush out the caliper bores and clean the pistons with Girling Cleaning Fluid.

8 Ensure that the new fluid seals are seated correctly in the caliper bore grooves.

9 Lubricate seals, caliper bores and pistons with brake fluid and push the pistons squarely into the bores.

10 Install the dust covers and fit the spring rings.

When installing calipers, renew the attaching bolts. These have nylon inserts as shown in **FIG 10:23**. Tighten the bolts to a torque of 33 lb ft. Install the friction pads as previously described. Bleed the brakes as described in **Section 10:14** and unseal the master cylinder cap air vent.

FIG 10:24 is an exploded view of the Lockheed brake caliper. It consists of a mounting half 12 and a rim half 8, bolted together by the special bolts 10. Each half of the caliper contains a self-adjusting hydraulic piston 3, the piston bores being connected by internal fluid channels. Fluid leakage past the pistons is prevented by rubber seals 6 located in grooves in the caliper bores. Dirt and moisture are excluded by grooved dust seals 5 secured in the mouth of the bores by retainers 4. The friction pads 1 are held in position by the retaining spring 7 held by splitpins 9. Anti-squeal shims 2 are fitted between the pistons and friction pads.

Friction pads must be renewed when the friction material has worn to a thickness of $\frac{1}{16}$ inch. To renew the pads, proceed as follows, referring to **FIG 10:24** for details:

1 Remove the road wheel. Siphon off fluid from master cylinder until reservoir is half full.
2 Withdraw the splitpins 9, depressing each end of the pad retaining spring 7 in turn. Lift out the pads 1 and shims 2. Do not depress the brake pedal when the pads are removed.
3 Thoroughly clean the exposed end of each piston with brake fluid and ensure that the pad recesses in the caliper are free from rust and grit.
4 Check that the relieved section of the piston is positioned as shown at A in **FIG 10:25**. Press each piston back into the caliper. This operation is facilitated by using the clamp tool No. D.1133 as shown in **FIG 10:26**.
5 Install the new friction pads and shims in the caliper, ensuring that the pad pressure plates do not bind in the caliper recesses. Renew the pad retaining spring if necessary and ensure that it is fitted the correct way up as shown in **FIG 10:24**. Depress the ends of the spring and insert new spitpins.
6 Depress the brake pedal two or three times to adjust the brakes. Top up the master cylinder with the recommended fluid to within $\frac{3}{8}$ inch of the top.

To remove Lockheed calipers:
1 Remove the friction pads as already described.
2 Temporarily seal the vent hole in the master cylinder filler cap to minimize fluid loss.
3 Disconnect the brake pipe from the caliper.
4 Remove the bolts and lockwashers securing the caliper to the steering knuckle. Do not remove the bolts securing the two halves of the caliper unless replacement bolts and fluid channel seal (items 10 and 11 in **FIG 10:24**) are available. The bolts are of special material and on no account must ordinary bolts be used. New bolts must always be used and tightened to 37 lb ft with clean dry threads.

To renew the piston seals in Lockheed calipers:
1 Remove the caliper as already described. Do not separate the two halves of the caliper.
2 Referring to **FIG 10:27**, fit the clamp D.1133 to the mounting half of the caliper to retain the piston. Insert a block of wood in the caliper to protect the other piston during removal. Apply compressed air to the inlet port and eject the piston from the rim half of the caliper. **Keep fingers clear of piston as compressed air will eject it forcibly.**
3 Remove the clamp. Referring to **FIG 10:24**, insert a blunt screwdriver between the dust seal 5 and the dust seal retainer 4 and carefully prise out the retainer.
4 Ease the dust seal and the fluid seal 6 out of the caliper, taking care not to damage the groove or bore. Clean the piston, groove and caliper bore with brake fluid.
5 Coat the new fluid seal (the seal without groove) with Lockheed Disc Brake Lubricant and install in the caliper bore, easing the seal round gently with the fingers to ensure it is seated correctly.
6 Assemble a new dust seal (grooved) to the seal retainer, coat with the same lubricant and place in the mouth of the bore. Press the seal and retainer home using the clamp D.1133.

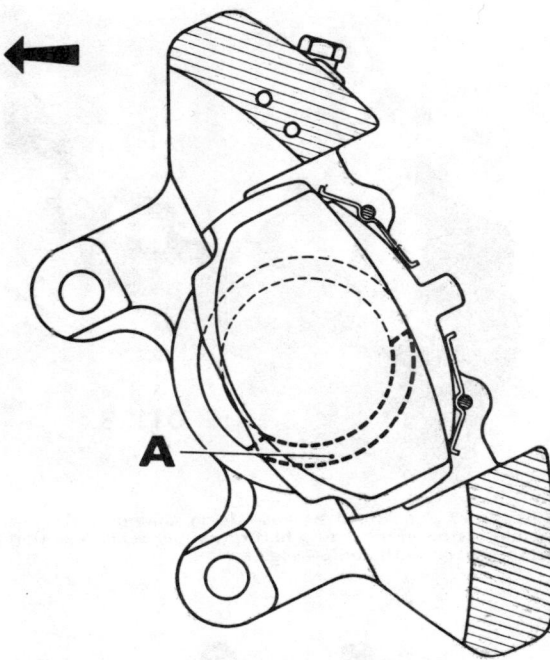

FIG 10:25 Lockheed caliper. Relieved section A of piston must be positioned facing downwards and to the rear as shown. Arrow indicates front of car

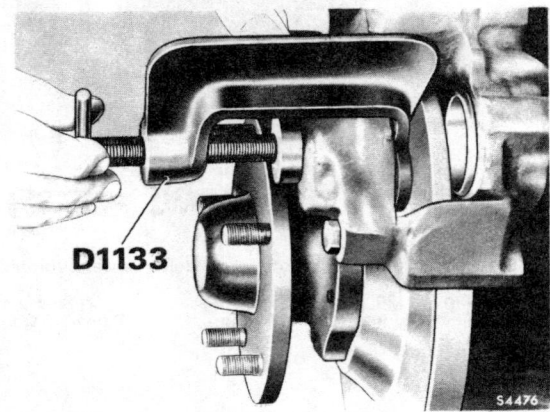

FIG 10:26 Lockheed brakes. Using clamp D.1133 to press piston into caliper before fitting new friction pads

7 Smear the piston with the recommended lubricant and enter it squarely in the bore so that the relieved portion is located as at A in **FIG 10:25**. Push the piston home, taking care it is not tilted in the process.
8 After completing installation of new seals in the rim half, repeat operations 2 to 7 for the mounting half. When installing calipers, renew the attaching bolts. These have nylon inserts as shown for the Girling brake in **FIG 10:23**. Tighten the bolts to a torque of 33 lb ft. Install the friction pads as already described. Bleed the brakes as described in **Section 10:14** and unseal the master cylinder cap air vent.

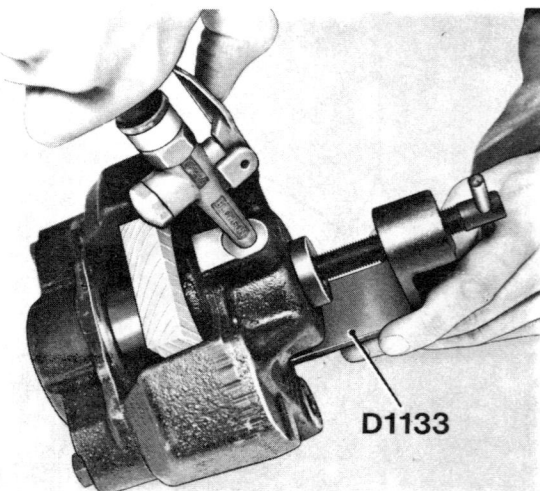

FIG 10:27 Lockheed brakes. Using Clamp D.1133 to retain piston in mounting half of caliper while ejecting other piston with compressed air

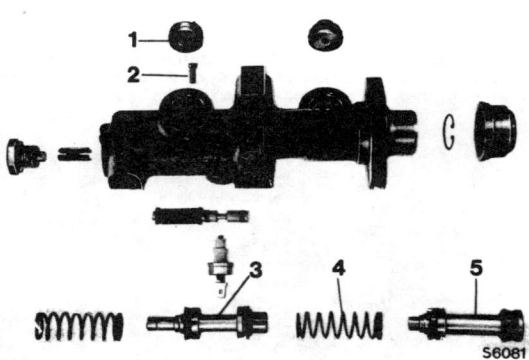

FIG 10:28 Components of the tandem master cylinder

Key to Fig 10:28   1 Rubber seal   2 Stop pin
3 Secondary piston   4 Spring   5 Primary piston

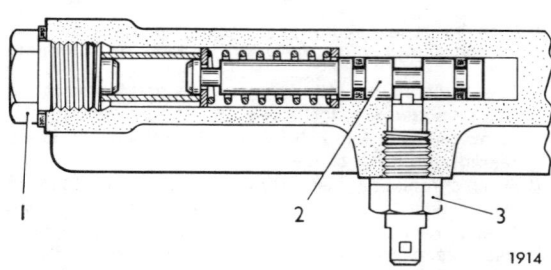

FIG 10:29 Section through pressure warning lamp switch

Key to Fig 10:29   1 Plug   2 Piston   3 Switch

10:14 Bleeding the system, disc brake models

The procedure for bleeding the hydraulic system where disc front brakes are fitted is the same as that given in **Section 10:8** for drum brakes, but the following additional points should be noted:
1 The engine must not be running whilst bleeding is carried out.
2 Before commencing operations, depress the brake pedal several times to eliminate residual vacuum in the servo system.
3 The bleed screw is on the mounting half of the caliper as shown in **FIGS 10:21** and **10:24**.

10:15 Lockheed tandem master cylinder

This is fitted to later cars and includes two pistons in a common bore as may be seen in **FIG 10:28**. The primary piston operates the front brakes through two separate pipes and the secondary piston operates the brakes on the rear wheels only. The plastic reservoir is divided internally and provides an independent supply of fluid for each piston. Should failure occur in either system the other system will provide an effective brake although brake pedal travel will be increased.

On some export models a pressure warning lamp switch is screwed into the cylinder between the two pistons as shown in **FIG 10:29**. This switch is actuated by a spring-loaded double-ended piston housed in a separate bore in the casting.

On cars without a servo this master cylinder has a non adjustable captive type pushrod and is bolted directly to the brake pedal support.

On cars fitted with a servo the master cylinder is bolted onto the servo unit.

Dismantling:

This will be simplified by reference to the exploded diagram in **FIG 10:28**. The primary piston 5 can be withdrawn after removing the circlip from the end of the cylinder. The spring 4 is used in servo-assisted installations.

Detach the fluid reservoir and withdraw the rubber seal 1 and stop pin 2, after which the secondary piston 3 and its spring can be removed.

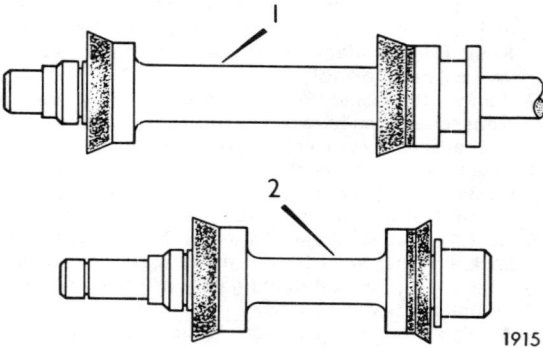

FIG 10:30 Showing correct fitting for piston seals

Key to Fig 10:30   1 Primary piston   2 Secondary piston

Referring to **FIG 10:29,** to remove the pressure warning lamp actuator piston 2, first remove the switch 3 and plug 1, then gently tap the cylinder on a wooden block to dislodge the piston assembly. The piston spring is retained by a circlip.

When refitting the pistons note that their return springs have retainer washers attached to one end. These washers must be located over the spigot end of the piston.

The seals must be well lubricated with brake fluid and if new seals are being used, see that they are correctly fitted to the pistons as shown in **FIG 10:30**. It will be seen that the lips of both seals on the primary piston 1 face towards the smaller end of the piston, while the lips of the seals on the secondary piston 2 face outwards.

10:16 Fault diagnosis

(a) Brakes ineffective

1 Worn brake linings
2 Linings contaminated by oil or fluid
3 Incorrect grade of linings
4 Scored brake drums
5 Incorrect brake fluid (leading to restricted hoses and swollen seals)

(b) Excessive brake pedal travel

1 Brake shoes need adjustment

(c) Pedal gradually sinks to the floor

1 External leaks in hydraulic system
2 Master cylinder seals defective
3 Leaking wheel cylinders (Check also 2 in (a))

(d) Pedal 'spongy' or needs 'pumping'

1 Check 2 in (c)
2 Air in hydraulic system

(e) Brakes bind

1 Check 5 in (a)
2 Shoe adjustment too close
3 Handbrake cable adjustment incorrect
4 Rear brake cylinder seized to backplate
5 Handbrake shoe levers seized
6 Weak pull-off springs
7 Slack hub bearings (brake drum tilting)
8 Reservoir overfilled or air vent restricted

(f) Brakes grab

1 Backplate loose
2 Hub bearings slack
3 Linings oily
4 Distorted brake drums
5 Incorrect grade of linings
6 Sususpension worn or loose

(g) Brakes pull to one side

1 Check 1, 2 3 and 4 in (f)
2 Unequal tyre pressures
3 Odd brake linings
4 One front brake hose restricted
5 Steering or front suspension worn
6 Front suspension control rod loose

In addition to faults already described, the following symptoms and diagnosis apply to disc brake models:

(h) Pedal travel excessive

1 Brake disc run-out excessive
2 Hub bearings slack
3 Defective caliper fluid seals or pistons
4 Defects in vacuum servo unit

(j) Excessive pedal pressure required

1 Defective vacuum hose
2 Faulty vacuum non-return valve
3 Servo air filter restricted
4 Defects in vacuum servo unit

Note that similar symptoms occur when coasting with the engine stopped. As soon as the residual vacuum is exhausted the brakes, although still working, lose the benefit of servo assistance.

(k) Brakes bind

1 Caliper piston seized
2 Caliper seals defective
3 Defects in servo unit

(l) Brakes grab or pull to one side

1 Brake disc distorted
2 Caliper mounting bolts loose
3 Friction pads contaminated by oil, grease or fluid

NOTES

CHAPTER 11

THE ELECTRICAL EQUIPMENT

11 : 1 The system, exchange units, test instruments

All cars covered by this manual are fitted with negative earth electrical systems. It is essential for replacement units to be of the correct polarity. This applies to the generator, battery connections, ignition coil and certain accessories such as a radio.

The system comprises the battery, generator (or alternator) starter, ignition system and ancillary equipment. The battery is of the normal lead/acid type. On cars fitted with the 1600 engine the standard equipment includes a 2-brush type generator whose output is regulated by a current/voltage control unit. Cars having the 2000 engine are supplied with an alternator charging system, consisting of alternator, regulator relay and warning lamp control as described in **Section 11 : 17**. The alternator is available as an option on cars with the 1600 engine.

Cars with the 1600 engine are fitted with either an inertia starter (popularly known as the Bendix drive), having a separate solenoid switch, or with a pre-engaged type of starter (see **Section 11 : 9**). All cars with the 2000 engine have pre-engaged starters.

The ignition system has been described in **Chapter 3**. The lighting system and auxiliary equipment include four headlamps, side tail and stop lamps, flashers, horn, windscreen wipers, interior lights and instruments.

Serious mechanical or electrical faults in units such as generator or starter can often best be dealt with by fitting a new unit on an exchange basis. Instructions for those adjustments which can be carried out by an owner with a basic knowledge of electricity are given in this Chapter, but many of them call for the use of accurate electrical measuring instruments. The wiring diagrams given in the Technical Data Section will assist in the tracing of wiring faults. In the absence of a voltmeter, a useful item of

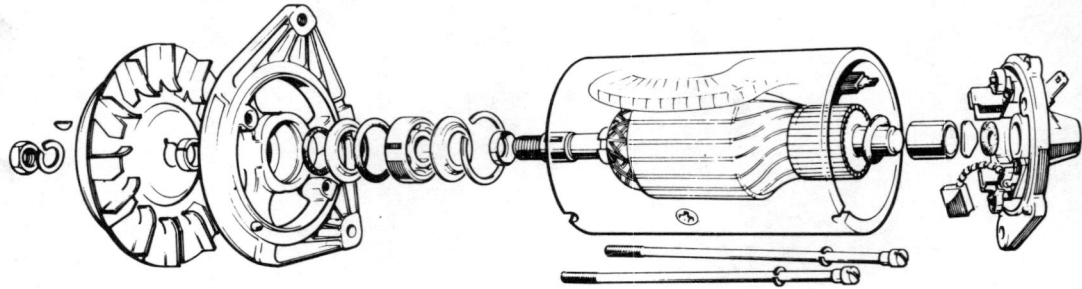

FIG 11:1   An exploded view of the generator

equipment which can be devised is a test lamp, consisting of a small 12-volt bulb in a holder with two well-insulated leads ending in crocodile clips. If one lead is earthed, the bulb will light if the other lead is connected to any terminal or point in the system which is 'live'.

Owners of cars fitted with alternator systems, however, should refer to **Section 11:17** before carrying out any electrical checks, as permanent damage may be caused to equipment by even a temporary wrong connection.

11:2 Battery maintenance and testing

The battery is of the lead/acid type using dilute sulphuric acid as an electrolyte. As on all modern cars the battery has an enormous amount of work to do and its life will be shortened by abuse or lack of regular maintenance. The outside of the battery should be kept clean and dry and any corrosion at the terminals should be eliminated. All affected parts, including the battery support and clamp, should be cleaned with dilute ammonia and then washed with clean water. The support and clamp should be painted with acid-resisting paint and the terminals and lugs smeared with petroleum jelly before reconnecting. Ensure that the battery is connected with its negative terminal to earth, as a reversal of polarity can cause serious trouble. In the case of alternator systems, permanent damage can be caused (see **Section 11:17**).

The level of the electrolyte in the cells should be checked regularly. Losses due to normal evaporation should be made up by adding distilled water only. Losses due to spilling or leakage call for the addition of dilute sulphuric acid at the correct specific gravity. The acid can be obtained ready diluted, but if strong acid is used, remember when diluting it to **add acid** to water. On no account must water be added to the strong acid.

The specific gravity of the electrolyte in each cell should be checked by using a hydrometer. This gives an indication of the state of charge as follows:

Fully charged—Specific Gravity 1.270 to 1.290
Half discharged—Specific Gravity 1.190 to 1.210
Discharged—Specific Gravity 1.110 to 1.130

These figures apply at a temperature of 16°C (60°F). Add or subtract .002 for a rise or fall respectively of 3°C (5°F). If the battery is unused for long periods it should be recharged at least once a month. It will deteriorate rapidly if left in a discharged condition. Also, on vehicles left in the open in severe winter conditions, it should be noted that while a fully-charged battery will withstand a temperature of minus 30°F, one that is completely discharged could freeze at a temperature only a few degrees below the freezing point of water.

11:3 Generator maintenance, tests in situ

FIG 11:1 is an exploded view of the generator. This is of the two-brush two-pole shunt type. The drive end of the armature runs in a ballbearing which is packed with lubricant during assembly and does not need periodic attention. The bush at the rear or commutator end is lubricated by a felt ring. This should be given a few drops only of SAE.20 engine oil through the hole provided. Do not over-lubricate as surplus oil may find its way on to the commutator.

The generator is driven by the same belt as the fan and water pump. The belt should be carefully adjusted as described in **Chapter 4, Section 4:2**, and renewed at the first signs of wear. A slipping belt will reduce generator output as well as affecting cooling.

To test the generator output on the car:

1 Check the armature circuit with the generator cold as follows (see **FIG 11:2**):
(a) Disconnect both wires from the generator.
(b) Connect the positive lead of a 0–20 range voltmeter to the output terminal 1 and the negative lead to earth.
(c) Start the engine and run at 1500 rev/min. The reading should be 2 to 4 volts.
(d) If no reading, this may be due to loss of residual magnetism in the polepieces. To rectify, flash the end of a lead attached to the battery positive terminal across the generator field terminal 2. If still no reading, dismantle the generator for examination. If reading satisfactory:

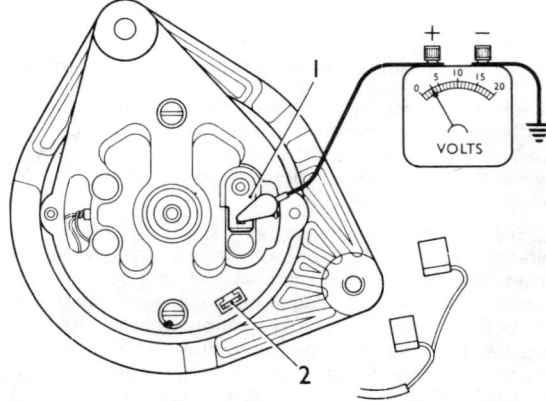

FIG 11:2   Generator output test 1

Key to Fig 11:2   1 Output terminal   2 Field terminal

2 Check the generator field circuit as shown in **FIG 11 : 3**:

(a) With voltmeter still connected as in the previous test, connect the positive lead of an ammeter to the terminal 1 and the negative lead to terminal 2.

(b) Start the engine and slowly increase speed until the voltmeter reads 12 volts. The ammeter reading should now be about 2 amps.

(c) If output is satisfactory when cold and no fault is apparent in the controller (see **Section 11 : 10**) or wiring to account for battery not holding charge, run the engine for 15 minutes at 1500 rev/min to warm up the generator, then recheck output.

(d) If no ammeter reading, remove and dismantle generator for examination.

11 : 4 Removing and dismantling generator

To remove the generator:

1 Disconnect both battery cables.

2 Disconnect the two wires from the generator.

3 If the generator is to be dismantled, undo the generator pulley nut before slackening drive belt.

4 Slacken the two generator pivot bolts and the brace nut on the engine. Remove the brace bolt from the generator.

5 Swing the generator towards the engine and disengage the drive belt.

6 Remove the two pivot bolts and lift away the generator. To dismantle the generator, referring to **FIG 11 : 1**:

1 Remove the pulley nut and lockwasher. If the nut has not previously been slackened, use an old fan belt to hold the pulley. Where a plastic pulley is fitted, this must on no account be held in a vice. Withdraw the pulley.

2 Remove the two through-bolts securing the end brackets to the yoke.

3 Withdraw the commutator end bracket from the yoke, if necessary tapping the bracket with a hide mallet.

4 Withdraw the drive end bracket and armature as an assembly from the yoke. Retain the fibre washer at the commutator end of the armature shaft.

5 It is not necessary to separate the drive end bracket and ballbearing assembly unless the armature or the bearing needs renewal, in which case a three-legged puller is needed for withdrawal and a press for assembly. The ballbearing is secured in the drive end bracket by a circlip. All armature tests can be carried out with the bracket in position, but these need specialized equipment and are best entrusted to a service agent.

6 Clean all parts before inspection and reassembly, but do not allow cleaning fluid to reach the armature, the field coils or the ballbearing.

The commutator end bracket bush is of the sintered-bronze type. It can be withdrawn by tapping a $\frac{5}{8}$ inch thread in the bush, then using a bolt, nut and a suitable distance piece as an extractor. Lubricate the new bush by placing the forefinger over one end and filling with engine oil. With the thumb over the other end apply pressure until the oil seeps through the porous walls of the bush. Repeat until the bush is saturated with oil. Press in the bush until flush with the end bracket.

11 : 5 Brushes and commutator, field coil testing

To remove the brushes, lift the springs, withdraw the brushes from their holders and disconnect the brush

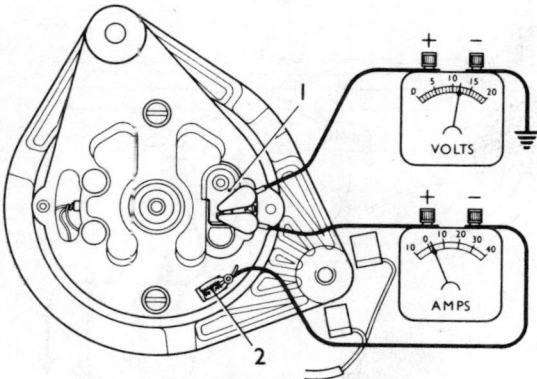

FIG 11 : 3 Generator output test 2
Key to Fig 11 : 3   1 Output terminal   2 Field terminal

leads. Brushes must slide freely in their holders but without shake. They can be eased by gently filing the sides of a brush with a smooth file. Brushes should be renewed if their length is less than .25 inch. New brushes are preformed and do not need bedding-in to the commutator, but if old brushes are refitted they must be installed in their original positions.

Test the tension of the brush springs with a spring balance. To carry out this test, temporarily assemble the commutator end bracket and brush gear to the armature without the yoke. The tension should be 30 oz with a new brush, or 15 oz with a brush worn to the minimum length of .25 inch.

Attention to the commutator is limited to cleaning off dust and grease with a rag moistened in petrol. The merest trace of petrol should be used, to avoid possible damage to the insulation. Commutators showing signs of scoring or pitting can be skimmed where this is possible without reducing the diameter below the specified limit. The commutator is of the moulded type and undercutting of the segments is not necessary.

The field coils and polepieces should not be removed from the generator yoke as a special expander tool is necessary for refitting. Field coil testing involves the use of mains test equipment, so that this work, as well as attention to the armature and commutator, is best entrusted to a service agent.

FIG 11 : 4 Location of generator brush leads, also showing method of wedging brushes in retracted position

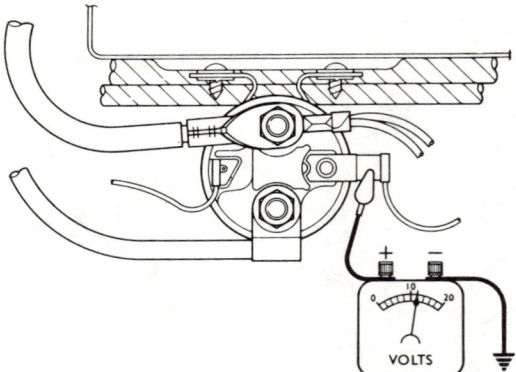

FIG 11:5 Inertia starter solenoid test 1

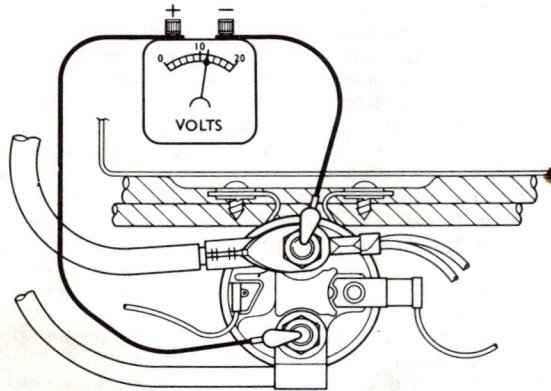

FIG 11:6 Inertia starter solenoid test 2

11:6 Generator reassembly and refitting

1 Referring to **FIG 11:1**, install the pulley spacer and key at the drive end of the armature shaft.
2 Assemble the pulley to the shaft with the fan blades facing the end bracket as shown. Secure with the lockwasher and nut.
3 Install the armature and drive end bracket assembly in the yoke and fit the fibre washer on the commutator end of the shaft.
4 The brushes should be assembled in their holders with the leads connected as shown in **FIG 11:4** and with the tags at 90 deg. to the brush holders. Wedge the brushes in a partly retracted position as shown by allowing the springs to bear on the sides of the brushes.
5 Assemble the commutator end bracket to the armature shaft sufficiently to bring part of the brushes over the commutator. Release the brushes by raising the spring arm with a screwdriver. Push the commutator end bracket fully home.
6 Line up the dowel in each end bracket with the recesses in the yoke and insert and tighten the two through-bolts.
To install the generator:
1 Fit the generator to the engine but do not fully tighten the two pivot bolts at this stage.

2 Fit the bolt securing the generator to the slotted brace and adjust the belt as described in **Chapter 4, Section 4:2**. Tighten the generator brace bolt and then the other three bolts and nuts and recheck the belt tension.
3 Reconnect the wires to the two generator terminals. Reconnect the battery leads.

11:7 Inertia starter, solenoid tests on car

This section applies only to the inertia type starter (popularly known as Bendix drive) fitted to the 1600 engine only. For details of the pre-engaged types fitted to some 1600 and all 2000 engines, reference should be made to **Section 11:9**.

When the starter switch (ignition key) is turned fully to the right a small current operates the solenoid (mounted on the battery support bracket) and closes its contacts. These contacts, which are capable of handling a heavy current, connect the battery direct to the starter by heavy cables. An additional contact on the solenoid feeds current to the 'cold start' ignition coil, without passing through the resistor. This provides a more powerful ignition current for starting (see **Chapter 3**).

When checking starter troubles, first ensure that the battery is in good condition and that all battery and starter connections are in good order. A corroded battery terminal or a bad earth connection may have sufficient electrical resistance to make the starter inoperative, though it may pass enough current for lamps and accessories.

To check the solenoid, operate the starter switch, when a click should be heard from the solenoid indicating that the contact bridge is moving. If no click can be heard, carry out the following tests using a 0–20 range voltmeter:

1 Connect the voltmeter positive terminal to the solenoid small terminal carrying the white/red wire as shown in **FIG 11:5**. On operating the starter switch a reading of 12 volts should be obtained. If no reading, the current is not reaching the solenoid owing to a faulty starter switch or wiring.
2 If test 1 is satisfactory, disconnect the distributor LT wire from the negative terminal on the ignition coil (to prevent the engine firing during this test and test 3).

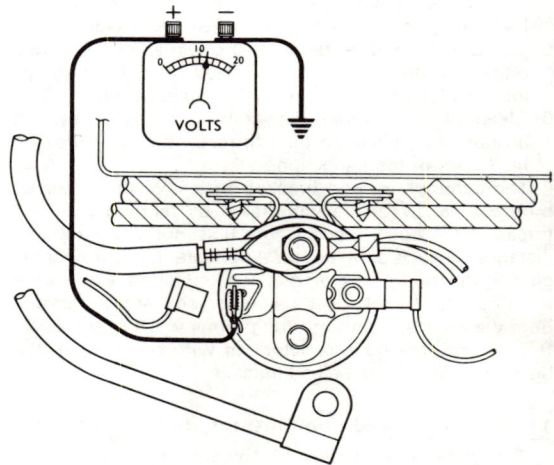

FIG 11:7 Inertia starter solenoid test 3

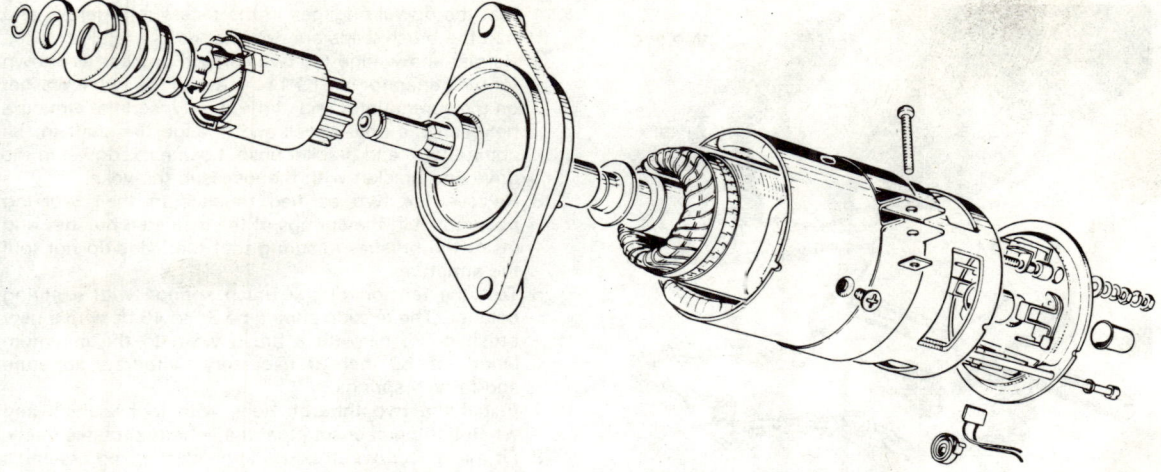

FIG 11 : 8   An exploded view of the inertia starter, type M.35G/1

Connect the voltmeter across the two large solenoid terminals as shown in **FIG 11 : 6**. A reading of 12 volts should be obtained. Operate the starter switch and if the solenoid contacts are closing the voltmeter reading should fall to not more than ½-volt. If the reading exceeds this figure renew the solenoid.

3 Disconnect the starter cable from the solenoid large terminal and the white/blue wire from the solenoid small terminal and connect the voltmeter between the latter terminal and earth as shown in **FIG 11 : 7**. On operating the starter switch a reading of 12 volts should be obtained. If no reading, the solenoid should be renewed, as although the starter will still operate, the solenoid is not completing the 'cold start' feed to the ignition coil.

11 : 8 Servicing inertia-type starter

The inertia-type starter M.35G/1 is shown in exploded form in **FIG 11 : 8**. To remove the starter:

1 Disconnect both battery cables.
2 Disconnect the cable from the starter.
3 Remove the dipstick. Remove the two bolts and lockwashers securing the starter to the crankcase. The starter can now be withdrawn but has a shallow spigot (see **FIG 11 : 8**) which is necessarily a tight fit in the crankcase orifice. In case of difficulty, rock the starter up and down by hand to release.

Inspect and test the starter as follows:

1 Remove the cover band and test the freedom of the brushes in their holders. Service the brushes as described for generator brushes in **Section 11 : 5**.
2 Clean the commutator with a petrol moistened cloth while rotating the armature. **Do not saturate as petrol is injurious to the windings.**
3 To test the starter, it must be firmly held in a vice or securely bolted to the bench. Connect the starter to a 12-volt battery by heavy cables, one cable going to the starter terminal while the other is earthed to the yoke. The starter should now 'motor' at high speed. If it does not it should be dismantled as follows:

1 If not already removed take off cover band and insulator.

2 Remove the two through-bolts. Tap the drive end bracket away from the yoke and withdraw the armature complete with the starter drive, and drive end bracket. Retain the washer from the commutator end of the armature.
3 Remove the two insulated brushes from their holders. Remove the terminal nut, lockwasher, plain washer and insulating washer from the terminal post. Remove the spacer from the insulating sleeve.
4 Remove the commutator end bracket and withdraw the plastic insulating sleeve from the terminal post.

If the starter drive is in good condition it need not be dismantled but should be washed in petrol. Oil must not be used as this will collect grit and cause the starter to fail to engage. If the drive has to be dismantled either for servicing or removal of the drive end bracket proceed as follows:

1 Compress the thrust spring using the special spring compressor JWP.376 as shown in **FIG 11 : 9**. Remove the circlip and release the spring. Remove the spring collar, spring and thrust washer.
2 Withdraw the pinion assembly and screwed sleeve from the armature shaft. If necessary, rotate the pinion slightly so as to line up the splined washer (inside the pinion barrel) with the splines on the shaft. Check that the light control (or anti-drift) spring which is also inside the barrel is undamaged. The pinion assembly should not be dismantled, being serviced as a complete assembly. The heavy thrust spring can best be checked by comparison with a new spring.
3 Clean the commutator as already described. The earthed brushes can be renewed by unsoldering the brush leads at the tags under the brush holders and soldering the new leads in position.
4 To renew insulated brushes, cut off the original brush leads .30 inch from the aluminium coil tags. Cut the leads of the new brushes to the required length, flatten and tin the ends. Clean and tin the remaining parts of the original brush leads and solder one flex of the new brush lead to each side of the original lead.

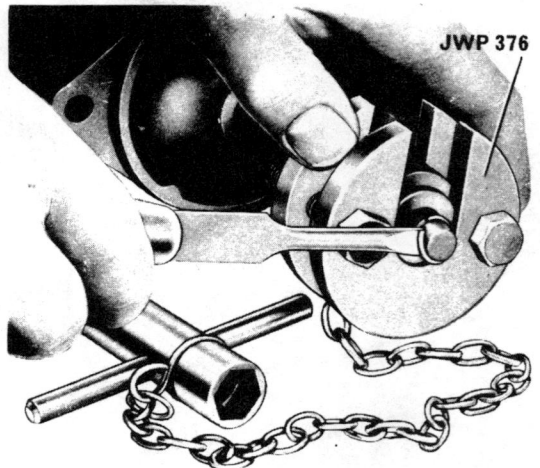

FIG 11:9 Inertia starter. Showing method of removing starter drive using compressor JWP.376

5 Attention to bearings or field coils should be entrusted to service agent.

Reassembly of the starter is a reversal of the dismantling procedure but the following points should be noted:

1 The starter should be waterproofed during reassembly by applying jointing compound to the following areas: Supply terminal and insulating sleeve; between each end bracket and the yoke; inside the cover band and dust cap. After assembly the yoke dowels should be sealed with Bostik 771.

2 If the starter drive end bracket has been removed, ensure that the thrust washer is installed before fitting the bracket. When fitting the starter drive pinion assembly, rotate as necessary to allow the splined washer (inside the pinion barrel) to engage the splines on the shaft. Compress the thrust spring with the tool JWP.376 and fit a new circlip on the shaft. Release the spring slowly while ensuring that the circlip is fully home in its groove.

3 Fit the insulating sleeve over the field coil terminal post with the extension located between the post and the yoke and install the commutator end bracket, ensuring

that the dowel engages in the recess in the yoke and that the brush leads are not trapped.

4 Retract and wedge the two earthed brushes as shown for the generator in FIG 11:4. Install the thrust washer on the commutator end of the shaft. Insert the armature between the pole shoes and engage the shaft in the commutator end bracket bush. Locate the dowel in the drive end bracket with the recess in the yoke.

5 Release the two earthed brushes to their working positions. Lift the springs of the insulated brushes and insert the brushes ensuring that the leads do not foul the armature.

6 Test the tension of the brush springs with a spring balance. The tension should be 34 to 46 oz with a new brush or 25 oz with a brush worn to the minimum length of .30 inch. If necessary, withdraw armature and fit new springs.

7 Install the two through-bolts with lockwashers and when tightened ensure that the armature rotates freely.

8 Fit the spacer over the insulating sleeve, and assemble an insulating washer, plain washer, two lockwashers and two nuts on the terminal post. Tighten securely but do not over-tighten.

9 Test the starter as previously described.

11:9 Pre-engaged starters

Three types of pre-engaged starters are used, namely M.35G/PE, M.418G/PE and M.35J/PE. FIG 11:10 shows an exploded view of the M.418G/PE which will serve to illustrate the basic principle of all three types. A two-stage solenoid is built-in to the starter. When the starter switch (ignition key) is turned a small current energizes the solenoid which, by means of a lever, moves the starter pinion into engagement with the flywheel ring gear. Only when engagement has taken place does the solenoid switch complete the main starter circuit. This circuit is automatically broken as soon as the starter pinion disengages. To prevent possible overspeeding of the starter armature if the switch is held in the on position after the engine starts, a one-way roller clutch is provided between the armature and the pinion.

On the M.35G/PE and on the M.418G/PE shown in FIG 11:10, the lever pivots on an eccentric pin by which the actuating position of the lever may be adjusted. On

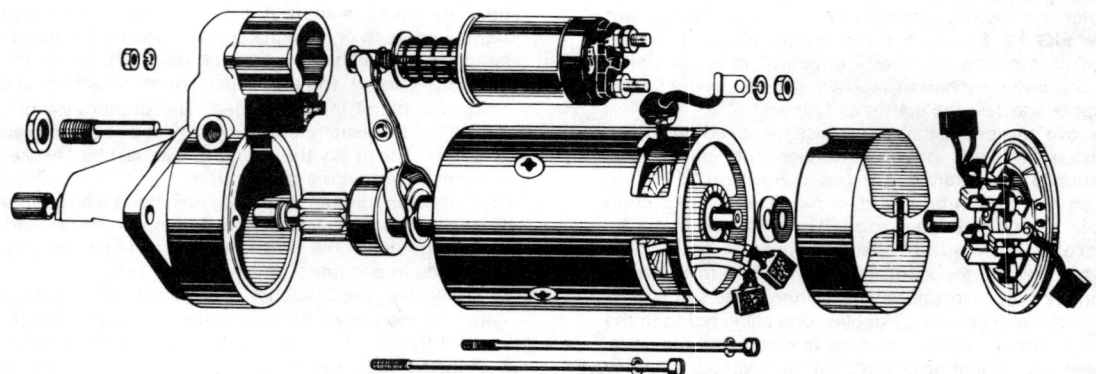

FIG 11:10 An exploded view of pre-engaged starter, type M.418G/PE. Type M.35G/PE is of basically similar construction

the M.35J/PE type starter, however, the position of the actuating lever is preset and cannot be altered.

When checking starter troubles, first ensure that the battery is in good condition and that all battery and starter connections are in good order. Particular attention should be paid to the earth connections.

When the starter switch is operated it should be possible to hear the solenoid movement. If not, the supply to the solenoid switch can be checked as shown in **FIG 11:11**. Disconnect the link from the STA terminal of the solenoid before commencing the test, to guard against possible operation of the starter. Disconnect the white/red wire from the solenoid and connect the positive side of a voltmeter to the wire and the negative to earth. Operate the starter switch, when the voltmeter should read 12 volts. No reading indicates a faulty starter switch or wiring. In the absence of a voltmeter, a test lamp (as described in **Section 11:1**) may be used.

Electrical tests of the solenoid windings, starter armature and field coils require the use of equipment which is unlikely to be available to the owner and such work is best entrusted to a service agent. Removal of the starter is carried out in the same way as in the case of the inertia starter (see **Section 11:8**) except that the solenoid switch is removed with the starter in the case of pre-engaged types.

Dismantling and reassembly of the pre-engaged starters types M.35G/PE and M.418G/PE follow the same basic principles as for the inertia starter described in **Section 11:8** with the following differences:

1 The solenoid can be withdrawn after detaching the connecting wire or strip and removing two nuts or bolts securing the solenoid to the drive end bracket, as shown in **FIG 11:12**.

2 On type M.35G/PE, the nut, washer and spacer securing the terminal to the commutator end bracket must be removed to allow the end bracket to be withdrawn.

3 Remove the eccentric pin before removing drive end bracket. Withdraw the drive end bracket from the yoke complete with armature. Take care of thrust washers at the commutator end.

4 On type M.35G/PE the rubber sealing grommet must be removed to allow withdrawal of the engagement lever together with armature from the drive end bracket. Take care of thrust washer at drive end of shaft.

5 To remove the drive assembly, free the thrust collar from the circlip by tapping the collar down with a piece of tube. Remove the circlip and withdraw the drive assembly. The latter is only serviced as a complete assembly.

6 Examine the roller clutch. This should provide instant take-up of drive in one direction and rotate smoothly and easily in the other. The assembly should move freely around and along the armature shaft splines without roughness or tendency to bind. If the assembly does not meet with these requirements it should be renewed. If the conductors are found to be lifting from the armature or solder appears to have melted, this indicates overspeeding of the armature and in such cases the roller clutch is suspect.

7 Armature shaft bushes are of the sintered-bronze type as described for the generator commutator end bush in **Section 11:4**.

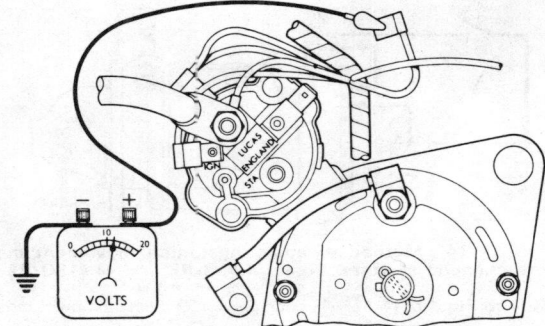

FIG 11:11 Pre-engaged starters. Testing of wiring supplying current to solenoid

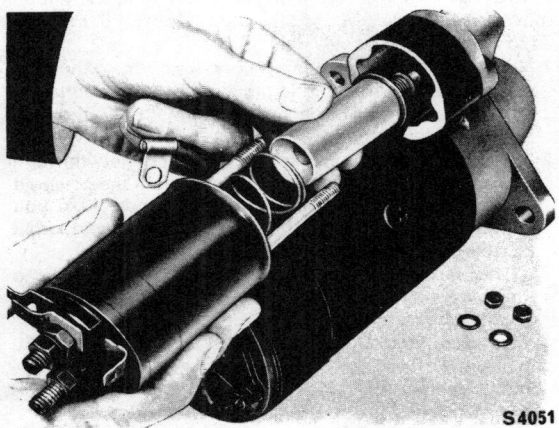

FIG 11:12 Removing solenoid from pre-engaged starters, types M.35G/PE and M.418G/PE

FIG 11:13 Rubber grommet must be installed in drive end bracket before assembling bracket and armature to yoke in pre-engaged starters, types M.35G/PE and M.418G/PE

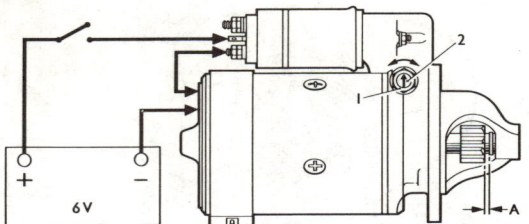

FIG 11:14 Method of adjusting pinion movement in pre-engaged starters, types M.35G/PE and M.418G/PE

Key to Fig 11:14   1 Locknut   2 Eccentric pivot pin

8 When reassembling starter, install the rubber sealing grommet, as shown in **FIG 11:13**, before fitting the drive end bracket and armature to the yoke.

FIG 11:14 shows the method of adjusting the pinion movement on types M.35G/PE and M.418G/PE. Proceed as follows:

1 Disconnect the wire or strip connection from the STA terminal on the solenoid to prevent rotation of armature during the check. Connect a lead from the STA terminal to the starter body.

2 Connect the postive terminal of a 6-volt battery through a switch to the small soldered terminal on the solenoid and the battery negative to the starter body. (A 6-volt battery is used as a safety measure to avoid rapid axial movement of the pinion).

3 Close the switch, thus throwing the drive forward into the engaged position. Dimension A between the pinion and the thrust collar should be .005 to .010 inch for the M.35G/PE and .005 to .015 inch for the M.418G/PE starters. To ensure accuracy when taking the measurement, press the pinion back lightly towards the armature, thus taking up any slack in the linkage.

4 If the dimension A is not within the specified limits, slacken the locknut 1 and turn the eccentric pivot pin 2 until the correct setting is obtained. The arc of adjustment is 180 deg. and the pivot pin must be set so that the arrow on its head is adjacent to the arrows on the end bracket.

5 Tighten the locknut to a torque of 15 lb ft while holding the pivot pin with a screwdriver.

The M.35J/PE pre-engaged starter shown in **FIG 11:15** operates on the same general principles as the two models already described, but has a face-type moulded commutator and a fully insulated plastic brush box which is riveted to the commutator end bracket. The wedge-shaped brushes, shown in **FIG 11:16** are kept in contact with the commutator by coil springs. The yoke has independently fixed end brackets, no through-bolts being used. Instead the drive end bracket is attached to studs incorporated in two of the pole shoes, while the commutator end bracket is secured to the yoke by two screws. Armature end float is controlled at the commutator end by a thrust plate and shims fitted on an external extension of the shaft and secured by a splitpin as shown in **FIG 11:19**. The actuating position of the engagement lever is preset and cannot be altered.

Dismantling procedure is similar to that described for other pre-engaged starters except for the independent fixing of the end brackets. Assembly is carried out on similar lines but the following points should be noted:

1 Lubricate the components of the engagement lever and drive assembly with the recommended grease. Referring to **FIG 11:17**, assemble the lever to the solenoid plunger so that the radiused edge of the lever 1 is towards the solenoid, and the solenoid retaining plate 2 is correctly positioned in relation to the lever.

2 Referring to **FIG 11:18**, assemble the solenoid plunger and engagement lever to the roller clutch drive operating plate 1 so that the locking shoulders 2 are located as shown.

3 Install the rubber grommet between the drive end bracket and the yoke before installing solenoid switch.

4 Before installing commutator end bracket, ensure that the thrust washer, arrowed in **FIG 11:16**, is in position.

5 Referring to **FIG 11:19**, after assembling thrust plate 1, temporarily install the splitpin so that the end float is not more than .010 inch. Adjust by varying the number of shims 2 between the thrust plate and the splitpin.

11:10 Current/voltage controller

On cars fitted with generator a current-voltage controller is used (see **FIGS 11:20** to **11:24**). It consists of three units, a cut-out relay, a current regulator and a voltage regulator. The three are housed under a single cover and

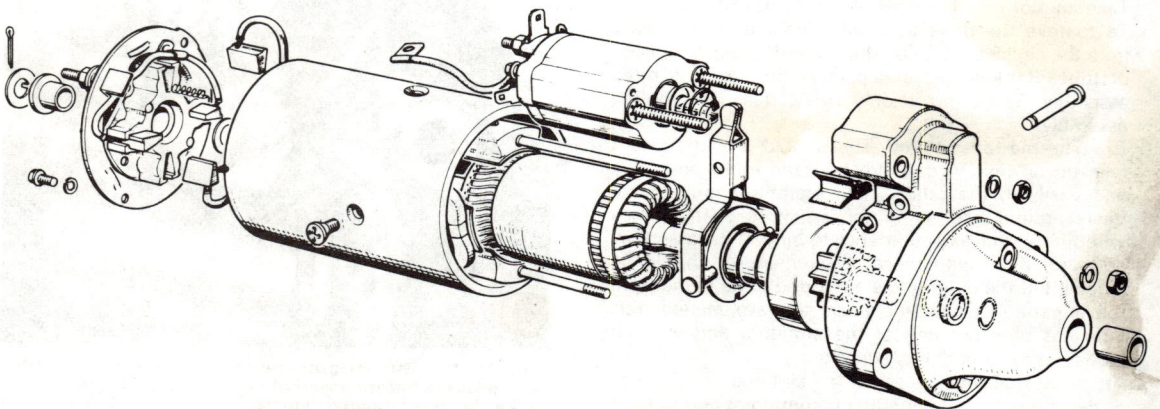

FIG 11:15   An exploded view of pre-engaged starter, type M.35J/PE

combine to regulate automatically the output of the generator under varying conditions. The controller should require little or no attention in normal service and in the case of electrical trouble other points should be checked first, such as generator belt, generator brushes and battery connections. Adjustment of the controller involves electrical and mechanical checks which call for accurate instruments, namely a 0—20 moving coil voltmeter, a moving coil ammeter and an air thermometer. The Lucas adjuster No. 54381742 will also be needed for the adjusting cams.

The four electrical tests which will be described can be made without removing the controller cover and should

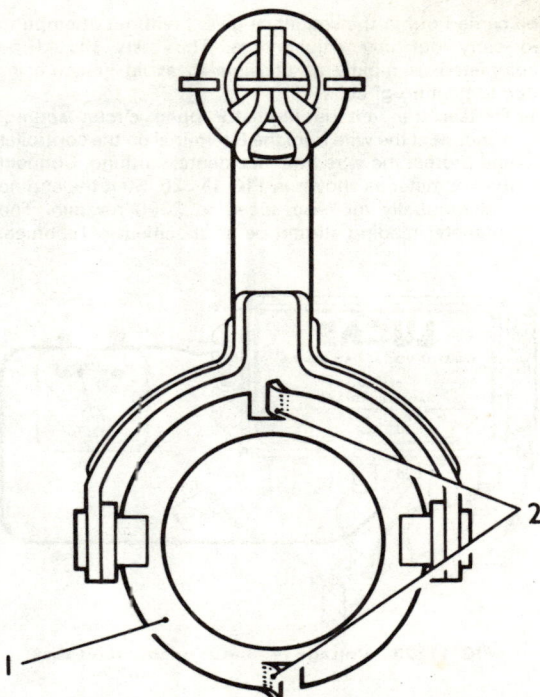

FIG 11:18 Pre-engaged starter type M.35J/PE. Solenoid plunger and lever must be assembled to roller clutch operating plate as shown

Key to Fig 11:18   1 Roller clutch drive operating plate
2 Locking shoulders

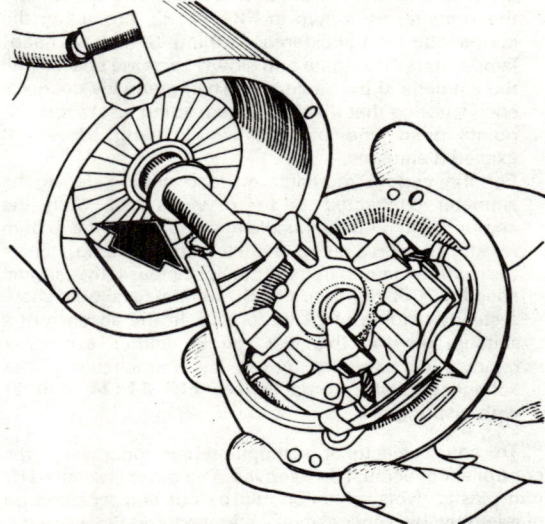

FIG 11:16   Pre-engaged starter type M.35J/PE, showing face-type commutator and commutator end bracket with wedge-shaped brushes. Arrow indicates thrust washer on armature shaft

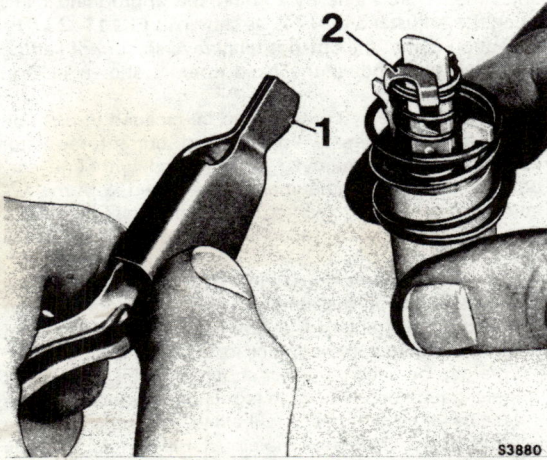

FIG 11:17   Pre-engaged   starter   type   M.35J/PE. Engagement lever must be fitted to solenoid plunger with radiused edge of lever 1 towards solenoid and with solenoid retaining plate 2 positioned as shown

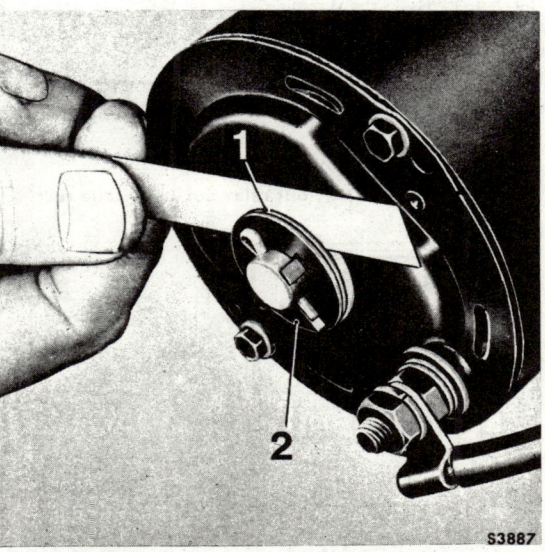

FIG 11:19 Method of checking end float on pre-engaged starter type M.35J/PE

Key to Fig 11:19   1 Thrust plate   2 Shims

be carried out in the sequence given, without attempting to carry out any adjustments. The tests should be completed as rapidly as possible to avoid inaccuracies due to heating of coils.

1 To test the voltage regulator open circuit setting, disconnect the wire from the B terminal on the controller and protect the wire from accidental earthing. Connect the voltmeter as shown in **FIG 11 : 20**. Start the engine and gradually increase speed to 2000 rev/min. The voltmeter reading should be as specified in Technical

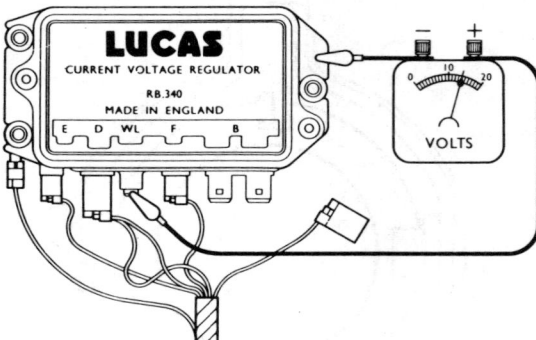

FIG 11:20   Voltage regulator open circuit test

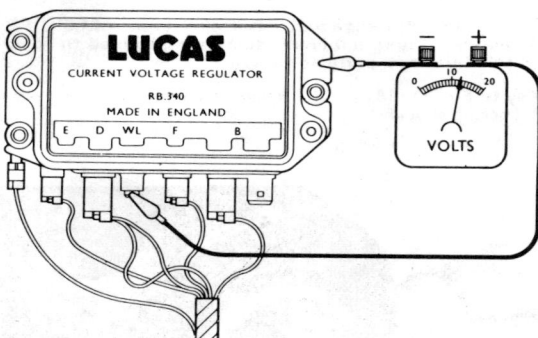

FIG 11:21   Cut-out relay cut-in voltage test

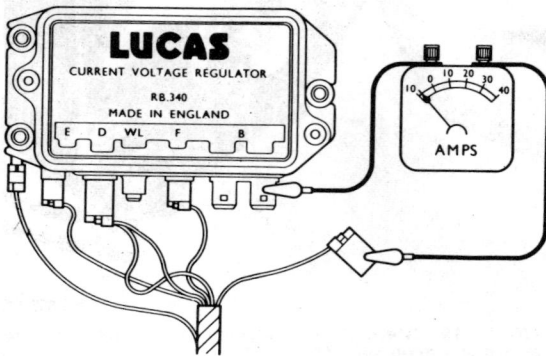

FIG 11:22   Cut-out relay reverse current test. Current regulator on-load test

Data. An unsteady reading may be due to dirty contacts. If the reading is steady but outside the limits by not more than $\frac{1}{2}$-volt, the electrical setting can be adjusted after completing the remaining tests. An error of more than $\frac{1}{2}$-volt, however, will probably mean that the controller will have to be renewed.

2 For the cut-out relay cut-in voltage test (see **FIG 11 : 21**), reconnect the wire to the B terminal. Leave the voltmeter connected as for previous test and switch on the headlamps. Start the engine and increase speed until the cut-out points close, indicated by the voltmeter needle flicking back. This should occur at 12.7 to 13.3 volts.

3 Test the cut-out relay reverse current by disconnecting the wire from the controller B terminal and connecting the ammeter as shown in **FIG 11 : 22**, protecting the connection from accidental earthing. Switch on headlamps, start the engine and slowly increase speed until the ammeter shows a charge. Then gradually decrease speed, noting that the discharge reading just before the points open (indicated by zero reading) does not exceed 8 amperes.

4 For the current regulator on-load setting, leave the ammeter connected as for previous test. Start the engine, switch on the headlamps and connect a .5 ohm resistor (having a rating of not less than 30 amp) across the battery terminals. Gradually increase the engine speed to 3000 rev/min, when the ammeter should show a steady reading of 24 to 26 amp. In the absence of a suitable resistor, this test can be carried out, after removal of controller cover, by shortcircuiting the voltage regulator contacts (see **FIG 11 : 24** item 1) with a spring clip.

To adjust electrical settings, where necessary, the controller cover must be removed. The cover is secured by two plastic rivets which should be cut and replaced on reassembly by service rivets supplied for the purpose. Adjustments must be carried out in the same sequence as the tests already described and as quickly as possible in order to avoid inaccuracies due to heating of coils. The adjustments are made by turning the appropriate cams using the Adjuster 54381742 as shown in **FIG 11 : 23**. The exception is that the cut-out relay reverse current setting is altered by bending the fixed contact shown at 3 in **FIG 11 : 24**.

The cut-out relay contacts can be cleaned in position using fine glasspaper. Voltage and current regulator contacts must be removed and cleaned with fine carborundum stone or emerypaper and wiped with methylated spirits. After cleaning the contacts, check the mechanical settings as follows, referring to **FIGS 11 : 23** and **11 : 24**:

1 Turn the current and voltage regulator cams clockwise to reduce lift on the armature control springs, leaving sufficient clearance for a box spanner on the current regulator adjustable contact locknut. The armature to core gap on each regulator should be .058 inch. Insert feeler gauge between each regulator armature and core face as far as rivet heads will allow. Press the armature firmly down and screw the adjustable contact inwards until it just touches the moving contact. Release the armature and check gap.

2 The cut-out relay contacts should just touch with a .015 inch feeler inserted between the armature and the core.

Adjust if necessary by bending the fixed contact. The armature to core gap should be .035 to .045 inch. Adjust if necessary by bending the backstop.

3 Recheck the electrical settings as previously described.

The controller terminals are connected to wires as follows (see **FIG 11:20**):

E and baseplate screw—black.
D (two wires)—brown/yellow.
F—brown/green.
B—brown.

11:11 Thermal circuit breaker and fuses. Switches

The push/pull lighting switch incorporates a thermal circuit breaker protecting the headlamp, sidelamp and foglamp circuits. It also has contacts for switching on the interior lamp and a rheostat and resistors for controlling the brightness of the instrument lamps. The thermal circuit breaker contacts are operated by a bi-metallic strip and should remain closed when carrying a current of 25 amps but should open within 30 to 180 seconds if the current increases to 33 amp at 20°C. (68°F). It can be tested after removal of the switch assembly by connecting to a 12-volt battery with a variable resistance and a 0–40 ammeter in series. If results obtained on test are not within these limits the switch unit must be renewed. On 1600 Super and 2000SL a self-contained thermal circuit breaker is fitted.

The fuse block (see **FIG 11:25**) is secured to the inside of the dash panel by two screws and the fuse cover and body project through an aperture into the engine compartment. Four 35-amp fuses protect the components listed:

Fuse No. 1: Windscreen wipers, cigarette lighter, radio.

FIG 11:24 Current/voltage controller showing contacts

Key to Fig 11:24 1 Voltage regulator contacts
2 Current regulator contacts 3 Cut-out contacts

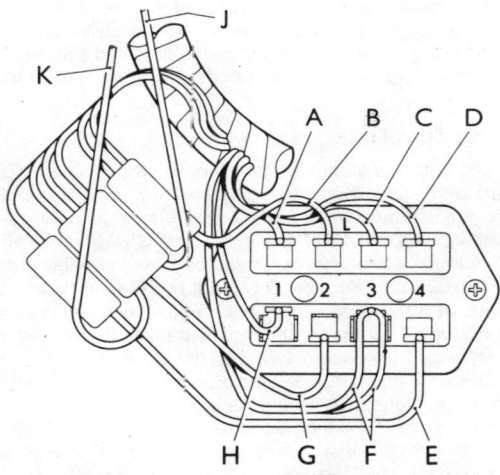

FIG 11:25 Fuse block and wiring connections

Key to cable colours Fig 11:25 **A** White/blue
B White **C** Brown/purple **D** Red/brown **E** Red
F Purple **G** Green **H** White/green
J Green (Brake pressure warning lamp LHD only)
K Green (Rear window demister where fitted)

Fuse No. 2: Stoplamps, indicators and warning lamps, oil and ignition warning lamps, fuel gauge, temperature warning lamp, heater motor, reverse lamps, overdrive unit (where fitted).

Fuse No. 3: Horns, interior lamp.

Fuse No. 4: Instrument lamps, rear lamps, number plate lamps, foglamps, cigarette lighter lamp.

FIG 11:25 shows the position of the fuses and gives a key to the cable colours of the connections. Check that wires have not been trapped by the pedal support bracket (see **Chapter 5, Section 5:3** and **FIG 5:4**).

The combined indicator, headlamp dip and flasher switch and horn push assembly is secured to two posts integral with the steering shaft top bearing housing, a

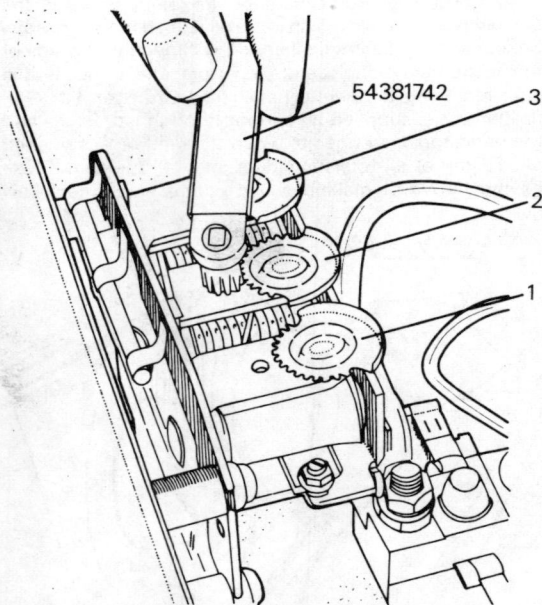

FIG 11:23 Current/voltage controller, with the special tool used to turn the controller cams

Key to Fig 11:23 1 Voltage regulator
2 Current regulator 3 Cut-out relay

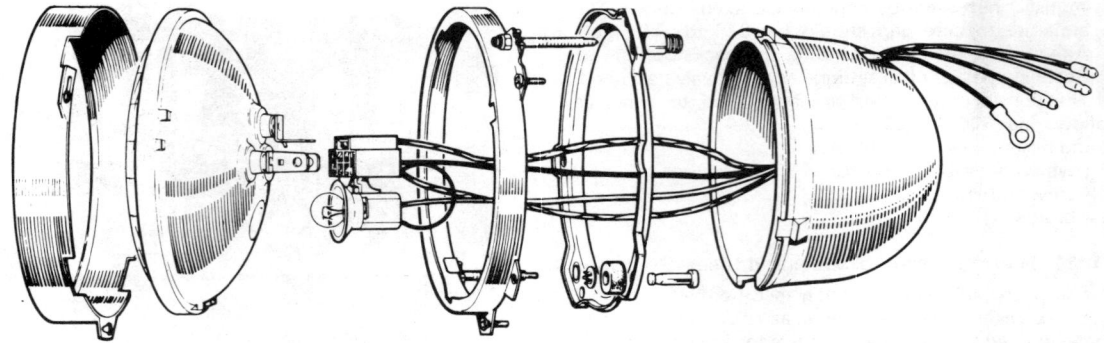

FIG 11:26 An exploded view of sealed beam headlamp components

square spigot on the switch body engaging in a recess in the housing to ensure positive location. Access to the horn push contacts is obtained by unscrewing the knob. The switch is accessible after removing the steering column canopy, which is secured by two screws.

The stoplamp switch is secured to the brake pedal support by two nuts threaded on the switch body. These enable the switch position to be adjusted. Stoplamps should operate with a brake pedal travel of .4 to .6 inch.

11:12 Headlamps, rear lamps

The four headlamp system incorporates sealed beam light units as shown in exploded form in **FIG 11:26**. The inner lamps have main beam filaments only (37.5 watt each on early cars. On later cars this was increased to 50 watts) while the outer lamps have supplementary main beam filaments of 37.5 watt and dipped beam filaments of 50 watt. When on main beam, all four lamps are in operation. Dipping the headlamps extinguishes the inner pair of lamps and switches the outer pair from main to dipped filament. A sidelamp bulb is incorporated in each outer headlamp, the bulb being located in a holder integral with the wiring adaptor and providing illumination through a transparent area in the light unit reflector.

Access to sidelamp bulbs and to wiring adaptors is obtained by squeezing the sides of the plastic cover (inside the bonnet) and withdrawing from lamp body. Access to the sealed beam light units is obtained after removal of the radiator grille. Slacken the three crosspoint screws in 'keyhole' slotted holes and turn the rim anticlockwise to release. When refitting light unit, the three screws should be fully tightened, as they are not used for aiming purposes.

Each headlamp is provided with two aiming screws. These are situated under the bonnet as shown in **FIG 11:27**. The screws can be rotated by using Adjuster VR.2024. Headlamp aiming should wherever possible be carried out by using an optical type beamsetter, so that this work will normally be carried out by a service agent. When checking headlamp aim the car must be on a level floor with tyres correctly inflated. The car must be at 'kerb weight' and if the car normally carries a heavy load at the rear end (as with an estate car) or draws a trailer, these loads should be on the car during checks. Inner lamps should be set so that the beam is $\frac{1}{2}$ deg. downwards with no lateral deflection. Outer lamps are checked on dipped

beam and set to give a deflection of 2 deg. downward and 2 deg. left.

Two makes of rear lamps are used, namely Lucas and Magnatex. These are similar in external appearance but their components are not interchangeable. The lamps are secured in the rear quarter panel by four studs and nuts. The two bulbholders in each lamp are mounted in a box retained by two or three screws according to make, or on later versions by screws and clips. The stop/tail bulb has offset pins to prevent incorrect fitting.

11:13 Direction indicators

Four lamp indicators are fitted, controlled by the combined switch on the steering column. The front indicators have separate lamps. Access to bulbs can be gained by removing the lens which is secured by two screws. The rear indicator bulbs are incorporated in the rear lamp assemblies which were described in the previous Section. The indicator flasher unit is clipped to the side of the instrument panel centre aperture and is accessible after removing the centre panel (see **Chapter 12**). The flasher unit is supplied by current through No. 2 fuse and the indicators only operate when the ignition is switched on. Failure of all four indicators may be due to the fuse having blown or making a bad connection. Check this

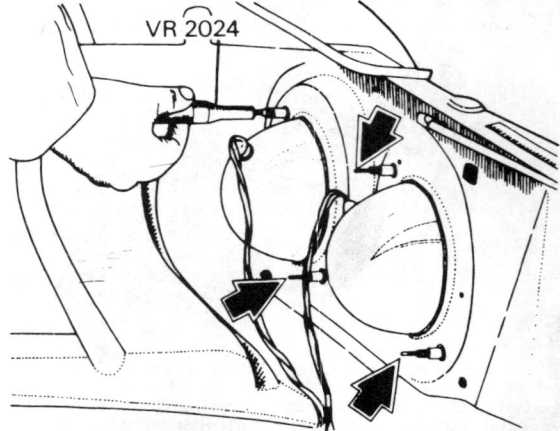

FIG 11:27 Headlamp aiming screws. Showing the special tool VR.2024 in use on one screw. Arrows indicate the other three screws

point by noting whether the other equipment controlled by the ignition switch and No. 2 fuse, such as petrol gauge, heater motor, still functions. If the fuse has blown, endeavour to ascertain the cause before renewing fuse. The flasher unit cannot be repaired and if faulty must be renewed. In this case the wiring should be carefully checked to ascertain the cause of the failure before fitting the new unit. Reference should be made to the wiring diagrams in the Appendix where the unit is shown as 'turn signal unit'.

11 : 14 Horn adjustment

On Victor models a single low-note horn is bracket-mounted to the righthand engine mount side rail under the front wing. On Victor 2000, and as an optional extra on Victor models, an additional horn (high-note) is fitted in a corresponding position on the other side rail. Ensure that the electrical connections are secure and that the bracket mountings are tight. To adjust the horn, rotate the slotted adjusting screw anticlockwise until there is no note from the horn, then turn clockwise until the horn is audible. Finally turn the screw another quarter of a turn clockwise. When adjusting twin horns, adjust each in turn, discon-necting the other one and protecting the cable from earthing.

11 : 15 Windscreen wipers

The windscreen wiper unit (see **FIG 11 : 28**) comprises a mounting bracket with a pivot housing riveted to each end and a single-speed electric motor secured to a centre

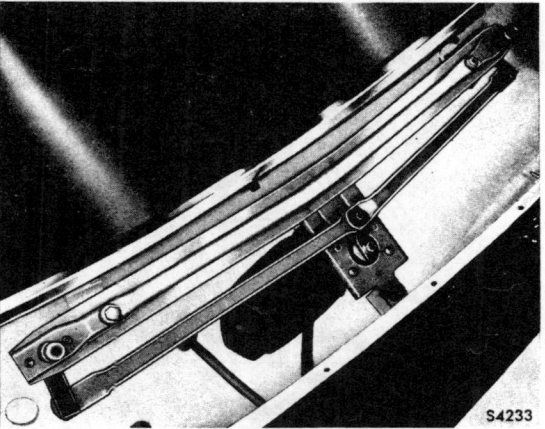

FIG 11 : 28 Access to windscreen wiper unit can be gained after removal of scuttle upper panel

plate by three screws. Two links connect the motor crank to pivot arms, one for each wiper. The driver's side pivot has a longer arm than that on the passenger side. A non-adjustable self-parking switch is incorporated in the motor. The wiper unit is housed in the plenum chamber (see Section on Heating and Ventilation System in **Chapter 12**). Access is gained by removing the scuttle upper panel (under the bonnet) as shown in **FIG 11 : 28**. After disconnecting the wiring harness plug, removing the

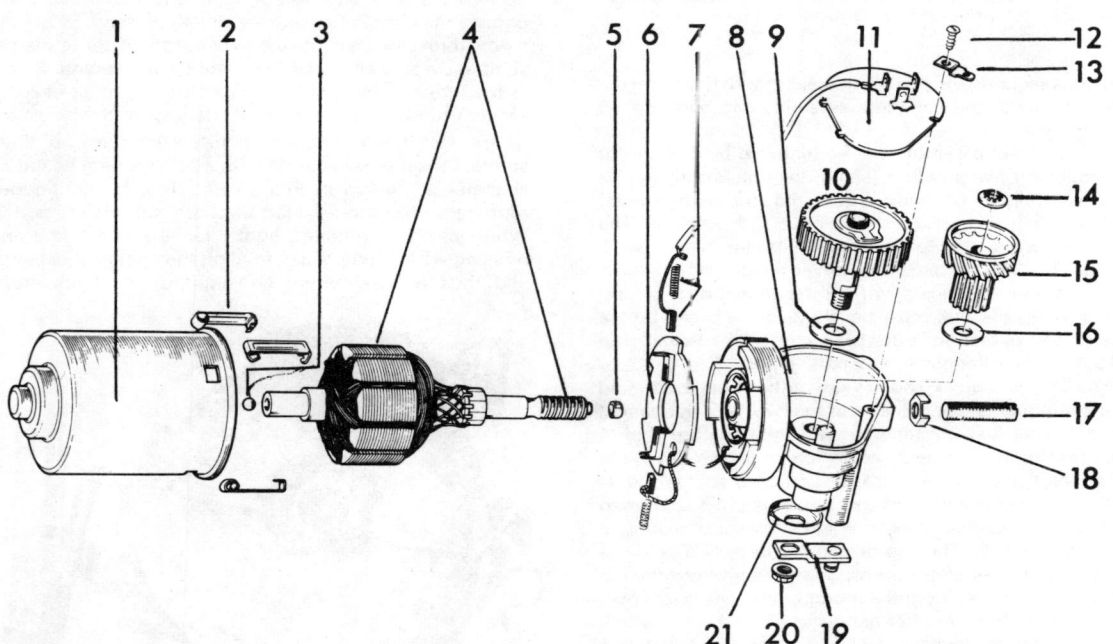

FIG 11 : 29 An exploded view of windscreen wiper motor

Key to Fig 11 : 29 1 End frame   2 Clips   3 Thrust ball   4 Armature and worm   5 Nylon thrust bearing
6 Brush plate   7 Brushes and springs   8 Gear housing   9 Cross shaft thrust washer   10 Gear and cross shaft
11 Gear cover   12 Gear cover screw   13 Terminal   14 Worm wheel retainer   15 Worm wheel   16 Worm wheel thrust washer   17 Armature thrust screw   18 Locknut   19 Motor crank   20 Cross shaft nut   21 Water shield

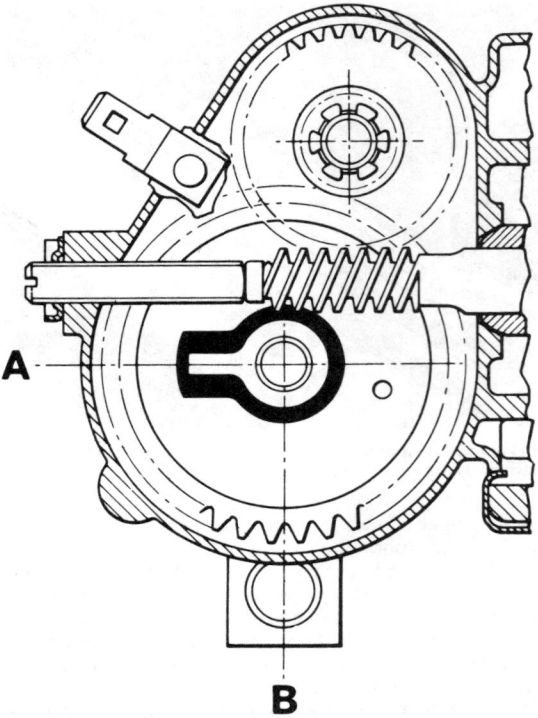

FIG 11 : 30 Windscreen wiper motor. Showing relative positions of A parking segment and B crank

two bolts securing the mounting bracket and detaching the rubber retainer, the complete assembly can be removed from the car.

A worn pivot assembly can be renewed by drilling out the attaching rivets with a $\frac{1}{8}$ inch dia. drill and riveting a new assembly in position. Ensure that the correct pivot for the specific side and for RHD or LHD is obtained. The motor is always fitted to the unit with its end frame (item 1 in **FIG 11 : 29**) towards the driver's side. When reassembling links lubricate with a recommended grease. The driver's side link must be fitted to the crank before that on the passenger side. Bushes must be installed in links with their flanges towards the crank.

FIG 11 : 29 is an exploded view of the wiper motor and gear components. The motor is of the two-pole permanent magnet type. A worm integral with the armature shaft 4 engages the worm wheel and pinion 15 which drives the cross-shaft gear 10. A crank 19 attached to the cross-shaft operates the wiper linkage. The armature is supported by a bush in the gear housing 8 and a spherical bearing in the end frame 1. The motor can be detached from its mounting bracket after removing wiper unit from the car and detaching links from the motor crank. The gear cover 11 can be withdrawn after removing the screw 12 which also secures the terminal 13. To release the end frame from the gear housing prise out the clips 2 from the slots in the frame. The end frame and armature can then be withdrawn taking care of the nylon thrust bearing 5 at the worm end of the shaft. Remove the brush plate 6 and gear cover 11 as an assembly. After removing the motor crank 19,

water shield 21 and armature thrust screw 17, prise off the worm wheel retainer 14 and withdraw the worm wheel 15 and the gear and cross-shaft 10. Take care of the thrust washers 9 and 16.

Motor bushes are not serviced separately, being supplied only with the gear housing and end frame respectively. Cross-shaft and gear are serviced as an assembly. To renew the earthed brush, cut the original brush lead $\frac{1}{4}$ inch from post and solder new brush lead to remaining part of old lead. Before installing the cross-shaft, pack the space between the bushes and coat the gear housing with a recommended grease. Do not omit thrust washer. The water shield and crank must be assembled so that relative positions of self-parking segment A and crank B are as shown in **FIG 11 : 30**. The cross-shaft should rotate freely without excessive end float after the crank nut is tightened to 12 lb ft. When installing worm wheel, a thrust washer must be fitted and the retainer pressed on the shaft until the wheel is free to rotate without excessive end float.

Before inserting the armature in the end frame, lubricate the bush with engine oil and apply anti-scuffing paste to the thrust ball recess in the shaft end. To ensure the ball is not misplaced, install it in bush before inserting the armature. Lubricate the bush in the housing with engine oil.

When assembling the armature and end frame to the gear housing, the brushes can be held in the retracted position by hooking their leads over the brush holder tags as shown in **FIG 11 : 31**. When armature and end frame are in position the brush leads can be released using a hooked piece of wire through the end frame clip slots. Engage the clips in the slots by thumb pressure. Fit a new nylon thrust washer on the worm end of the armature shaft and apply anti-scuffing paste to the bearing. Screw in the thrust screw until it is just clear of thrust bearing. Tighten the locknut to 12 lb ft. Refit gear cover.

To test the motor and adjust armature end float, connect the motor in circuit with a 12-volt battery and an ammeter as shown in **FIG 11 : 32**. Test for continuous running with a jumper lead between terminals 2 and 3. Whilst motor is running, lightly tap the end frame and housing with a hide mallet to align the spherical bearings and thus reduce current consumption to a minimum.

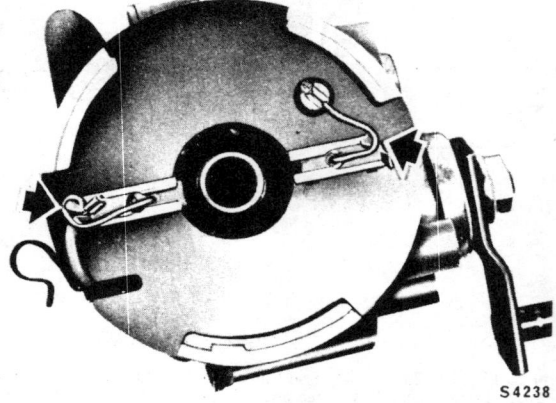

S4238

FIG 11 : 31 Showing method of retaining wiper motor brushes in retracted position during assembly

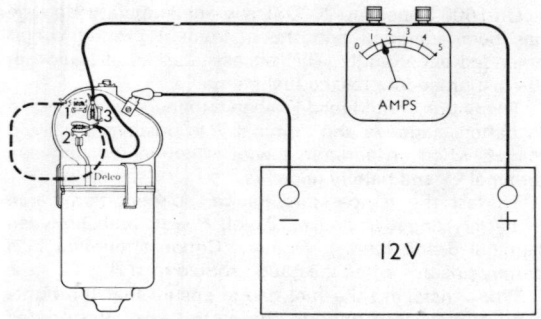

FIG 11:32   Wiper motor test circuit

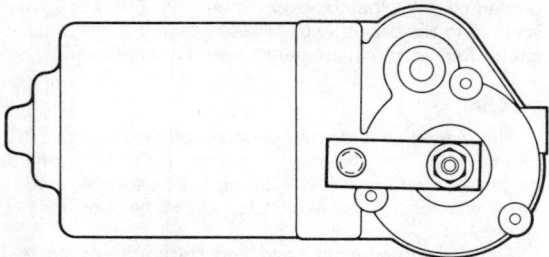

FIG 11:33   Wiper motor crank should come to rest in position shown

Adjust the armature end float by screwing in the thrust screw until the current increases by not more than .1-amp. Current should be checked after running light for 5 to 10 minutes. Retighten the locknut to 12 lb ft. To check for correct self-parking, transfer jumper lead from terminal 3 to terminal 1. Crank should come to rest in position shown in **FIG 11:33**. If it does not, the self-parking segment is incorrectly assembled.

Two alternative makes of windscreen wiper blades and arms are used, stamped 'Aeramic' or 'Tex'. They are interchangeable only as complete assemblies. The Aeramic arm is removed by easing from the spindle with a screwdriver. To remove the Tex arm, slacken the screw and tap screw inwards to release tapered wedge from spindle. The arms must be located on their spindles so that with the wiper motor in the parked position the centre of each blade is $1\frac{1}{2}$ inch above the lower edge of the windscreen.

11:16 Instruments

The instrument head assembly comprises a speedometer and matching instrument assembly including a fuel gauge and warning lamps for ignition, main beam, oil pressure and water temperature. A printed circuit attached to inner face of the combined instrument assembly connects the fuel gauge, instrument lamps and warning lamps via a multi-socket connector to the wiring harness. Access to the two instrument lamp holders and warning lamp holders can be gained through the centre panel aperture after releasing the instrument head assembly from the instrument panel. It is not necessary to detach the switches from the facia. For details of trim and panel removal, reference should be made to **Chapter 12**. The instrument lamp holders are the bayonet type and are withdrawn by turning anticlockwise. Warning lamp

holders are of the pull-out type. All the holders have capless wedge type bulbs.

If the fuel gauge is inoperative, first ensure that No. 2 fuse is not defective, by noting if oil and ignition warning lamps light when ignition is switched on. Also check connections to fuel gauge and to the tank unit.

FIG 11:34 shows the instrument head assembly with (left) speedometer and (right) the combined instrument assembly. To remove the fuel gauge from the casing, detach the instrument casing from the facia and withdraw all warning lamp bulb holders. Remove the clips (arrowed) securing the front glass and clips 1 securing instrument lamp lens. After removing two small screws (at front of instrument assembly) securing mask and lens, and two nuts 4, the fuel gauge can be withdrawn. **FIG 11:34** also shows the printed circuit, four square apertures for warning lamps and two bayonet sockets for instrument lamp holders. The speedometer can be removed from the casing after detaching clips (arrowed) securing front glass and clips 3 securing speedometer lamp lens, then removing the two screws 2.

After removal, the fuel gauge on early cars can be checked using a 12-volt battery and a spare multi-

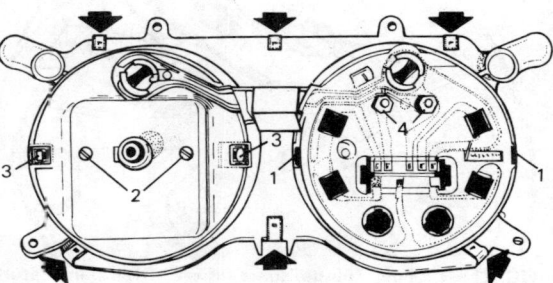

FIG 11:34   Instrument casing withdrawn from facia. Arrows indicate clips securing front glass

Key to Fig 11:34   1 Clips securing instrument lamp lens
2 Securing screws   3 Clips securing speedometer lamp lens
4 Nuts securing speedometer head

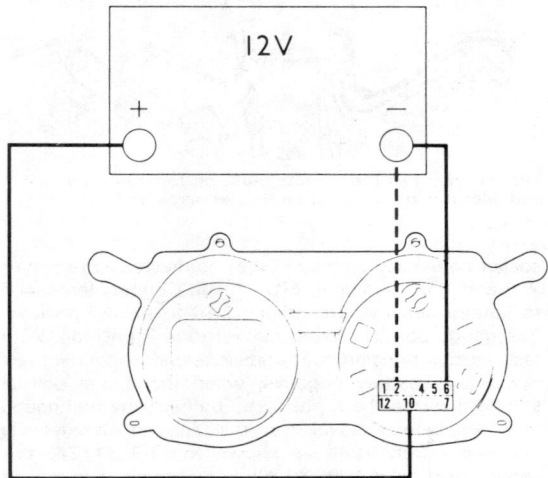

FIG 11:35   Fuel gauge test circuit

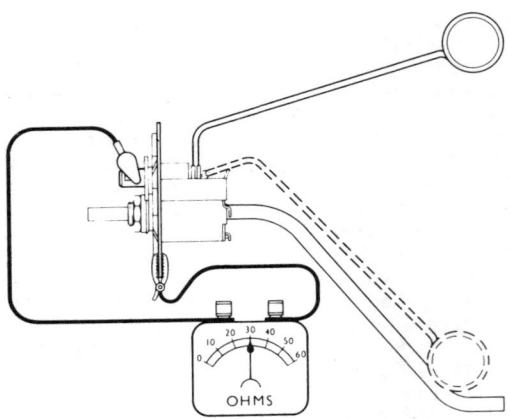

FIG 11:36 Fuel gauge tank unit test circuit

FIG 11:37 Fuel gauge installation. Righthand stud must pass through earth tag of printed circuit

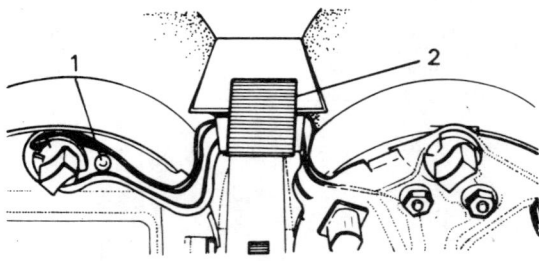

FIG 11:38 Printed circuit must be located over peg 1 and secured to casing by adhesive tape at 2

socket connector with test wires connected to terminals 2, 6 and 10 as shown in **FIG 11:35.** Connect terminal 6 to battery negative and terminal 10 to battery positive. The gauge pointer should move to the F position. With test wires connected as for previous check, connect terminal 2 to battery negative, when the gauge pointer should move to the E position. To check the fuel gauge tank unit, after removal from the tank, an ohmmeter is necessary. Connected as shown in **FIG 11:36,** this should read from 1 to 30 ohms as the float is moved through its complete arc.

On 1600 Super and 2000SL a water temperature gauge has been included and the instrument printed circuit amended accordingly. This necessitates an alteration in the test procedure for the fuel gauge.

The gauge should read F when terminal 4 is connected to battery negative and terminal 7 to positive. It should read E when an additional wire is connected between terminal 11 and battery negative.

To test the temperature gauge, connect terminal 4 to battery negative and a 12-volt 6 watt bulb between terminal 6 and battery negative. Connect terminal 7 to battery positive when the gauge should read H.

When installing the fuel gauge ensure that the right-hand stud passes through the earth tag of the printed circuit inside the casing (arrowed in **FIG 11:37**). Before installing the instrument head assembly ensure that the printed circuit is located over the peg 1 in **FIG 11:38** and secured to the casing with adhesive tape 2 to prevent the circuit fouling the instrument panel reinforcement.

VX4/90:

The individual water temperature, oil pressure and fuel gauge, and the ammeter, together with the ignition, oil pressure and low fuel warning lamps are mounted in the lower facia panel which is held in position by five screws.

The main instrument head and surround is detached from the instrument panel by removing four screws after removing the lower facia panel.

Warning lights for main beam, lights on and turn signals can be withdrawn by prising out the appropriate assembly with a screwdriver.

The switches for the two-speed windscreen wipers and the screen wash are mounted in the centre console which can be prised upwards for access.

11:17 Alternator

An alternator charging system, comprising alternator, regulator, relay and warning lamp control, is fitted to all cars with the 2000 engine and is available on cars with the 1600 engine as an alternative to the standard generator.

In the event of trouble being experienced with the alternator system, the owner is recommended to seek the advice of a service agent. Not only is specialized equipment needed for electrical checks and repairs, but a wrong connection can cause instant and irreparable damage to the diodes incorporated in the alternator. In any case, the following precautions must be observed when carrying out any work on cars fitted with alternators:

1 All alternator systems have negative earth. **Great care must be taken not to connect the battery wrongly, as accidental reversal of the leads will burn out the diodes in the alternator and can damage the wiring harness.**

2 Battery leads and any wires in the charging system must not be disconnected while the engine is running.

3 When charging the battery from an outside source, disconnect the car battery leads. If the battery is not disconnected and the car is inadvertently started during boost charging, the transistors in the regulator will be damaged.

Although the owner is not advised to attempt repairs, a brief description of alternator principles may be of

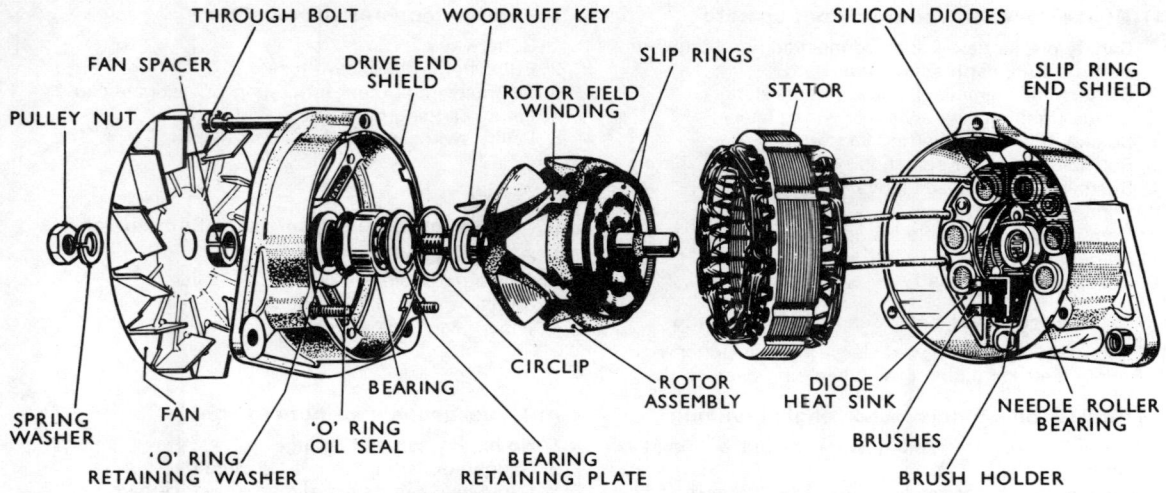

FIG 11:39   An exploded view of the Lucas 10AC alternator

THROUGH BOLT
WOODRUFF KEY
SILICON DIODES
FAN SPACER
DRIVE END SHIELD
SLIP RINGS
ROTOR FIELD WINDING
STATOR
SLIP RING END SHIELD
PULLEY NUT
BEARING
CIRCLIP
ROTOR ASSEMBLY
DIODE HEAT SINK
NEEDLE ROLLER BEARING
SPRING WASHER
FAN
'O' RING OIL SEAL
BEARING RETAINING PLATE
BRUSHES
BRUSH HOLDER
'O' RING RETAINING WASHER

interest. In the more familiar dynamo or DC generator, the output windings of the armature revolve in the magnetic field of stationary magnets energized by the fixed field coils. In the alternator, or AC generator, the position of the components is reversed, as will be seen from the exploded view in **FIG 11 : 39**. The stator or fixed element carries the output windings, while the rotor or rotating component carries the field magnets and field coils. These are supplied with the necessary energizing current through brushes acting on plain, face-type slip rings. The alternating current produced in the output windings is rectified by six silicon diodes carried in the end bracket. The main advantages of the alternator are that the output windings, being stationary, can be larger, thus giving greater output especially at low speeds. Absence of a commutator obviates brush troubles and at the same time permits a higher maximum speed.

The alternator is self-regulating in regard to current output, the only external control being a regulator to keep the voltage within the necessary limits. In the Lucas system the 4TR regulator, a transistorized unit, is employed. No cut-out is necessary, as the diodes will only pass current in one direction, so that it cannot flow back from the battery through the output winding at low speeds. A relay is needed, however, to disconnect the battery from the field circuit when the engine is stationary and the Lucas 6RA relay is fitted for this purpose. Owing to the absence of a reverse current, the normal method of warning lamp operation cannot be used. In the Lucas system the 3AW warning lamp control, which is a thermally-operated relay, is used. To distinguish the relay from flasher units of similar external appearance it has a green label. A diagram showing wiring connections for alternator systems is shown in the Appendix.

As previously stated, the advice of a service agent should be sought in cases of trouble with the alternator system. It should be noted, however, that an alternator when functioning correctly produces a characteristic magnetic hum. This should not be confused with the much louder hum caused by a faulty diode, which will be accompanied by serious loss of output, or with the noise caused by a faulty alternator bearing.

On the later cars covered by this manual alternators with built-in regulators are used, either Lucas 15ACR or 17ACR, or AC-Delco 28 amp or 35 amp types.

11 : 18 Fault diagnosis

(a) Battery discharged

1 Terminals or earth connection loose or dirty
2 Lighting circuit shorted
3 Generator not charging
4 Cut-out contacts not opening
5 Battery internally defective

(b) Insufficient charging current

1 Loose or corroded battery terminals
2 Generator or alternator drive belt slipping
3 Alternator system defects (see **Section 11 : 17**)

(c) Battery will not hold charge

1 Low electrolyte level
2 Battery plates sulphated
3 Electrolyte leaking from casing or top sealing compound
4 Plate separators ineffective

(d) Battery overcharged

1 Controller needs adjustment

(e) Generator or alternator output low or nil

1 Belt broken or slipping
   The following apply to generators only (for alternator defects refer to **Section 11 : 17**).
2 Controller needs adjustment
3 Worn generator bearings, loose polepieces
4 Commutator worn, burnt or shorted
5 Armature shaft bent or worn
6 Insulation proud between commutator segments
7 Brushes sticking, springs weak or broken
8 Field coil wires shorted, broken or burnt

(f) Starter lacks power or will not operate

1 Battery discharged. Loose connections on battery or starter. Faulty earth connection
2 Starter pinion jammed in mesh (inertia starter)
3 Starter (ignition key) switch or wiring faulty
4 Solenoid switch faulty (inertia starter)
5 Solenoid switch or actuating lever faulty (PE starter)
6 Brushes or brush leads faulty
7 Commutator dirty or worn
8 Commutator or field coils faulty
9 Starter shaft bent
10 Engine abnormally stiff

(g) Starter revolves but does not turn engine

1 Pinion sticking on screwed sleeve (inertia starter)
2 Broken teeth on pinion or flywheel ring gear

(h) Starter pinion noisy when engine running

1 Anti-drift or control spring weak or broken (inertia starter)
2 Actuating lever incorrectly adjusted (PE starter)

(j) Starter motor rough or noisy

1 Check 2 in (h) (PE starter)
2 Mounting bolts loose
3 Damaged pinion or ring gear
4 Main pinion spring broken (inertia starter)

(k) Lamps inoperative or erratic

1 Battery low
2 Bulbs burnt out, blown fuse
3 Thermal circuit breaker opening (investigate cause)
4 Faulty earthing of lamps or battery
5 Faulty switches or wiring

(l) Wiper motor sluggish, takes high current

1 Faulty armature
2 Commutator dirty or brushes defective
3 Armature end float incorrectly adjusted
4 Wiper gearshafts seized, linkages seized

(m) Fuel gauge does not register

1 No battery supply to gauge
2 Gauge not earthed to printed circuit
3 Cable between gauge and tank unit earthed
4 Tank unit faulty

(n) Fuel gauge registers 'Full'

1 Wire between gauge and tank unit broken

CHAPTER 12

THE BODYWORK

12:1 Removing door trim

The trim pads are attached to the inside of the doors by clips at the bottom and sides and by retainer brackets at the top. On the back door (tailgate) of the estate car the trim pad is attached by clips only. The front and rear doors on all models have a polythene water deflector attached to the door inner panel by adhesive. Before removing trim pads it is necessary to remove inside handles, ashtray container, locking knob and door pull or armrest according to model.

Door inside handles are secured by a screw in the centre of each handle boss. The screws are concealed by inserts sprung into position in the handles. A wearing disc or spacer is fitted between each handle and the trim pad except in the case of remote control handles on cars fitted with armrests. Where an armrest is fitted, this must be removed before removing the remote control handle. Each armrest is attached by a screw which is accessible when the remote control handle is lifted, and by a bracket attached to the door. Door pulls are attached by screws concealed by finishers. To remove, slide each finisher away from the pull and remove screws.

FIG 12:1 shows the method of prising the door trim pad away from the door panel using a thin blade. Release the bottom and side clips in this way and then lift the pad upwards to release retainer brackets, taking care not to dislodge the rubber retainers in the top edge of the door inner panel.

Carefully peel away the polythene water deflector. This should be renewed if defective. Remove all traces of old adhesive from the door panel. Ensure that the drain holes in the bottom of the door are clear. Renew drain hole dust seals if necessary, applying trim adhesive to the mating surfaces of seal and door except for the flap of seal which must be free to open. When fitting water deflector, smooth out any wrinkles, especially along the lower edge, otherwise water may percolate past the door inner panel and soak the trim pad.

12:2 Servicing door locks, remote control gear

The outside handle of each door incorporates a push-button and lock barrel. A rotary bolt type lock assembly is mounted inside the door shut face and engages an adjustable striker on the body pillar. The lock and handle components are shown in **FIG 12:2** while the striker is shown in **FIG 12:3**. Periodic attention is a follows. First wipe off all old lubricant and dirt. Apply a thin coating of high melting point grease to the rotary pinion teeth, the shoe spring plunger (in the striker) and to the striker teeth. Apply a drop of light oil to the pinion spindle. Close and open the door several times and then wipe off all surplus lubricant from the side of the striker teeth and the lock extension. Door hinge pins and check link rivets (see **FIG 12:6**) should be lubricated with engine oil, a thin coating of high melting point grease sufficing for the check links themselves. Lock barrels should be lubricated sparingly with a special lock oil such as Slip, which prevents freezing down to —40°F.

To remove the door lock:

1 Remove inside handles, trim pad and water deflector as described in the previous Section.

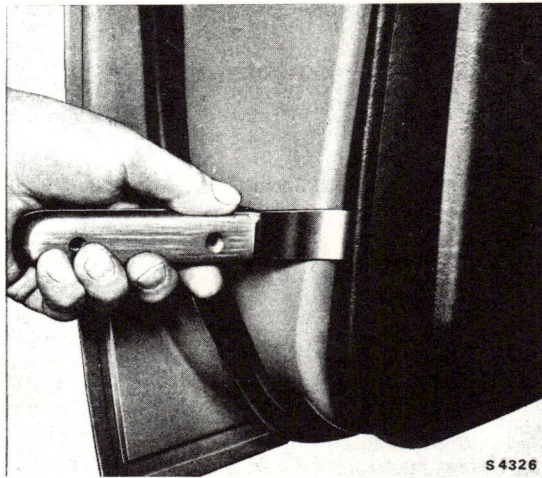

FIG 12:1   Method of removing door trim

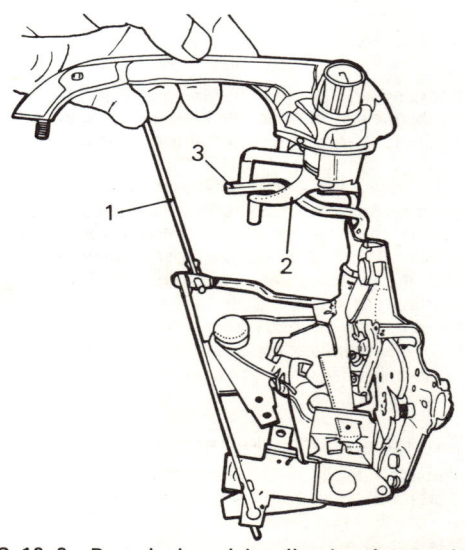

FIG 12:2   Door lock and handle showing method of assembly. Components are shown removed from door for purposes of illustration

Key to Fig 12:2   1 Locking rod   2 Handle locking lever
3 Lock bar

2 Remove the outside handle. This is secured by two nuts inside the door panel. The window should be in the fully closed position for access to these nuts. The handle can then be withdrawn after turning until its free end is uppermost.

3 Disconnect the remote control rod 2 in **FIG 12:4**.

4 Remove the glass run channel retainer attaching screws.

5 Remove the three screws securing the lock to the door shut face. The lock can now be withdrawn complete with locking rod.

To release the push-button from the handle, remove the spring clip (see **FIG 12:5**) from the boss of the handle. To release the lock barrel from the push-button, press down the spring-loaded plunger in the end of the barrel, then remove extension and withdraw lock barrel.

Before reassembling lock barrel, lubricate barrel wards with light oil or with a special lock oil. Smear friction surfaces of barrel extension with high melting point grease. When assembling locking lever, place gaskets in position on handle and ensure that the key of the retaining plate, arrowed in **FIG 12:5**, engages the groove in the handle boss before easing the spring clip into position. Before installing the door lock, lubricate the friction surfaces with high melting point grease. Referring to **FIG 12:2**, which shows the components removed from the car for clarity of illustration, assemble the locking rod 1 to the lock bar. When installing the outside handle, ensure that the forked ends of the handle locking lever 2 are positioned on either side of the lock bar 3.

When refitting the remote control (see **FIG 12:4**), ensure that an anti-rattle spring is securely attached to each end of the connecting rod 2 and that the rod is fitted to the lower hole in the door lock upper plate 3. Before tightening the control attaching screws, gently ease the control 1 towards the front lower corner of the door to take up any slackness between the lock upper plate and lock. All friction surfaces should be lightly smeared with high melting point grease.

FIG 12:3   Door lock striker adjustment. After taking impression of lock in plasticine, dimension A must not exceed .18 inch

VERNONS COPY COUPON

RESULTS

6 GOES A PENNY — TREBLE CHANCE — 4 DRAWS-9 HOMES-5 AWAYS

	A	B	C	D	E	F	No.	Home	Away						
							1	ARSENAL	LIVERPOOL						
			✗				2	ASTON VILLA	SUNDERLAND						
							3	COVENTRY	NOTTS C.						
			✗				4	EVERTON	SOUTH'PTON						
							5	IPSWICH	MAN. UTD.						
							6	MAN. CITY	STOKE						
							7	MIDDLESBRO'	BRIGHTON						
							8	NOTT'M FOR.	BIRMINGHAM						
							9	WEST HAM	TOTTENHAM						
							10	WOLVES	LEEDS						
							11	BARNSLEY	NORWICH						
							12	BLACKBURN	CHARLTON						
							13	CHELSEA	CARDIFF						
		✗					14	CRYSTAL P.	SHEFF. WED.						
							15	DERBY	SHREWSBURY						
		✗					16	GRIMSBY	ORIENT						
							17	LUTON	Q.P.R.						
							18	NEWCASTLE	BOLTON						
							19	OLDHAM	WATFORD						
							20	ROTHERHAM	CAMB'GE U.						
							21	WREXHAM	LEICESTER						
		✗					22	BRISTOL R.	CHESTERF'LD						
							23	CARLISLE	EXETER						
							24	DONCASTER	BRISTOL C.						
		✗					25	FULHAM	LINCOLN						
							26	GILLINGHAM	READING						
							27	HUDDERSF'LD	OXFORD UTD.						
							28	NEWPORT	SOUTHEND						
							29	PLYMOUTH	BURNLEY						
							30	PORTSMOUTH	PRESTON						
		✗					31	WALSALL	BRENTFORD						
							32	ALDERSHOT	STOCKPORT						
							33	BLACKPOOL	SCUNTHORPE						
							34	BOURNEM'TH	MANSFIELD						
		✗					35	BRADFORD C.	HULL						
							36	BURY	HEREFORD						
							37	HARTLEPOOL	ROCHDALE						
							38	NORTH'PTON	YORK						
							39	PETERBORO'	HALIFAX						
							40	PORT VALE	DARLINGTON						
		✗					41	SHEFF. UTD.	WIGAN A.						
							42	BUXTON	BURTON A.						
							43	GAINSBORO'	WORKINGTON						
							44	GOOLE	MATLOCK						
		✗					45	KING'S LYNN	MOSSLEY						
							46	ABERDEEN	HIBERNIAN						
							47	AIRDRIE	ST. MIRREN						
							48	DUNDEE	PARTICK						
							49	MORTON	DUNDEE UTD.						
		✗					50	RANGERS	CELTIC						
							51	AYR	MOTHERWELL						
							52	CLYDEBANK	RAITH						
							53	DUNF'MLINE	QUEENS PK.						
							54	FALKIRK	KILMARNOCK						
		✗					55	HAMILTON	DUMBARTON						

A B C D E F

Treble Chance Stakes
MIN. ½p. MAX. 1p. PER LINE

5 DIVIDENDS

TREBLE CHANCE POINTS. 3 points for a SCORE-DRAW (1-1, 2-2 etc.) 2 points for a NO SCORE DRAW (0-0)
1½ points for an AWAY WIN (1-2 etc.) 1 point for a HOME WIN (2-1 etc.) 1½ points for a void match.

FOR MATCHES PLAYED SAT.

JAN. 9 1982

Printed by Norman B Burgess, Liverpool.

VERNONS POOLS. Proprietors: VERNONS ORGANISATION LTD. Directors: R. E. Sangster, (Chairman) V. E. Sangster (Deputy Chairman) G. R. Kennerley (Managing Director) K. A. Paul F.C.A. J. R. Kennerley, Executive Directors: T. Thatcher, R. R. Stephenson, K. R. LeFauve.

© The Football League Ltd. 1981 and © The Scottish Football League 1981

FIG 12:3 shows a door lock striker plate. The striker can be adjusted up or down or in or out as required. To check fore and aft location of striker, apply plasticine to notch of striker and push door towards striker to form an impression. If the dimension A is greater than .18 inch, a packing plate or plates should be installed between the striker adjusting plates and the body panel to correct.

To remove a front door check link (see FIG 12:6), place the door in the fully open position and remove the screw 1 from the end of the link, then ease the spring over the pip on the hinge plate 2 and pull check link and spring away from the roller 3. When installing check link, lubricate friction surfaces of the roller with high melting point grease.

To remove the back door (tailgate) catch on estate cars, remove the door trim pad. Push the turn button retainer plate towards the turn button and release the turn button from the connecting rod. When installing, lubricate the door catch and rod ends with high melting point grease and engage the end of the rod in the catch release plate hole furthest from the turn button. The door striker plate bolt holes are slotted for adjustment. An adjusting plate with non-slip surfaces is fitted between the striker and the body panel. After lowering the door gently into position, it may be necessary to move the striker sideways to maintain door alignment. The striker can then be adjusted up or down until the door closes with normal firm hand pressure.

12:3 Servicing window winders, renewing glass

FIG 12:7 is a cutaway view of the door panel showing the window winder mechanism. This incorporates two balance arms riveted to a main arm. The balance arms pivot about the rivet to ensure an equal lift at the front and rear of the glass. The lower balance arm engages a support channel (arrowed in FIG 12:7) bolted to the door inner panel. To remove a window winder, remove the trim pad and deflector as described in Section 12:1. Wedge the glass in the fully closed position and remove the lower balance arm support channel and the window buffer bracket from the inner panel. The winder mechanism can then be withdrawn. When refitting the window winder mechanism, adjust the lower balance arm support channel

stud (arrowed in FIG 12:8) up or down until the upper edge of the window glass is parallel with the door frame.

To renew door window glasses, on cars not fitted with ventilators, the glass can be removed after removing the window winder as described. On cars fitted with door

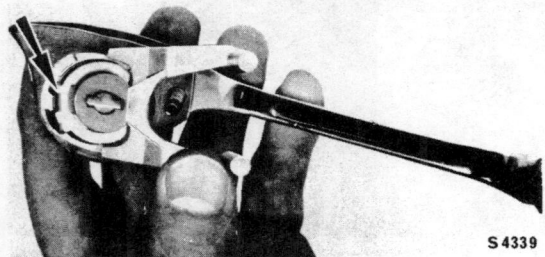

FIG 12:5 Assembling locking lever. Key of retaining plate (arrowed) must engage in handle boss before fitting spring clip

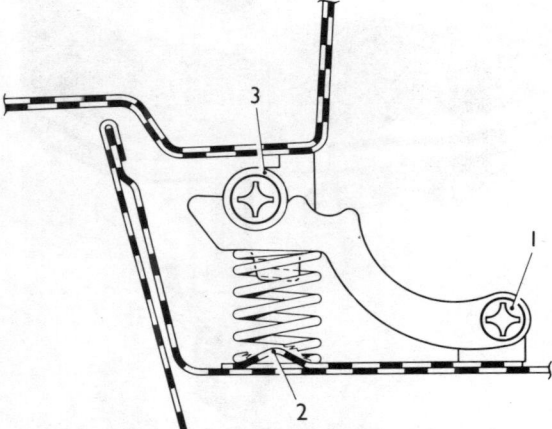

FIG 12:6 Sectional view showing front door check link details

Key to Fig 12:6   1 Screw   2 Hinge plate   3 Roller

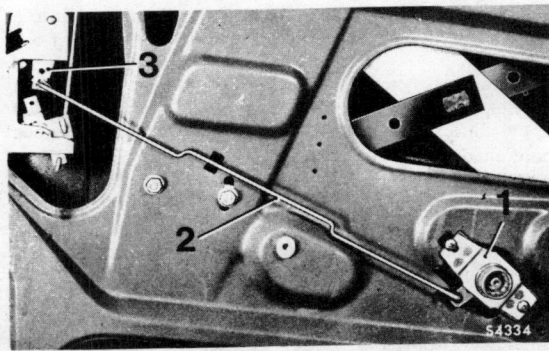

FIG 12:4 Front and rear door inside handle remote controls. Rod must be assembled to lower hole in door lock upper plate

Key to Fig 12:4   1 Remote control   2 Connecting rod
3 Door lock upper plate

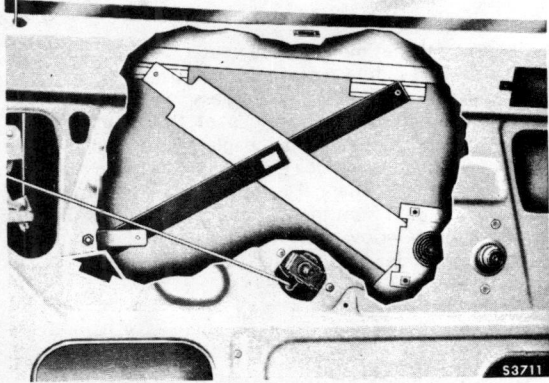

FIG 12:7 Cutaway view of door panel showing details of front door window winder mechanism. Rear door window mechanism is similar but includes an additional vertical guide channel to control sideways movement of glass

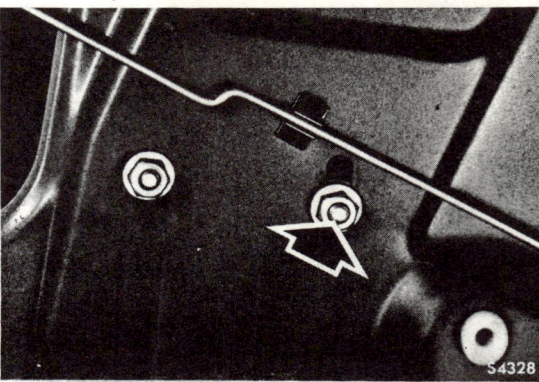

FIG 12:8 After installing window winder, adjust lower balance arm support channel stud (arrowed) up or down until upper edge of glass is parallel with door frame

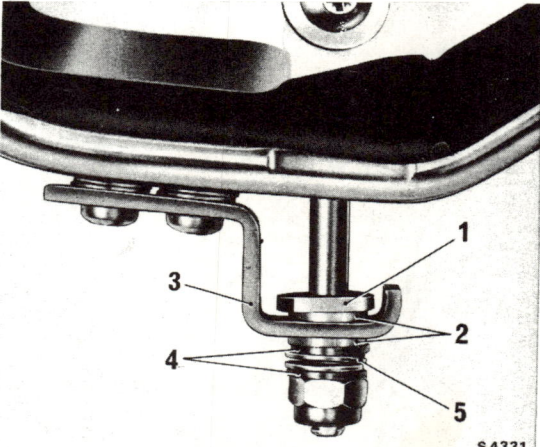

FIG 12:9 Ventilator lower pivot and friction control
Key to Fig 12:9   1 Ventilator stop   2 Plastic washers
3 Support bracket   4 Plain washers   5 Spring washer

ventilators, these must be removed as described in **Section 12:4** before removal of window glass.

When renewing a window glass or glass support channel, smear the inside faces of the channel with engine oil and assemble to the glass so that the open sides of the channel guides are towards the inside face of the glass and the channel is positioned so that its rear edge is 4.30 inch from the rear edge of the glass. Before installing the window or winder, smear friction surfaces of channel guides and winder with high melting point grease.

12:4 Removing door ventilators

On some models the front doors incorporate pivoting ventilator windows. The lower pivot has an adjustable friction control (see **FIG 12:9**) which retains the window in any set position. A swivel handle attached to the glass locks the ventilator in the closed position.

To remove the ventilator:
1 Remove door trim and deflector (see **Section 12:1**).
2 Ease the door weatherstrip out of its channel to give access to two screws in the front of the door. These hold the ventilator frame.
3 The rear edge of the ventilator frame is riveted to the division channel. Remove the screw securing the bottom end of the division channel to the door inner panel. Remove the window sealing strips (see **FIG 12:10**).
4 Withdraw the ventilator complete with division channel by easing towards the rear and lifting out.

To renew ventilator window glass, remove the friction control (see **FIG 12:9**), including the support bracket 3, from the lower pivot. Push the window downwards to release the upper pivot and withdraw window. Upper pivot and locking handle are serviced as an assembly with the glass. Before fitting the window, the upper pivot and the tapered face of the lower pivot should be smeared with silicone grease. Referring to **FIG 12:9**, assemble the friction control as follows. With window in closed position, locate the stop 1 as shown, followed by a plastic washer 2, support bracket 3, plastic washer 2, plain washer 4, spring washer 5, plain washer 4 and nut. Before tightening the friction control nut, ensure that there is a clearance of .020 to .040 between the mating faces of the upper pivot brackets. Adjust if necessary by adding a plain washer between the stop and the plastic washer, or fibre washers between the support bracket and the frame. Next tighten the support bracket screws, after adjusting the bracket backwards or forwards so that the window closes firmly on the weatherstrip when in the locked position. Tighten the friction control nut sufficiently to prevent the window closing under wind pressure.

12:5 Windscreen and fixed glasses

The windscreen is either of toughened glass incorporating a wide safety zone, or of laminated glass. Each type of glass can be identified by the manufacturer's symbol with 'kite' mark etched in the centre at the top or bottom of the screen.

Windscreen, backlight and estate car rear quarter lights are bonded into the body apertures using a special caulking adhesive and primer. This is available in kit form. The renewal of windscreen glasses may be entrusted to a service agent with the required facilities for carrying out this work.

Water leaks around the windscreen or other fixed glasses can, however, often be rectified without removal of the glass, using the special primer and caulking adhesive contained in the kit mentioned. It will be necessary first to remove the reveal mouldings which cover the edge of the glass. The windscreen side reveal mouldings are attached with rustless pop rivets, while the lower reveal is retained by clips fitted over the body flange. The windscreen upper reveal and the backlight reveals are held by clips which are secured by pop rivets or fitted to pegs welded to the body. If any of these clips become detached from the body, special replacements are available which can be attached with a No. 4 self-tapping screw: a $\frac{3}{32}$ inch hole is first drilled in the body flange. When removing or installing a reveal moulding, care must be taken to avoid damaging paintwork, scratching the glass, or bending the moulding itself.

Referring to **FIG 12:11** proceed as follows. Trim off adhesive protruding beyond edge of glass in the affected area, as shown at A. Brush a thin coating of primer over the surfaces indicated by arrows at A. Do not allow the primer to come into contact with polished surface of paintwork. Apply caulking adhesive as indicated by the arrow at B. Then work adhesive into leak area 1 using a flat bladed tool 2 as shown at C. When carrying out a water test, do not apply high pressure water supply directly on to freshly applied caulking adhesive as this takes several hours to set.

The backlight glass (or rear window) is of toughened glass except for the heated type which is laminated. When cutting adhesive caulking around this type of glass, care must be taken to avoid cutting the wire connection.

12:6 Heating and ventilating system

Controlled ventilation of the car interior is provided by a ventilator assembly mounted under the bonnet on a full width plenum chamber which is integral with the body structure. Fresh air enters the ventilator through two intakes in the scuttle upper panel and is distributed to various points inside the car. It is eventually extracted through slotted holes at each side of the rear window, or on estate cars at the back of the roof. In addition to the main ventilation system, air outlets at each side of the instrument panel, with individual volume and direction controls, provide a direct flow of unheated fresh air as required.

Where a heater is fitted, this is incorporated in the main ventilator assembly and consists of a radiator, electric blower unit and a thermostatically-controlled water valve. The ventilator and heater controls, shown in exploded form in **FIG 12:12** are mounted in the centre of the instrument panel.

The individual air outlets are each attached to the instrument panel by one screw. Each outlet has a tubular extension protruding into the plenum chamber, where it is sealed by a rubber grommet. When refitting air outlet, ensure that the grommet is seating against the plenum chamber panel, otherwise water may leak into the car at this point.

The scuttle ventilator assembly is secured to the plenum chamber by fourteen screws. To gain access to four of the screws the front outlet duct must first be removed. Two screws are concealed by a rubber plug. After releasing the control wire from the nipple in the air distribution valve lever, the ventilator can then be removed as an assembly.

To remove the distribution valve, referring to **FIG 12:13**, bend back the tab 2, ease out the key 3 and withdraw spindle 4. The valve 1 can then be lifted out.

When reassembling, the valve can be installed either way round. After aligning the keyway on the spindle with the cutaway in the valve, press in the key with its flat side edges against the valve, then bend up the valve tab to retain the key.

After installing the ventilator casing, set the ventilator control to the SCREEN position and hold the air distribution valve against the stop on the casing boss, then tighten the nipple screw to secure the control wire. Operate the control knob to CAR position and check for full movement of the valves.

The ventilator control is attached to an escutcheon by two screws (see **FIG 12:12**). Where a heater is fitted, a

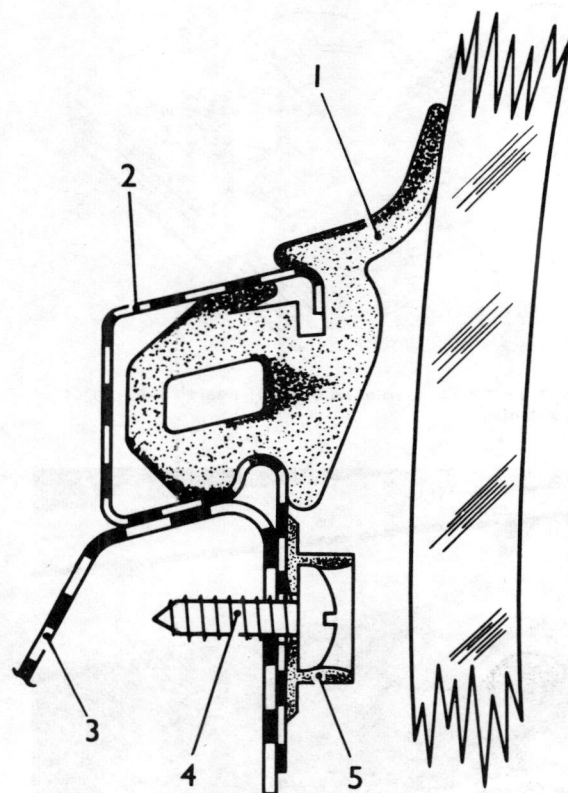

FIG 12:10 Sectional view of door outer sealing strip

Key to Fig 12:10 1 Outer sealing strip 2 Waist moulding 3 Door outer panel 4 Securing screws 5 Centre screw buffer (front doors only)

FIG 12:11 Rectifying windscreen water leaks. For details of operations A, B and C, see text

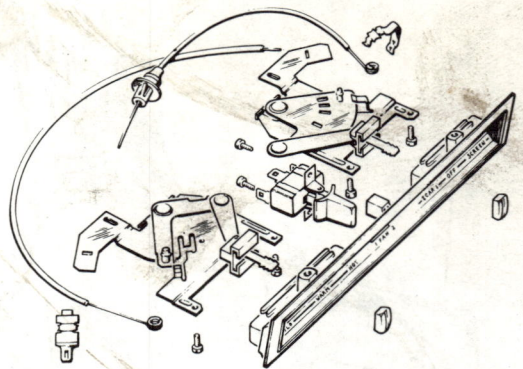

FIG 12:12 An exploded view of heater and ventilator controls

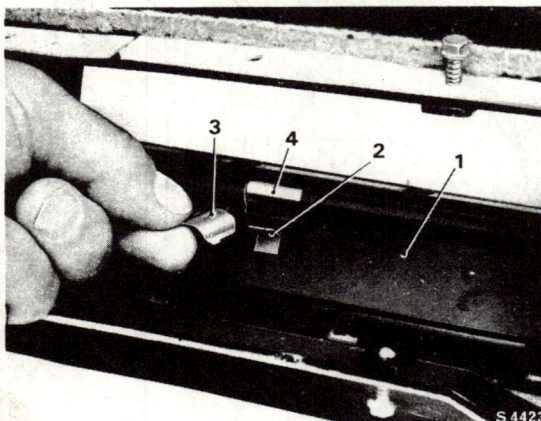

FIG 12:13 Air distribution valve

Key to Fig 12:13   1 Valve   2 Tab   3 Key   4 Spindle

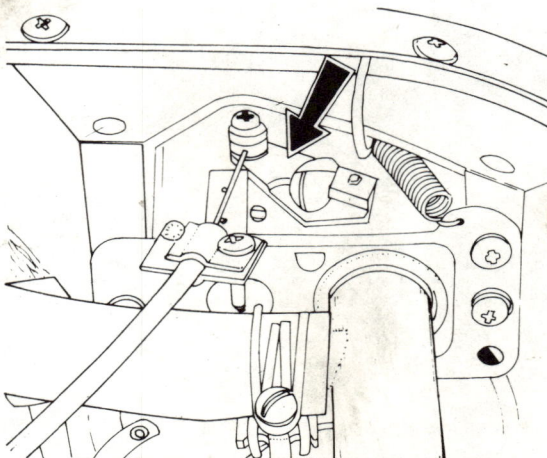

FIG 12:14 Heater water valve adjustment. Arrow indicates water valve lever

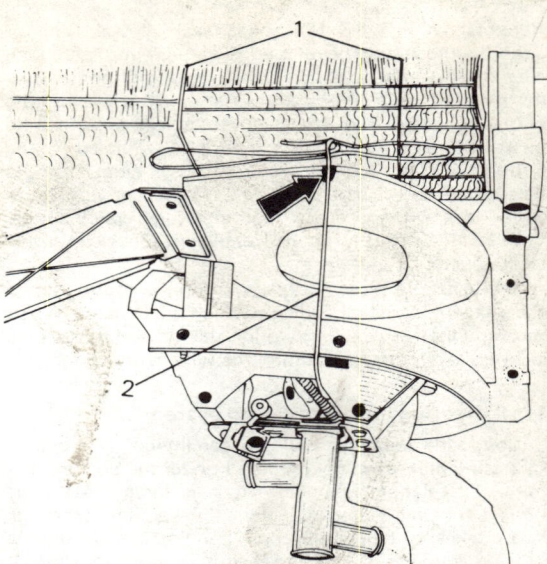

FIG 12:15 Heater water valve and thermostat. Arrow indicates slot in lower casing for capillary tube
Key to Fig 12:15   1 Clips   2 Capillary tube

FIG 12:16 Heater connections. Arrow indicates water valve inlet pipe which should be connected to hose from engine thermostat housing

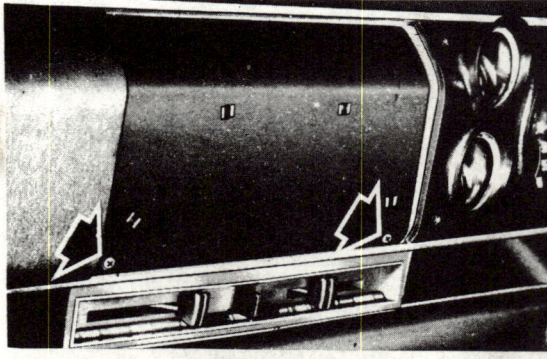

FIG 12:17 Facia centre panel is attached to instrument panel by two screws (arrowed) and two clips at the top. Screws are accessible after easing centre cover away from panel

separate heater control and fan switch are attached to the same escutcheon. The controls are connected by cables to the ventilator air distribution valve and heater water valve respectively. The control unit can be removed as a complete assembly after removing the instrument centre panel (see **Section 12:7**) for access to the four securing screws and also releasing inner and outer cables from controls and wires from fan switch. The control knobs are a press-fit on levers and must be withdrawn carefully to prevent damage to escutcheon.

When refitting control knobs, note that the one with the blue stripe goes on the ventilator control lever and the knob with the red strip on the heater lever. The heater motor fan switch should be assembled to the control unit with its centre terminal uppermost. Connect the heater harness black wire to the switch centre terminal, black/blue wire to lefthand terminal and green/yellow wire to the remaining (smaller) terminal. The black/blue and green/yellow wires must be connected so that they lead upwards from the switch, otherwise they may be damaged or dislodged when the controls are operated. After connecting the cables to the control unit, check the operation of the control levers. With the ventilator control in the SCREEN position the air distribution valve inside the ventilator casing should be against its stop. With the heater control lever in the COLD position, the heater water valve should be completely closed. Referring to **FIG 12:14**, check by temporarily releasing the cable from the clip on the water valve and pushing the water valve lever (arrowed) rearwards against its stop.

To remove the heater water valve and thermostat unit, first remove the ventilator and heater assembly and release the ventilator upper casing to provide access to the two clips 1 shown in **FIG 12:15** which attach the thermostat capillary tube 2 to the heater radiator. If the water valve or thermostat are defective they must be renewed as an assembly. When installing, ensure that the

capillary engages in the slot (arrowed in **FIG 12:15**) in the lower casing, and that the water valve lever return spring does not contact the capillary tube when the lever is on the fully closed position. When installing ventilator and heater assembly, thread the heater control cable through the hole in the ventilator lower casing. Adjust the ventilator and heater control cables as already described.

Referring to **FIG 12:16**, note that the hose from the engine thermostat housing should be connected to the water valve inlet pipe (arrowed) and the hose from the heater radiator inlet (lower) pipe connected to the water valve outlet pipe.

12:7 Facia panel. Centre console

The instrument panel facia covers are in four sections and are attached to the instrument panel and centre panel by wingnuts and spring retainers. The centre panel is attached to the instrument panel by two screws (arrowed in **FIG 12:17**) and by two clips at the top. The screws are accessible after easing the centre cover away from the panel. The long facia cover can be removed after removing the centre panel and instrument panel air outlet (see previous Section) but before removing the intermediate and short facia covers the instrument assembly (see **Chapter 11**) must be released.

To remove the centre console on cars with automatic transmission, proceed as follows. Remove the selector lever grip. Remove the screws securing the console insert and carefully ease the insert away. This will provide access to the screws securing the console, which can then be withdrawn by lifting over the handbrake lever. When installing the console, ensure that a spacer is fitted over each console attaching screw between underside of console and the transmission tunnel. Before fitting the console insert, ensure that the spring friction bushes are fully engaged in the holes in the console.

NOTES

APPENDIX

TECHNICAL DATA

Engine details   Fuel system   Ignition system   Cooling system
Clutch   Gearbox (Synchromesh)   Automatic transmission
Propeller shaft, rear axle, rear suspension   Front suspension and steering
Brakes   Electrical equipment   Alternator charging system
Tightening torques

WIRING DIAGRAMS

HINTS ON MAINTENANCE AND OVERHAUL

GLOSSARY OF TERMS

INDEX

NOTES

TECHNICAL DATA

Dimensions are in inches unless otherwise stated

ENGINE DETAILS

Engine type		4-cylinder in-line OHC
Dimensions:	*1600*	*2000*
Bore	85.73 mm (3.375 inch)	95.25 mm (3.75 inch)
Stroke		69.24 mm (2.726 inch)
Capacity	1599 cc (97.5 cu. inch)	1975 cc (120.5 cu. inch)
Firing order		1—3—4—2
No. 1 cylinder		At front
Compression ratios:		*Fuel grade (min)*
High-compression engine	8.5:1	97 Octane
Low-compression engine	7.3:1	90 Octane

Valve stem diameter, standard—Inlet	.3410 to .3417
Exhaust	.3403 to .3410
Stem clearance in head—Inlet	.0010 to .0027
Exhaust	.0017 to .0034
Valve head thickness—Inlet	.025 minimum
Exhaust	.035 minimum
Assembled height of valve in head	1.13 maximum
Valve seat angle	44 deg.
Valve seating in head	45 deg.
Valve seating width—Inlet	.035 to .060
Exhaust	.055 to .085
Valve springs:	
Nominal free length—Inner	1.40
Outer	1.64
Spring load—Inner	72 lb at .83 inch
Outer	139 lb at 1 inch
Tappet diameter	1.4365 to 1.4370
Clearance in housing	.0010 to .0015
Valve clearance, hot—Inlet	.007 to .010
Exhaust (early camshaft) ...	.010 to .013
Exhaust (later camshaft) ...	.015 to .018
Camshaft:	
Journal diameters:	
No. 1 (front)	2.3735 to 2.3740
No. 2	2.3575 to 2.3580
No. 3	2.3425 to 2.3430
No. 4	2.3265 to 2.3270
No. 5	2.0605 to 2.0610
Clearance in housing	.0010 to .0025
End float	.001 to .007
Thrust washer thickness	.157 to .160
Auxiliary shaft:	
Front journal diameter	1.749 to 1.750
Rear journal diameter	1.686 to 1.687
Clearance in bearings	.001 to .003
Thrust washer thickness	.116 to .118
End float	.002 to .008
Piston clearance in cylinder bore:	
1600 engine	.0015 to .0017
2000 engine	.00125 to .00175

VIC1600/2000

Piston rings:

   Ring gap cylinder bore:

Top ring 1600 engines	.010 to .015
Top ring 2000 engine	.011 to .016
Centre ring	.010 to .020

   Thickness (top to bottom face):

Top and centre rings	.077 to .078

   Clearance in grooves :

Top ring	.0015 to .0035
Centre ring	.0010 to .0030

Crankshaft and bearings:

Crankpin diameter	1.9975 to 1.9985
Crankpin clearance in bearing	.0010 to .0032
Crankpin fillet radius	.125
Crank throw	1.360 to 1.365

Main journal diameter :

Nos. 1 (front) 2, 3, 4	2.4995 to 2.5005
Rear journal	2.5000 to 2.5005

Main journal clearance in bearing

Nos. 1, 2, 3, 4	.0008 to .0028
Rear journal	.0008 to .0025
Main journal fillet radius	.125
Minimum crankshaft regrind size	.040 undersize
Main bearing housing bores	2.6655 to 2.6660
Crankshaft end float	.002 to .010
End float controlled by	Flanged rear bearing
Main bearing shells 1600 engine	Whitemetal lined
Main bearing shells 2000 engine	Copper/lead lined

   (Copper/lead bearings may be used as replacements on 1600 engines)

Oil capacity:

Total, dry engine	8½ pints
Refill	7½ pints
Refill, with filter change	8¼ pints
Oil pressure, hot	45 to 55 lb/sq in at 3000 rev/min

FUEL SYSTEM

Mechanical fuel pump:

Type	AC.FG
Drive	Eccentric on auxiliary shaft
Delivery pressure	2 to 3½ lb/sq in
Diaphragm spring load at .64 inch	8 to 8½ lb

Carburetter:

Make and type	Zenith 36.IV

Identification number:

1600 engine	3139 early—3202 later
2000 engine (manual gearbox)	3140
2000 engine (Automatic transmission) ...	3141
Main jet	100 (90 on later 1600)
Compensating jet—1600 engine	125 (130 later)
2000 engine	145
Idling jet	50 (45 on later 1600)
Pump jet	55
Air bleed screw	Not fitted
Needle valve	1.75 mm
Needle valve washer thickness	2 mm

Make and type	...	...	...	...	Zenith/Stromberg 175 CD-2S(T)
Identification number	...	...	...	...	3269
Metering needle	...	...	...	...	2 AM
Air valve spring	...	...	...	...	Blue
Float level	...	...	...	...	15.5 to 16.5 mm
Make and type	...	...	...	...	Zenith/Stromberg 175CD-2SETV

Identification number:

Synchromesh	...	...	...	...	3355
Automatic	...	...	...	...	3354
Metering needle	...	...	...	...	B2AP
Float level	...	...	...	...	16.0 to 16.5

Automatic cold start needle:

Synchromesh	...	...	...	...	J7
Automatic	...	...	...	...	JK

Twin carburetter installations:

Make and type	...	...	...	...	Zenith/Stromberg 175CD-2S

Identification number:

Synchromesh—early engines	...	...	...	3295 Rightdrive 3297 Leftdrive
later engines	...	...	...	3438
Automatic ...	...	...	...	...	3312 Rightdrive 3313 Leftdrive

Metering needle:

Early engines	...	...	...	...	1AS
Later engines	...	...	...	...	1BJ
Air valve spring	...	...	...	...	Red
Make and type	...	...	...	...	Zenith/Stromberg 175CD-2ST
Identification number	...	...	...	...	3439
Fast idle cam	...	...	...	...	A6
Cold start needle	...	...	...	...	K
Air cleaner type	...	...	...	...	Pleated paper element

IGNITION SYSTEM

Coil	...	...	...	...	...	Oil-filled resistor type ('Cold start')

Distributor:

Make and type	...	...	...	...	...	Delco-Remy D.300
Drive	...	...	...	...	...	Skew driven from auxiliary shaft
Rotation	...	...	...	...	...	Anticlockwise viewed from top

	2000 HC engine	Other engines
Mainshaft identification number:	26	36
Cam number	22	20
Advance weights	53	Unmarked
Advance weight springs	Orange/blue	Orange/green
Mainshaft diameter	.4895 to .4900	
Mainshaft end float	.085 to .175	

Contact points:

Gap setting—new points	...	...	...	.022
Service gap setting	...	...	...	.020
Contact arm spring tension	...	...	...	22 to 26 oz
Ignition timing	...	...	...	9 deg. BTDC

Sparking plugs:

Standard	...	...	...	...	AC.42TS (tapered seating)
High-speed running	...	...	...	AC.41T (tapered seating)
Plug gap	...	...	...	...	.030
Plug socket spanner	...	...	...	VR.2040, used with $\frac{3}{8}$ inch square drive torque wrench

COOLING SYSTEM

Capacity—without heater		$12\frac{1}{2}$ pints
Capacity—with heater...		$13\frac{1}{2}$ pints
Drain taps		2
Radiator filler cap opening pressure		$13\frac{1}{2}$ to $17\frac{1}{2}$ lb/sq in

Thermostat:	*Western Thomson*	*AC*
	(upward opening valve)	*(downward opening valve)*
Valve opening temp.	85° to 89°C (185° to 192°F)	80° to 84°C (177° to 183°F)
Valve fully open temp.	99° to 102°C (210° to 214°F)	98°C (208°F)
Valve fully open position (measured from flange)	.51 minimum	.48 minimum

Fan belt tension ... ... 53 lb equivalent to $\frac{3}{8}$ inch deflection midway between water pump and generator pulleys with applied load of 10 lb

CLUTCH

Clutch type	Diaphragm spring
Operation	By cable
Fork free travel	.20 inch
Clutch disc hub springs:	
Number of springs—1600 engine ($7\frac{1}{2}$ inch clutch) ...	4
2000 engine (8 inch clutch) ...	6
Identification colour—1600 engine	Yellow/light green
2000 engine...	Light grey/violet

Some 2000 engines were fitted with $7\frac{1}{2}$ inch clutch. Disc used with this assembly has woven facings with wire instead of plain moulding facings.

GEARBOX (SYNCHROMESH)

Gearbox ratios:		*1600 engine*	*2000 engine*
Threespeed—1st		3.200	2.879
2nd		1.671	1.671
Top		Direct	Direct
Reverse		3.064	3.064
Fourspeed—1st		3.300	2.786
2nd		2.145	1.981
3rd		1.413	1.413
Top		Direct	Direct
Reverse		3.064	3.064
Overdrive—3rd		1.100	1.100
Top		.778	.778

Speedometer driven gear housing:	
Positon of flat locating eccentric:	
15 tooth gears	Adjacent to upper LH housing screw
17 and 18 tooth gears	Adjacent to upper RH housing screw
19 tooth gears	Adjacent to lower RH housing screw
Oil capacity:	
Threespeed	$2\frac{1}{8}$ pints
Fourspeed	$2\frac{1}{2}$ pints
Fourspeed with overdrive	3 pints
Overdrive (with fourspeed gearbox only):	
Type	Laycock Type J
Residual hydraulic pressure...	20 lb/sq in maximum
Operating hydraulic pressure	300 to 340 lb/sq in

AUTOMATIC TRANSMISSION

Transmission type	Borg-Warner Model 35
Oil capacity, nominal	11 pints
Converter stall speed	2000 rev/min
Converter stall speed line pressure—1600 engine ...	130 to 140 lb/sq in
2000 engine ...	150 to 160 lb/sq in
Transmission type	GM
Oil capacity	9 pints
Identification colour	Green

PROPELLER SHAFT, REAR AXLE, REAR SUSPENSION

Universal joints:
Make	Hardy Spicer or BRD
Number of needle rollers	34 in each bearing

Rear axle:
Type	Semi-floating, hypoid
Oil capacity—nominal	2½ pints
Ratios—1600	8/33 (4.125)
2000	10/39 (3.9)
Special	11/38 (3.455)

Rear standing height:
Standard suspension:

Tyre size:

	Standing height
5.60 x 13	9.39 to 10.15
6.20 x 13	8.89 to 9.65
6.90 x 13—Saloon	9.49 to 10.25
Estate	9.46 to 10.22
165 x 13—Saloon	8.85 to 9.61
Estate	8.82 to 9.58

Heavy duty suspension:
5.60 x 13	9.74 to 10.50
6.20 x 13	9.24 to 10.00
6.90 x 13—Saloon	9.84 to 10.60
Estate	9.74 to 10.50
165 x 13—Saloon	9.20 to 9.96
Estate	9.10 to 9.86

Variation between left and right not to exceed .24 inch.

FRONT SUSPENSION AND STEERING

Front standing height
Standard suspension:

Tyre size:

	Standing height
5.60 x 13	10.42 to 11.18
6.20 x 13	9.92 to 10.68
6.90 x 13—Saloon	10.52 to 11.28
Estate	10.40 to 11.16
165 x 13—Saloon	9.88 to 10.64
Estate	9.76 to 10.52

Heavy duty suspension:
5.60 x 13	10.70 to 11.46
6.20 x 13	10.20 to 10.96
6.90 x 13—Saloon	10.80 to 11.56
Estate	10.70 to 11.46
165 x 13—Saloon	10.16 to 10.92
Estate	10.06 to 10.82

Toe-in	.04 inch toe-out to .04 inch toe-in
Camber angle	Nil to 2°30′ positive
	(Angle to be within 1°30′ side for side)
Steering pivot inclination	5°23′ to 8°23′
Castor angle	2°30′ to 4°
	(Angle to be within 1° side for side)
Toe-out on turns	Outside wheel 19° from straight-ahead with inside wheel at 20°
Steering gear type	Rack and pinion
Make	Burman or Cam Gears
Oil capacity	$\frac{1}{4}$ pint
Steering column	Energy-absorbing type

BRAKES

Type	Hydraulically operated
Rear brakes	Drum, leading and trailing shoes
Front brakes	Drum, 2-leading shoe type or self-adjusting disc brakes
Vacuum servo	Fitted to all disc brake models, (servo-assistance to both front and rear brakes)
Brake drum diameter:	9.000 to 9.005
Maximum permissible diameter after refacing ...	9.06
Maximum permissible run-out:	
Front drums—checked on hubs	.002
Rear drums—checked on axle shafts	.004
Brake discs	.004

ELECTRICAL EQUIPMENT

Polarity of system	Negative earth
Voltage	12-volt
Battery:	
Standard—Exide 6.VTAZ 9 BR or Lucas BH9 ...	38 amp/hr
Large capacity—Exide 6VTA 11 BR ...	55 amp/hr
Generator:	
Make and type	Lucas C.40.L
Cutting-in speed—maximum	1350 rev/min at 13 volts
Output	25 amps 2275 rev/min at 13.5 volts on .54 ohm resistance load
Field resistance	5.9 ohms
Commutator minimum diameter after skimming ...	1.430
Brush length—minimum	.25
Brush spring tension	30 oz with new brush
	15 oz with brush at minimum length
Current/voltage controller:	
Make and type	Lucas RB.340
Voltage regulator:	
Open circuit setting—engine speed 2000 rev/min:	
Air temperature 0° to 25°C	14.5 to 15.5 volts
Air temperature 26° to 40°C	14.25 to 15.25 volts

Cut-out:
    Cut-in voltage ... ...   12.7 to 13.3 volts
    Reverse current—maximum ... ...   8 amps
    Armature-to-core gap ... ...   .035 to .045
    Follow-through of moving contact ... ...   Contacts just touching with .015
        armature-core gap

Current regulator:
    Load setting—engine speed 3000 rev/min ... ...   24 to 26 amps
    Armature-to-core gap 058

Starter:
    Inertia type ... ...   Lucas M.35G/1
    Pre-engaged types ... ...   Lucas M35G/PE, M35J/PE or
        M418G/PE

	M35G/1	M35G/PE	M418G/PE
Brush length—minimum	.30	.30	.30
Brush spring tension—minimum with new brush ...	34 to 46 oz	25 oz	36 oz
Brush spring tension—minimum with brush at minimum length	25 oz	—	—
Commutator—minimum diameter after skimming ...	1.281	1.422	1.531

M.35J/PE Starter (Face-type commutator):
    Brush length—minimum 30
    Brush spring pressure ... ...   28 oz when brush protrudes $\frac{1}{16}$
        from holder
    Commutator—minimum thickness after skimming 080

ALTERNATOR CHARGING SYSTEM

Polarity of system ... ...   Negative earth
    Make and type ... ...   Lucas 15 ACR or AC/Delco 28
    Output ... ...   28 amps
    Make and type ... ...   Lucas 17 ACR or AC/Delco 35
    Output ... ...   35 amp
    Make and type ... ...   Lucas 10.AC
    Output ... ...   33 amps
Regulator ... ...   Lucas 4.TR
Relay ... ...   Lucas 6.RA
Warning lamp control ... ...   Lucas 3.AW

TIGHTENING TORQUES (lb ft)

Figures are for clean dry threads except where otherwise stated

Connecting rod bolts (oiled threads) ...	47
Crankshaft main bearing bolts (oiled threads)	83
Flywheel or flexplate to crankshaft bolts	48
Cylinder head bolts	83
Camshaft housing bolts	15
Clutch to flywheel bolts	14
Converter to flexplate bolts	30
Sparking plugs	15
Overdrive relief valve plug	16
Overdrive pump plug	16
Overdrive pressure filter plug	16
Automatic transmission torque converter housing front cover bolts	10
Rear axle coupling flange nut	75
Panhard rod to underbody mounting bolt	24
Panhard rod to rear axle mounting nut	24
Rear spring upper mounting bolt	24
Rear spring lower mounting bolt	24
Rear suspension arm to underbody mounting and rear axle mounting nuts	38
Front suspension control rod to lower arm nuts	38
Front suspension control rod rear nut	47
Front damper upper mounting nut	38
Front damper to lower mounting bracket nut	57
Steering arm to steering knuckle nuts	25
Steering ball joint to steering arm nut	24
Steering knuckle to ball joint nuts—tighten to next splitpin hole	33
Upper arm service ball joint nuts	22
Upper arm fulcrum bolt nut	57
Lower arm fulcrum bolt nut—rubber bush	38
Lower arm fulcrum bolt nut—sleeve bush	68
Crossmember mounting to engine side rail nuts	38
Steering wheel nut	57
Steering column mounting bracket bolts	17
Steering universal coupling cotter nut	7
Steering universal coupling clamp bolt nut	14
Flexible coupling to intermediate shaft nuts	12
Flexible coupling cotter nut	7
Steering gear to crossmember nuts	19
Steering ball joint to steering arm nut	24
Front brake backplate to steering knuckle nuts	25
Lockheed brake caliper bolts	37
Brake caliper to steering knuckle bolts	33
Pre-engaged starter pivot pin locknut	15
Wiper motor crank locknut	12
Wiper motor thrust screw locknut	12 lb in

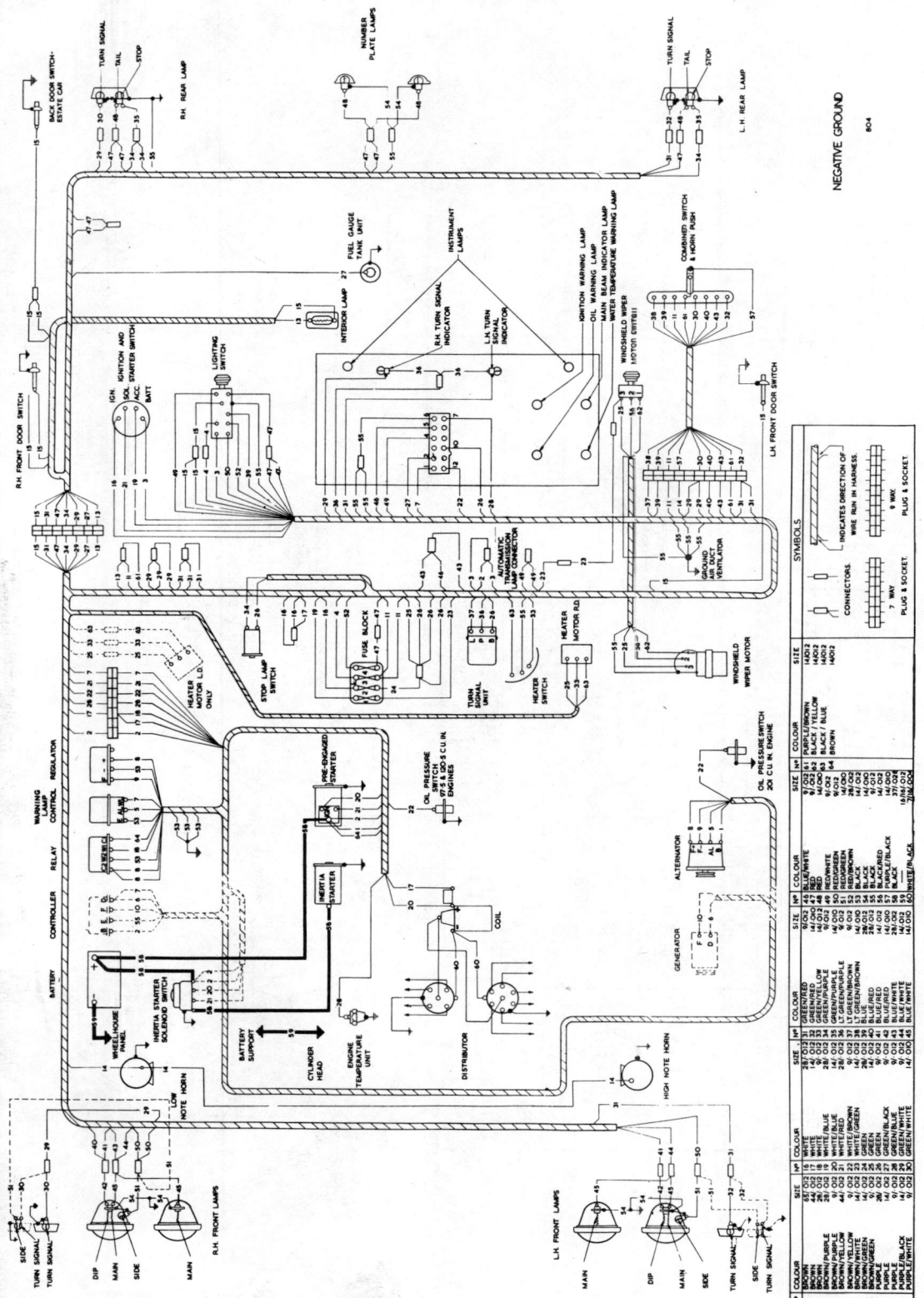

FIG 13:1 Wiring diagram (physical)

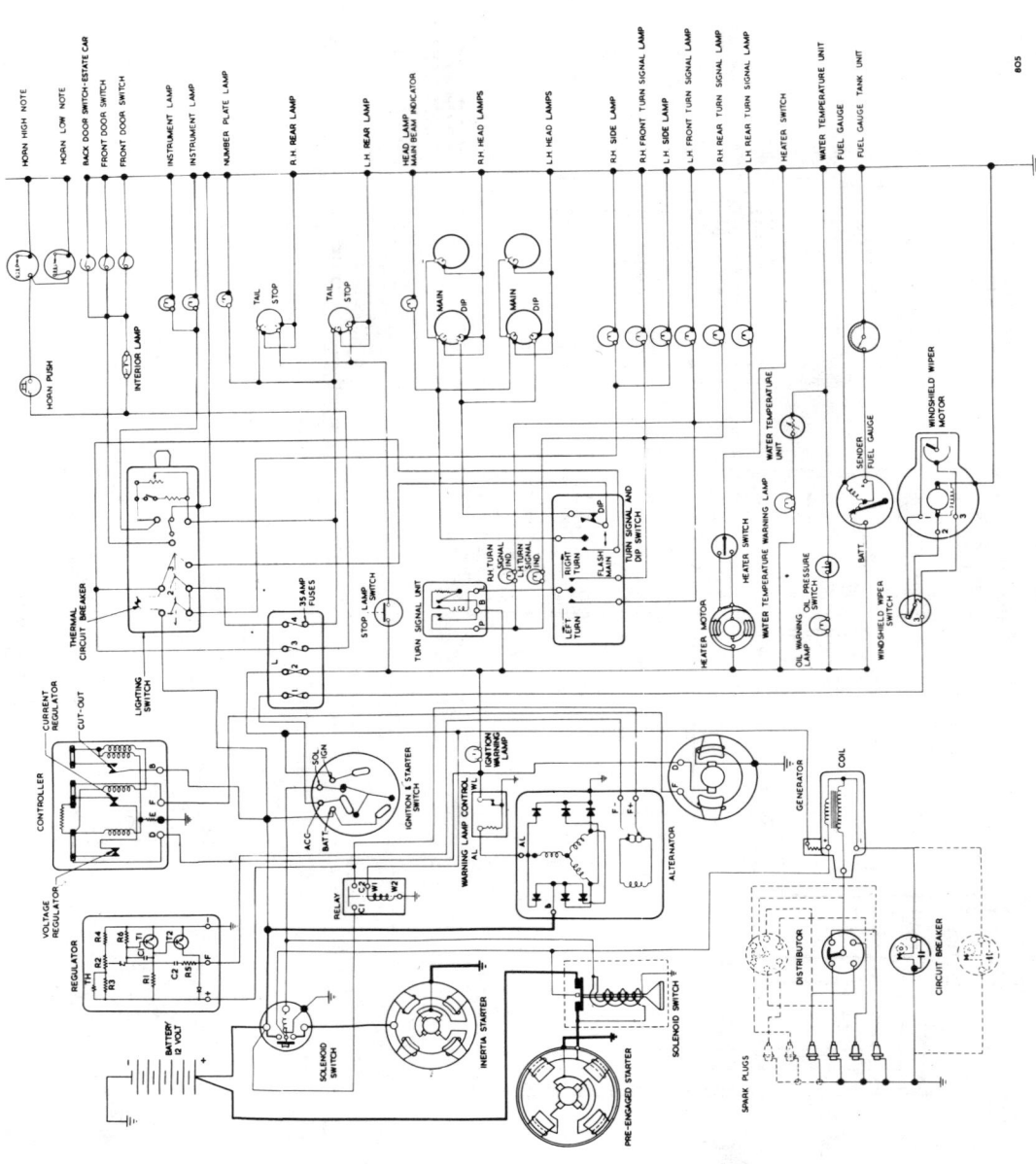

FIG 13:2 Wiring diagram (theoretical)

805

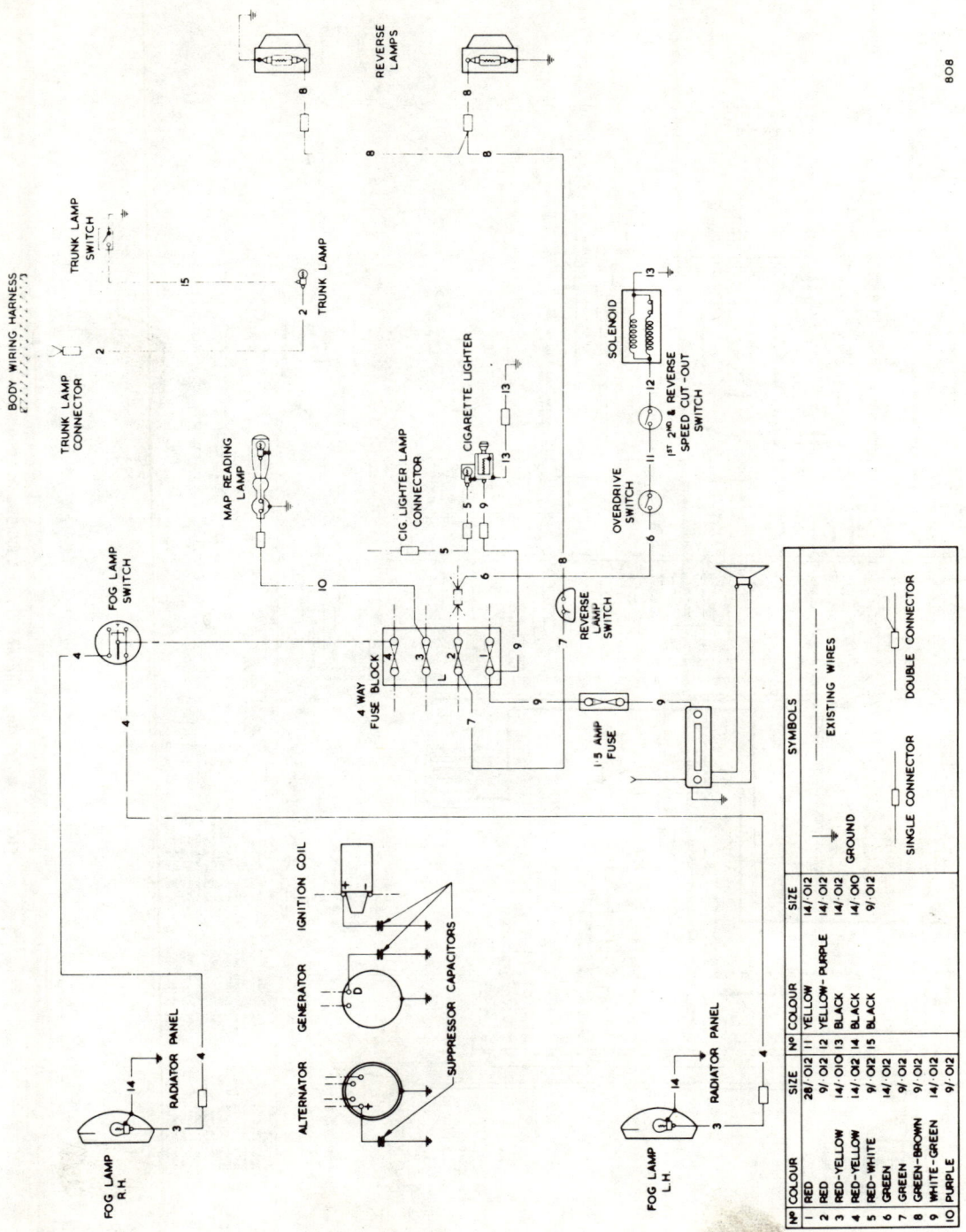

FIG 13:3 Accessory wiring diagram

Nº	COLOUR	SIZE	Nº	COLOUR	SIZE
1	RED	28/.012	11	YELLOW	14/.012
2	RED	9/.012	12	YELLOW–PURPLE	14/.012
3	RED–YELLOW	14/.010	13	BLACK	14/.010
4	RED–YELLOW	14/.012	14	BLACK	14/.010
5	RED–WHITE	9/.012	15	BLACK	9/.012
6	GREEN	14/.012			
7	GREEN	9/.012			
8	GREEN–BROWN	9/.012			
9	WHITE–GREEN	14/.012			
10	PURPLE	9/.012			

SYMBOLS		
EXISTING WIRES		
GROUND	SINGLE CONNECTOR	DOUBLE CONNECTOR

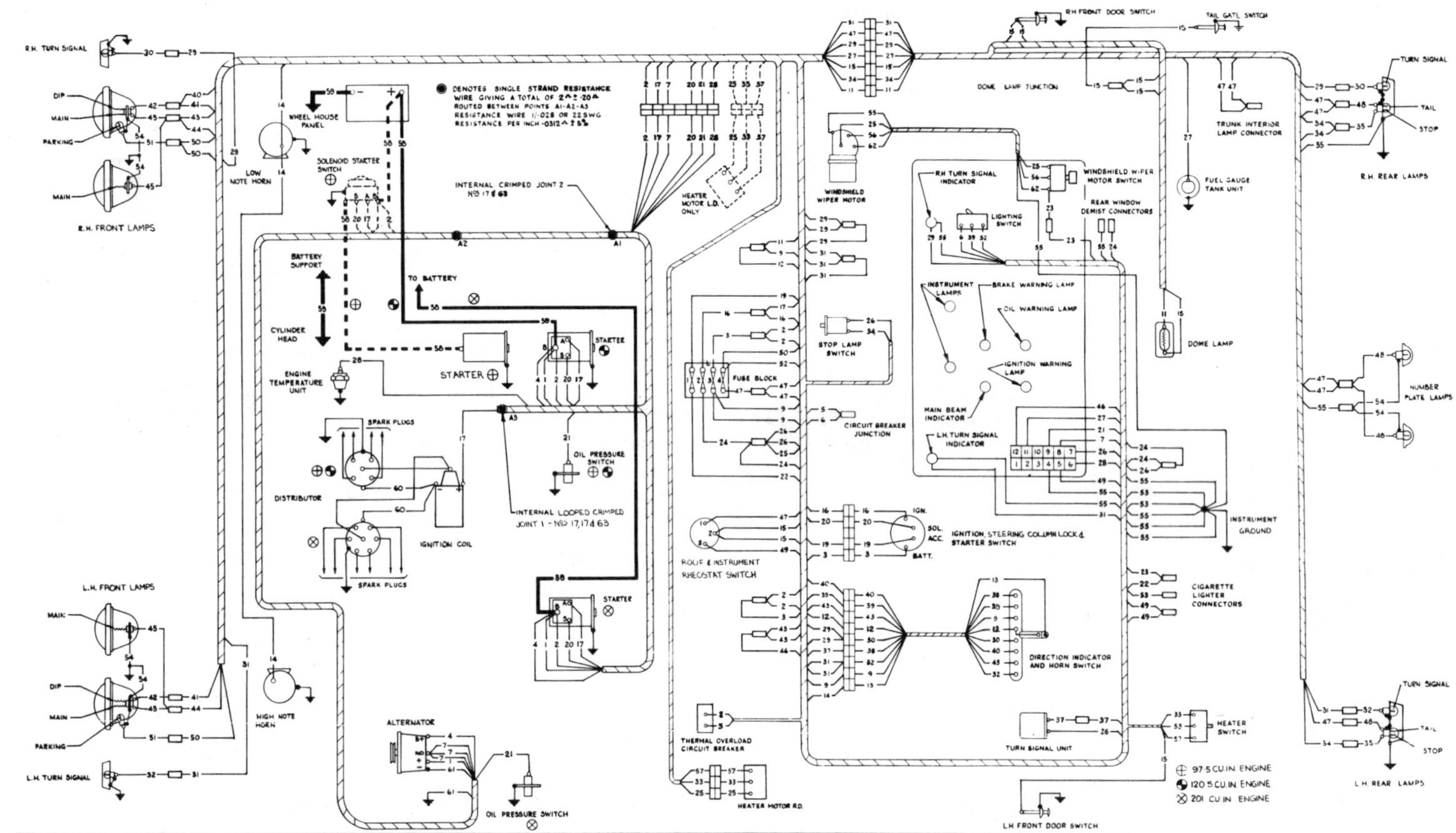

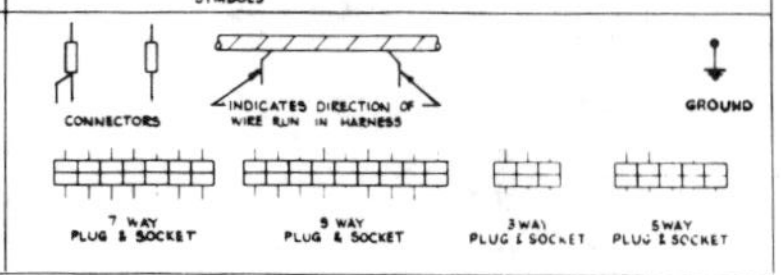

FIG 13:4 Wiring diagram Victor 1600 Super, 2000 SL

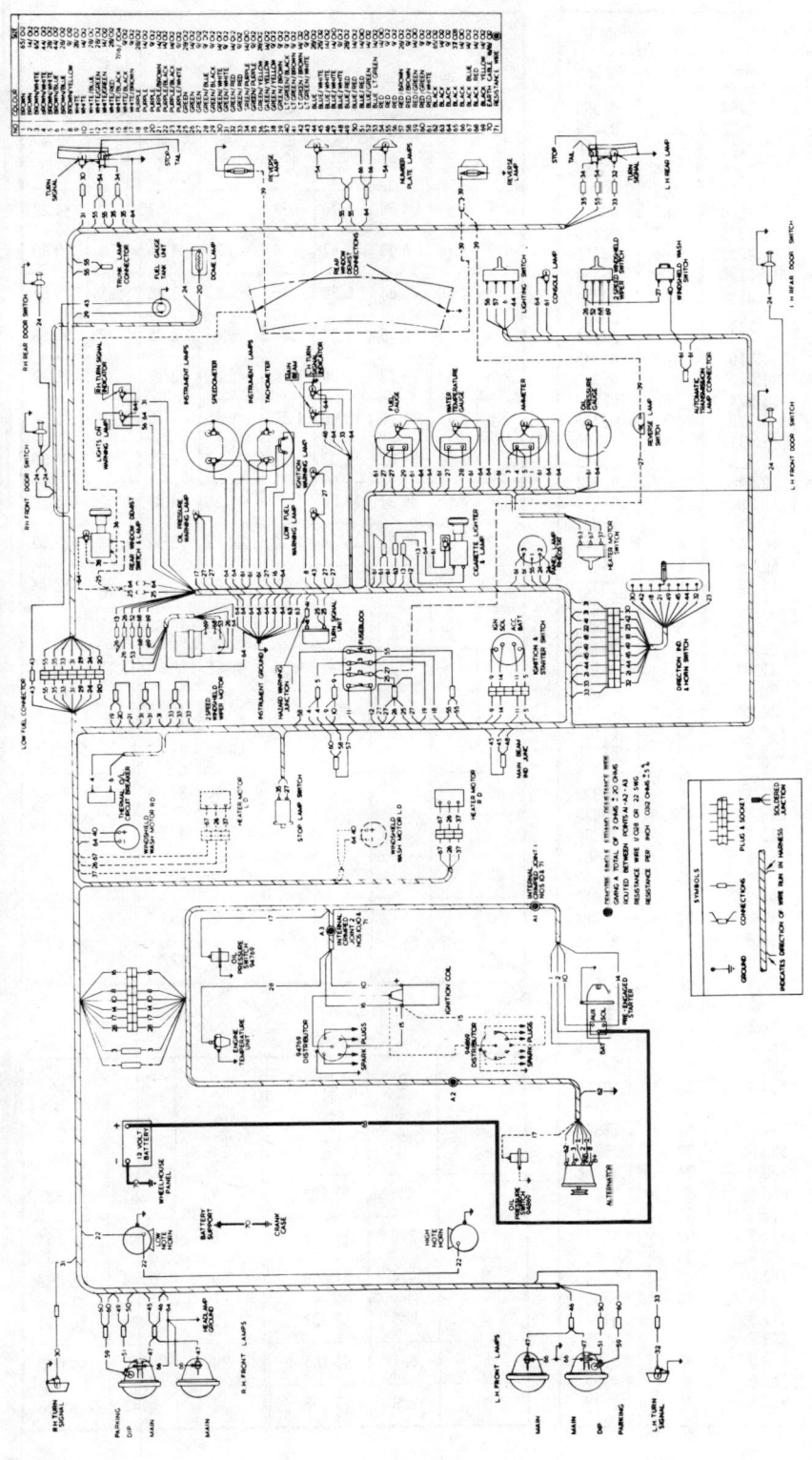

FIG 13:5 Wiring diagram VX4/90

Inches	Decimals	Milli-metres	Inches to Millimetres — Inches	Inches to Millimetres — mm	Millimetres to Inches — mm	Millimetres to Inches — Inches
1/64	.015625	.3969	.001	.0254	.01	.00039
1/32	.03125	.7937	.002	.0508	.02	.00079
3/64	.046875	1.1906	.003	.0762	.03	.00118
1/16	.0625	1.5875	.004	.1016	.04	.00157
5/64	.078125	1.9844	.005	.1270	.05	.00197
3/32	.09375	2.3812	.006	.1524	.06	.00236
7/64	.109375	2.7781	.007	.1778	.07	.00276
1/8	.125	3.1750	.008	.2032	.08	.00315
9/64	.140625	3.5719	.009	.2286	.09	.00354
5/32	.15625	3.9687	.01	.254	.1	.00394
11/64	.171875	4.3656	.02	.508	.2	.00787
3/16	.1875	4.7625	.03	.762	.3	.01181
13/64	.203125	5·1594	.04	1.016	.4	.01575
7/32	.21875	5.5562	.05	1.270	.5	.01969
15/64	.234375	5.9531	.06	1.524	.6	.02362
1/4	.25	6.3500	.07	1.778	.7	.02756
17/64	.265625	6.7469	.08	2.032	.8	.03150
9/32	.28125	7.1437	.09	2.286	.9	.03543
19/64	.296875	7.5406	.1	2.54	1	.03937
5/16	.3125	7.9375	.2	5.08	2	.07874
21/64	.328125	8.3344	.3	7.62	3	.11811
11/32	.34375	8.7312	.4	10.16	4	.15748
23/64	.359375	9.1281	.5	12.70	5	.19685
3/8	.375	9.5250	.6	15.24	6	.23622
25/64	.390625	9.9219	.7	17.78	7	.27559
13/32	.40625	10.3187	.8	20.32	8	.31496
27/64	.421875	10.7156	.9	22.86	9	.35433
7/16	.4375	11.1125	1	25.4	10	.39370
29/64	.453125	11.5094	2	50.8	11	.43307
15/32	.46875	11.9062	3	76.2	12	.47244
31/64	.484375	12.3031	4	101.6	13	.51181
1/2	.5	12.7000	5	127.0	14	.55118
33/64	.515625	13.0969	6	152.4	15	.59055
17/32	.53125	13.4937	7	177.8	16	.62992
35/64	.546875	13.8906	8	203.2	17	.66929
9/16	.5625	14.2875	9	228.6	18	.70866
37/64	.578125	14.6844	10	254.0	19	.74803
19/32	.59375	15.0812	11	279.4	20	.78740
39/64	.609375	15.4781	12	304.8	21	.82677
5/8	.625	15.8750	13	330.2	22	.86614
41/64	.640625	16.2719	14	355.6	23	.90551
21/32	.65625	16.6687	15	381.0	24	.94488
43/64	.671875	17.0656	16	406.4	25	.98425
11/16	.6875	17.4625	17	431.8	26	1.02362
45/64	.703125	17.8594	18	457.2	27	1.06299
23/32	.71875	18.2562	19	482.6	28	1.10236
47/64	.734375	18.6531	20	508.0	29	1.14173
3/4	.75	19.0500	21	533.4	30	1.18110
49/64	.765625	19.4469	22	558.8	31	1.22047
25/32	.78125	19.8437	23	584.2	32	1.25984
51/64	.796875	20.2406	24	609.6	33	1.29921
13/16	.8125	20.6375	25	635.0	34	1.33858
53/64	.828125	21.0344	26	660.4	35	1.37795
27/32	.84375	21.4312	27	685.8	36	1.41732
55/64	.859375	21.8281	28	711.2	37	1.4567
7/8	.875	22.2250	29	736.6	38	1.4961
57/64	.890625	22.6219	30	762.0	39	1.5354
29/32	.90625	23.0187	31	787.4	40	1.5748
59/64	.921875	23.4156	32	812.8	41	1.6142
15/16	.9375	23.8125	33	838.2	42	1.6535
61/64	.953125	24.2094	34	863.6	43	1.6929
31/32	.96875	24.6062	35	889.0	44	1.7323
63/64	.984375	25.0031	36	914.4	45	1.7717

UNITS	Pints to Litres	Gallons to Litres	Litres to Pints	Litres to Gallons	Miles to Kilometres	Kilometres to Miles	Lbs. per sq. In. to Kg. per sq. Cm.	Kg. per sq. Cm. to Lbs. per sq. In.
1	.57	4.55	1.76	.22	1.61	.62	.07	14.22
2	1.14	9.09	3.52	.44	3.22	1.24	.14	28.50
3	1.70	13.64	5.28	.66	4.83	1.86	.21	42.67
4	2.27	18.18	7.04	.88	6.44	2.49	.28	56.89
5	2.84	22.73	8.80	1.10	8.05	3.11	.35	71.12
6	3.41	27.28	10.56	1.32	9.66	3.73	.42	85.34
7	3.98	31.82	12.32	1.54	11.27	4.35	.49	99.56
8	4.55	36.37	14.08	1.76	12.88	4.97	.56	113.79
9		40.91	15.84	1.98	14.48	5.59	.63	128.00
10		45.46	17.60	2.20	16.09	6.21	.70	142.23
20				4.40	32.19	12.43	1.41	284.47
30				6.60	48.28	18.64	2.11	426.70
40				8.80	64.37	24.85		
50					80.47	31.07		
60					96.56	37.28		
70					112.65	43.50		
80					128.75	49.71		
90					144.84	55.92		
100					160.93	62.14		

UNITS	Lb ft to kgm	Kgm to lb ft	UNITS	Lb ft to kgm	Kgm to lb ft
1	.138	7.233	7	.967	50.631
2	.276	14.466	8	1.106	57.864
3	.414	21.699	9	1.244	65.097
4	.553	28.932	10	1.382	72.330
5	.691	36.165	20	2.765	144.660
6	.829	43.398	30	4.147	216.990

HINTS ON MAINTENANCE AND OVERHAUL

There are few things more rewarding than the restoration of a vehicle's original peak of efficiency and smooth performance.

The following notes are intended to help the owner to reach that state of perfection. Providing that he possesses the basic manual skills he should have no difficulty in performing most of the operations detailed in this manual. It must be stressed, however, that where recommended in the manual, highly-skilled operations ought to be entrusted to experts, who have the necessary equipment, to carry out the work satisfactorily.

Quality of workmanship:

The hazardous driving conditions on the roads to-day demand that vehicles should be as nearly perfect, mechanically, as possible. It is therefore most important that amateur work be carried out with care, bearing in mind the often inadequate working conditions, and also the inferior tools which may have to be used. It is easy to counsel perfection in all things, and we recognize that it may be setting an impossibly high standard. We do, however, suggest that every care should be taken to ensure that a vehicle is as safe to take on the road as it is humanly possible to make it.

Safe working conditions:

Even though a vehicle may be stationary, it is still potentially dangerous if certain sensible precautions are not taken when working on it while it is supported on jacks or blocks. It is indeed preferable not to use jacks alone, but to supplement them with carefully placed blocks, so that there will be plenty of support if the car rolls off the jacks during a strenuous manoeuvre. Axle stands are an excellent way of providing a rigid base which is not readily disturbed. Piles of bricks are a dangerous substitute. Be careful not to get under heavy loads on lifting tackle, the load could fall. It is preferable not to work alone when lifting an engine, or when working underneath a vehicle which is supported well off the ground. To be trapped, particularly under the vehicle, may have unpleasant results if help is not quickly forthcoming. Make some provision, however humble, to deal with fires. Always disconnect a battery if there is a likelihood of electrical shorts. These may start a fire if there is leaking fuel about. This applies particularly to leads which can carry a heavy current, like those in the starter circuit. While on the subject of electricity, we must also stress the danger of using equipment which is run off the mains and which has no earth or has faulty wiring or connections. So many workshops have damp floors, and electrical shocks are of such a nature that it is sometimes impossible to let go of a live lead or piece of equipment due to the muscular spasms which take place.

Work demanding special care:

This involves the servicing of braking, steering and suspension systems. On the road, failure of the braking system may be disastrous. Make quite sure that there can be no possibility of failure through the bursting of rusty brake pipes or rotten hoses, nor to a sudden loss of pressure due to defective seals or valves.

Problems:

The chief problems which may face an operator are:
1 External dirt.
2 Difficulty in undoing tight fixings.
3 Dismantling unfamiliar mechanisms.
4 Deciding in what respect parts are defective.
5 Confusion about the correct order for reassembly.
6 Adjusting running clearance.
7 Road testing.
8 Final tuning.

Practical suggestions to solve the problems:

1 Preliminary cleaning of large parts—engines, transmissions, steering, suspensions, etc.,—should be carried out before removal from the car. Where road dirt and mud alone are present, wash clean with a high-pressure water jet, brushing to remove stubborn adhesions, and allow to drain and dry. Where oil or grease is also present, wash down with a proprietary compound (Gunk, Teepol etc.,) applying with a stiff brush—an old paint brush is suitable—into all crevices. Cover the distributor and ignition coils with a polythene bag and then apply a strong water jet to clear the loosened deposits. Allow to drain and dry. The assemblies will then be sufficiently clean to remove and transfer to the bench for the next stage.

On the bench, further cleaning can be carried out, first wiping the parts as free as possible from grease with old newspaper. Avoid using rag or cotton waste which can leave clogging fibres behind. Any remaining grease can be removed with a brush dipped in paraffin. If necessary, traces of paraffin can be removed by carbon tetrachloride. Avoid using paraffin or petrol in large quantities for cleaning in enclosed areas, such as garages, on account of the high fire risk.

When all exteriors have been cleaned, and not before, dismantling can be commenced. This ensures that dirt will not enter into interiors and orifices revealed by dismantling. In the next phases, where components have to be cleaned, use carbon tetrachloride in preference to petrol and keep the containers covered except when in use. After the components have been cleaned, plug small holes with tapered hard wood plugs cut to size and blank off larger orifices with greaseproof paper and masking tape. Do not use soft wood plugs or matchsticks as they may break.

2 It is not advisable to hammer on the end of a screw thread, but if it must be done, first screw on a nut to protect the thread, and use a lead hammer. This applies particularly to the removal of tapered cotters. Nuts and bolts seem to 'grow' together, especially in exhaust systems. If penetrating oil does not work, try the judicious application of heat, but be careful of starting a fire. Asbestos sheet or cloth is useful to isolate heat.

Tight bushes or pieces of tail-pipe rusted into a silencer can be removed by splitting them with an open-ended hacksaw. Tight screws can sometimes be started by a tap from a hammer on the end of a suitable screwdriver. Many tight fittings will yield to the judicious use of a hammer, but it must be a soft-faced hammer if damage is to be avoided, use a heavy block on the opposite side to absorb shock. Any parts of the steering system which have been damaged should be renewed, as attempts to repair them may lead to cracking and subsequent failure, and steering ball joints should be disconnected using a recommended tool to prevent damage.

3 It often happens that an owner is baffled when trying to dismantle an unfamiliar piece of equipment. So many modern devices are pressed together or assembled by spinning-over flanges, that they must be sawn apart. The intention is that the whole assembly must be renewed. However, parts which appear to be in one piece to the naked eye, may reveal close-fitting joint lines when inspected with a magnifying glass, and, this may provide the necessary clue to dismantling. Left-handed screw threads are used where rotational forces would tend to unscrew a right-handed screw thread.

Be very careful when dismantling mechanisms which may come apart suddenly. Work in an enclosed space where the parts will be contained, and drape a piece of cloth over the device if springs are likely to fly in all directions. Mark everything which might be reassembled in the wrong position, scratched symbols may be used on unstressed parts, or a sequence of tiny dots from a centre punch can be useful. Stressed parts should never be scratched or centre-popped as this may lead to cracking under working conditions. Store parts which look alike in the correct order for reassembly. Never rely upon memory to assist in the assembly of complicated mechanisms, especially when they will be dismantled for a long time, but make notes, and drawings to supplement the diagrams in the manual, and put labels on detached wires. Rust stains may indicate unlubricated wear. This can sometimes be seen round the outside edge of a bearing cup in a universal joint. Look for bright rubbing marks on parts which normally should not make heavy contact. These might prove that something is bent or running out of truth. For example, there might be bright marks on one side of a piston, at the top near the ring grooves, and others at the bottom of the skirt on the other side. This could well be the clue to a bent connecting rod. Suspected cracks can be proved by heating the component in a light oil to approximately 100°C, removing, drying off, and dusting with french chalk, if a crack is present the oil retained in the crack will stain the french chalk.

4 In determining wear, and the degree, against the permissible limits set in the manual, accurate measurement can only be achieved by the use of a micrometer. In many cases, the wear is given to the fourth place of decimals; that is in ten-thousandths of an inch. This can be read by the vernier scale on the barrel of a good micrometer. Bore diameters are more difficult to determine. If, however, the matching shaft is accurately measured, the degree of play in the bore can be felt as a guide to its suitability. In other cases, the shank of a twist drill of known diameter is a handy check.

Many methods have been devised for determining the clearance between bearing surfaces. To-day the best and simplest is by the use of Plastigage, obtainable from most garages. A thin plastic thread is laid between the two surfaces and the bearing is tightened, flattening the thread. On removal, the width of the thread is compared with a scale supplied with the thread and the clearance is read off directly. Sometimes joint faces leak persistently, even after gasket renewal. The fault will then be traceable to distortion, dirt or burrs. Studs which are screwed into soft metal frequently raise burrs at the point of entry. A quick cure for this is to chamfer the edge of the hole in the part which fits over the stud.

5 **Always check a replacement part with the original one before it is fitted.**

If parts are not marked, and the order for reassembly is not known, a little detective work will help. Look for marks which are due to wear to see if they can be mated. Joint faces may not be identical due to manufacturing errors, and parts which overlap may be stained, giving a clue to the correct position. Most fixings leave identifying marks especially if they were painted over on assembly. It is then easier to decide whether a nut, for instance, has a plain, a spring, or a shakeproof washer under it. All running surfaces become 'bedded' together after long spells of work and tiny imperfections on one part will be found to have left corresponding marks on the other. This is particularly true of shafts and bearings and even a score on a cylinder wall will show on the piston.

6 Checking end float or rocker clearances by feeler gauge may not always give accurate results because of wear. For instance, the rocker tip which bears on a valve stem may be deeply pitted, in which case the feeler will simply be bridging a depression. Thrust washers may also wear depressions in opposing faces to make accurate measurement difficult. End float is then easier to check by using a dial gauge. It is common practice to adjust end play in bearing assemblies, like front hubs with taper rollers, by doing up the axle nut until the hub becomes stiff to turn and then backing it off a little. Do not use this method with ballbearing hubs as the assembly is often preloaded by tightening the axle nut to its fullest extent. If the splitpin hole will not line up, file the base of the nut a little.

Steering assemblies often wear in the straight-ahead position. If any part is adjusted, make sure that it remains free when moved from lock to lock. Do not be surprised if an assembly like a steering gearbox, which is known to be carefully adjusted outside the car, becomes stiff when it is bolted in place. This will be due to distortion of the case by the pull of the mounting bolts, particularly if the mounting points are not all touching together. This problem may be met in other equipment and is cured by careful attention to the alignment of mounting points.

When a spanner is stamped with a size and A/F it means that the dimension is the width between the jaws and has no connection with ANF, which is the designation for the American National Fine thread. Coarse threads like Whitworth are rarely used on cars to-day except for studs which screw into soft aluminium or cast iron. For this reason it might be found that the top end of a cylinder head stud has a fine thread and the lower end a coarse thread to screw into the cylinder block. If the car has mainly UNF threads then it is likely that any coarse threads will be UNC, which are not the same as Whitworth. Small sizes have the same number of threads in Whitworth and UNC, but in the $\frac{1}{2}$ inch size for example, there are twelve threads to the inch in the former and thirteen in the latter.

7 After a major overhaul, particularly if a great deal of work has been done on the braking, steering and suspension systems, it is advisable to approach the problem of testing with care. If the braking system has been overhauled, apply heavy pressure to the brake pedal and get a second operator to check every possible source of leakage. The brakes may work extremely well, but a leak could cause complete failure after a few miles.

Do not fit the hub caps until every wheel nut has been checked for tightness, and make sure the tyre pressures are correct. Check the levels of coolant, lubricants and hydraulic fluids. Being satisfied that all is well, take the car on the road and test the brakes at once. Check the steering and the action of the handbrake. Do all this at moderate speeds on quiet roads, and make sure there is no other vehicle behind you when you try a rapid stop.

Finally, remember that many parts settle down after a time, so check for tightness of all fixings after the car has been on the road for a hundred miles or so.

8 It is useless to tune an engine which has not reached its normal running temperature. In the same way, the tune of an engine which is stiff after a rebore will be different when the engine is again running free. Remember too, that rocker clearances on pushrod operated valve gear will change when the cylinder head nuts are tightened after an initial period of running with a new head gasket.

Trouble may not always be due to what seems the obvious cause. Ignition, carburation and mechanical condition are interdependent and spitting back through the carburetter, which might be attributed to a weak mixture, can be caused by a sticking inlet valve.

For one final hint on tuning, never adjust more than one thing at a time or it will be impossible to tell which adjustment produced the desired result.

NOTES

GLOSSARY OF TERMS

Allen key   Cranked wrench of hexagonal section for use with socket head screws.

Alternator   Electrical generator producing alternating current. Rectified to direct current for battery charging.

Ambient temperature   Surrounding atmospheric temperature.

Annulus   Used in engineering to indicate the outer ring gear of an epicyclic gear train.

Armature   The shaft carrying the windings, which rotates in the magnetic field of a generator or starter motor. That part of a solenoid or relay which is activated by the magnetic field.

Axial   In line with, or pertaining to, an axis.

Backlash   Play in meshing gears.

Balance lever   A bar where force applied at the centre is equally divided between connections at the ends.

Banjo axle   Axle casing with large diameter housing for the crownwheel and differential.

Bendix pinion   A self-engaging and self-disengaging drive on a starter motor shaft.

Bevel pinion   A conical shaped gearwheel, designed to mesh with a similar gear with an axis usually at 90 deg. to its own.

bhp   Brake horse power, measured on a dynamometer.

bmep   Brake mean effective pressure. Average pressure on a piston during the working stroke.

Brake cylinder   Cylinder with hydraulically operated piston(s) acting on brake shoes or pad(s).

Brake regulator   Control valve fitted in hydraulic braking system which limits brake pressure to rear brakes during heavy braking to prevent rear wheel locking.

Camber   Angle at which a wheel is tilted from the vertical.

Capacitor   Modern term for an electrical condenser. Part of distributor assembly, connected across contact breaker points, acts as an interference suppressor.

Castellated   Top face of a nut, slotted across the flats, to take a locking splitpin.

Castor   Angle at which the kingpin or swivel pin is tilted when viewed from the side.

cc   Cubic centimetres. Engine capacity is arrived at by multiplying the area of the bore in sq cm by the stroke in cm by the number of cylinders.

Clevis   U-shaped forked connector used with a clevis pin, usually at handbrake connections.

Collet   A type of collar, usually split and located in a groove in a shaft, and held in place by a retainer. The arrangement used to retain the spring(s) on a valve stem in most cases.

Commutator   Rotating segmented current distributor between armature windings and brushes in generator or motor.

Compression   The ratio, or quantitative relation, of the total volume (piston at bottom of stroke) to the unswept volume (piston at top of stroke) in an engine cylinder.

Condenser   See capacitor.

Core plug   Plug for blanking off a manufacturing hole in a casting.

Crownwheel   Large bevel gear in rear axle, driven by a bevel pinion attached to the propeller shaft. Sometimes called a 'ring gear'.

'C'-spanner   Like a 'C' with a handle. For use on screwed collars without flats, but with slots or holes.

Damper   Modern term for shock-absorber, used in vehicle suspension systems to damp out spring oscillations.

Depression   The lowering of atmospheric pressure as in the inlet manifold and carburetter.

Dowel   Close tolerance pin, peg, tube, or bolt, which accurately locates mating parts.

Drag link   Rod connecting steering box drop arm (pitman arm) to nearest front wheel steering arm in certain types of steering systems.

Dry liner   Thinwall tube pressed into cylinder bore

Dry sump   Lubrication system where all oil is scavenged from the sump, and returned to a separate tank.

Dynamo   See Generator.

Electrode   Terminal, part of an electrical component, such as the points or 'Electrodes' of a sparking plug.

Electrolyte   In lead-acid car batteries a solution of sulphuric acid and distilled water.

End float   The axial movement between associated parts, end play.

EP   Extreme pressure. In lubricants, special grades for heavily loaded bearing surfaces, such as gear teeth in a gearbox, or crownwheel and pinion in a rear axle.

Fade	Of brakes. Reduced efficiency due to overheating.
Field coils	Windings on the polepieces of motors and generators.
Fillets	Narrow finishing strips usually applied to interior bodywork.
First motion shaft	Input shaft from clutch to gearbox.
Fullflow filter	Filters in which all the oil is pumped to the engine. If the element becomes clogged, a bypass valve operates to pass unfiltered oil to the engine.
FWD	Front wheel drive.
Gear pump	Two meshing gears in a close fitting casing. Oil is carried from the inlet round the outside of both gears in the spaces between the gear teeth and casing to the outlet, the meshing gear teeth prevent oil passing back to the inlet, and the oil is forced through the outlet port.
Generator	Modern term for 'Dynamo'. When rotated produces electrical current.
Grommet	A ring of protective or sealing material. Can be used to protect pipes or leads passing through bulkheads.
Grubscrew	Fully threaded headless screw with screwdriver slot. Used for locking, or alignment purposes.
Gudgeon pin	Shaft which connects a piston to its connecting rod. Sometimes called 'wrist pin', or 'piston pin'.
Halfshaft	One of a pair transmitting drive from the differential.
Helical	In spiral form. The teeth of helical gears are cut at a spiral angle to the side faces of the gearwheel.
Hot spot	Hot area that assists vapourisation of fuel on its way to cylinders. Often provided by close contact between inlet and exhaust manifolds.
HT	High Tension. Applied to electrical current produced by the ignition coil for the sparking plugs.
Hydrometer	A device for checking specific gravity of liquids. Used to check specific gravity of electrolyte.
Hypoid bevel gears	A form of bevel gear used in the rear axle drive gears. The bevel pinion meshes below the centre line of the crownwheel, giving a lower propeller shaft line.
Idler	A device for passing on movement. A free running gear between driving and driven gears. A lever transmitting track rod movement to a side rod in steering gear.
Impeller	A centrifugal pumping element. Used in water pumps to stimulate flow.
Journals	Those parts of a shaft that are in contact with the bearings.
Kingpin	The main vertical pin which carries the front wheel spindle, and permits steering movement. May be called 'steering pin' or 'swivel pin'.
Layshaft	The shaft which carries the laygear in the gearbox. The laygear is driven by the first motion shaft and drives the third motion shaft according to the gear selected. Sometimes called the 'countershaft' or 'second motion shaft.'
lb ft	A measure of twist or torque. A pull of 10 lb at a radius of 1 ft is a torque of 10 lb ft.
lb/sq in	Pounds per square inch.
Little-end	The small, or piston end of a connecting rod. Sometimes called the 'small-end'.
LT	Low Tension. The current output from the battery.
Mandrel	Accurately manufactured bar or rod used for test or centring purposes.
Manifold	A pipe, duct, or chamber, with several branches.
Needle rollers	Bearing rollers with a length many times their diameter.
Oil bath	Reservoir which lubricates parts by immersion. In air filters, a separate oil supply for wetting a wire mesh element to hold the dust.
Oil wetted	In air filters, a wire mesh element lightly oiled to trap and hold airborne dust.
Overlap	Period during which inlet and exhaust valves are open together.
Panhard rod	Bar connected between fixed point on chassis and another on axle to control sideways movement.
Pawl	Pivoted catch which engages in the teeth of a ratchet to permit movement in one direction only.
Peg spanner	Tool with pegs, or pins, to engage in holes or slots in the part to be turned.
Pendant pedals	Pedals with levers that are pivoted at the top end.
Phillips screwdriver	A cross-point screwdriver for use with the cross-slotted heads of Phillips screws.
Pinion	A small gear, usually in relation to another gear.
Piston-type damper	Shock absorber in which damping is controlled by a piston working in a closed oil-filled cylinder.
Preloading	Preset static pressure on ball or roller bearings not due to working loads.
Radial	Radiating from a centre, like the spokes of a wheel.

Radius rod	Pivoted arm confining movement of a part to an arc of fixed radius.
Ratchet	Toothed wheel or rack which can move in one direction only, movement in the other being prevented by a pawl.
Ring gear	A gear tooth ring attached to outer periphery of flywheel. Starter pinion engages with it during starting.
Runout	Amount by which rotating part is out of true.
Semi-floating axle	Outer end of rear axle halfshaft is carried on bearing inside axle casing. Wheel hub is secured to end of shaft.
Servo	A hydraulic or pneumatic system for assisting, or, augmenting a physical effort. See 'Vacuum Servo'.
Setscrew	One which is threaded for the full length of the shank.
Shackle	A coupling link, used in the form of two parallel pins connected by side plates to secure the end of the master suspension spring and absorb the effects of deflection.
Shell bearing	Thinwalled steel shell lined with anti-friction metal. Usually semi-circular and used in pairs for main and big-end bearings.
Shock absorber	See 'Damper'.
Silentbloc	Rubber bush bonded to inner and outer metal sleeves.
Socket-head screw	Screw with hexagonal socket for an Allen key.
Solenoid	A coil of wire creating a magnetic field when electric current passes through it. Used with a soft iron core to operate contacts or a mechanical device.
Spur gear	A gear with teeth cut axially across the periphery.
Stub axle	Short axle fixed at one end only.
Tachometer	An instrument for accurate measurement of rotating speed. Usually indicates in revolutions per minute.

TDC	Top Dead Centre. The highest point reached by a piston in a cylinder, with the crank and connecting rod in line.
Thermostat	Automatic device for regulating temperature. Used in vehicle coolant systems to open a valve which restricts circulation at low temperature.
Third motion shaft	Output shaft of gearbox.
Threequarter floating axle	Outer end of rear axle halfshaft flanged and bolted to wheel hub, which runs on bearing mounted on outside of axle casing. Vehicle weight is not carried by the axle shaft.
Thrust bearing or washer	Used to reduce friction in rotating parts subject to axial loads.
Torque	Turning or twisting effort. See 'lb ft'.
Track rod	The bar(s) across the vehicle which connect the steering arms and maintain the front wheels in their correct alignment.
UJ	Universal joint. A coupling between shafts which permits angular movement.
UNF	Unified National Fine screw thread.
Vacuum servo	Device used in brake system, using difference between atmospheric pressure and inlet manifold depression to operate a piston which acts to augment brake pressure as required. See 'Servo'.
Venturi	A restriction or 'choke' in a tube, as in a carburetter, used to increase velocity to obtain a reduction in pressure.
Vernier	A sliding scale for obtaining fractional readings of the graduations of an adjacent scale.
Welch plug	A domed thin metal disc which is partially flattened to lock in a recess. Used to plug core holes in castings.
Wet liner	Removable cylinder barrel, sealed against coolant leakage, where the coolant is in direct contact with the outer surface.
Wet sump	A reservoir attached to the crankcase to hold the lubricating oil.

NOTES

INDEX

Alfa Romeo Giulia 1600, 1750 1962 on
Aston Martin 1921-58
Auto Union Audi 70, 80, Super 90, 1966 on
Audi 100 1969 on
Austin, Morris etc. 1100 Mk. 1 1962-67
Austin, Morris etc. 1100 Mk. 2, 3, 1300 Mk. 1, 2, 3 America 1968 on
Austin A30, A35, A40 Farina
Austin A55 Mk. 2, A60 1958-69
Austin A99, A110 1959-68
Austin J4 1960 on
Austin Maxi 1969 on
Austin, Morris 1800 1964 on
Austin, Morris 2200 1972 on
Austin, Morris 1300, 1500 Nomad 1969 on

BMC 3 (Austin A50, A55 Mk. 1, Morris Oxford 2, 3 1954-59)
Austin Healey 100/6, 3000 1956-68
Austin Healey, MG Sprite, Midget 1958 on
Bedford Beagle HA Vans 1964 on
BMW 1600 1966 on
BMW 1800 1964 on
BMW 2000, 2002 1966 on
Chevrolet Corvair 1960-69
Chevrolet Corvette V8 1957-65
Chevrolet Corvette V8 1965 on
Chevrolette Vega 2300 1970 on
Chrysler Valiant V8 1965 on
Chrysler Valiant Straight Six 1966-70
Citroen DS 19, ID 19 1955-66
Citroen ID 19, DS 19, 20, 21 1966 on
Daf 31, 32, 33, 44, 55 1961 on
Datsun 1200 1970 on
Datsun 1300, 1400, 1600 1968 on
Datsun 240C 1971 on
Datsun 240Z Sport 1970 on
De Dion Bouton 1899-1907
Fiat 124 1966 on
Fiat 124 Sport 1966 on
Fiat 125 1967 on
Fiat 128 1969 on
Fiat 500 1957 on
Fiat 600, 600D 1955-69
Fiat 850 1964 on
Fiat 1100 1957-69
Fiat 1300, 1500 1961-67

Ford Anglia Prefect 100E 1953-62
Ford Anglia 105E, Prefect 107E 1959-67
Ford Capri 1300, 1600 OHV 1968 on
Ford Capri 1300, 1600, 2000 OHC 1972 on
Ford Capri 2000, 3000 1969 on
Ford Classic, Capri 1961-64
Ford Consul, Zephyr, Zodiac, 1, 2 1950-62
Ford Corsair Straight Four 1963-65
Ford Corsair V4 1965-68
Ford Corsair V4 2000 1969-70
Ford Cortina 1962-66
Ford Cortina 1967-68
Ford Cortina 1969-70
Ford Cortina Mk. 3 1970 on
Ford Escort 1967 on
Ford Falcon 6 1964-70
Ford Falcon XK, XL 1960-63
Ford Falcon 6 XR/XA 1966 on
Ford Falcon V8 (U.S.A.) 1965-71
Ford Falcon V8 (Aust.) 1966 on
Ford Pinto 1970 on
Ford Maverick 1969 on
Ford Mustang V8 1965-71
Ford Thames 10, 12, 15 cwt 1957-65
Ford Transit 1965 on
Ford Zephyr Zodiac Mk. 3 1962-66
Ford Zephyr Zodiac V4, V6, Mk. 4 1966-72
Ford Consul, Granada 1972
Hillman Avenger 1970 on
Hillman Hunter 1966 on
Hillman Imp 1963-68
Hillman Imp 1969 on
Hillman Minx 1 to 5 1956-65
Hillman Minx 1965-67
Hillman Minx 1966-70
Hillman Super Minx 1961-65
Holden V8 1968 on
Holden Straight Six 1948-66
Holden Straight Six 1966 on
Holden Torana 4 Series HB 1967-69
Jaguar XK120, 140, 150, Mk. 7, 8, 9 1948-61
Jaguar 2.4, 3.4, 3.8 Mk. 1, 2 1955-69
Jaguar 'E' Type 1961 on
Jaguar 'S' Type 420 1963-68

Jaguar XJ6 1968 on
Jowett Javelin Jupiter 1947-53
Landrover 1, 2 1948-61
Landrover 2, 2a, 3 1959 on
Mazda 616 1970 on
Mazda 1200, 1300 1969 on
Mazda 1500, 1800 1967 on
Mercedes-Benz 190b, 190c, 200 1959-68
Mercedes-Benz 220 1959-65
Mercedes-Benz 220/8 1968 on
Mercedes-Benz 230 1963-68
Mercedes-Benz 250 1965-67
Mercedes-Benz 250 1968 on
Mercedes-Benz 280 1968 on
MG TA to TF 1936-55
MGA MGB 1955-68
MGB 1969 on
Mini 1959 on
Mini Cooper 1961 on
Morgan 1936-69
Morris Marina 1971 on
Morris (Aust.) Marina 1972 on
Morris Minor 2, 1000 1952-71
Morris Oxford 5, 6 1959-71
NSU 1000 1963 on
NSU Prinz 1 to 4 1957 on
Opel Ascona, Manta 1970 on
Opel GT 1900 1968 on
Opel Kadett, Olympia 993cc 1078cc 1962 on
Opel Kadett, Olympia 1492, 1698, 1897cc 1967 on
Opel Rekord C 1966 on
Peugeot 204 1965 on
Peugeot 304 1970 on
Peugeot 404 1960 on
Peugeot 504 1968-70
Porsche 356A, B, C 1957-65
Porsche 911 1964-69
Porsche 912 1965-69
Porsche 914 S 1969 on
Reliant Regal 1952 on
Renault R4, R4L, 4 1961 on
Renault 6 1968 on
Renault 8, 10, 1100 1962 on
Renault 12, 1969 on
Renault R16 1965 on
Renault Dauphine Floride 1957-67
Renault Caravelle 1962-68
Rover 60 to 110 1953-64
Rover 2000 1963 on
Rover 3 Litre 1958-67
Rover 3500, 3500S 1968 on

Saab 95, 96, Sport 1960-68
Saab 99 1969 on
Saab V4 1966 on

Simca 1000 1961 on
Simca 1100 1967 on
Simca 1300, 1301, 1500, 1501 1963 on
Skoda One (440, 445, 450) 1955-70
Sunbeam Rapier Alpine 1955-65
Toyota Corolla 1100 1967 on
Toyota Corona 1500 Mk. 1 1965-70
Toyota Corona 1900 Mk. 2 1969 on
Triumph TR2, TR3, TR3A 1952-62
Triumph TR4, TR4A 1961-67
Triumph TR5, TR250, TR6 1967 on
Triumph 1300, 1500 1965 on
Triumph 2000 Mk. 1, 2.5 PI Mk. 1 1963-69
Triumph 2000 Mk. 2, 2.5 PI Mk. 2 1969 on
Triumph Dolomite 1972 on
Triumph Herald 1959-68
Triumph Herald 1969-71
Triumph Spitfire, Vitesse 1962-68
Triumph Spitfire Mk. 3, 4 1969 on
Triumph GT6, Vitesse 2 Litre 1969 on
Triumph Toledo 1970 on
Vauxhall Velox, Cresta 1957-72
Vauxhall Victor 1, 2, FB 1957-64
Vauxhall Victor 101 1964-67
Vauxhall Victor FD 1600, 2000 1967 on
Vauxhall Victor 3300, Ventora 1968 on
Vauxhall Victor FE Ventora 1972 on
Vauxhall Viva HA 1963-66
Vauxhall Viva HB 1966-70
Vauxhall Viva, HC Firenza 1971 on
Volkswagen Beetle 1954-67
Volkswagen Beetle 1968 on
Volkswagen 1500 1961-66
Volkswagen 1600 Fastback 1965 on
Volkswagen Transporter 1954-67
Volkswagen Transporter 1968 on
Volkswagen 411 1968 on
Volvo 120 1961-70
Volvo 140 1966 on
Volvo 160 series 1968 on
Volvo 1800 1960 on